E-learning Theory and Practice

E-learning Theory and Practice

Caroline Haythornthwaite
and Richard Andrews

Los Angeles | London | New Delhi
Singapore | Washington DC

First published 2011

SAGE Publications Ltd
1 Oliver's Yard
55 City Road
London EC1Y 1SP

SAGE Publications Inc.
2455 Teller Road
Thousand Oaks, California 91320

SAGE Publications India Pvt Ltd
B 1/I 1 Mohan Cooperative Industrial Area
Mathura Road
New Delhi 110 044

SAGE Publications Asia-Pacific Pte Ltd
33 Pekin Street #02-01
Far East Square
Singapore 048763

Library of Congress Control Number: 2010937863

British Library Cataloguing in Publication data

A catalogue record for this book is available from the British Library

ISBN 978-1-84920-470-5
ISBN 978-1-84920-471-2 (pbk)

Typeset by C&M Digitals (P) Ltd., Chennai, India
Printed in Great Britain by CPI Antony Rowe, Chippenham, Wiltshire
Printed on paper from sustainable resources

MIX
Paper from
responsible sources
FSC® C013604
www.fsc.org

Contents

About the Authors

Caroline Haythornthwaite

Caroline Haythornthwaite is Director and Professor, School of Library, Archival and Information Studies, The University of British Columbia. She joined UBC in 2010 after 14 years at the University of Illinois at Urbana-Champaign where she was Professor in the Graduate School of Library and Information Science. She has an international reputation in research on information and knowledge sharing through social networks and the impact of computer media and the Internet on learning and social interaction.

Her research includes empirical and theoretical work on social networks and media use, the development and nature of community online, distributed knowledge processes, the nature and constraints of interdisciplinary collaboration, motivations for participation in crowds and communities, and the development of automated processes for analysis of online learning activity.

Richard Andrews

Richard Andrews is Professor in English and Dean of the Faculty of Children and Learning at the Institute of Education, University of London, where he teaches an online research methods course as well as supervising the work of doctoral students in the field of e-learning. He is the editor of *The Impact of ICT on Literacy Education* and on the editorial boards of the journals *Learning, Media and Technology* and the China-based *International Journal of Computer Assisted Language Teaching*.

Research interests include argumentation in schools and higher education; writing development; English from a multimodal perspective; world Englishes; and the discourses of e-learning. He has held professorships at the universities of Middlesex, Hull and York, and taught at New York University in the Steinhardt School of Culture, Education and Human Development. He has also held research fellowships at the University of Illinois at Urbana-Champaign and the University of Western Sydney.

Acknowledgements

All scholarship is a result of multiple interactions, conversations and support of others. As authors we wish to acknowledge the support of many people and institutions in providing the opportunity to complete this book. We thank first the Leverhulme Trust. This book was written during Caroline Haythornthwaite's tenure as Visiting Leverhulme Professor at the Institute of Education, University of London in 2009/10. We are greatly indebted to the Trust for timely production of this work which was begun and completed over the year in conjunction with a public lecture series associated with the Professorship. The support of Vivien Hodgson (Lancaster University), Brian Loader (The University of York) and Barry Wellman (University of Toronto) was instrumental and much appreciated in the process of applying for the grant. The ability to be resident in London for the Visiting Professorship to work, combined with the support of individuals at various institutions made it possible for Caroline to present papers and interact with colleagues across the UK during the year. For their support, she thanks Richard Noss, Bernie Hogan, Richard Andrews, David Prytherch, Mike Thelwall, Robin Goodfellow, Vivien Hodgson, Mary Hamilton, David Barton, Chris Bissell, Chris Jones, and Bill Dutton.

Other support and activities helped to inform the writing. These include an Economic and Social Research Council grant for a seminar series entitled: 'New forms of doctorate: the influence of multimodality and e-learning on the nature and format of doctoral theses in education and the social sciences', awarded to the Institute of Education which ran from 2008 to 2010, directed by Richard Andrews in collaboration with Stephen Boyd Davis (Middlesex University), Erik Borg (Coventry University) and Jude England (The British Library). An earlier version of Chapter 3 was given as a paper by Richard at the European Conference on Educational Research at The University of Vienna in September 2009, and also appeared under the title 'Does e-learning need a new theory of learning?' in the *Journal for Educational Research Online*. Thanks go to the editors of that journal, Wilfried Bos and Cornelia Gräsel, for permission to rework the paper as a chapter.

We are also grateful for the support of our institutions: for Caroline, the Graduate School of Library and Information Science, University of Illinois at Urbana-Champaign, and for both Caroline and Richard, the Institute of Education, University of London. Of importance to Caroline's work on e-learning has been personal and research participation in the fully online Masters degree option at Graduate School of Library and Information Science (GSLIS) known as LEEP (Library Experimental Education Program). Thanks go to participants in studies as well as to the many colleagues who have provided input over the years. Particular thanks go to Associate Dean Linda Smith whose administrative, teaching and research efforts have been instrumental in making the LEEP program the success it is, and to former GSLIS Dean Leigh Estabrook, as well as to GSLIS colleagues who have contributed ideas about LEEP over the years (most included as authors in Haythornthwaite and Kazmer [eds] [2004a] *Learning, Culture and Community in Online Education*). Thanks also go to GSLIS Dean John Unsworth for facilitating the leave to take up the Leverhulme Visiting Professorship.

We are grateful to Geoff Whitty, Chris Husbands, Sue Rogers and Richard Noss at the Institute of Education for hosting the Professorship, and to Celia Hoyles for the share of her office for the duration. Colleagues whose involvement helped shape the project include Gunther Kress, Diana Laurillard, Rebekah Willett, Susie Andretta, Fred Garnett, Caroline Daly, Norbert Pachler and Kyoko Oi, plus participants at the Leverhulme lectures and other presentations on e-learning given by each of the authors. The professional help afforded by Andrew Copeland, Kar-wing Man, Kevin Walker, Jess Stachyra, Sarah Smith, Sarah Gelcich and Rachel Shaw made sure arrangements were seamless and smooth-running.

We are particularly grateful to Marianne Lagrange at SAGE for her belief in the idea that we proposed, and for her commitment throughout the project; and to Monira Begum for excellent administrative support.

The book would not be the same without the inclusion of our case study writers. Thanks go to Chris Bissell, Pauline Cheong, Sun-young Choi, Juel Chouinard, Myrrh Domingo, Christine Greenhow, Yoram Kalman, Michelle M. Kazmer, Christie Koontz, Marcus Leaning, Paul Marty, Gale Parchoma, Rosanna de Rosa, Lesley Scope, Lisa Tripp, and a contributor who wished to remain anonymous, for the cases that appear here (and to Loretta Horton, Betsy Stefany and others who contributed through informal conversations) for sharing their innovative practices and experiences with us so generously.

The authors and publisher would like to thank the following for permission to use the figures in the book: Cope and Kalantzis, *Multiliteracies* (2000). Reproduced with permission of Taylor and Francis.

Introduction: New Learning Practices

What's New in Learning?

How we learn, with whom, and by what means is changing. Rapid changes in knowledge and technology are driving the need for new approaches to dissemination and integration of new information into workplaces and work practices, and new learning paths for adults. Education is no less affected. Universities, colleges, and secondary schools are rapidly adopting and integrating learning and course management systems into regular use. Distance learning, once supported through television broadcast and one-to-one correspondence between learners and teachers, has been transformed by the online spaces available for online or e-learning. Resources, in the form of published texts or subject experts, are increasingly easily available through the web, from anywhere, at any time, and to anyone. Moreover, learners, who have traditionally been readers and receivers of information, are taking on a new role as information providers, contributing to ongoing dialogues in public forums, adding local information into global contexts, and engaging with others online for work, learning and play.

The net result is a radically changed landscape of who can and does learn from whom, where, and under what conditions. These circumstances challenge current models of education. The bricks-and-mortar school or university no longer bounds knowledge when learners attend classes from multiple sites within and across countries. Set curricula and set technology plans with a multi-year lifespan are seriously challenged by a knowledge and technology base that changes every year. Authoritative texts are also challenged by such rapid change, but also by the information posted daily to the web through news, opinion articles, and, increasingly, in academic pre-prints and open access repositories. If we view these changes as an assault on accepted paradigms of teaching and learning – the teacher as the authority, online information as unacceptable, students as receivers of knowledge – we miss the opportunity to learn with these changes and take them in our stride as a way of embracing newer forms of education.

This book argues for the need, but also the enjoyment of new ways of teaching and learning. We see the changes accompanying online knowledge acquisition, sharing and production as momentous, signifying a marked change in learning for the 21st century. But it should not be an unexamined change. Thus, this book grapples with the currently unfolding new paradigms of learning that accompany the continuing expansion of the Internet, online learning, and online learning relationships.

As a whole, we refer to this new approach as e-learning. There are, of course, other names for this area: asynchronous learning, online learning, networked learning; and, there are other areas that concern themselves with distributed, online or technology-supported learning: distance learning, educational informatics, educational technology. There are also newly emerging areas that address technological and philosophical aspects of learning transformation, such as mobile learning (Pachler, 2007; Pachler et al., 2009; Sharples et al., 2007; Vavoula et al., 2009) and ubiquitous learning (Cope and Kalantzis, 2009). Along with glowing reports of transformations, there is the reality of the technical, social and organizational work it takes to create successful e-learning environments. Some of this reality has led to interpretations of e-learning that see it as only a diminished version of learning in physical spaces, and as an added burden placed on teachers by their administrations. Despite potential negative connotations, and the choice of alternate names, we have deliberately chosen e-learning as our overarching term and we define it as follows.

First, we see e-learning as a transformative movement in learning, not just the transfer of learning to an online stage, and we use the prefix 'e-' in keeping with usage in the emerging areas of e-research and e-science. Second, we do not see e-learning as bounded by institutional structures of courses, programs or degrees, but instead as embracing the way learning flows across physical, geographical and disciplinary borders. Third, we see e-learning as perpetual, sustained over a lifetime and enacted in multiple, daily occurrences as we search for information to satisfy our learning needs and contribute content that promotes our and others' understanding. This kind of learning is mobile, in the sense of learning from and in new and different locations as needed and on the devices at hand. Fourth, we see e-learning as an engaged act created through both technical and social decisions. A technology does not make e-learning, but rather teachers and learners use technology to create the social space in which learning occurs. This may be a psychological space, sustained across multiple devices and activities; it may be a cyberspace, providing one-stop entry into the learning experience; and it may be a physical space, using technology to connect learning to locations or objects in cities and museums.

This grounds our view of *practice*. Where e-learning embodies a transformation in learning, it entails more than just a change in delivery mechanism, it changes the way we learn. Some of the transformative effects include greater learner responsibility in formal learning settings through collaborative learning as a practice and online conversations as rhetorical platforms, as self-directed, even entrepreneurial learners search and contribute in informal contexts on and through the web. As Jenkins et al. (2006) point out regarding participatory cultures, attention should be paid as much to these new practices as to the knowledge content so that learners become effective members of this emerging culture.

To provide a connection to real-world experience, throughout the book we include cases provided by e-learning teachers and researchers. These help to highlight particular areas of discussion, but also stand on their own as examples of current experiences – both successful and not – in the context of emerging e-learning practices. Also, throughout the book we provide definitions offset in boxes that provide extra clarification on topics or concepts we are using.

This book is directed toward all who engage in learning online, including teachers, course designers, course providers, instructors, trainers, tutors and academic faculty. It is equally directed to new e-learners, particularly those embarking on professional certification, and college or university degrees that are partially or fully online. The former will gain an understanding of the way learning is changing everywhere with the presence of the Internet and participatory media, and the theoretical and practical aspects that help in approaching new learning practices. Students of all levels will gain a sense of their new role as participants in new learning, whether related to class participation or lifelong learning. As presented in the case by Kalman (p. 4), we hope that new e-learners will come to realize the potential of this environment for learning. We also hope that any who use, learn and contribute online will gain from this book. E-learning extends well beyond the classroom, and the practices described here also extend to how people pursue personal learning agendas, leisure learning and online learning as an adjunct to daily life. Lastly, we direct this book to those studying, researching and learning about learning online. We hope our discussions of theory, new learning roles, participatory transformations, research methods and references to the growing literature on e-learning, will provide a basis for informing researchers and research directions in the new and exciting area of learning and the Internet.

While this book primarily addresses adults engaged in part- or full-time higher education via partial or full use of online learning, the kinds of changes explored here neither originate from nor are bound by the institution. Instead, new learning practices are leaking from the Internet into higher education. Widespread use of the Internet for online communication, knowledge discovery, deliberation and building community online outside learning institutions is making these activities essential components of what it means to learn and to engage in the practice of learning. Information practices from workplaces, social venues and gaming are all affecting how and what is expected in educational settings, and hence are all part of the landscape for new learning practices.

CASE I.1: CONVINCING THE SKEPTICS: THAT SPECIAL MOMENT

Yoram Kalman, The Open University of Israel

I have spent about 10 years of my life as an entrepreneur in the field of international online higher education. One of my favorite moments working in this field comes when I am talking to a prospective e-learning student, or having a discussion with an academic committee that needs to approve some aspect of the online program. Before I tell you about that moment, I note that a prerequisite for reaching it is that whoever I am speaking to has never participated in a well-designed online collaborative class. Most people haven't, and they assume that e-learning is a substitute for 'real' learning. We know that substitutes can be similar to the real thing, and even almost like the real thing, but we also perceive them as second-rate: think 'sugar substitute' or 'cream substitute', and the immediate associations are after-taste, compromise, and inferiority. Is it any wonder that people who have not experienced a well-designed online collaborative class are skeptical about its qualities?

Take Jessica for example, a 34-year-old IT manager at a British telecommunication company. She was very attracted by the online program we offered, but shared with me her concern about being all alone online, working only with the learning materials, and being isolated from real interaction with people. I explained to her that that is not the way online collaborative learning works. The first thing she and her classmates would do when they join the program would be to get to know each other, and learn how to behave in an online classroom in a manner that builds a sense of community. This socialization phase is critical to the success of the class. I described to her, for example, how students use the 'café' section of the online classroom to share good news of births, engagements and marriages with their instructor and their classmates. I reassured Jessica that online students are not lonely users banging away at their keyboards, but rather part of a community of people who know and care about each other.

A candidate like Jessica also wonders about academic quality: 'Can you really get a high quality of education online?' My answer is that the quality of an online academic program is as high as the quality of the university offering the program. I show her, for example, how a well-designed discussion question leads to a week-long intellectual exchange between students, and how such a discussion reveals to the instructor much more about each student than a traditional face-to-face setting. Not only is the instructor able to assess how well the students understand this week's topics, but can also see to what extent they can apply academic theory to real-world situations. These examples help candidates realize that online learning might even be more interactive and engaging than more traditional face-to-face classrooms, and that the online format does not diminish the academic quality of the course.

But I am not done there. I explain to students and academics about those with special circumstances who would otherwise be prevented from gaining this education, and describe the magic that takes place when you place under one virtual roof a diversity of students who live in different circumstances, time zones and countries. From real life cases, I describe the busy CEO who had to forgo face-to-face classes that could never fit into a busy schedule in which family and work commitments are juggled; the quadriplegic consultant whose home-based business is an exemplary success story; and the ambitious account manager at an advertising firm who heads a single-parent family. I tell them about real classes that bring together people from around the globe, such as the one that included a marketing manager at a Chinese financial firm, an accountant at a Swedish high-tech company, and a security manager at a casino in Las Vegas. Where would these students have an opportunity to understand each other's perspective were it not for the power of online collaborative education?

At this time I begin to see in the eyes of my audience that the 'special moment' has arrived, and that they are starting to understand that online collaborative education is not a substitute for 'real education', but rather something that is new and different. 'But there is one more thing you need to know', I tell Jessica. 'Our online classes are also a lot of work. That part won't go away.' I have her CV in front of me, and know her professional achievements so far. I am thus not surprised that this only encourages her further. I can see she is excited at the opportunity, and eager to begin exploring this new way of getting an education. Her only question now is 'What do I need to do to apply?'

It is said that innovation often starts by doing old things in new ways, but that it really makes an impact when it allows doing new things in new ways. That is what online collaborative education is all about: an education that can accomplish what traditional forms of education could not have accomplished before. Are you still a skeptic?

Dr Yoram Kalman researches the impact of digital communication technologies on individuals, organizations and society, at the Department of Management and Economics, The Open University of Israel. Formerly, Dr Kalman served as Senior Vice President at Laureate Online Education, B.V., collaborating with the University of Liverpool. His homepage is at www.kalmans.com

What is Driving New Conditions for Learning?

Throughout this book we engage with the question of what is driving change in our teaching and learning environments, how this affects practice, and how to come to terms with these rapid changes in technologies in the service of teaching and learning. The question to ask then is: What are the trends in information and communication technology that are creating these new conditions and new opportunities for learning?

The first obvious trend is the increased use of electronic communication in our daily lives, supported through increased access to the Internet via a combination of mobile devices (laptops, mobile and smart phones) and communication infrastructures (broadband and wireless), and providing access to a growing library of information in electronic formats (articles, books, news, movies, music and videos). Few campuses today are without their own email, online file storage systems, digital libraries, and a virtual learning environment (VLE)/ learning management system (LMS, or CMS for course management system; VLE is the usual term used in the UK and Europe; LMS or CMS in North America). New students are increasingly comfortable and savvy in the use of online tools and techniques, including searching for and evaluating online information, selecting and downloading applications, using social networking sites, and contributing to private or public discussions and news through participatory media. Together, these changes mean that all participants in the learning process are tied to a greater or lesser extent to online learning. It is no longer a separate realm for specific courses, teachers and students, but is instead a common method of working and learning across all learning experiences.

Online technologies provide both the infrastructure and the drive for distributed learning. While forms of distance learning have been with us for many years using media such as paper-based correspondence, video and television, and with asynchronous learning networks used in formal education as early as the mid-1970s (Hiltz et al., 2007), the new media – alone or in combination – are greatly increasing the options for providing comprehensive, distributed, interactive learning. As we discuss these developments, it is important to bear in mind the difference between changing the *medium* used for teaching or learning, and the *mode*. Putting text resources online is a change in medium, but a transition from linear text to hypertext is a change in mode. As we will discuss primarily in Chapter 7, a change in medium is often the first step to later changes and transformations in social and technical practices.

As well as the trend to computer-mediated communication, a number of further trends are driving change in how, where, and from whom we learn. First, the presence of vast quantities of information online is driving a need to keep up with such information by applying advanced search skills and by acquiring new knowledge through online discussion. The combination of new media options and the pressing need to keep up with current knowledge is driving a tremendous growth in programs that use online means to reach and interact with distributed students. Other changes affect the learning relationship with people and resources found on the web, for example, in the ease with which anyone can now post to the web. The simpler web posting supported by blogs, and the ease of gaining access to and using new computers and communication infrastructures, has removed the academic, publishing and news media gatekeeping from the web. The result is a new quantity and quality of information online, and a tipping of evaluation from the point of publication to the point of retrieval (Haythornthwaite, 2009a). This has added greater weight to the need to teach, learn and practice information literacy skills.

Another trend involves the acquisition of new literacies associated with online discourse and online practice. Operating online entails learning new skills in discourse, group management and participation. One such new skill for contemporary learning is engaging online, with distributed, previously unconnected others. Whether taking one of the many online courses for formal education, or joining an online learning group, such as those devoted to health issues, rock bands, poetry or academic areas of interest, these new collaborations bring in people from vastly different regions, with communication and group maintenance all managed online. Learning to be a productive member of these groups is a set of practices we are only now beginning to acquire, and beginning to learn how to teach.

Trends such as these – in the use of new media, greater access to information and people, acquisition of new literacies, and adoption of participatory practices – form the substrate on which new learning practices are developing and being driven. As we address e-learning theory and practice, we will return repeatedly to these themes and trends as we address topics in each of the chapters outlined below.

BOX I.1: TERMINOLOGY

A short note is needed on our use of terminology. Bridging North American and UK/European traditions and institutions, we are mindful of the interpretation of labels for those who provide instruction. As a general rule, we use 'instructor' or 'teacher' as generic terms to signify the professional who is responsible for a course and its instruction, whether a tutor, lecturer, reader or professor in UK traditions, a teaching assistant, instructor, assistant professor, associate professor or professor in North American traditions, or whether a teacher in secondary school (UK) or high school (N. America). Where a separate role of course designer is intended we refer to that role specifically.

The term 'faculty' is used to refer to the individual member of a department (a 'faculty member') and indicates someone with an academic appointment in a university, but the term also refers to larger units such as a 'Faculty of Arts

(Continued)

(Continued)

and Science'. We have tried to avoid the use of the term 'staff', which means faculty members in the UK context, and office and support staff in the US context. Where the word 'staff' appears we have tried to define its use more specifically.

The term 'course' is generally used to refer to a single, semester (aka term) long class, and 'program' as the set of courses that make up the requirement for a degree or a specialization. We have avoided the use of the term 'module' (UK) for these 12–15 week units ('courses' in the US).

By contrast with the largely US use of terms for people and courses, we chose to use the UK/European term Virtual Learning Environment (VLE) over Learning or Course Management System (LMS, CMS). This is in part because the term describes a better objective for the kind of environment in which we hope learning will occur. It captures better the idea of a place for learning than a place for management of course administrative details.

We hope that any inadvertent inconsistencies in the use of these terms will be understandable from the context in which they are used.

Chapter Contents

Chapter 1 begins the examination of e-learning by highlighting the major features of *new media* and their impact on interaction, relationship building, teaching and learning. In particular, this chapter highlights the differences between computer-mediated and face-to-face communication, and the opportunities each provides.

Chapter 2 looks at how the contemporary processes we are seeing and experiencing through e-learning fit with *existing theories of learning*. The questions we ask in this chapter include: Do we need a new theory of learning to address learning online? If so, what are the implications of new learning practices for learning theory in general?

Chapter 3 also addresses learning theories, but now for online learning. Here we wrestle further with the question of whether we need *new theorizing for online learning*. This chapter considers where existing theory can be taken up or extended to address new learning platforms, as well as proposing new theoretical positions specifically tailored to learning in the age of collaborative peer production, multiple literacies, and distributed participants.

Chapter 4 addresses in more depth the range and challenge of *new literacies and new discourses* needed for new modes of learning and production. While text and conversation have dominated, and may well continue to dominate online, new discourses also include facility with image, audio and video. This chapter provides a theoretical grounding in approaching new discourses, and in particular draws on the idea of reciprocal co-evolution to draw out understanding of the continuously emergent relationship between literacy and technology.

Chapter 5 addresses how learning is affected by the rise of *participatory culture* (Jenkins et al., 2006), and the change from learner as consumer to learner as producer with the rise of participatory media. New social media and contributory practices join together to drive participative practices. While collaborative products such as final assignments may still be in the future for many institutions, peer production is already becoming well entrenched as a work and social practice, from the many open source development projects to Wikipedia and other online collaborations sustained by crowds and communities. Indeed, from the first bulletin board for discussion, online learning has engaged in collaborative, participatory practice. This chapter explores the impact of these changes on the authoritative voice of teachers and information gatekeepers, and the emerging transformations this creates for learning practices.

Chapter 6 addresses the specific social outcome of developing and nurturing *learning communities*. The promise of using online venues for creating the safe space for collaboration and sharing of ideas has engaged scholars with interests as diverse as business and the community. This chapter explores what it takes to make a learning community for e-learning settings and beyond.

Chapter 7 picks up the theme of *social and technical* literacy and practices with an eye to the way these are co-constructed. A learning environment may be actualized through technology, but it gains its life and meaning through social interaction. This chapter explores how the social and the technical are balanced in online interaction and online learning environments, bringing attention to what might be called a new literacy of sociotechnical practice.

Chapter 8 looks at the embedded nature of e-learning and the *e-learning ecologies* that form the context for learning. The chapter discusses both a bird's eye view of ecologies that supports analysis and design, and also a personal view of the multiple ecologies and social worlds an individual navigates as an e-learner. With a view to overlapping ecologies and worlds, we can ask how the embedding in multiple environments – both online and off – affects the learning experience; or, we can ask how a learner manages engagement in these multiple worlds. This chapter engages with the issue of e-learning ecologies as a means of making visible the concurrent work and social lives in which today's online learners are embedded. The idea of invisibility is returned to again in Chapter 11 in relation to cross-cultural participation in e-learning.

Chapter 9 discusses how the ubiquity of information online, and the many access points available in our daily lives is creating a state of *ubiquitous learning*. We explore the way learning on, through and by means of the web provides a wealth of resource potential, both to documents, audio and video and also to people with expertise or common interest. We explore in this chapter what it means to become an e-learner in the sense of an engaged, ubiquitous learner, active in participation and contribution supported through online means.

Chapter 10 examines who is able to take advantage of the revolution in information and learning practices and who is not, considering *e-inclusion and exclusion*. E-inclusion for learning involves not just access to and use of technology, but also adoption and fluency with the social practices of online participation and learning. In this chapter, we look at current approaches to considering inclusion and exclusion in relation to Internet use and educational and learning opportunities.

Chapter 11 addresses *cross-cultural issues in e-learning*. Distributed learners are not only spread across countries, they are also spread across cultures. As more e-learning programs reach beyond national borders, more teachers and students engage with multiple cultures within a single class. In the same way that new learning practices require understanding of participatory culture, so too these must be learnt against the backdrop of different national, social and pedagogical cultures. This chapter continues the idea of e-learning ecologies, here with an emphasis on cross-cultural issues. Recognizing that differences will be present is the first step for cross-national e-learners and teachers. This chapter offers examples and suggestions of practices for both learners and teachers to help uncover and bridge cultural and local practices.

Chapter 12 turns our attention to *researching e-learning*. As an emerging field, it is important to create a common base on which to compare strategies and practices, as well as consider ways to examine e-learning in practice and by practitioners. This chapter presents a starting point for considering research questions and methods relating to e-learning. While this chapter concentrates on the process of research, throughout the book we highlight research areas and questions that we see as particularly relevant and important for the development of the e-learning field. These questions we leave as invitations to research fellow learners about e-learning.

These chapters provide a beginning for exploration of the major trends affecting teaching and learning. For some, these changes are a given, already part of their daily life and activity. However, for many, the transition to new, online conditions is still an ongoing process as they remember, and often prefer to adhere to, earlier modes of teaching and learning. The aim here is not to throw away older practices, but to outline how these are affected and (potentially) transformed with online, anywhere, anytime, anyone connectivity, and how newer practices overlap with and affect older practices.

Looking Forward

E-learning sits now much as discussions of the Internet did in 2000 – as a separate realm of activity, distinct from everyday life. E-learning has been about the online class, designed to meet the needs of distributed, off-campus students, and more recently co-opted to serve the on-campus class, extending information access and contact outside class times. But both options still work within the boundaries of institutional practices, established and monitored to conform to educational practices within the framework of higher education, and with membership limited to participants who have passed the entry bar based on pre-evaluation of qualifications and payment of fees. Teaching and learning options in these environments have been limited – or, perhaps, safeguarded – to what could be managed through the supported educational systems, and to the resources (e.g. readings) available and distributable from the institution delivering the program.

Now, e-learning, as has been found before for the Internet, has become part of everyday life, from the handy reference sources of Wikipedia, the Internet Movie Data Base (IMDB), and online newspapers, to the tumble of citizen-generated, annotated and tagged texts, pictures and videos. The result is that the information practices that serve learning now merge with, flow across, and pervade on and offline activity, both inside and outside the defining frame-work of a physical or virtual class.

As we maintain our focus on learning practices for higher education, we can-not ignore how institutionally-based learning is subject to influences from information and Internet practices in general. Hence, as we proceed through the book, expect to find that as we address e-learning in gated communities of learners in higher education, we also address the contemporary trends in infor-mation and knowledge practices that spill over into educational environments and affect learning success within these institutions and across the Internet.

Further Reading

Brown, J. S. and Adler, R. P. (2008). 'Minds on fire: Open education, the long tail, and learning 2.0', *EDUCAUSE Review, 43*(1): 16–32.

1

The New Media

Introduction

The new media – from email to blogs to YouTube to Twitter – have driven major changes in who we communicate with, from where, and when. Similarly, they are driving changes in what we can and want to do in the online and on-campus classroom, and when searching and learning via the web. The differences and affordances of each of these modes of communication underpin the revolution in e-learning. Thus, it is well worth reviewing some of the fundamental differences between communicating via computer media and communicating face-to-face. This serves as a starting point for understanding what makes e-learning different from face-to-face learning.

We use computer media so frequently and in such an integrated manner with daily life that it is no longer practical to talk about computer-mediated communication (CMC) *versus* face-to-face communication. Yet, there are major differences between face-to-face and online communication, such as the text interface and asynchronous communication. Awareness and attention to these differences helps in understanding how these technologies can best be used, or adjusted for use, for e-learning. Also important is unbundling the medium from the desired outcome. For example, often people feel that in a move from face-to-face to CMC, they lose the richness of the intimate circle of others. But if we unbundle the intimate circle from the medium, we may find that what is lost is the immediacy of interaction and the close attention of others. The desired outcome of 'immediacy' and 'attention' can then be addressed with social or technical enhancements, for example more rapid feedback in asynchronous discussions or a synchronous connection with a critical mass of remote learners. In looking at CMC 'versus' face-to-face communication, there may be some losses, but there are also gains. Many studies and many successful online programs and collaborations indicate that learning and working together online and through computer media can be a satisfying and productive experience. Our task is to find out how best to make that happen.

We feel the aim is not to judge whether online is better than offline, but rather to work from the idea that if you cannot meet face-to-face, how are you going to make the best effort to create and sustain a productive learning environment? What do we need to know – about learning, media and social interaction – that can help inform our participation in learning environments whether as a novice, expert, student or teacher? This approach applies equally to the now common blended or hybrid learning environment that combines face-to-face meetings with deliberately designed online activity. What do we need to know to appropriately distribute learning experiences across these offline and online settings? The first answer to these questions is that we need to understand the basic differences between offline and online communication on our way to making deliberate use of these features for learning.

Features of Computer-mediated Communication

The earliest observers of CMC noted that computer media convey far fewer communication cues between speaker and audience than face-to-face communication (e.g. Kiesler, 1997; Kiesler and Sproull, 1987; Sproull and Kiesler, 1986; Walther, 1996). Email lists, for example, permit communication via text from an unseen speaker to an unseen audience of indeterminate size and composition. Email – and many forms of CMC that follow – hide visible signs of gender, race and age, prevent us from picking up cues associated with how people dress, and remove from the communication a range of nuances normally added through voice, hand gesture and body language. Unless explicitly stated in messages, the status and provenance of the speaker are also invisible. At first this all seems a terrible loss, particularly if you are the person losing status by the inability to be seen. But, this status flattening has had positive effects for those who are shy about responding, or were previously prevented or inhibited from contributing because of low work status.

A key aspect – even a benefit – of CMC is the way it allows unbundling of the message from cues which are tightly bound with face-to-face communication, in particular cues about individual identity and setting. Along with unbundling, CMC can also be combined and used in ways that allow a rebundling that suits the new setting (Haythornthwaite and Nielsen, 2006). This is a particularly salient point for addressing issues of shyness, turn-taking, or remote participation in e-learning settings. While it is possible to try to re-introduce all the cues of a face-to-face setting, for example through multiple video feeds from different sites, a rush to recreate the many cues can lose the benefits that a lean, text-based, asynchronous setting confers. Such benefits include the ability to post simultaneously, to post after reflection, and to form thoughts into text, a prime communication mode in learning and education.

Both face-to-face and CMC *afford* different possibilities for communication, but both have their merits for communication outcomes. Face-to-face communication in small groups permits a richness of communications cues that provide multiple types of information about others; lean CMC permits selective presentation of cues, providing control over what kinds of information are conveyed to others. Anonymity – or the relative anonymity possible when so many cues about an individual are missing – is one of a number of *affordances* of CMC. Box 1.1 provides background on the idea of affordances. Other major affordances of CMC are listed in Table 1.1, highlighting those that differ from the affordances of face-to-face communication. These include anonymity, but also the way CMC affords asynchronous (anytime), mobile (anywhere) communication that potentially connects widely to other people (anyone), both locally and globally. New forms of data capture, such as digital cameras, and of communication, such as blogs and blog comments, afford rapid updating and aggregation of information.

Affordances of CMC technologies – whether email, bulletin boards, wikis, chat or video – create opportunities for conversation, learning and the creation of common understanding and purpose, just as face-to-face conversation can and does. Yet, the conditions are different. Awareness of differences and possibilities helps in planning their adoption and use, as well as in recognizing where changes are happening outside the traditional learning setting that will affect supposedly 'closed-room' learning (e.g. as laptops enter the classroom). The following sections discuss some of the ways that features listed in Table 1.1 can be considered for their effect on interaction in learning contexts.

BOX 1.1: AFFORDANCES

The idea of affordances stems from the work of Gibson (1979) referring to what an environment affords an animal in that context. This idea was adapted for discussion of design of material artifacts by Norman (1988), and for computing technology by Gaver (1991, 1996). It has also been extended to design that considers patterns of social interaction in the idea of *social affordances* proposed by Bradner, Kellogg and Erickson (1999; see also Wellman, et al., 2003). Each of these writers addresses the latent potential of the object of interest (environment, artifact, interface) for the actor approaching the object. While there is some distinction among them on how much an actor needs to be aware of the potential dangers and/or use, considering what an object allows or makes possible is useful for many areas of endeavor. Thus, we can think about the way social networking *affords* interaction among distributed participants, but also affords transmission of computer viruses and loss of privacy. The idea of affordances is particularly useful as a way to approach design and is well used in this area for computer systems design (for a critique of the use of the concept with reference to technology and learning, see Oliver, 2005a). In some cases this is taken at the very close level of what a computer screen feature allows: radio buttons afford clicking; windows allow separation of application uses; scroll bars afford navigation within a window. Attending to affordances can also be used to focus on the capabilities of a system rather than the particular instantiation of its use: the way a system allows remote connection, asynchronous communication, data collection, navigation, awareness of others, etc. While systems may afford certain features, it is often not until a combination of social and technical features align that a particular affordance reaches its potential. Chapter 7 goes into more depth on this sociotechnical perspective.

Table 1.1 Major Features of Computer-mediated Communication

Feature	Computer-mediated Communication
Anonymous	Relative or actual anonymity is possible because participants are only identified through an online name, email address, or personally chosen identifier. The lack of visual and contextual cues afforded by remote, online, text-only communication allows speakers to choose what they reveal about themselves. Anonymity also holds in online worlds, where individuals can choose what image of themselves they want to present in an avatar.
Asynchronous (Anytime)	Since communications are stored on a server for retrieval at the convenience of the recipient(s), speaker and audience do not need to be present at the same time, in the same place. This permits communication in parallel with other activities, and conversations that can spread over longer periods of time than face-to-face interaction. It also permits communication at any time of the day or night, across time zones, and across work, home or school settings; and affords simultaneous contribution, eliminating the turn-taking found in single-speaker settings and technologies.
Mobile (Anywhere)	Rapidly spreading communication infrastructures and shrinking mobile devices make anywhere communication a reality, allowing people to keep in touch and to follow and contribute to ongoing activities from multiple locations. Internet connectivity also puts the resources of the web in the hands of individuals at all times, from the resources of wikis to electronic journals and books.
Connected (Anyone)	A critical mass of online resources, in the form of web pages, digital libraries, online news and blogs, is permitting increasing access to online information. Similarly, the increasing presence of online profiles, maintained in the form of at least an email address, but also elaborated through home pages, social networking sites, diary blogs and Flickr photo accounts, provides the ability to find many people and to initiate connections worldwide.
Rapid	Although opening and reading email or web pages may be deferred until convenient by the recipient, publication of data and information online can be accelerated where gatekeeping of publication review, and requirements of computer format and device are removed. The current mélange of CMC technologies – from mobile phone to Internet to search engine to laptop retrieval – provide quicker submission, publication and commentary on new information.

(Continued)

Table 1.1   (Continued)

Feature	Computer-mediated Communication
Global	A critical mass of users combined with ready access to technologies and infrastructure stretches contributions and retrieval well beyond national borders. Devices complementary to computers, such as mobile phones, are helping to make connection in regions where other infrastructures and devices are unavailable.
Text-based	While new technologies are rapidly appearing that provide easy audio and video capture and integration, our major communications online continue to be text-based, whether via email, bulletin boards, wikis or Twitter. This creates a major transition as the many cues present in face-to-face communications are reduced to those chosen to be conveyed through text.
Persistent	Supporting asynchronous communication necessarily means storing messages for later retrieval. Discarding a message becomes a choice made separately by message senders *and* receivers, with a record of the message also inhabiting a place on computer servers and backups from where it may also be retrievable long after deleted by both message participants. How long a message persists is bound up in the habits of individuals and the intentions of system designers. This has had a profound effect on conversations, which become retainable and reviewable (email, listservs, discussion boards, online communities), putting such communications somewhere between text and speech. Similarly, posting content online (web page, blog, links to documents) puts such communications somewhere between correspondence and publication.
Serial, Pooled or Composite Logic	Most CMC supports serial posting of messages (email, discussion lists, blogs, blog commentaries, Twitter) as its *logic of representation*. Yet the web as a whole supports a pooled interdependence, with each page contributing independently to the whole. Wiki contributions create a third kind of logic, with the visible entry as a composite, no longer obviously attributable to any particular individual.
Multimodal	While *media* support different platforms for communication (e.g. a text may be provided as a printout, a bound book, an editable word processing file, a fixed document file (pdf), or as a picture), *modes* support different means of expression (verbal, iconic, visual). Contemporary computing interfaces are inherently multimodal, from the texts that appear on screens to pictures, icons, menus, etc.

Anonymity

Anonymity can be highly important for gaining contributions from people who are not comfortable with participating, whether from shyness, lack of familiarity with ways of contributing, second language use, or concerns about how they will be judged for their submission. Thus, anonymity may be a good way to begin online contribution among new e-learners. However, longer term, it becomes important to trust what is happening to freely submitted ideas and information, and thus to get to know others in the learning group. Face-to-face, physical cues such as gaze and body language help confirm the spoken message, helping to build trust between people. Since these are lacking when only CMC is used, other means of building trust need to be established. Identifying others is a first step, and that can be done by knowing who is talking (see Case 1.1). This provides continuity in identity over time as conversations continue and allow participants to build a mental model of the people with whom they are interacting. Even if not using a real name, continuity in identity at least creates a known history within the group and helps participants know who is talking. Sharing a history provides a common ground that can reduce the amount of joint work needed to facilitate discussion (Clark and Brennan, 1991). Over time, individuals gain reputations as experts, information providers, information gatekeepers, and synthesizers of knowledge (Montague, 2006; Preston, 2008; see also Haythornthwaite, 2006a, 2006b). When we recognize that certain group members hold specific skills or knowledge it becomes easier to know what to do with information or information requests and for the group as a whole to operate effectively (Haythornthwaite, 2006a; Wegner, 1987; for more on this, see Chapter 9).

CASE 1.1: PLEASE POST YOUR STORY!

Christie Koontz, Florida State University, USA

Each semester I ask the students in my online classes to write a mini-biography and post it along with a photo during the first week. The bio includes their name and professional background, where they are physically located (and hence where they are coming in from for the distance class), favorite web links expressing personal and professional interests, and career goals. Then, in that first week, I write each one an email in response and welcome them to the class, mentioning something they shared with me, so they know my response is not canned. In the next class, I allow time for students to peruse these bios and post a response to at least one. This activity introduces students to each other, some of whom may be in the same town. Privacy issues do not allow us to post who is where, so this activity provides a mechanism to facilitate a personal touch in several directions. My online mentor, a fellow faculty member at Florida State, introduced this activity to me. I share it with new faculty who observe my classes as a really successful online technique. I teach marketing, storytelling, management, foundations and supervise internships and it works well for all these classes.

Christie Koontz is a faculty member in the School of Library and Information Studies, Florida State University, USA.

Asynchronous, Mobile and Connected

Asynchronicity sets the stage for anywhere, anytime, and anyone communication. It removes the necessity for all participants to be in the same physical or online meeting place at the same time. Thus, it is an ideal solution for distributed, on-the-go learners. It fits well with our contemporary, cluttered schedules which are filled with work, family and social obligations. It also serves ubiquitous learning well since it can be managed on a just-in-time and as-time-is-available schedule: formal learners can choose when to dip into and join online class discussions; lifelong learners can pick up new information and skills as and when needed; and everyday learners can search the web now for information on today's activity.

In discussing media affordances, we should note in the context of e-learning that asynchronicity and distributed participation – in time or location – are not just the purview of structured classes, nor only of online classes. Those who attend traditional classes may manage out of class tasks asynchronously through computer media, for example in the management of group projects. Similarly, online classes may meet synchronously, through chat, audioconference or videoconference. What is of interest is the way the uses of these technologies, individually or collectively, create opportunities for communication and interaction.

BOX 1.2: DESCRIBING LEARNERS

Basic distinctions between *formal* and *informal* learning already exist in the literature. The *formal learner* follows their study in the context of degree or certificate-granting institutions (e.g. schools, colleges and universities). Once 'formal' describes the space, 'informal learning' becomes what's left. It is marked by a lack of the specific teacher–student relationship, but may retain a hierarchical aspect: parent–child, supervisor–employee, master–apprentice, expert–novice, guru–newbie. It can entail learning of a serendipitous nature that happens without an agenda; it can mean self-directed learning to personal goals, hence with an agenda but not one set by a teaching authority; and it often refers to acquiring process (how-to) knowledge rather than content (know-what) knowledge. Thus, the *informal learner* is found engaged in many kinds of activities. (For more on informal learning and education, see the online resource, The Encyclopedia of Informal Education at http://www.infed.org/). Building on definitions from the UK Department for Education (DfE), Garnett and Ecclesfield (2009) make a distinction between formal, informal, and *non-formal* learning, with the latter as structured learning without formal learning outcomes. These authors model the relationships between these types of learning to pursue the idea of *learner-generated contexts* (Luckin, 2010; Luckin et al., 2007, 2009; see also Chapters 3 and 7).

In relation to e-learning, it is useful again to make the distinction between *formal e-learners*, those engaged in online or blended classes in support of gaining a degree or certificate, and *non-formal* or *informal e-learners*, including those surfing the web for entertainment, facts, news, or opinion, or for dialogue and engagement in knowledge construction. (See also Stebbins, 2006, 2009 for distinctions between casual and serious leisure pursuits.)

We might go further and suggest that web surfers may be 'serendipitous e-learners' – browsing the net in the way many browse book shelves in the traditional library, not sure of what they will find, but ready to follow an interesting thread. Along with lifelong learners, we might add a class of 'everyday e-learners' who surf the web for answers to today's questions, a group that might formerly have looked at an encyclopedia. Finally, we might consider 'salon e-learners' who join online communities to discuss the latest arts, news or events, and 'coterie e-learners' who share their creative products with others (e.g. see Rebaza, 2009, regarding such activity in *LiveJournal*). As a whole, we might call the phenomenon of learning anywhere, anytime, from anyone, *ubiquitous learning*, and those engaged in a continual immersion of knowledge seeking, retrieval, integration and creation as *ubiquitous learners* (Cope and Kalantzis, 2009; see Chapter 9).

While we are now getting very used to online communication, and developing new personal routines to deal with keeping up with our email, Twitter stream, online news reading, and social networking, asynchronicity introduces a new time management challenge for those learning or working online. It generates an extra time management load as individuals juggle the multiple worlds that put demands on their time. Anytime connectivity brings work into home hours, and formal learning into work hours. The relative invisibility of this work – for example, that the student does not leave the house or workplace and go to class – can fail to convey to others that the learner is 'in class' and occupied. The task of managing expectations across these overlapping, multiple, invisible worlds adds to what it means to be an online learner (Kazmer and Haythornthwaite, 2001; Star and Strauss, 1999). This aspect of e-learning life is discussed further in Chapter 8 on e-learning ecologies.

A major side-effect of asynchronicity for learning is the delay between post and response, question and answer. The immediacy of interaction in a face-to-face setting, combined with the multiple cues of facial expression, vocal tone, and body language, as well as the ability to use impromptu drawings or models, can allow quicker feedback on ideas and questions and more elaboration on the way to creating common understanding. While new technologies can address these limitations, for example with tablet PCs for drawing, computer simulation models, or video presentations, it is often the social solution that addresses these shortcomings. Communication practices can increase responsiveness: teachers and learners can check for questions and answers more frequently; care can be taken in explaining; and workarounds can be developed for conveying models and drawings. Mobile infrastructures help in increasing connectivity, but it is the social pattern that adjusts – for better or worse in terms of time use – to create a responsive learning environment (see also Chapter 7 for more on synergies between social practice and technical features).

Since many teachers find the load of responding individually to each and every question and post online very demanding, the practice of collaborative learning has been taken up as one way out of this potentially show-stopping overload. Collaborative learning, and its online version computer-supported collaborative learning (CSCL; Koschmann, 1996; Koschmann et al., 2002; Miyake, 2007), involves a shift of control from delivery of knowledge by a teacher to shared evaluation and contribution from all learners. This is discussed further in Chapter 5 on participatory culture.

Rapid and Global

Computer-mediated and asynchronous communication increase opportunities for interaction and learning, and thus the rapidity of input and feedback. Rapidly spreading communication infrastructures – Internet access and wireless connections – and shrinking mobile devices – laptops and smart phones – make anywhere communication a reality. People can stay aware of others' activities through Twitter feeds and social networking site information; they can stay connected on tasks with mobile email; and they can update data and status information to central sites for others to view and use. All this is possible from multiple locations, and thus can bring experiences and information from individuals across town or across the world. Perhaps the most well-known examples of this kind of contribution are the mobile phone images uploaded to the web following disasters such as the Asian Tsunami (December, 2004), Hurricane Katrina in New Orleans, Louisiana (August, 2005), and the bombing attacks in London (July, 2005); and photo and Twitter feeds during political demonstrations in Iran (2009; dubbed a 'Twitter revolution' by the *Washington Post*, 2009; see also Smartmobs, 2009).

As well as supporting in-group communication, Internet connectivity also puts a vast range of rapidly updated online resources in the hands of individuals at all times. Web pages, online databases, digital libraries, online news, news blogs, and other online texts represent just a few of the kinds of resources that can be accessed for information retrieval. Combined with search engines and other information retrieval mechanisms, these resources greatly enhance the range of resources available at our fingertips anytime, anywhere. Of course, many of these resources are not the peer-reviewed and publisher-approved articles and books that teachers would like students to use. Widespread use of online information is becoming such a reality for all learners that the evaluation of such resources becomes a skill for today's learners to master, and for today's teachers to integrate into their practices (e.g. see Tripp, 2009).

Access to online resources is also having an effect in an unexpected location – the physical classroom. While the idea of an online student using online resources sounds like a natural fit, teachers in the physical classroom are beginning to deal with students also consulting online resources during face-to-face classes. Computer-free or Internet-free face-to-face settings constrain participants to the resources in the room – both textual and interpersonal. But, the general trend for more Internet and wireless access in physical classrooms, to serve both the teachers and the students, is driving a hybrid situation in face-to-face educational settings. While few of us would resist bringing laptops to meetings, or searching for relevant information during those meetings, there is a continuing reluctance to extend that to classroom settings, and many teachers have yet to come to terms with the presence of Internet-connected computers in class during class time. Indeed, there are now many instances of individual faculty and programs banning laptops in the classroom as distracting from the face-to-face class (e.g. Bone, 2010; Fang, 2009; Fried, 2008; de Vise, 2010).

Text-based

Our heavily text-based communication represents a major transition from the oral and visual stimulations of a classroom or co-located setting. Missing from text are nuances in voice such as deliberate or unconscious variation in vocal pitch, pace, volume, accent, etc.; hand-gestures, eye gaze and body language; and visual cues of age, dress and race. Gone is the information on in-group interaction that can be gleaned from seating arrangement and positioning in group settings, and observation of side-conversations and attention.

The lack of these cues can be useful in the same way anonymity is useful – allowing individuals to be judged based on what they type rather than on other aspects of their person. But, many find the text-based environment too lean to maintain the kind of interpersonal connectivity they desire. They find it easy to fade back and become invisible online, and without extra effort it can be difficult to feel present or be perceived to be present online (Bregman and Haythornthwaite, 2003; Haythornthwaite and Kazmer, 2004a; Haythornthwaite et al., 2000).

Many kinds of cues have been re-introduced in daily CMC use, from emoticons to signature lines and personal icons that add nuance to a message and status to an identity. These can be used deliberately in e-learning to enhance the sense of others in the community and to introduce a greater range of interaction via text. Personality can be expressed through profile pages with personal details (see Case 1.1). Signatures, shorthands, and personal online writing styles can be developed that convey personal identity through the medium of text and the creativity afforded by keyboard characters. Online class texts may introduce variety by bringing in styles from other media, for example commands from online chat or games, or short message text, to dramatize a point or make a joke. A teacher may need to model a lighter tone in text to promote conversation and/or a 'heavier' tone if the discussions get too much off topic. Teachers and students can work toward adopting common use of terms or styles, both those associated with the course content or career and those specific to the particular class. Common use signals solidarity with other members in an online community, and can reinforce group cohesiveness toward their joint learning goal.

Persistent

Another feature that proves useful for learning is that CMC provides a ready-made transcript of communications that can be reviewed and reused, a *persistent conversation* (Erickson, 1999) that can be revisited, reviewed, and (in some cases) revised (see also Chapter 5). The persistent record facilitates asynchronous participation but with synchronous awareness of the discussion, that is, a learner can enter anytime and catch up on the conversation before responding. Such transcripts may be openly available online from lists with open archives or gated and accessible only to registered participants, as in environments open only to those invited or granted access because of enrollment in classes.

Knowing the record is persistent can make some participants shy about writing online and adding to ongoing information streams (Haythornthwaite et al., 2000). This may particularly be the case when teachers use the persistent text to evaluate contributions to classes. Ephemeral face-to-face conversations disappear, providing a freer environment for impromptu conversation, trying out ideas, and fooling around. Again, teachers can make a choice about such conversational features, manipulating the use of CMC to recreate ephemeral conversations, for example by turning off recording and archiving for some forums, or reducing the evaluation burden on early contributions (see Case 1.2).

CASE 1.2: 'LOW STAKES' MEDIA USE

Lisa M. Tripp, Florida State University, USA

This online class in 'Digital Media: Concepts and Production' is designed for novices in Web 2.0 and digital media authoring. To get these students started in a non-threatening way, the first strategy used is to get students active in the learning space.

'For the first eight weeks of the class, students do "low stakes" media production exercises each week. These exercises are graded pass/fail; submitting an exercise constitutes a passing grade. This is done so as to lower students' stress levels about being assessed in an unfamiliar area, and encourage students to learn something new with little risk of failure. The exercises require minimal preproduction planning and move quickly; each exercise lasts approximately one week, and some weeks involve multiple exercises. This creates a fast pace right from the start, in which students get exposed to a wide variety of "Web 2.0" tools and media production applications within a relatively short period of time. The exercises are also sequenced so as to move from the more basic competencies of using collaborative, web-based software for communication and collaboration among students, and for sharing and circulating media online, to the more advanced skills involved in using media production software to create simple, short image, audio, and video projects. In this way, each exercise helps scaffold the skills needed for the next, more complicated exercise; and, together, the exercises prepare students to do more creative, ambitious media production work in the second half of the class.' (Tripp, 2009: 3107).

Four strategies are recommended to support this kind of high tech, distributed class for novice learners: (1) use a 'low stakes' start-up strategy; (2) use an open source software to reach students with diverse, and often limited resources; (3) foster a culture of collaboration for peer support and assistance; and (4) teach ethical and legal practices for finding, remixing and circulating media, including creative commons licensing.

Lisa M. Tripp is an Assistant Professor in the School of Library and Information Studies, College of Communication and Information, Florida State University, USA. This case summarizes the strategies and recommendations presented in Tripp (2009).

Outside the domain of formal learning, attitudes to what can and should be posted online are emerging and are influencing social norms associated with the practice of online self-disclosure. Use of personal data from the persistent conversations in general online participation, for example personal disclosures on health or drug support sites, and social networking sites, are raising concerns about the future ramifications for individuals. Individuals are taking time to consider how they will enact their presentation of self online. As societal norms continue to change in reaction to online information use, new attitudes, practices and expectations of use will enter formal learning environments as well, potentially affecting rules and norms for e-learning practices in institutional settings. (For more on changing conditions and attitudes to privacy in relation to online interaction, see the Pew Internet and American Life Project report on young adults and privacy considerations, Lenhart and Madden, 2007; for more on privacy and surveillance concerns, see also Lyon, 2007; for discussion of legal aspects of assuring student privacy in education, see Varvel et al., 2007).

Logics of Representation

Different logical organization of communications is possible with CMC. Some media provide a primarily sequential ordering of messages, dictated by time of arrival at a central server. This applies to email, discussion lists, blog commentaries, Twitter. The delay between receiving a message and responding to it has often been referred to as a useful learning opportunity, providing time for reflection and thought, and the opportunity to compose a message with revision and without haste. However, this delay also creates confusion as messages appear to be out of sequence. A question may lead to an answer and further comment, and then another answer appears. Over time, we have become more accustomed to these visible traces of asynchronous interaction and interweaving of answers. We have, in essence, adopted another concept or mental model about the logic of message sequencing in asynchronous conversations, one that allows us to follow multiple threads of conversation in a sequential list (sometimes with help from the software design). However, sequential ordering is not the only option. For example, a quite different kind of sequencing – or logic – is involved with media such as wikis, where the visible presentation is of a single composite, and where each participant can overwrite another's copy. Adopting a wiki means adopting different ideas of the goals of online participation and can entail a learning process in making the switch from identifiable contributions in discussion to pooled result. Box 1.3 provides more on logics of representation, tying this to the way we read media according to different logics.

BOX 1.3: LOGICS OF REPRESENTATION

It is possible to think of the modes of communication in terms of the logics of their presentation. The conventional, print-based logic of writing (and speech) is *sequential*. That is to say, words follow other words; sentences (writing) or utterances (speech) are arranged in sequences; paragraphs follow paragraphs, and so on. Whether the writing moves vertically from top to bottom of the page (as in Chinese), or horizontally from left to right (as in English), the connecting links are sequential and we 'read' the information accordingly.

Written or spoken language, however, can embody *hierarchies* via abstraction. An idea or concept is considered to be at a 'higher' level than a fact. In science, categories and concepts are generated from observable data. *Hierarchy* assumes, then (at least in Western discourse) a more vertical logic than a sequential one. It is as if a set of smaller boxes fitted inside larger boxes. The relationship is one of larger categories embracing and including smaller ones. (While hierarchy is perhaps the most commonly known organizing principle, other kinds of relational logic are inherent in entity-relationship models used for designing relational databases, and in network models (e.g. semantic networks) that do not presuppose a higher or lower level of importance or earlier or later place in a sequence.)

These logics of sequence and hierarchy, which metaphorically can be characterized in Western discourse as horizontal and vertical, have many variations. For example, a *stack* assumes a pile of phenomena that are all more or less of equal status and size; a *still image* will have a different kind of presence (hardly a logic, unless it is arrayed with other images); a *composite* logic will move between the two main axes or logics and possibly include other kinds too, including still images (moving images, of course, take on a sequential logic).

These logics provide us with expected ways to approach communications and to organize thought. Some media present commonly agreed upon paths for reading and production, for example reading a book from beginning to end, reading sequentially through a list of postings on a discussion list, and adding a contribution at the end of a list or the end of a thread. Some reading paths are more flexible, for example reading an image or a multimodal web page, or designing a web page. Wikis provide separate but interrelated logics of the surface level text and the behind-the-scenes talk pages.

Analysis of contemporary learning resources communicated via computer interfaces will find such logics useful. See Bayne, Williamson and Ross (2010) for an analysis of 'webquests' provided in a UK National Museums project that suggests that such logics are sometimes in conflict, to the detriment of the resource as a whole.

Multimodal

In the main, widely adopted e-learning educational platforms depend on relatively monomodal forms of verbal language exchanges, that is, words presented in written form, whether these are conversations, explanations, reports, assignments or assessments. To some extent this can be seen as modelling the kind of discourse needed for academic work and even for much of today's business operations. However, the written form has drawbacks for many kinds of learning content where modelling, drawing, crafting, or working with objects, patients or animals is important for explaining concepts or demonstrating practice. To date, the lack of such facilities on a routine basis has led to much in the way of workarounds – pictures drawn and scanned to be sent electronically, videos of interaction as sidebars to the discussion in the class, simulations of physical processes to be run as exercises, and collaborations with off-campus sites for laboratory or field experience. However, driven by new developments in e-science, ongoing processes are more readily available to be monitored and analyzed in real time, providing continuous updating of observed processes. Greater computing power, broadband connectivity and new technologies combine to push the limits of what can be combined in the process of e-learning. Thus, virtual worlds begin to become a real possibility for reaching and engaging learners, at a distance and in real-time, in environments that make it possible to do and see and contribute in ways not previously possible in traditional learning, nor in current mainstream e-learning.

The move to such avant garde means of e-learning turns our attention to the multimodality of currently common CMC and its relation to e-learning. The very form of the screen has changed the way we read online, including at its most basic our options about where and what to read, and in what order when web pages present framed areas of text, image, icon, video and audio, as well as conventions of menus, scroll bars and size adjustment. Reading the screen now entails choices of reading path, as well as familiarity with the common language of visual shorthands. Such shorthands serve in CMC as known conventions that compress the need to explain and negotiate understanding in the same way they do in other settings (e.g. in pidgin languages, technical languages, acronyms, metaphors, and other textual shorthands used among members of a discourse community; Clark, 1996; Clark and Brennan, 1991; Hjørland, 2004; Thagard, 2005; Lakoff and Johnson, 1980; Miller, 1994). Miller (1987) notes that icons fulfil a half-way function between words and images. The same may be said for other on-screen communicative devices such as status displays, toolbars, screen sliders and menus, each of which compresses communication and yet also, and importantly, retains our peripheral attention (e.g. as a twitter stream may flicker at the edge of attention). Beyond fixed features of text and textual compressions, still images, moving images and sound round out the common current features of the computer interface and make interaction through it more widely and more obviously multimodal.

Being conversant with the reading and writing of words, whether on paper or on screen, is what is wrapped up in the term *literacy*. However, as reading texts also becomes reading screens and multimodal communications, the term literacy becomes overly strained by the load it must bear. We pick up this discussion in Chapter 4, where we propose that as we move beyond words into other modes, that the discussion should likewise move from literacy (or even literacies) to *new discourses*.

Conclusion

In this chapter we have looked briefly at the features of CMC that allow for the creation of a new kind of discourse space, one largely free of (or lacking) the identifying features and communication cues carried in a face-to-face setting. While a key benefit of CMC has been the unbundling of communication from face-to-face co-presence, the cues lost have left a perception of a diminished interaction. As CMC use has increased, many cues to personality, style, status and group membership have reappeared, with features rebundled to suit new settings and new purposes.

While only a few features and media combinations were discussed here, CMC is now much more than a single email channel of text-based memos. Expansion of medium and mode, and particularly their combination, create spaces as simple as a tweet and as complex as an online community supported through web space, blogs and commentaries, digital repositories, synchronous and asynchronous discussion spaces, and wiki spaces. E-learning fits anywhere and everywhere in this creative mix: on one medium or via multiple media, in an authority-driven virtual learning environment or in an idiosyncratic user-designed mash-up of applications and communications technologies.

As new forms of CMC, alone or in combination, appear at a rapid pace, any treatise on them is unlikely to keep up. This chapter has chosen some classic features of CMC to discuss, but the major point of the chapter has been to give a proactive cast to the use of CMC, to direct attention to what a medium offers, and to advocate for use of that information to make informed choices about communication and learning environments for each e-learning experience.

Further Reading

Andrews, R. and Haythornthwaite, C. (Eds.) (2007). *The Sage Handbook of E-learning Research*. London: Sage.

Haythornthwaite, C. and Nielsen, A. (2006). 'CMC: Revisiting conflicting results'. In J. Gackenbach (Ed.), *Psychology and the Internet*, 2nd edn. San Diego, CA: Academic Press. pp. 161–83.

Lyon, D. (2007). *Surveillance Studies: An Overview*. Cambridge, UK: Polity.

Pachler, N., Bachmair, B. and Cook, J. (2009) *Mobile Learning: Structures, Agency, Practices*. New York: Springer.

Tripp, L. M. (2009). 'Teaching digital media production in online instruction: Strategies and recommendations', in *Proceedings of World Conference on Educational Multimedia, Hypermedia and Telecommunications 2009*. Chesapeake, VA: AACE. pp. 3106–11. http://www.editlib.org/p/31922

Theories of Learning

Introduction

What can conventional learning theory contribute to the development of e-learning theory? Learning theory provides an understanding of what it means to learn, and how learning can be seen by others to have taken place. It articulates the *psychological* process of learning based on an internal change in what we bring to a situation and how that transforms our understanding to a new state. It addresses how we make sense of the world around us, including people, technology and society, and how we assign meaning to situations as the basis of interpretation or action. In developing a sense of the world, we also gain an understanding of our place in the world, and thereby assume and learn to express our identity. Learning theory also provides an understanding of *social* and *environmental* aspects of learning in the way that what we are exposed to, attend to and experience is tied up with our social setting and inter-actions with others. This then ties into *political* aspects of learning, involving power relations in who speaks and who listens, as well as the way learning requires choices among materials and how achievement is recognized through conformance to rhetorical conventions.

Conventional learning theory and e-learning theory are best conceived as over-lapping circles in a Venn diagram: they have their own spheres of application, but also have much in common. These commonalities include understanding learning as a psycho-social process, intrinsic and extrinsic motivations to learn, and a distinction between 'development' (as a naturally occurring and integra-tive process) and 'learning' geared to shorter and medium-term changes in states of mind and knowledge. Both are distinguished from teaching which is an external pedagogic act that may or may not induce learning.

In our discussion, we do not try to distinguish and articulate differences between behaviourist, cognitivist and constructionist theories of learning. These might have been useful categories in the past to distinguish different aspects of the learning process, but they are so inevitably connected that it is hard to give an account of learning from a purely behaviourist point of view for example, or from one of the other viewpoints. Rather, it is more helpful to assume that the three traditions each have something to offer the theory of learning in combination with the others. (For a recent cogent and comprehensive account of learning theory which attempts to cover the three traditions, see Illeris, 2007; for another cogent review specifically written with e-learning in mind, see Mayes and de Freitas, 2006). Since it is beyond the scope of this chapter and this book to review all learning theories for their applicability to e-learning, we select instead aspects that appear most relevant and useful for addressing e-learning. In doing so, we also bring in theoretical perspectives from other domains as they apply to learning and knowledge construction by individuals and other collectives.

Transformation, Framing and Emergence

There are three foundational notions associated with learning theory that help lay our groundwork for making sense of e-learning. The first is *transformation* which is considered in many theories to be the hallmark of learning, that is, that some kind of change in understanding occurs that transforms cognition from an initial state to a modified state, and is also somehow observable in behavior, speech, writing, or other forms of production. The second is *framing*, a concept that turns our attention to the complex of knowledge, past experience, mindset and mental construct of the scope and borders of an endeavor, that characterizes what we, or our learners, bring into the learning experience and bring to bear on the learning itself. Third, we highlight the notion of *emergence*, that is, the way learning and knowledge construction are happening continuously from the interplay of elements in the environment we operate in, and the meaning, interpretation and actions that individually and collectively add to the communal frame. The following sections follow through these three notions in more detail before considering further the tie to e-learning.

Transformation

Transformation is at the heart of the learning. Mezirow (2009) traces the origins of transformative learning theory to adult (specifically, women's) learning communities in the US in the 1970s, and finds the theory on the work of, amongst others, Habermas (with the idea of communication-as-social-action), as having 'a test of validity until new perspectives, evidence or arguments are encountered and validated through discourse as yielding a better judgement' (2009: 92). Such mindsets, suggests Mezirow, are the results of cognitive, emotional and value-based frameworks and specific frames that are brought to bear on perception and experience. When these frames are changed, learning takes place. Such changes in the shape of interpretive frames are brought about by 'critical assessment of the sources, nature and consequences of our habits of mind' and by 'participating fully and freely in dialectical discourse to validate a best reflective judgement' (2009: 94).

Transformation can be seen as both the goal of pedagogical effort and the outcome of successful learning intervention. We can characterize this process and outcome as manifesting itself in changes of understanding along personal, social and political dimensions and do so in the following sub-sections. However, in preparation for this and later discussions in Chapters 3 and 4, we note here that our selection and integration of theories of learning into e-learning hinges on three conditions. First, is the assumption that the way we manifest learning, or observe that it has happened, necessarily entails some production on the part of the learner. The second condition is that such productions are: (a) *rhetorical*, that is, made up of consciously formed discourses and able to be placed in a political and social environment; and (b) multimodal, that is, expressed and expressible not just linguistically (through words, either written or spoken), but through multiple modes of words, images, movement, sound, etc., singly or in combination. The third condition is that the signs and semiotic systems that we use for these productions combine learning at the personal, social and political levels (even as we discuss them separately below). These three conditions represent a move onward from most contemporary theories of learning, building on those that examine socially situated discourse from the view of (verbal) language by extending the discussion both to multiple modes and to the rhetorical domain. Further theoretical exploration of the multimodal and rhetorical dimension to communication and learning is picked up in Chapter 4 (and in Andrews, forthcoming).

Personal, Social and Political Understandings of Learning

We examine here the levels represented in manifestations of learning. While in general, the assumption is that the personal, social and political are fully integrated in learning, nevertheless, it is possible to analyze each of the levels separately.

Personal Learning

Personal learning (cf. personal knowledge in the thinking of Polanyi, 1958) is what most of us assume, for most of the time, that learning actually is. We may hold this assumption for a number of reasons: our experience of the world, and of the world of knowledge, seems undeniably personal in that we are aware of it through *our own* senses and consciousness. We can, if we are articulate, say that we *know* something, that we have *learnt* something, but not be sure that others know or have learnt the same thing. Above all, we *feel* individually a sense of having learnt something. That feeling can be both tacit (embedded, unspoken) and explicit (articulated). Following Polanyi, we could say that the mind creates meanings actively, making sense and meaning from phenomena; and, again, that the experience of mindfulness seems indubitably personal. However, we would not follow Polanyi in his association of the tacit with the personal, as we believe that the personal can be both tacit and articulated as can the social and political. In other words, we are arguing for the integration of the personal into the social and political; and for the acceptance of the tacit and articulated in all three domains.

There are further aspects of the personal dimension of learning that can be characterized – first, our propensity to organize our own learning and knowledge. We mean here activities as seemingly mundane and everyday as the way we organize our desks and our filing systems – the ways in which we categorize learnt experience. The metaphors of filing and of the desktop are pervasive in electronic communication and in e-learning: the business of placing material in folders and files; of search, research and composition (putting things together) are replicated on the computer screen, even as it sits on a desk. In mobile learning, that desktop is transported, often in micro versions, on handheld devices. Second, a driving and informing metaphor for learning (and thus personal learning theory), is the notion that we are, individually, on a journey through life (from the cradle to the grave), the metaphor of learning and development. Learning here takes on a spiritual as well as human (and humane) function: it acts as a guide for us, morally and experientially, as we make our small trajectories through life. Very few theories of the pre- or after-life posit the notion that they are states of development or learning; rather it is assumed that they are relatively more static states, and that we learn in between birth and death. Learning, therefore, is seen from this perspective to be an existential (and sometimes lonely) endeavor.

Social Aspects of Learning

Perhaps of particular importance to the views of e-learning we present here are the *social aspects of learning*, including work by a number of writers that addresses learning as occurring at the nexus of individual, social (group, community, culture), and technological (tools, artifacts, policies and procedures) components (e.g. Bandura, 1977; Brown and Adler, 2008; Engeström, 2009; Engeström and Middleton, 1996; Engeström et al., 1999; Vygotsky, 1986). Inherent in these theories is the idea of active engagement by learners with their environment and with others. Although there is a strong acceptance of the internal processes associated with learning and knowledge acquisition, and that learning means a change in understanding, learning is observed in its end result, that is, changes in behavior, use of tools or language, facility with tasks, production of texts or artifacts, and relations with others.

The very recognition that we have learnt something, or indeed are learning something, may occur as a social act rather than a personal one. That social dimension manifests itself in a number of ways. One of the most salient is via social semiotics (the science of signs systems, like written languages, icons, visual images, etc.), where we contribute to both the creation and development of sign systems in which to communicate, but also are informed by them, use them, and learn via them. Another way in which the social dimension is manifested is via 'socially situated' learning which is both informed by its environment (this leading to the notion of social cognition) and contributes to it. Meaning, from such a perspective, is created by communities who share the same values and discourses, and is thus deeply social. We could say, following Vygotsky (e.g. 1986), that meaning is generated from the social interaction of individuals; that cognitive development is essentially social in its inception; that what can be achieved collaboratively becomes internalized and part of the repertoire of what one can do alone; and so on. Social semiotics takes Vygotskian thinking a step further in that it sees social interaction as the informing agent in the development of sign systems and communication via these systems. For example, social semiotics would be interested in the semiotic resources available to a child as he/she makes meaning in a classroom activity. He/she watches a flower unfold on a slow-motion film and then re-presents the movement in a cut-out collage, in words, in animation, in music or in any combination of these. We operate with a set of discourses in our heads; but those discourses have been created before us, historically and socially, and are the tools via which we can make sense of the world and of ourselves in the world.

BOX 2.1: SOCIAL SEMIOTICS

If semiotics is the science of (meaningful) signs, then social semiotics is simply about signs in their social environment or setting.

Anything from an arrow on a road sign, to a word, to an image, to a gesture or to a mark on the ground can be a sign, indicating to us something beyond itself – some 'meaning'. Semiotics is the science of this range (and more) of signs, but it is essentially interested in the signs themselves and in sign systems, that is, the constituent elements in a 'vocabulary' of signs that work together to form a 'syntax' and 'grammar' (note that these terms derive from verbal language!).

Social semiotics expands in two ways upon this science of signs. First, it suggest that all signs are indicative of a socially constituted reality; that is to say, they point outwards to socially recognizable meaning. Second, because in communication 'the social is prior', then signs can be found to communicate such prior meaning. In other words, the social and the sign are inextricably connected in the generation and reception/interpretation of meaning.

Social semiotics is the theory behind multimodality, in that it allows the choosing of any modes in any combination to convey meaning.

But learning is social in another way. A second layer of perspectives address the *group, organizational or community level* of learning. These theories draw our attention to the way the relations with others lead to observable outcomes that imply learning among a set of individuals. Organizations learn in a spiral of knowledge creation that exploits synergies between the specification of procedures (explicit knowledge) and their internalization (tacit knowledge; Nonaka, 1994; Nonaka and Takeuchi, 1995). Learning at the collective level does not just create a set of individuals with greater knowledge, but creates a whole that is more capable of performing their functions and that learns *to be* a different kind of collective, for example as the organization studied by Orlikowski (2002) learned to be a distributed organization. Networks and communities learn by holding among their members resources of knowledge, skills and practices that enable responses to external and internal needs, that is, its *social capital* (Lin, 2001; Putnam, 2000).

Learning can then be seen as the outcome of the network (Haythornthwaite and de Laat, forthcoming). The idea of social capital has been applied to technologies in the idea of 'sociotechnical capital' (Kazmer, 2006; Resnick, 2002).

The exchange of ideas, the dialogic exploration of learning and interpretation of old knowledge – and the creation of new knowledge – usually involves more than one person. Learning is framed socially in classrooms, chatrooms, online, offline, in groups on the street and in the family, and in ('learned') societies. These social groupings around the act of learning are important because they provide a *forum* or *space* (Gee, 2005a, 2005b; Jenkins et al., 2006) for the collective creation and exploration of knowledge. They also form spaces within which aspects of norms of language, knowledge domain, and production are defined, for example in *epistemic communities*, *discourse communities* and *rhetorical communities* (Danet et al., 1998; Knorr-Cetina, 1999; Miller, 1994).

Learning the epistemological frame is particularly evident in the organization of disciplinary knowledge. What, for example, belongs in education as opposed to management in terms of learning, or in history, sociology or information science in terms of use of technology? Epistemological discovery and domain recognition take place in the gradual, often life-time, initiation into a discipline, for example from an initial interest in biology driven by pleasure in life forms, through engagement with biology as a subject at school and as a discipline at university, into a commitment to developing the field more thoroughly as an expert. The whole trajectory from interested naïf to accomplished expert traces a steep and long learning curve, but the individual acts of learning along the way take place when the existing knowledge is transformed, with the aid of pedagogical scaffolding, into a new state of knowledge and understanding. The process is not so much one of learning goals and outcomes (the discourse of a target-driven mindset) but of motivation, application, transformation and re-framing.

Consonant with our emphasis on emergence, the very act of learning – the minor or major breakthrough at the edge of knowledge, as well as the manner and mode of its expression – itself transforms and is transformed by such a social nexus. Moreover, driving such change is often the work of experts as they co-construct new knowledge (Scardamalia and Bereiter, 1996). We can say with some certainty that the public world of knowledge changes moment by moment, and that changing picture is the result of individual and collective contributions to it. That changing picture is also the backdrop to each person's new learning journey. For example, we are able to communicate in a range of languages by email because people who have gone before us have not only shaped the language(s) that we use, but have created the media infrastructure to enable email to take place across the world. Some of our learning, then, takes place along well-worn tracks that others have trod before us; that does not mean to say that we could not wander off the track, or take the path further.

Finally, learning is social in that it is an effect of the communities in which we operate (Rogoff, 1992); the social capital that results from the network of communal operation (Lin, 2001; Putnam, 2000). Inspired by Vygotsky, Rogoff (1992) introduced the idea that *learning is an effect of community*. This idea suggests that learning is not a psychometrically measurable entity that individuals register irrespective of their connection to other people, rather, that it *happens as a result of* close connection in cohesive social groupings or communities. Whereas Rogoff's Vygotskian conception was that 'learning is an effect of community', we develop the notion further in the present book by acknowledging that most individuals operate in a number of interrelated communities, for example family, interest groups, classrooms, schools or colleges, friendship groups, gangs, and various electronic communities (see also Chapter 8). One of the major challenges for learning theory is to explore whether the *nature* of learning changes in these different *environments*, or whether it remains constant. It is our contention that the nature of learning not only changes from community to community, but that the interfaces of these various communities are crucial in terms of what counts as learning, and how it is mediated or used by the different communities. We explore the nature of communities in learning in Chapter 6.

Political Aspects of Learning

Social theories of communication and learning have been prevalent for some time. The notion that learning is a private, psychological act that only takes place in the brain or the mind of an individual is one that is scarcely creditable. How could it be thus if it is clear that learning is socially situated and contributes to social well-being and development? But it is our contention that a social perspective on learning theory is not enough; we wish to take learning into yet another dimension – that of the political and rhetorical.

At the personal level, questions of 'What do we know?' and 'How do we know what we know?' can be answered by meta-awareness of the processes of learning and how they advance personal knowledge. At the social level, they can be answered by verification and argumentation. At the political level, the issue of *power* manifests itself. A theory of learning that takes in the political dimension recognizes that knowledge is a selection of possible outcomes; that the settling of arguments about knowledge often emerges from the predominance of a particular paradigm and thus, in Toulminian (1958) terms, a particular set of backing and warrants that verify the connections made between claims and grounds or evidence. The dominant paradigm of the time can itself be challenged and unsettled, and such changes 'call all in doubt'.

At a more local but no less political level, learning can be affected and influenced by micro-politics. A teacher's conception of how the connections are made in a particular discipline, or on a particular topic, can be highly influential to his or her students. Teacher attitudes to what a classroom means and how it will operate represent a political stance – in effect, a stance of power relations. But it does not have to be the person who conventionally holds most power in a social network – that is, the teacher in the classroom or the e-learning course or program – who wields influence. Rather, a student who voices a perceived set of connections logically and powerfully can influence the thinking of the remaining students, and indeed change the views of the teacher. Learning, in such contexts, is seen to be a political act: it is influenced by power relations, but the very creation of new knowledge in such a collective is itself also a political act, changing the configuration of knowledge in the social network that hosts it (and perhaps influencing other social networks that are marginally connected).

The servant of politics in this respect is rhetoric, that is, the 'arts of discourse' that present and influence others to a form of understanding, perhaps to adoption of a new viewpoint, carried through whichever mode and medium it manifests itself. Learning, from a political perspective, would at its best be reciprocal and open to discussion and potential change, while a situation in which there was hegemony or tyranny would limit the potential for learning and for change. It would become merely a matter of 'learning' (i.e. parroting or reciting) existing knowledge and following well-trodden pathways. Such extreme conservatism in learning perspective is seen in some political states which are repressive in their operation; ultimately, they would rather do away with new understanding altogether. At the other end of the spectrum, learning is not just the product of enlightenment belief in the advancement of scientific thinking; it is intimately tied up with the process of democracy itself, which, by the reconciliation or at least toleration of difference, has the means by which it can move forward.

As suggested in Chapter 1, we see e-learning as a transformative movement in learning. We are using 'transformation' in a somewhat different sense there, to mean large-scale cultural change. But the advent of e-learning and its practices that has prompted us to re-visit learning theory is a significant movement in itself. We follow this up further in the next chapter where we focus more sharply on e-learning. In the present chapter so far, and in what follows, we consider the implications that e-learning has for understanding learning more broadly.

Framing

Framing is a helpful concept in thinking about learning. It refers to the way we use certain kinds of rules and experiences as interpretive *frames* for action. For example, we use the context of the formal classroom as a frame for behavior that includes paying attention to the main speaker, refraining from talking to others, taking notes, remaining seated, using language to discuss matters instrumentally (rather than emotionally or in a play mode, e.g. with jokes), and using culturally appropriate language (e.g. without slang or swear words, or derogatory epithets). Contrast this with behavior in a pub or bar, particularly as the evening wears on. We take the classroom or the pub as carrying a certain meaning that is framed by our past experience, using them as a frame for behavior.

Learning is involved in this process. Just as meaning and experience are framed, so too is learning (see also Andrews, 2010 for the application of framing in literacy teaching). What we experience in the classroom or pub adds to our understanding of behavior in that frame, modifying what we understand

| A. Initial ontological state of being, framed by personal, social and political experience | → | B. The learning act, also framed by personal, social and political experience but with the addition of a pedagogical framing | → | C. Subsequent ontological state of being, framed by personal, social and political experience |

Figure 2.1   Stages in the Learning Process

as relating to the frame for future reference. When we learn, we make *further sense* of or discover meaning in our surroundings, whether that 'sense' is psychological, scientific, logical, social and/or affective, and whether the learning is explicit or tacit. That further sense is based on the knowledge we already have, plus the new knowledge that we acquire in the act of learning. We could represent the framing diagrammatically as in Figure 2.1 as three states and stages of learning. The state of being in the initial state (A), is transformed by the learning act (B) into the new state of knowledge (C). Each stage is framed. The learning act makes little sense if it does not correspond in some way to the frames in the initial state. Without a base on which to build the learning act has no purchase. The correspondence can be made by the learner on his or her own, but it can be aided by a teacher who mediates for the learner between initial and subsequent states of knowledge by providing pedagogical framing or learning constructs. It goes without saying that those pedagogical frames have to be appropriate to the learner and his or her situation, otherwise there may be no learning resulting from the encounter with the teacher.

What are *pedagogical frames* like, and how do they operate? They usually take the form of types of discourse (usually in words) which are designed to offer different perspectives on the states of knowledge characterized in the initial state (A). They may offer a completely different framework for understanding phenomena; or they may operate with the same frames and frameworks, and add new knowledge. They may challenge the existing frames and assumptions associated with the initial state. Whichever way they operate, their intention is to change the state of knowledge in the learner from some initial (A) to some subsequent state (C). Schooling, tuition and instruction at school level and in further and higher education is a formal way in which such learning can take place. In these contexts, teachers and lecturers are trained in the arts of pedagogic framing and re-framing in order to maximize learning opportunities and effects. Within the framing of the institution (school, college, university) and of the particular curriculum slot and classroom, the teacher or lecturer organizes the time available to bring about learning in the students. Outside formal learning contexts, the frames are less tightly defined, operating on a spectrum from evening classes and short courses at one end (often unaccredited) to everyday situations like conversations, family gatherings, groupings on the street, etc., which hardly look on the surface like learning opportunities, but which may be more conducive to learning for some students than formal situations.

The use of verbal language to define the pedagogic frames is most common; but physical language and movement in sports education or in dance, musical language in music education and visual language in art and/or film education operate too (usually in combination with words) in order to frame the learning experience. The mode of communication is principally that of the original state of knowledge, as part of learning is exploring meaning through that mode of communication. But the media (forms of delivery, like computer interfaces, film, etc.) can change. Additional modes can be used to shed light on the core meaning in one particular mode.

Kegan (2009), provides an interesting twist to consideration of learning in terms of transition and frames. In developing Merizow's definition of transformative learning, he notes that precision is necessary in the use of the term. Kegan suggests that 'transformational kinds of learning need to be more clearly distinguished from informational kinds of learning'; that 'the *form* that is undergoing transfor-*ma*tion needs to be better understood'; and that, if framing means that learning is always epistemological as well as behavioral, then transformational learning must recognize that dimension (Kegan, 2009: 41). Kegan is thus advocating limiting 'transformational' to describe frame-changing experiences (e.g. the development of new perspectives), as opposed to more information-based learning within existing frames (e.g. learning well understood structures). This is a useful description, but one that leaves open the question of who will determine what is 'frame-changing' – the learner or some outsider. We could instead follow Rogers (1995) who considers adoption of an innovation to apply to anything that is new to the adopting unit. Or, we could reserve the term transformation for the grander idea of new knowledge that is held to be the pinnacle of academic and entrepreneurial production. We leave this at present with the understanding that we use the term here to address both small-scale transformations, such as the acquisition of a new fact, and large-scale ones (the adoption of a different framework for solving a problem, for example the discovery of a new strategy for NATO involvement in Afghanistan, or a new approach to the problem of teaching writing to school-age students). Kegan's limiting of the use of the term 'transformational' as applied to learning is helpful in the sense that it increases clarity, but is less helpful in contributing to the understanding of learning theory and its application or development in relation to e-learning.

Emergence

Once a new state of knowledge is attained and consolidated (as in the last stage of Figure 2.1), the individual is again in an initial ontological state, ready to experience and integrate new learning. In this way, frames are continuously re-framed, sometimes with pedagogical intervention, sometimes by personal exploration and enlargement. Thus, the third concept of central importance to e-learning is the *emergent nature of learning*. Through observation and active engagement with environmental elements, learners experience 'expansive learning' leading to (continuously emerging) new understandings of the object of interest (Engeström, 2009).

Emergent learning entails more than just individual learning, although that is an important aspect. It also entails learning by and with a *community*. Individual learning emerges from the relationship between a learner and their environment (in what Bandura (1977) called a 'reciprocal determinism'), but the reintroduction of that learning into the community creates a continuous refinement and generation of new knowledge (what Cook and Brown (1999) called a 'generative dance'), and a modified environment. Individuals observe, react and contribute to the elements of the environment in which they are immersed. Social reality is constructed through the multiple actions and interactions of individuals as they engage with their community, environment, tools, etc. This is the underpinning of a number of views of social construction and of the continuously emergent nature of social construction (Berger and Luckmann, 1966), as well as of the state of the actor within an environment and the social structures of networks or societies that shape social outcomes (Giddens, 1984 re 'structuration'; for social network views see Monge and Contractor, 2003). These ideas have been applied to the use of technology in ideas of the 'social shaping of technology' (Bijker, 1995; MacKenzie and Wajcman, 1999; Pinch and Bijker, 1984), and the adaptive structuration of the use of technology by groups (Poole and DeSanctis, 1990) and in organizations (Fulk and Steinfield, 1990).

The many perspectives on emergence also promote attention to the way learning encompasses many aspects of personal, professional, social and societal growth. As ideas and attitudes change – for example from classroom to online learning – the frame that bounds a learning activity changes, as does what is considered viable to bring into such a domain. Acknowledging frames and emergence is particularly relevant in current conditions of rapid change in knowledge and technology base, and as these both challenge disciplinary boundaries and discourses (see also Haythornthwaite, 2006b).

Building Further

Transformation, framing and emergence may be said to be the constructs upon which our theory of learning is based. In this conceptualization transformation captures the action that mediates between the different states of knowledge construction – the frame and its re-framing – and emergence characterizes the continuity of this practice and its emanations at personal, social and political levels. What else is there in learning that we need to capture before we go on to consider e-learning in more depth? We see the following as secondary aspects of learning, but nevertheless important ones that will have a bearing on our understanding of e-learning: learning and community which we develop in Chapter 6; and a trio of aspects that relate to the learner: risk-taking, readiness, and the act of not-learning.

Risk-taking is an interesting element in learning, partly because it is often either taken for granted or ignored. To move from a state of knowing something to another state involves taking a risk, becoming a pioneer (Haythornthwaite et al., 2000), being an early or late adopter of an innovation (Rogers, 1995). To feel one knows something is comforting, even if that knowledge is unpleasant. So our initial state A, in our simple diagram (Figure 2.1), is a conservative state bolstered by experience that helps us consolidate our knowledge. This state is not a state of learning *per se*, because it is not in action. To keep learning, we need to generate a hypothesis, take a step into the unknown, feel comfortable in a state of un-knowing or uncertainty and question our own existing assumptions. To do so takes courage. What drives us to step out from a state of certainty is inner motivation, extrinsic motivation, or the very fact of finding that phenomena and experience do not match our existing frames and frameworks (see also Rogers, 1995 for why innovations are adopted). The motivation – or even more deeply, the drive from within us to explore – can be spiritually, emotionally and/ or intellectually driven. Being a learner requires such risk-taking, and being an e-learner requires a particular kind of confidence in reaching out to new applications, new networks and new technologies that might at first seem daunting.

Linked to notions of risk-taking is the condition of *readiness*. In some situations, however rich the possibilities of transformation are, an individual learner may resist learning or simply not see the situation's potential for it. Individuals may be unaware of or resist new ideas (Rogers, 1995); groups may succumb to 'group think' and refuse to consider outside knowledge, or be unprepared with insufficient knowledge to recognize opportunities (Cohen and Levinthal, 1990). We can transpose this state of affairs to the classroom or lecture theatre: not all pedagogic constructions and interventions are going to make a difference to students. A learner, or a student in a more formal situation, will be a more proactive learner if prepared for the moment of learning, or ready and willing to learn something. For example, pioneers in versions of e-learning in the 1980s and 1990s faced greater risk in being early adopters before general use of computer-mediated communication made e-learning more attuned to existing patterns of daily life. In education, the cycle of adoption appears to be technological advance followed by overstatement of its transformative potential for learning; then gradual adoption (or not) and an integration of technology and learning, so that use of a new technology or device seems 'natural' and disappears from view (Bruce and Hogan, 1998).

The converse of readiness to learn is the state of *not-learning*. It is worth reflecting on such a state, for it will help us characterize more clearly what happens when we *do* learn. There are various types of conditions in which learning might *not* take place. First, as learners and/or students, we may simply not want to learn from a particular situation. Second, we may not be ready (in terms of immediate preparation or longer-term disinclination) to learn. Third, something specific may prevent us from learning, like a distraction (e.g. the death of a relative, the anticipation of a positive event). Fourth, our own expectations of what we might learn may be disappointed by poor pedagogy or poor material. Fifth, we may not know the rules and conventions for learning, whether these conventions are epistemological, procedural, cross-cultural or multimodal. Sixth and finally, being and experience do not constitute learning *per se*: one can imagine living a life with little learning in it, but it would be a minimal, impoverished life.

Challenges for Assessment

If we take the lineaments of learning to be those set out earlier in the chapter – transformation, framing and re-framing, emergence, and individual readiness, risk-taking and the interaction within and between communities (Chapter 6), how do we assess such complex activity? Given that learning can involve transformations (turnarounds, changes of direction) from anywhere between one and 360 degrees, and the state of the art is necessarily moving and emergent, what kinds of assessment are appropriate?

The first and probably most useful kind of assessment of individual learning is self-assessment. From a state of C, one can look back to A and ask oneself 'What have I learnt?' and 'What was the process that got me from A to C?'. Such self-reflection can be scaled upwards to the social, political and institutional levels. At those levels, the questions tend to be framed as 'What lessons have we learnt as a result of that process?' Self-assessment gives learners the power to make sense of their own learning and prepare themselves for more learning.

A second kind of assessment is diagnosis of development. If this is carried out by a third party – for example, a teacher or counsellor – that third party needs to take time to find out what the state of the learner was at A, what kinds of intervention have taken place in the process of learning (B), and what the current state of development is (C). The responsibility of the third party is to be sensitive to the states of knowledge and learning of the individual in question; such sensitivity requires not only time and patience, but a good deal of knowledge about the nature of knowledge and the learning process. Ultimately, the diagnosis by a third party needs to be taken on board by the learner if he or she is to develop in relation to it.

Thirdly, assessment of a more summative or synchronic type needs to take into account the benchmarking that is necessary at A in order to measure how far the learning has taken the individual to C. We have already seen that the framing of knowledge at point A is influenced by personal, social, political and epistemological dimensions; in a work context, it may also be framed by professional constructs. Such benchmarking, then, has to address these different framings in order to understand the state of the learner. And as different pedagogical approaches at B can lead to different types of learning and different outcomes, the nature of the intervention at B needs to be recorded and understood. The state of learning and/or knowledge at C has to be described and recorded in order to measure the difference that the journey from A to C has made.

The present book does not address questions of assessment in any depth. Here, we merely set out the problems that assessors of the learning experience need to address if they are to design an appropriate model for assessing learning both in the general sense and in specific e-learning contexts. We will return to the question of assessment, but merely in terms of the *implications* of our theorizing for assessment practices.

Toward E-learning Theory

The bulk of the present chapter has been concerned with learning theory in general. We have taken this approach because we feel that e-learning requires its own theory (see Chapter 4) but that: (a) we need to know what we mean by learning before we can address such issues; and (b) e-learning itself has posed challenges to conventional learning theory. Building on the exposition of computer-mediated communication in Chapter 1, we now begin to move towards a theory of e-learning by considering some of the features and affordances of e-learning.

In the first chapter, we outlined the major features of computer-mediated communication as anonymity, asynchronicity, mobility, connectivity and rapidity, with the potential for global reach and the predominance of a verbal, text-based mode. It is the last of these to which we turn attention now, as we see this aspect of e-learning as problematic. We need to first consider how texts are used in learning theory in general, to define some terms, and then embark in the following chapter on a further exploration of the nature of communication in e-learning.

Texts

It is true to say that the bulk of communication in e-learning has been, to date, through verbal printed texts. The reduction to a seemingly monomodal form of communication has its problems when compared to face-to-face learning, with its physical co-presence, its sensitivity to nuance, its multimodal channels. In terms of learning generally, this is an interesting dilemma, because teaching has often stripped down multimodal representations of experience and phenomena into monomodal systems in order to teach them. Take, for example, the teaching of reading or writing. Although there are undoubtedly many multimodal cues that are used by learners to gain command of the reading and writing systems, teachers often reduce the process of teaching reading and writing to the verbal (i.e. words) system itself, as if reading and writing have no visual or aural identity in themselves, and as if they exist in a vacuum, unconnected to the wider experience of movement, visual and aural modes. So whereas teaching has often been monomodal, learning is usually not monomodal. It draws on cues in all the modes to make sense of and bring meaning to the particular sign system it is trying to understand. The fact that early e-learning programs tended to use verbal printed text as their preferred mode and medium of communication (and even of programing) is ironic. It is as if a new learning approach, powered by new technologies, has reverted to a more primitive and reduced form of learning. But such ironies are not uncommon as new technologies open up new ways of approaching learning. They tend to draw on conventional and, as suggested, primitive, forms of communication in fields in which they are not expert or cutting-edge.

Learning is inevitably multimodal in that it involves *transduction* – the change from one mode to another (e.g. from speech to dance), as opposed to *remediation* which is the shift from one medium to another (e.g. from printed book to e-book). However, the transduction or remediation of material across modes and media *can be* a transformative act of learning. Where there is more than one mode of communication ostensibly present, these need to be configured and the relationship between them thought out. What happens to them in the process of learning/transformation needs to be considered. The affordances of each mode, the gains and losses that take place in transduction, have to be reflected upon in the process of learning. Even where there seems to be only one mode in operation (a plainly printed verbal text, or pure sound, for example) other modes are *implied*. That implication – part of the work of the imagination – supplies experience that the text itself may not supply. Think of two examples: the reading of a poem, and the reading of a manual for the construction of a shed. In each case, the reader is asked to supply information (auditory and visual in the case of the poem, spatial, visual and physical in the case of the shed manual) that will complete the communication process. The initial text in each case – printed words on a page in the case of the poem, and printed words plus diagrams in the case of the manual – is not enough to complete the process of interpretation and understanding.

For example, a short story is read aloud by a teacher from a printed (mode = verbal language in print) book (medium). Already we have a complex set of interactions. The teacher is transducting the printed verbal text into the spoken/read form. He or she is a physical presence in the classroom, with the nature of the voice playing a particularly key role in the listening experience for the students. He or she may move around the room or stay in one place. The students may keep their eyes on the teacher, on a copy of the text itself, or they may gaze out of the window. Their attention may move backward and forward, and be more focused and less focused in relation to the sound of the story. But once the story is finished, the students are asked to do something else: first, talk in small groups about what they remember as the key points; second, pool those memories and ask questions of the teacher about what they did not understand; third, write the script of a short radio play based loosely on the story; and fourth, rehearse and perform (and/or record) the play. Each stage of the action following the listening to the story involves transductions, remediations and transformations. These, we suggest, are what is learnt.

This raises the question of what is learnt in the transduction, remediation and transformation to an e-learning environment. Many teachers have reported on how the act of re-creating the learning materials in a form suitable for a VLE has made them re-think their pedagogy. E-learning thus acts as a transductive learning environment for professional development. Students have found themselves re-defining their identities as their e-learning presence provides them with a set of skills that then become marketable because they are e-learning savvy. They also develop from being socio-technological naïfs to adepts as they transduct social interaction from conversation to persistent conversation, and assignment production from paper to web-based output. What is also evident in the development and spread of e-learning is the way it adopts emergent practices. Thus, becoming an e-learner includes the learning and adoption of emergent practices (this is discussed further in Chapter 10).

It can be seen that the theory of learning that has been developed in this chapter, and which will inform our thinking about e-learning theory, is informed by *activity*. In other words, learning is an active process that involves: engagement; movement from one's state of knowledge into another state; transduction, remediation and transformation; re-framing; and positive consolidation. The theory of learning that we are proposing here does not sit easily with a practice that is passive. We do not think that much learning takes place when the mind is conceived as a *tabula rasa* and teaching is imprinted upon it. Rather, learning takes place when the individual or community reaches out and up to teaching, and meets it along the way.

Conclusion

This chapter started with the proposition that it is unproductive for contemporary learning, and e-learning in particular, to approach learning theory via separate behaviorist, cognitivist and constructionist camps. To do so relegates e-learning to the role of a technologically driven addendum or site for learning, rather than a complex set of social practices in itself. The opportunities that e-media offer, and the mix of different modes that are possible in the e-learning environment, may be missed by those who see information and communication technologies as an add-on rather than as an integral part of the world of communication. When new technologies are integrated into the practice of the e-learner and e-teacher, they are seen to offer opportunities not to enhance learning as we knew it, for example as in the term 'technology-enhanced learning', but to transform it through the processes of transduction, remediation and transformation.

Building on suggestions from conventional learning theory, we have explored in this chapter notions of transformation, framing and re-framing, and emergence as three main elements of contemporary learning. These we see as taking place personally, socially, politically and epistemologically. Our accent is on the *acts of framing* or framing as a process, both as a recipient and as a composer of communication, which is why we have not built an elaborate model of frames within frames à la Goffman (1986). Rather, we have proposed a simple model of a state of knowledge, (A) which is transformed by learning acts (B) into state of knowledge (C), operating again at individual, social and political levels (and in terms of a body of public knowledge). The third stage in the process – arrival at state of knowledge C – is a process of re-framing, and necessarily builds into the next iteration of the cycle. At the heart of the overall learning process are the learning acts that take place at stage B: these may or may not be scaffolded by pedagogic framing, whether by textbooks, virtual learning platforms, teachers/instructors or even self-directed learning practices. As we will elaborate more in the rest of the book, one of the key actors at this stage in the learning process are the communities that individuals are part of and/or subscribe to. We see this central stage (B) as transformative in that it changes the state of knowledge A into the state of knowledge C. In keeping with Kegan (2009), we also acknowledge that the transformation is as likely to affect the frame itself as it is the understanding within the frame. Without transformation, of understanding and/or frame, there is no learning. Although our definition of learning might seem tautological and self-referential, we feel that active learning is learning that transforms the individual (or society or state) by smaller or larger degrees.

Finally in this chapter we have addressed other aspects of learning that we feel are important to consider: learner risk-taking and readiness to learn, and the problem of assessing what at times seems a moving target of learning. Leaving the fuller discussion of communities of learning, how they interact and how individuals navigate between them, to later chapters, we started to chart the passage toward e-learning theory by discussing the multimodal nature of learning as opposed to the sometimes monomodal systemic teaching, pointing out the ironies that whereas e-learning had advanced social practices and affordances of learning, much of its actual practice has been disappointingly narrow in the range of modes used to engender learning.

In the next chapter, we build on the present one to dive more fully into e-learning. What we carry forward from the present chapter is a conception of learning that is framed, transformative, risky and multimodal. The conception is deliberately and necessarily tentative, because we do not think that a fixed and too-certain, static model of learning is going to be helpful as new technologies, new social practices interact with learning. Our learning theory, then, is dynamic, simple and flexible. We hope it will provide a strong basis for further thinking in the fast changing field which we are exploring in this book.

Further Reading

Andrews, R. (2010). *Re-framing Literacy: Teaching and Learning in English and the Language Arts*. New York: Routledge.

Greeno, J. G. (2006). 'Learning in activity', in R. K. Sawyer (Ed.), *The Cambridge Handbook of the Learning Sciences*. New York: Cambridge University Press. pp. 79–96.

Illeris, K. (2007). *How We Learn: Learning and Non-learning in School and Beyond*. Abingdon: Routledge.

Illeris, K. (Ed.) (2009). *Contemporary Theories of Learning: Learning Theorists ... in their own Words*. London: Routledge.

Mayes, T. and de Freitas, S. (2006). 'Learning and e-learning: The role of theory', in H. Beetham and R. Sharpe (Eds.), *Rethinking Pedagogy for a Digital Age: Designing and Delivering E-learning*. London: Routledge. pp. 13–25.

3

Theorizing Online Learning

Introduction

The principal question considered in the present chapter is whether the practices of e-learning require a new theory of learning, or whether existing theories of learning are adequate to account for what happens, and what is possible in e-learning. Our premise, which we will explore throughout the chapter and the rest of the book, is that e-learning is more than just an environment or site for conventionally conceived learning. Instead it is a new practice that calls for a new theoretical perspective. In this chapter, we highlight some existing theoretical positions that address the different learning experience and practice of the distributed, online learner.

'E-learning' itself is a term that is complex, and that attracts a degree of controversy and disagreement. Anderson (2004), for example, claims a wide territory, referring to online learning as embracing all forms of learning other than face-to-face. Others view e-learning more narrowly as that which takes place in educational settings and through the technologies of virtual learning environments. Yet others include ideas of 'open learning' as part and parcel of e-learning, predicated on the principles of open access and open courseware.

Earlier, in *The* SAGE *Handbook of E-learning Research*, we charted in more detail what we saw as the boundaries and identity of e-learning. In our introduction to that book, we stated:

> By e-learning research, we mean primarily research *into*, *on*, or *about* the use of electronic technologies for teaching and learning. This encompasses learning for degrees, work requirements and personal fulfilment, institutional and non-institutionally accredited programmes, in formal and informal settings. It includes anywhere, anytime learning, as well as campus-based extensions to face-to-face classes. (Andrews and Haythornthwaite, 2007: 1)

While holding with this definition, in this book we find more need to consider the greater pervasiveness of learning on and through electronic technologies in all aspects of daily life. At the time, we emphasized the reciprocal, co-evolutionary processes of *literacy and technology*. While the earlier emphasis was on literacy, we now take that idea to learning, or more specifically e-learning. We see the co-evolutionary aspects as evident and in need of analysis at both the level of local e-learning experiences associated with educational institutions and pedagogical practice, and wider societal levels of impact of online learning in general.

We continue to hold our preference for the term 'e-learning' over formulations such as 'technology-enhanced learning'. This is because we do not see 'learning' as a process or state of being which is necessarily 'enhanced' by technology. The phrase 'technology-enhanced learning' seems unduly technicist, technologically deterministic, and unrealistically positive, suffering from what Rogers (1995) terms a 'pro-innovation bias'. There are many scenarios we can envisage in which learning *is* enhanced by technology, but equally there are others where technology can interfere with learning. Indeed, the point is made in several locations in this book that it is deliberate choices about both *social and technical* features that lead to an enhanced, comprehensive learning experience. In other words, there is a social dimension to e-learning that gets lost if the concept and its practice are discussed as if they were a mere technological intervention. Thus, the focus, in our conception of e-learning, is on *learning* and its personal, social, political and technological dimensions.

The term 'e-learning' is helpful because it is a hybrid, compound term. It suggests that there is something distinctive about e-learning, and that it is different from 'learning'. This difference is captured in the idea noted above of the *reciprocally co-evolutionary* relationship between technology and learning (for more on this model, see Chapter 4). What is distinctive about e-learning is, then, the way the two components – the 'e' and 'learning' – develop independently and alongside each other, yet are also interrelated, and contribute to each other's development. A change in one precipitates a change in the other. This is not the same as a symbiotic relationship because symbiosis exists to maintain a status quo. By contrast, e-learning is dynamic, changing and modifying with new social situations, new politics, new technologies, and new forms of learning. We may be criticized for drawing boundaries around e-learning as an area of social practice that cannot always be distinguished from learning itself, and for attempting to build theory on the site of learning that is already well provided for theoretically. But part of our motivation is that existing theories of learning *do not account fully* for what happens in e-learning because those theories do not adequately include the effects of the 'e-' portion of this social practice, nor the theoretical ground from other areas of 'e-'endeavors. Thus, here and throughout the book, we bring forward and begin to blend theories from learning, technology adoption, and social practices on the way to theorizing e-learning.

Existing Theoretical Positions

There is a new wealth of material on learning theory (e.g. Illeris, 2007, 2009); and a parallel strand on e-learning and its variant (e.g. Danaher et al., 2009; Garrison and Anderson, 2003; Pachler, 2007; Siemens, 2004: on mobile learning communities; Latchem and Jung, 2009 on distance and blended learning in Asia; Conole and Oliver, 2007; Dirckinck-Holmfeld et al., 2009; Steeples and Jones, 2002 on networked learning; see also the chapters in Andrews and Haythornthwaite, 2007a). But these very different sources of material do not come together to help us think about the *theoretical* nature of e-learning.

On the one hand, while struggling with the real world task of implementing e-learning, e-learning studies have emphasized strategies, social contexts, design and/or pedagogies for e-learning implementation (although see Koschmann, 1996, for theoretical positions on computer-supported collaborative learning). Methodologically, most of the studies published, and most papers given at conferences, are ethnographic and/or descriptive studies. While these are important in themselves, and are also important for working from the ground up toward theory, they do not in themselves constitute a theoretical contribution. Without such overarching theory or theories, the field will be unable to chart and gauge its progress; nor will it reach a degree of coherence that allows further discussion of complex tensions and complementarities in the field.

On the other hand, many theories of learning only consider the online context as an add-on or remediation of conventional learning. Illeris (2007), for example, sees e-learning as a site for learning, a 'virtual' space. So he first conceives of the notion of learning as a psycho-social activity, and then assigns it 'different learning spaces' in which to operate. The notion of socially situated learning, for Illeris, is about sites for learning; the social situations in which learning takes place are not seen as integral to the nature of that learning. As a result, he plays down the idea of 'learning as an effect of community' (Rogoff, 1992) and the transformative power of community for effecting learning, as well as the way that learning is mediated through social semiotic and multimodal communication. In his discussion of 'net-based learning' (the term 'e-learning' is quickly dropped), there is scant recognition of the transformations possible through electronic communication. The two pages devoted to net-based learning acknowledge the practical usefulness of learning at distance (best combined, he suggests, with some face-to-face interaction, as in blended or hybrid learning) but see it very much as merely another *site* for learning.

It is our contention that e-learning constitutes more than a specific *environment* or site for learning; and that something is happening to the *nature* of learning itself that makes it different from learning as it has been conventionally conceived. There is support from a number of directions for a view that treats e-learning as more than just a variant of conventional learning. Keegan (1993) explores theoretical principles of distance education, with the student at the center of considerations and thus has a focus on learning rather than teaching; similarly Luckin (Luckin, 2008, 2010; Luckin et al., 2007) centers the learner within the ecology of their own learning resources (discussed further in Chapter 8).

From another angle, Holmes and Gardner (2006) work toward a theory of *communal constructivism* that underpins their approach to e-learning. In a brief chapter on e-learning theory, these authors see a development from behaviourism through cognitive constructivism and socio-constructivism to communal constructivism. In communal constructivism, the individual contributes to and benefits from a community which provides a living repository of learning: an idea like that of social capital discussed in Chapter 2. Siemens (2004) concentrates on the connectivity features of networks, advocating a connectivism theory of learning which is an 'integration of principles explored by chaos, network, and complexity and self-organization theories' (online) (see also Rennie and Mason, 2004). Building from a social network perspective, Haythornthwaite (Haythornthwaite, 2005a, 2010; Haythornthwaite and deLaat, forthcoming) addresses learning as constituted at several levels of the networks. Learning can be the 'glue' that holds people together in a network (e.g. in the content of their social network ties), identifying a community (e.g. a community of inquiry such as a class or research group), and an outcome of knowledge and resources held within the network (i.e. social capital).

Along the same lines is Rogoff's (1992) position that *learning is an effect of community*, noted in Chapter 2. As for a social network perspective, learning is seen as the product of an individual in relation to the community and its members. Effects of e-communities or online/offline communities are no different, whether gathering in social networking sites, virtual learning environments, or via email, or combining face-to-face with Internet communication. The collectives supported on and through these various means all constitute learning communities. Where they operate entirely online, it is not appropriate to call these mere sites for the application of learning. As Haythornthwaite and colleagues have observed, in such cases it can be the face-to-face that is the add-on for the community (Haythornthwaite et al., 2000). In their operation, these communities provide the very fabric of learning which is both 'read off' and 'woven' from involvement with the communities in question, through processes of dialogic exchange, exchange of resources, and active and 'passive' peripheral participation. For example, immersion as an intern in a particular workplace means that the individual not only learns specific skills, but also learns the ethos of the company, the dynamics of social interaction at work, the loci of information, and the professional rules of conduct that are often not spelled out from the start (Lave and Wenger, 1991; Wenger, 1998; see also Chapter 9).

We also need to extend Rogoff to consider learning as not just the effect of community in the singular, but *learning as the effect of communities* in the plural. As we increasingly maintain partial commitment and identity in multiple communities, we find ourselves, as individuals, operating simultaneously in different communities (social worlds in Strauss' [1978] terminology) in which we may take on different roles (e.g. employee in one world, parent in another, gamer in a third; Haythornthwaite and Kazmer, 2002; Kazmer and Haythornthwaite, 2001; Merton, 1957). In our 'networked individualism' (Wellman, 2001; see also Chapter 8), we not only learn from (and add knowledge to) multiple communities, but also exploit the synergies between communities. Thus, along with extending Rogoff to consider learning as the effect of communities, we also extend it to consider *learning as the effect of interconnection between communities*.

While each of these different approaches requires further discussion for e-learning, and some are picked up in subsequent chapters, in the next sections we expand on two conceptions: Moore's (1997) articulation of a theory of *transactional distance* that suggests more than physical distance is at work in distance learning and which has been the most long-standing view of distributed learning; and Kress (2003, 2009) and Jewitt's (2008) approach which sees learning as being informed and constituted through multimodality, and which is particularly relevant for understanding the multimodal, screen-based life we inhabit. This provides a background for the longer discussion of multimodality in relation to new discourses in Chapter 4.

Transactional Distance

Moore (1997) articulated a theory of transactional distance, developing a notion first mooted in the 1970s that distance education is not just a matter of geographical separation, but is instead a pedagogical concept. The notion of transactional distance is a relative one, and involves a set of three variables that operate in relation to the degree of transactional distance between the teachers and learners: dialogue, program structure and learner autonomy. In particular, there was reference to the (then) newly available practice of 'teleconferencing', enabling distributed learners to converse simultaneously with each other and the teacher. The potential increase in the number of lines of communication in such an e-learning situation, compared to those in a conventional face-to-face learning situation, is considerable. In e-learning, co-presence is replaced and compensated for by more extensive and potentially busier electronic networking along a number of lines of connection. While early work on designing systems to support connectivity emphasized heavily involved, collaborative work participants (e.g. from group decision support systems to computer-supported cooperative work and computer-supported collaborative learning), new forms of organizing are appearing, particularly in relation to participatory culture. E-learning, particularly where it involves multiple memberships in a variety of communities, supports both weak and strong engagement with others and with the enterprise as a whole. Thus, we see lightweight engagement by lurkers or occasional posters in open forums and discussion lists, as well as heavyweight engagement by core, altruistic contributors in the same contexts (Haythornthwaite, 2009a). E-learning also transforms relationships; 'participatory learning entails instructors ceding leadership and control of learning, giving it over to participants, and encouraging a new form of co-learning pedagogy' (Haythornthwaite, 2009b: 38).

Part of this new responsibility for learners is the need for choice as to how their research is conducted, that is, what sources are used, what degree of cross-checking is employed, and so on. Such a wealth of choice can be disorienting for a student who is not used to such freedom, or is wedded to the conventional face-to-face teaching situation where the student tends to defer to the teacher/lecturer. It is likely that neither students nor institutions are sufficiently prepared for the choices that present themselves in an e-learning context. 'Learner autonomy', mentioned as one of the key variables in Moore's theory of transaction distance, is one that requires more attention from all concerned (see Luckin, 2010; see also this volume, Chapter 9). The next step from learner autonomy is 'learner agency' in which the learner is empowered to construct for him- or herself the nature, sources, styles and pathways for learning.

Multimodality

Another significant body of thinking is that centered on multimodality. Although not all e-learning is obviously multimodal, a theory of e-learning must now take account of the multimodal nature of contemporary communication. Such a perspective is highly relevant because most e-learning communication is via computer interface (whether on a desktop, laptop or handheld), and these computer interfaces are multimodal in nature. Even if communication of this sort is relatively monomodal (as, for example, in a page of verbal text or, alternatively, the presentation of a single un-captioned image), the contemporary computing environment is not without other conventions and modes that appear in the complex of the application, window, and operating system structuring of a screen (from scroll bars to menus and icons; see Chapters 1 and 2). We would argue that while remediation (Bolter and Grusin, 1999) has been the necessary focus in response to new media in a time of conversion from offline to online, now that materials and communities are constituted online first, remediation takes second place to the issues of learning and meaning-making in and across multiple modalities.

In exploring issues of multimodality, we return to the ideas of transformation and transduction described in Chapter 2. Kress (2003) suggests in relation to learning (although not e-learning specifically) that *transformation* is a key concept in a theory of meaning-making and refers to how users re-shape meaning according to the available resources; *transduction* is the more specific term used to denote the modal shift from one set of resources to another. As Kress describes, transformation is 'the process of inward meaning-making and the resultant change to the state of an inner semiotic resource' (2003: 40). Transformation is also central to a theory of learning. Learning transforms a person's state of mind or knowledge from one stage to the next.

If we make the jump from learning to e-learning, we can see that transduction takes place in the re-casting of meaning from one mode to another; and transformation takes place where the transduction has the effect of changing a person's state of mind or knowledge. Transformation becomes prominent in the e-learning context in the *reading* of multimodal texts since connections have to be made between the different modal elements of the text, for example between menu items, headlines, pictures, videos. (Here 'reading' is proposed as a process without transduction, although it could be argued that transduction is taking place too, for example from the printed text into 'thought' or the impression upon the reader). A note of caution is that, in the same way that not all e-learning programs are 100 percent online and yet online is the primary medium for learning, not all e-learning is obviously, primarily or pedagogically multimodal. Many e-learning courses and pedagogic approaches privilege the verbal over other modes, making primary use of textual resources and persistent conversations. Verbal written text has been the default mode because of technical considerations of storage and transmission of data. But, it has also been incorporated into e-learning practice because it emulates academic production (as well as a lot of business production) in the generation of essays, reports, and records of interaction. Remaining with text can be a response to legacy systems, including aging VLEs, but also to the need to maintain the use of low bandwidth distribution to accommodate remote users and those with poorer personal equipment, or to reach places that lack regional infrastructure for high speed telecommunications. While these problems may abate, providing the opportunity to use a wider range of modes, formal e-learning may always be constrained to systems that operate on less than the most recent hardware, software and telecommunications (see Chapter 10).

Jewitt (2008) also addresses multimodality and learning, and sets out 'a framework for re-thinking learning from a multimodal perspective in order to explore what real difference the use of new technology can make for learning' (2008: 2), where learning is seen as 'internalising the representational and communicative means of the subject discourse' (2008: 25). Jewitt's framework also includes activity theory (Engeström, 1987) and its Vygotskian basis in thinking about transfers from the social plane to the internal plane. Both these perspectives allow an insight into learning 'from the outside in'; they chart the resources, social semiotic and social constituents of learning.

Drawing on Volosinov (1973), Jewitt suggests that the mind is nurtured on signs and that it makes sense of the world and of its own consciousness through such mediation. She suggests that most theories of the internalization of social relations are based on (verbal) language, but that 'from a multimodal perspective *all* modes contribute to learning' (Jewitt, 2008: 27). Jewitt thus points us in the direction of: (a) a multimodal conception of semiotic resources and relationships that are internalized as thought and transformed as learning; (b) a multimodal and kinaesthetic approach to what psychologists and those whose theories derive from psychology call 'input'; (c) seeing student 'output' as one form of evidence of their learning; and (d) a question regarding the relationships of new technologies and computer interfaces to multimodality, that is, largely in the multimodal nature of the computer screen interface.

In these conceptions, both by Kress and Jewitt, the social dimension of e-learning is addressed through the lens of social semiotics. This perspective encompasses not only how signs become signifiers for creating a socially agreed upon meaning, but also how such signs can develop and change over time. This holds promise for informing both social and emergent aspects of e-learning practice. In his recent work, Kress (2009) establishes multimodality firmly within the social semiotic approach, arguing that learning takes the form of augmentation of life experience and thus affects identity. A multimodal social semiotic approach sees learning as 'the result of the transformative engagement with an aspect of the world which is the focus of attention by an individual ... leading to a trans-formation of the individual's semiotic/conceptual resources' (2009: 182). Of particular relevance in this work, is its attention to media as well as modes. Kress discusses how the internalization and transformation of identifiable semiotic resources in the external world, via smartphones and other devices as well as multimodal interfaces, is mirrored in a realignment in internal semiotic resources, which in turn can be manifested again in the *productions* of learners. As per Jewitt, 'output' is available that can be used as evidence of learning. How else, we might ask (barring brain scans) is it possible to *see* evidence of learning? In e-learning environments, such traces are evident in discussion lists, blogs, commentaries, and wiki talk pages that leave formal and informal productions in association with class discussions, online support groups, news responses, etc. as publicly shared archives of interaction available for review and examination. But, the important point is not that such traces exist, but that they represent the internalization of signs and then their externalization within the e-learning environment, thus both weaving and becoming the fabric that is the learning community.

In keeping with our earlier articulation of the reciprocal co-evolutionary model of learning and literacy, Kress' position above suggests another use of the same ideas. The more we function as multimodal e-citizens in an e-world, the more we change our expectations and productions to fit that world view. Multimodality, and e-learning, as an input will produce a mindset for multimo-dal, e-learning production – transforming both the frame and the media associ-ated with learning. As in the past, we may have heard the words in our heads as we read and write; now we are beginning to 'hear' the inner voice of multi-modality. This transformation is already well underway, demonstrated in the initial remediation of academic discourse from paper to online publication, and the accompanying transduction that has occurred as online publication and creative commons licensing combine with ideas of open access to change the permanence, visibility, use, re-use and re-mix of texts (Haythornthwaite, 2009a; forthcoming). Similar transformations have hit university campuses as e-learning distance classes change possibilities for education on campus; and students and faculty change their information searching and use patterns around increased demand for easy, online access to resources.

Further Theories

What further theory or theories extend our understanding of e-learning? One of the major issues in learning is always, how much depends on the individuals themselves to make the transformation from one state of knowledge to another versus the efforts of an outside agent (teacher, author, etc.). In Chapter 2, we discussed risk-taking and readiness as attributes relating to individuals (although an argument can always be made for how even these are socially situated). Motivation is another learner-centric area that is gaining considerable attention in relation to online participation, particularly as research is underway to understand the motivations for participation in online crowds and communities, for example such as Wikipedia or OpenStreetMap. Two other considerations for theory in relation to e-learning are social informatics and digital media theory.

Intrinsic Motivation

Learning is never an entirely passive activity. Even the most instrumental of learning activities requires some accommodation of existing learning patterns and configurations to new learning. In e-learning, because the learner is often isolated physically from other learners in the network, he or she has to make an extra effort to contribute to the e-learning community. Learning is never a simple 'read-off' from the tissue of connections made by others, it requires some engagement and contribution on the way to transformation of understanding, albeit that some e-learners may contribute little, and simply feed off the contributions of others; but it still takes some awareness and engagement to benefit, even from such a seemingly parasitic position. Illeris (2007), along with many others involved in e-learning programs, has suggested that net-based learning requires greater motivation than traditional learning:

> Net-based learning or e-learning can constitute an appropriate supplement [to learning] in many contexts, but it presupposes that the relevant multi-aspect programs are available and – to an even greater extent than other learning – that the participants have considerable motivation. (Illeris, 2007: 2003)

It is not clear why e-learning should require more motivation than other forms of learning (everyday, school-based, work-based or voluntary-driven); or why, in an age in which electronic access to texting, voicemail, email, the net, virtual learning environments, etc. is prevalent in the developed world, e-learning is seen as so peripheral. We believe this view by Illeris, and others, stems from early use of e-learning where self-motivated learners were considered the only ones with sufficient drive to be successful at the relatively new practice of communicating online, involving motivation to learn the technical platform, social norms, and idiosyncracies in a time when books were mailed out to students – that is, it was distance education, only more unfamiliar. Thus, this bias of 'considerable motivation' appears to be based on a distance/correspondence view of learning rather than on a more contemporary picture in which young people in particular seem to see online learning as more potentially social, more accessible and more responsive than conventional face-to-face learning.

Yet, questions do remain about motivation. Why, for example, do individuals participate in online communities, multiplayer gaming, or creation of knowledge bases – often with unknown others from around the globe? Among the interesting and emerging areas looking at motivation is the entrepreneurial behavior necessary to be a self-motivated, self-directed learner. Related to that is the idea that the kind of learning an open-web e-learner engages in is more like that of an expert creating knowledge at the edge of their field. These ideas are taken up later in Chapter 9 on ubiquitous learning (see also Bransford et al., 1999; Scardamalia and Bereiter, 1996; Senges et al., 2008).

While it is beyond the scope of this book to review motivational literature in general, and motivations for online activity in particular, a body of work is emerging on precisely this latter question. Studies and theories of motivation from an array of perspectives contribute ideas that inform practices in small to large, and anonymous to named joint enterprises (see also Chapters 5 and 6) that may prove useful for e-learning, including: communications (coorientation theory, Chaffee and McLeod, 1973; participatory culture, Jenkins et al., 2006), gaming (theories of play), leisure studies (theories of serious leisure; Stebbins, 2006), law (economic and legal perspectives on peer production; Benkler, 2006; Lessig, 2006), and systems design and use (for online communities and crowdsourcing; Bryant et al., 2005; Budhathoki, 2010; Haythornthwaite, 2009a).

Social Informatics
Social informatics is an interdisciplinary body of theory that includes consideration of the design, uses and affordances of information and communication technologies, particularly in social, institutional and cultural contexts (Kling et al., 2005). Here we provide just a basic outline of the area, but take this up in more depth in Chapter 7 on the sociotechnical perspective (see also, Andrews and Haythornthwaite, 2007b: 27–31; Haythornthwaite, 2006d).

Social informatics addresses the ways in which new information and communication technologies change the patterns and potentialities of social interaction, and vice versa. Effects are studied at the task, group, organizational and/or societal level, with methods and theoretical approaches brought in from social psychology, sociology, communications, management and information science to name a few. The interacting effects of the social and the technical makes for 'more than just a re-purposed version of offline learning' (Andrews and Haythornthwaite, 2007b: 29). For e-learning contexts, it creates a larger, more complex space for interaction, with multiple media and modes of communication, greater distances of potential interaction, and compressed and/or enhanced synchronous and asynchronous means of communication.

Sawyer and Eschenfelder (2005: 428) suggest that social informatics 'is neither a theory nor a single domain', but a field of research focusing on the relationship between ICTs and the larger social context in which they exist. As such it is a field of inquiry that has overlaps with e-learning practices, but does not provide a theoretical perspective on the problem of whether e-learning requires a new theory of learning. Social informatics itself is undergoing transformation, being subsumed under a broader category of the science of sociotechnical systems (e.g. see http://sociotech.net/). As the field forms its theoretical base, it may be more or less useful for developing theory about e-learning. At present, ideas from the constituent fields – sociology, communications, management – already provide a good theoretical underpinning for understanding group and organizational dynamics around e-learning, and particularly for e-learning implementation, a topic not covered in depth here (see chapters in Haythornthwaite and Kazmer, 2004a).

Among other perspectives that address both social informatics and e-learning are management theories of group processes (e.g. Haythornthwaite, 2006a; McGrath, 1984; Poole and Hollingshead, 2005; see also Chapter 6); sociological theories of social networks and of community (Wellman, 1999; Wellman et al., 1996); and the social construction theories from sociology and the social studies of science (see Chapter 2). Another transformative initiative to follow that will likely have a bearing on e-learning in the future is the move to e-research (American Council of Learned Societies, 2006; Hine, 2006; Jankowski, 2009; Schroeder and Fry, 2007).

Digital Media Theory
This particular body of theory tends to accentuate the visual, concentrating on still and moving images. As such, it focuses on only one mode of communication, but in doing so draws attention to the power of that mode in contemporary communication. Its relevance to understanding e-learning and to the building of e-learning theory is mainly in its exploration of the variety of media that are available for learning, from hand-held devices to desk-top computers and their screens, and from interactive television to portable radio and recording devices. As such, it takes multimodality for granted, preferring to concentrate on the variety of media via which messages can be communicated. Its focus, therefore, is on the ubiquity of learning, and on questions of access and accessibility, rather than on the nature of the message itself. As the web pages at the University of Sussex's Centre for Visual Fields has it:

> scholars in this field re-assess forms of practice and forms of thinking about new media technologies as visual digital cultures. They work with the visual, material and symbolic properties, the affective or sense perceptive regimes, and the political economies that are invoked under the banner of digital media, particularly in visual forms. (http://www.sussex.ac.uk/cvf/)

Interim Summary
Considering a move toward e-learning theory has identified several perspectives on e-learning that need to be taken into account: the principle of distance; communal constructivism (which underpins the notion that learning is an effect of communities and their interaction); multimodality; and transformation. In addition, we have identified intrinsic motivation, social informatics, and digital

media theory as being helpful in gaining further perspective. These are all useful in beginning to define what e-learning theory could be, and now need to be built upon further. Each of them could constitute the beginnings of a theory, but none of them achieves sufficient theoretical scope in itself to cover the ground of e-learning. The next stage of theory-building needs to answer some difficult challenges.

Does E-learning Require a New Theory of Learning?

E-learning 'is a re-conceptualization of learning that makes use of not only instructor-led pedagogy but all the flexibility that asynchronous, multi-party contribution can bring' (Andrews and Haythornthwaite, 2009: 19). It is also continuously emergent, enjoying the dynamic that the co-evolution of learning and technology provides. That dynamic is mediated and experienced by people. Just as the emergence of a new technology changes the way people interact, and how they access and use information, so, too, these changing social patterns change the possibilities of how we learn and how we use new technologies as part of that learning. E-learning, then, is an inextricably *social* act; and it is more than a socio-technical alignment to address efficiency. At the same time it is not just social. The technology has a real role to play, making the 'e-' in e-learning work. Our perspective on e-learning includes changes – transformations – in the platform of practice as an intrinsic part of the phenomenon, and emergence of new practices. In doing so, we follow ideas of structuration and social shaping of technology and society. However, we add to that learner agency, particularly entrepreneurship, as demonstrated in proactive, human expansion of use, from the simplest outcome of SMS turning up in email to the more complex user-generated mash-ups, collaboratories, and learner-centered ecologies of resources.

In the Introduction to *The SAGE Handbook of E-learning Research* (Andrews and Haythornthwaite, 2007), while charting some of the constituent elements and factors in building a theory of e-learning, we backed off on whether a 'grand theory' of e-learning was needed. At the time, we felt that the field was not in a sufficiently mature state for such theorizing. However, we now say in our 'answer' to the question posed by the present section, yes, new theory is needed, and e-learning as an activity and as a way of learning requires its own theoretical treatment.

How far has the argument for a theory of e-learning been taken in the present chapter, and to what extent have questions been answered that were set at the end of the theoretical section of the Introduction to *The SAGE Handbook of E-learning Research* (Andrews and Haythornthwaite, 2007: 32)? The questions posed in that Introduction are quoted and re-formatted here. We have italicized the questions that seem to be particularly relevant to the concerns of the present chapter, namely, does e-learning require a new theory of learning, and if so, what would it look like?

In the *Handbook*, we suggested these questions for future work:

1 What do we mean by a community of enquiry?
2 *How do e-communities relate to situated, real-world communities?*
3 What kinds of community experience are best suited to high-quality learning?
4 Where and what are the boundaries between being and acting in the world, and in learning?
5 What could an ecology of learning mean, and, once defined, how would e-learning fit into it?

A central theme emerging from such questions is the relationship between the social control of learning and individual agency in learning. From the identification of such a theme – one that is not confined to e-learning, but which applies to learning more generally – further questions arise:

1 *When engaged in e-learning, what are you learning?*
2 Whose model of learning and whose selection of knowledge are you adopting?
3 *What are the unexpected consequences of the drive for e-learning initiatives, such as the continued exclusion of non-ICT users?*
4 What is the digital spectrum in terms of access to and use of ICT in learning?

Three Questions Answered

We will take the three italicized questions in a different order: first, when engaged in e-learning, what are you learning? Second, how do e-communities relate to situated, real-world communities? And third, what are the unexpected consequences of the drive for e-learning initiatives, such as the continued exclusion of non-ICT users? The sequence therefore addresses questions of what and how, followed by the implications of the answers. The question about an ecology of e-learning is addressed in Chapter 8.

When Engaged in E-learning, What Are You Learning?

This question brings us back to epistemological concerns, which earlier we had tried to side-step in a focus on the act of e-learning. We suggest that engagement in e-learning makes for a different kind of learning. In conventional learning and scholarship, there is an authoritative, hierarchical power system at work. The teacher acts as mediator for the student between the body of knowledge, as enshrined in books, journals and other forms of print. 'Knowledge' is seen to exist, to be 'added to' by research, and to be guarded by editors of journals who, among others, protect and preserve the discourses of induction into that community. The student voice is always subservient to the authoritative power, unless, through debate and discussion, a critical stand is taken and then committed to print. By engaging with print, the authoritative voice of knowledge is *taken on in its own terms* (e.g. in book reviews, in replies to journal articles, in letters, in books that provide a counter-argument). No amount of talk or blogging will dent what appears to be a hegemony of knowledge that is reified in print.

In e-learning, however, the canonical texts are themselves committed to digital format and thus become at once more malleable, more open to critique that is actioned on the same level as the original text. A digital electronic text can more easily be broken up, annotated, re-aligned, and incorporated as part of a dialectic or at least dialogical exchange. The 'voice(s)' of the original author can be placed alongside the student voice or voices. The learning process becomes more like speech, is more democratic, and is less hierarchical than one based conventionally on print.

So, to focus again on the question, when engaged in e-learning, what are you learning? The answer must be: first, the content can remain the same in either a conventional learning or an e-learning context. But the means by which the learning takes place changes the position of the learner in relation to the content/existing knowledge. As an e-learner, you are learning that knowledge is *provisional*, that what is enshrined in print is only the transduction of what was said or thought in speech, and that you have a part to play in the acceptance and/or critique of that presented knowledge. This is an understanding of content that was normally (or formerly) kept for the expert end of knowledge construction, particularly for younger learners. Thus, as we note throughout the book, the way e-learners are asked to operate is more like experts than novices, and like entrepreneurs. 'Knowledge', from an e-learning perspective, can be conceived conventionally as an existing and authoritative *body of knowledge*; but it can also be seen as a continually moving, fluid set of relationships between propositions on the one hand, and supporting or contrary evidence on the other. Knowledge, from this e-learning perspective, is the result of argued social and rhetorical practice; it is situative.

How Do E-communities Relate to Situated, Real-world Communities?

Another argument to be made about what you are learning when engaged in e-learning is that you are learning *to be* an e-learner both individually, and communally. You are learning how to behave online, how to converse with others, when to lurk and when to step (figuratively) forward and speak out. While as an individual you learn this, the community also develops and learns. The community substrate provides a means for those not yet engaged with others in the community to become peripherally involved, perhaps motivated by a coorientation to the topic of the community (Haythornthwaite, 2005a, 2009a). A stable community can sustain partial involvement of some members. While geography has been the stable substrate for many communities, e-communities rise and fall on their network structures. Thus, the basis for 'community', that is, the mechanics that make it survive, are somewhat different from traditional ideas of community. Patterning is also different for individuals, who can maintain a more partial membership in many communities, both offline and online, than is possible when geographically bound. While some have seen these multiple memberships as too much to manage, taking individuals away from 'real' relationships, e-learning as a transformative event facilitated through computer means has the potential to ramify benefits to multiple communities. Thus, what is learned in the e-learning community can be used to make sense or add to the learning of another community. Overall, simplistic assumptions about the detrimental or positive effects of e-learning on learner well-being need to be replaced by more complex depictions of the relationship between on- and offline learning (Haythornthwaite and Kazmer, 2002). Part of that complexity is that the texture of relations between e-learning and conventional learning is rich, and the two types of learning interpenetrate each other's domains. This is also something we are learning about: how to 'juggle' our multiple social worlds and their multiple intersecting platforms of operation.

If learning is an effect of community, there are two further questions to ask: what is the nature of learning in each of these two types of community? And how are they interconnected? It is again the case, as with the nature of knowledge and learning in the two types of community discussed above, that the real-world contexts tend to be more hierarchical. It can only be speculation as to whether such a context determines the nature of learning (e.g. in making hierarchies of concepts more acceptable) but such an effect is unlikely. Rather, a more likely effect is that learning itself is more fully *locked into* local social and political contexts. In e-learning contexts, on the other hand, learning is apparently less constrained (even though the computer interface is heavily framed as a social and political construct) because the individual user has more control of the format in (through transductive possibilities) and pace at which he or she encounters and processes the material on offer. He or she also has more scope in searching out material. Learning, for an e-learner, is thus less locked to one context, more 'parcelled' and re-workable in different shapes and formats, and more open to re-configuration. Interestingly, at the same time, site specificities change because learning gets re-embedded in new local environments (e.g. home, in transit, at the workplace) and *moves with the learner* (hence the notion of mobile learning).

Associated with learning on the move is the practice of 'just-in-time' learning; that is, learning that takes place very close to the point where it is 'needed' (described as 'everyday learners' in Chapter 1). For example, a nurse working on a ward may need to consult a database of best practices in the dressing of wounds, or a teacher with a particularly intractable pedagogic problem may need instant advice on the best ways of teaching a particular spelling rule. We might, somewhat awkwardly, term such learning 'just-in-place' learning: it is highly contextualized, highly specific and operating in *praxis* – such learning will almost inevitably be remembered as it is closely allied to solving a problem in the real world (assuming it works, and assuming the quality of synthesized evidence is high). In learning to use sources in this way, the learner is also experiencing a transduction of the learning process itself. They are, in effect, learning not only from the retrieved information, but also from the transactional process. They are learning how well this approach (of just-in-time learning) works for gaining the information they need. Thus, a layer of meta-learning is also wrapped into the process of independent e-learning.

What Are the Unexpected Consequences of the Drive for E-learning Initiatives, such as the Continued Exclusion of non-ICT Users?

The final question takes us further away from the core focus of the present chapter and toward the implications of a new theory of learning. The digital spectrum of access and use (rather than a simplistic 'digital divide'; see Chapter 10) is evident not only internationally, but also within societies. 'Access' is distinguished from 'use' in that it is one thing to have access to a networked computer, and another to use that privilege to good and full effect. But we know that many people in society do not have access to a computer, and if they do they may not have access to fast broadband connectivity. There is thus a spectrum of access which means that some learners will be relatively disadvantaged. Such disadvantage may not affect the quality of learning, but it will most certainly affect the type of learning and the range of resources that are available. Access is an issue of systemic economic inequality. Use is more a matter of individual engagement with the possibilities and affordances of new software and connectivity, and manifests itself generationally as well as socio-economically. See Haythornthwaite (2007) for a fuller discussion of the 'digital divide' and e-learning.

As far as e-learning theory goes, those of us who generalize about e-learning practices need to continue to bear in mind that there is a wide spectrum both of access and use. We need to remember also that learning expectations, paradigms and practices will not be the same the world over, and that cross- and inter-cultural issues will arise (see also Chapter 11).

Further Thoughts

The distillation of rhetorical and social informatics approaches in relation to knowledge creation and transformation means this: that e-learning occurs when the available resources for learning are transformed by the learner to result in personal, social and/or political change, with the added dimension of peer as well as teacher discussion, asynchronously as well as synchronously. Available and existing texts may be transducted (Kress and van Leeuwen, 2001) in the process of learning; that is to say, they may change their modal or multimodal composition, and the very change may embody the learning that takes place (e.g. in the transduction of a printed text into an image, or vice versa), but transduction is only part of the overall process of transformation that is at the heart of learning.

Such e-learning is distinctively different from conventional face-to-face learning, or solitary learning by an individual in a library or a monastic cell, in three main ways: the digitization of text makes for easier and more rapid transduction; the availability of an extended community of learners, with the teacher taking his/her place alongside learners, extends the possibilities of learning as an effect of that community (and as an effect of its connection with other communities); and the affordance of asynchronicity makes for a potentially more dynamic relationship between the individual learner and his/her interaction with the wider group/community.

This last point resonates with those made by Castells (2001), who suggests that the Internet has enabled a new system of social relationships based on the individual; a 'networked individualism' (Wellman, 2001; see also Chapter 8). In short, the individual is able both to define and be defined by the social networks he/she plays a part in. When applied to e-learning, the freedom of the individual is clear. Within (and beyond) the confines of the course or program and its requirements, the individual learner has the freedom to define his or her network of learning. Because the learner moves in and out of the electronic environment of learning, even in so-called '100% online' learning programs, he or she builds a web of discourses and patterns for learning that becomes distinctive. E-learning, then, transforms the nature of learning for the contemporary learner; it does more than 'enhance' an existing state of affairs, and much more than provide a re-situated version of conventional learning. It creates a web of networked communities that in themselves are generative of learning, but in combination and association, provide a richer, more extensive opportunity for learning.

Conclusion

In summary, what is the answer to the overall question which this chapter addresses: Does e-learning require a new theory of learning? We have attempted to argue that e-learning changes the nature of learning in a number of significant ways. First, if we accept the premise that learning is socially situated, and that e-communities are different from conventional learning communities in classrooms in schools and universities, then it follows that e-learning is different from conventional learning. Crucially, e-learning extends the horizons of learning in space, resource and time. The notion of transactional distance is important to understanding how e-learning is different from conventional face-to-face learning. Such extension requires more from the learner in that he/she has to make selections from the possible available resources, as well as decide how and when to engage in the e-learning community. Second, the nature of knowledge itself (and therefore the learning of that knowledge) is affected by digital technology, particularly in the leveling out of the relationship between existing knowledge, the teacher and the student. Rather than a hierarchical conception of knowledge, e-learning and its technologies promote a 'flatter', more democratic, more potentially dialogical relationship between the learner and knowledge. Third, transduction is easier with a multimodal computer interface than without it. Transduction is one aspect of transformation, which in itself is a major aspect of learning theory. Lastly, any new theory of e-learning needs to bear in mind that just as learning was always subject to a spectrum of access and use, according to socio-economic, geographic, cognitive and motivational factors, e-learning stretches that spectrum still further.

The answer to the question that has driven this chapter – does e-learning need a new theory of learning? – must therefore be 'yes'. The first three points made in the previous paragraph, distilled from the chapter as a whole, suggest that in terms of learning as (a) a psycho-social construct, (b) an epistemologically informed entity, and (c) a multimodal process, e-learning is bringing about a new theory of learning. How that theory is manifested or expressed in new literacies discourse is the subject of the next chapter, where we will look more closely at the combination of word, image and sound in e-learning, both from the point of view of the learner but also from the perspective of the instructional designer, the teacher and others involved in the management of learning.

Further Reading

Haythornthwaite, C. and Kazmer, M. M. (Eds) (2004). *Learning, Culture and Community in Online Education: Research and Practice.* New York: Peter Lang.

Haythornthwaite, C., Andrews, R., Bruce, B. C., Kazmer, M. M., Montague, R-A. and Preston, C. (2007). 'New theories and models of and for online learning', *First Monday, 12*(8). Available online at: http://firstmonday.org/issues/issue12_8/haythorn/index.html

Jewitt, C. (2008). *Technology, Literacy, Learning: A Multimodal Approach.* Abingdon: Routledge.

Kress, G. (2010). *Multimodality: A Social Semiotic Approach To Contemporary Communication.* London: Routledge.

New Literacies, New Discourses in E-learning

From New Literacies to New Discourses

This chapter continues the theme from the previous two in looking at how theories of learning and e-learning are manifest in communicative practices. In this chapter, we explore how e-learning affords opportunities for different kinds of communication than are traditionally used in learning. In a sense, whereas other chapters in this book look through transparent glass to the topic under discussion, this one regards the stained glass of the medium itself through which the understanding of the field is filtered. In this chapter we work simultaneously on seeing the stained glass, and also on looking through it to the focus of our book as a whole: e-learning theory and practice.

Because online communication demonstrates an array of forms – words, images, sound, icons, diagrams, and more – read and produced through computing interfaces, and because the social contexts for communication are so different from those in conventional learning, we can hardly remain satisfied with the narrow notion of literacy (or 'new literacies') as the reading and writing of words. Instead, to move beyond words into other modes, we need to *shift the discussion from literacies to new discourses*. Such a shift enables us not only to move beyond words into other modes, but also to locate the communication process in a different range of social situations and contexts.

Multimodality, Multiliteracies, and the New London Group

In the 1990s, the New London Group (1996, 2000) – so called because they met at a seminar in New London, New Hampshire – presented and explicated a new literacies model that addressed multimodality. The model is depicted in Figure 4.1.

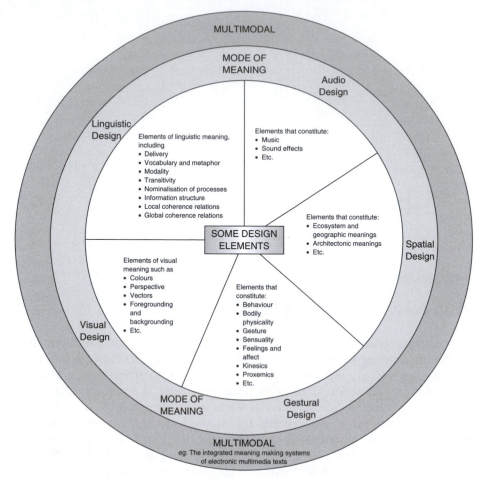

Figure 4.1   New London Group model. Cope and Kalantzis (2000). Reproduced with permission of Taylor and Francis

The New London Group's new literacies model appears to hold promise for making sense of communication in e-learning. The *context* in which that model was composed took into account the 'burgeoning variety of text forms associated with information and multimedia technologies' (2000: 9). However, beyond this, the focus of the model has been on multimodality and design within a framework of socially informed sign systems (social semiotics, see Box 2.1). The social context addressed by this model included attention to late-twentieth-century capitalism, changing social patterns and influences on changing public and personal lives, as well as implications for schooling. But, new information and communication technologies remained somewhat outside the focus of this seminal discussion on multiliteracies and pedagogy. Thus, while the New London Group's work has drawn attention to multimodality (and the computer interface is certainly one site of multimodal design and potential learning), issues of digitization and e-learning have largely remained separate from those of multimodality. This then leaves the possibility of taking the multiliteracies model further.

This chapter focuses on extending the multiliteracies model by moving the discussion from 'literacy', and its pluralistic form 'literacies', to 'discourse'. Here we look at why 'literacy' as a term is no longer sufficient, and return later to describe the use of discourse. At present we find that 'literacy' and 'literacies' carry too much to be useful in describing the kinds of communication that take place in e-learning. The burdens are manifold. First, literacy as a term has been used to mean 'cultural competence' rather than the ability to read and write verbal language. It has been used in phrases like 'computer literacy', 'information literacy', and 'digital literacy', partly metaphorically, and partly in terms of the discourses used in a particular field, to account for awareness and capability in those and other fields. It has even been used to describe human capabilities, for example 'emotional literacy'. Such use has dissipated the power of the term. Second, 'literacy' has been pluralized to cover the various codes which can be mastered, and also to refer to a range of social practices in which communication takes place. So, for example, we can talk of one form of literacy in a high-level banking board meeting, and another in a street conversation between members of the same gang. These 'literacies' are more than mere jargons; they are worlds of communication, sometimes almost mutually incomprehensible, which presuppose different sets of values, assumptions, diction, vocabulary and delivery.

BOX 4.1: MEDIUM AND MODE

E-learning issues are neither the domain of *multimedia* nor of the *multimodal* exclusively. Both are important to e-learning, but while *multimedia* provide the hardware vehicles via which e-learning might take place, *multimodality* is a semiotic issue which has to be addressed in any kind of learning. A *mode* is a type of communication language, like speech, writing, or the still image. We tend to think of media as the hardware via which messages are conveyed (computers, television, etc.), but e-learning escapes confinement to either multimedia or multimodality. It is transmitted via these media and it uses a range of modes, but essentially, it is a type of learning, and is thus more closely allied to learning theory and practices.

Exploring Modes

As noted in Chapter 1, one of the ironies of e-learning is that, despite the potential affordances of computing and multimodality, much e-learning has confined itself to the relatively monomodal written form of verbal language exchanges, that is, words in their written form. Yet, even these basic forms still use and exploit the medium of the screen, with a wide range of modes including text, icon, image, audio and video, and the conventions of computing practice. In this section we use some examples to demonstrate what we mean by a wide range of modes for communication, and how even the most limited of e-learning interfaces goes beyond the verbal (an adjective denoting association with the word, but which we use in this book to refer to both spoken and written language).

Key concepts discussed here that help unpack the complexity of modality and multimodality include:

- *Frames*: Real or imagined constructs which help shape the communication between the speaker(s)/composer(s) and the audience/reader.
- *Literacy*: In its narrow form, the ability to write and read; more broadly, communication capability in a range of social and electronic literacies.
- *Discourse*: Although originally used to denote spoken communication, now it is used to refer to any kind of 'stretch' of communication, using a range of modes and media.

Example: Multimodality in a Virtual Learning Environment Page

In the screenshot from a virtual learning environment (VLE) page shown in Figure 4.2, there are three modes in operation, all arranged by framing. The first mode is the *verbal*, through words placed across the whole page on buttons, in direct communication with the students, in instructions and for other functions. The second mode is the *iconic*, where in almost every case a small visual logo is attached to a word to denote a function that the computer can perform for you. However, there are some icons that are taken for granted and

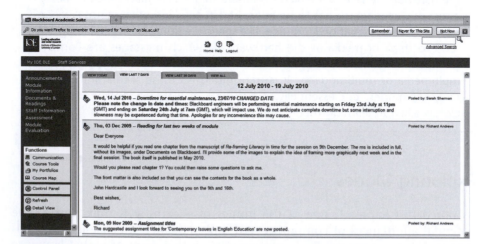

Figure 4.2 Screenshot from Blackboard Academic

which are not accompanied by words, such as the 'x' in a box at the upper right corner (which most will immediately understand to mean the whole verbal phrase 'click here to close this window'), or the icon showing a small piece of paper pinned with a large (relative to the size of the paper) push pin, which must be interpreted within the context of this application to signal a resemblance to a note on a bulletin board and hence an instruction to 'read this note'. The third mode is the *visual*, represented in the folder-like arrangement of banks of information. The visual is amplified in the framing of the page. An outer frame is provided by the operating system (in this case, Windows), and within it sit a number of sub-frames in the VLE itself. These are arranged to make navigation, and therefore reading, an easy process, and can suggest a reading path through the complexity of a multimodal page. Each of the framed boxes has a different function; each has its own set of words and icons and, in some cases, further visual features. Each mode has a different way of communicating, and a different message to communicate. The term used to refer to what these means and content make possible is *affordances* (Gaver, 1991; Gibson, 1979; see also Chapter 1).

Example: Multimodality, Opportunity Gained

In a more sophisticated interface, the visual and aural modes can play a greater part, for example, in the inclusion of a video clip. While not a VLE in itself, the possibilities for learning from the BBC website, for example, are considerable. Represented here are all the modes that were present in the VLE screenshot example, but additionally the facilities of sound, still and moving image, plus the possibility of blogging, a selection from a range of weather forecast locations, the chance to donate to disaster relief, the chance to set a location for the channelling of further information, access to 'live' information from sporting events and other interactional functions (see Figure 4.3). The pages shown here were accessed in 2010. By the time you read this such interfaces may have many more features.

Example: Multimodality, Opportunity Lost

That features and communicative possibilities are available does not mean they are necessarily used. This is the paradox of affordances: they are possibilities, not uses. Many screens fail to live up to multimodal expectations, particularly in their first instantiation. As will be discussed later in Chapter 7, the affordances of Web 2.0 technologies can be lost in a Web 1.0 approach. So, too, in capitalizing on the possibilities of multimodality and for new learning presentations, an implementation may miss the mark. Bayne, Williamson and Ross (2010) demonstrate precisely this point in the case of a museum website. In their multimodal analysis, the authors find that the game interface provided at the time on a 'webquest' site for young adults intended to facilitate access to museum digital resources. The issue in terms of multimodality is that the space prescribes a learner's progress throughout the site. Color-coded screen spaces delimit learner and teacher spaces; navigation 'traps' learners in a 'determined learning and working path with no options for foraging for his or her own

Figure 4.3   Screenshot from the BBC website (retrieved 19 July 2010)

direction through the activity' (Bayne et al., 2010: 4). Despite the high quality of the digital resources, for example of the objects displayed, textual elements dominate the interface design. There is 'no user-generated content, no shared space for knowledge construction or discussion, no user-defined pathway through the text'. The result is a 'driving sense … of a digital learning space which works against its own digitality' (2010: 5).

By contrast, Greenhow (Case 4.1) presents a case where the features of the media, and particularly the features of Web 2.0 social media, are brought in to encourage civic engagement by young adults.

CASE 4.1: THE 'HOT DISH' SOCIAL NETWORKING APPLICATION: A SOCIAL LEARNING RESOURCE

Christine Greenhow, University of Maryland, USA

Teenagers and young adults are thought to be disengaged from school and civic lives. According to traditional measures, they are less well informed, read less, engage in communities less, and achieve less in school than their predecessors. At the same time, the future world of work in a global economy demands higher levels of preparedness and acquisition of new competencies. When preliminary studies suggested the educational and social potential of social network sites for high school age students, we decided to explore whether users would participate authentically through a social network site. To examine this, we developed an open source online social networking application called 'Hot Dish' and implemented it within young people's existing social network on Facebook. The goal was to engage young people (ages 16–24) in literacy and socio-scientific inquiry around a pressing social issue of interest to them: environmental issues and climate change. The project also sought to engage them in related environmental activism through offline and online challenge activities. Along with questions about how participation would progress, we were also interested in whether their interest in and knowledge of environmental science and climate change issues would increase, and if so, how? Would a sense of community develop? Perhaps most importantly, would their online contributions translate into real-world actions or consist solely of virtual activism?

The Hot Dish social networking application is the first of its kind to prominently feature editorial alongside user-generated content all enveloped by the unique socializing, profiling, sharing, and inviting features that are hallmarks of social network sites like Facebook. Launched in March 2009, Hot Dish quickly attracted around 5,000 monthly active users (at peak) with 2,174 total users, including nearly 150 Facebook fans. The application positions participants in the role of producers of content: within Hot Dish, young people *read, rank, annotate, post* and *share* digital content relevant to the topic at hand; *vote* up others' stories; and craft *blog* entries, *comments* and *documentation* of their offline and online civic engagement. The site supports individual identity within this niche network: each member constructs a '*My Profile*' which is featured prominently on the home page and separate from his or her Facebook profile. Hot Dish also emphasizes the link between *online* debate and action and civic participation *offline*, helping to make this connection more transparent for young people. An 'Action Team' feature provides opportunities to complete problem-solving challenges (e.g. writing a letter to the editor, writing to lawmakers, starting a recycling program, participating in activist-oriented events in their local communities). Completing challenges bolsters members' involvement in the application and showcases how they are making environmental change. Team members are publicly recognized with accumulating point awards, rankings and titles (e.g. 'Climate Czar').

Over the course of a three-month study period, young people contributed two-thirds of the content available within the network (i.e. posted articles, blog entries, multimedia comments). Overall the program looks to be a success. Contributions indicate increased interest in the topic, in self-expression, and in civic involvement. For instance,

(Continued)

(Continued)

surveys revealed that overall interest in environmental science and climate change increased among all users. Young people appeared to use current events to connect more meaningfully with career interests and concepts or fields of study (i.e. environment-related or journalism majors) they were learning in school. Comment threads revealed online debate about editorially driven and user-generated commentary on environmental science findings, policies and other environment-related topics. The majority of articles available on the site were read. In addition, users completed impressive numbers of environmental activist challenges, engaging the issue locally or through online civic actions.

Christine Greenhow is an Assistant Professor, College of Education & College of Information Studies, University of Maryland, College Park. The 'Hot Dish' application was funded by the John S. and James L. Knight Foundation, and designed by developers at NewsCloud, a social media company, in collaboration with Dr Greenhow as principal investigator, and graduate research assistants from the University of Minnesota. For more on this project, see Greenhow and Robelia, 2009a, 2009b; Greenhow et al., 2009a, 2009b.

From 'Literacy' to 'Discourse'

The examples above show the possibilities of communicative modes in e-learning. Even when failing to embrace the full range of possibilities, the most minimal interface moves well beyond the verbal in its facilities, modes and affordances, and in the relations between modes. Thus, we find it is problematic to describe what is needed to read, respond to, create and recreate with and through such interfaces as merely 'literacy'. We find a better way to refer to such multimodal interaction is to say there are *discourses* that need to be engaged in.

BOX 4.2: LITERACY, LITERACIES AND DISCOURSE

Literacy is the most commonly used term, and signifies, at its simplest, the ability to read and write. But it is made more complex by at least two dimensions: first, an understanding that the apparently simple act of reading and writing is not the same in all cultures and societies, nor in a range of specific situations. What it means to be literate in the urban, post-industrial twenty-first-century US may not be the same as what it means to be literate in rural Afghanistan. Second, reading and writing are transformed by new technologies so that the ability to read and interpret websites, for example – and the ability to write or compose them – adds a further dimension to literacy. Hence the term *litera-cies*. There is one further step that this chapter takes in sharpening the tools to discuss e-learning developments. The term *literacy/literacies* is predicated on engagement with script and print and so, essentially, with what we have described as *verbal* language (including speech). The term *discourse* is useful because it refers to a wider range of communicative codes or modes, including not only speech, listening, reading and writing, but also icons, still and moving images, gesture, movement, etc.

In the e-learning context, multimodal interactions are *new discourses* in the sense that their combination is new in the pursuit of learning compared to conventional learning. One key difference that is evident from the examples above is that e-learning requires attention to spatial arrangements – of screens, menus, icons, text and image features – as well as to linear presentations – of texts within screen layouts, of threaded discussions, etc. Spatial awareness pertains to locating screen management features (where menus are located, where to move the cursor to save work), and managing on- and off-screen pages and series of multimodal pages. Knowledge of where to find currently open but invisible windows is held in mental maps of multi-window activity, following learned logics about visual display within a specific operating system. Navigation tools such as sliders that bring 'off-screen' elements into view give a sense that we are looking through a window at a scroll rather than at a page (Agarwal-Hollands and Andrews, 2001), and hot keys permit cycling through series of open windows as we simultaneously cycle through screens of attention (from working with a local application, to reading email, to searching on the web). (For further discussion of the reading of images within a social and multimodal semiotic framework, see Kress and van Leeuwen, 1996.)

The Implications of a 'Discourse' View of E-learning

What are the implications of seeing e-learning in terms of discourses rather than literacy or literacies? In particular, what design demands are made? And what are the implications for the reader/learner? We premise our approach to answering these questions on the recognition that, while being highly textual, e-learning interfaces have more than textual work to accomplish in the service of learning. Of primary significance is that *the e-learning interface is both text and learning space* (whether we think of that space as a classroom, workshop, or workplace). It is on this interface that learners talk, read, interpret and provide feedback. While conventional face-to-face learning situations can rely on physical, spatial, time-bound and co-present interaction to aid the mediation of texts that are brought into the classroom, e-learning interfaces must do this work. Thus, e-learning interfaces have the added work of providing a context and home for textual and learning practices. The computer screen, and the way the virtual learning platform configures the screen, act to determine the kinds of interaction that can take place.

Most commonly, functions and activities in e-learning implementations try to replicate those of the spatially-located classroom. In fact, the frame that is the conventional classroom is 'replaced' by the virtual learning environment itself. But the medium via which the VLE is conveyed – a laptop, a tablet, a handheld (phone) or desktop computer – itself is located in different places according to where the learner is operating: at home, in a bedroom or office; on a train; in the street; or on location in the workplace. These locations are in one way irrelevant to the process of learning, in that the activity and interaction take place via the screen; but in another way the locations determine the 'position' of the learner. What is meant by 'position' is not only whether the individual is working alone, but also his or her 'stance' in relation to learning and to the community of learning.

Let's for a moment reflect on the individual e-learner and the screen. He or she is most probably operating physically independently and alone. Learning alone is one dimension of the e-learning/ubiquitous learning experience, and when in that dimension, the e-learner is making sense of material by him/ herself – possibly connecting with others in an e-learning group or community to do so. He or she is isolated from other learners by being distributed, but connected online, and isolated from local conditions by being online, and engaged in an e-learning activity, while connected to these locales physically.

On the other hand, he or she might be in a social situation, in a workplace, where the learning takes place both in relation to the screen and in relation to an immediate social grouping that will be fed the results of the learning. Individuals can engage in 'over-the-shoulder' learning in association with local colleagues for just-in-time learning (Twidale, n.d.; Twidale and Ruhleder, 2004). This relationship between what the screen can offer and what is required by the immediate social situation was also evidenced for us by observation of two people conversing on a train about the origin of the phrase 'Pandora's box'. One of the conversants made several forays into the Internet (via Wikipedia and search engines), all on a handheld phone, to explore in layers of deeper analysis the origin and significance of the Pandora story. This small example is a case of ubiquitous learning, an aspect of e-learning discussed more fully in Chapter 9.

Interface Work

We ask a lot of an e-learning interface. Because the conventional learning situation is (ideally) multimodal, rich in interactional possibility, and (hopefully) engaging and transformational, the screen interface has to fulfil a large number of functions via a range of modes in order to compete as a learning space – whether for a learner working in relative isolation, or for two or more learners clustered around a screen or working via a network. It is not as if the online/offline space relating to the screen is impoverished in relation to face-to-face possibilities, merely that it is a different space, with different affordances.

Both formal learning and e-learning share the experience of removal from day-to-day life. The 'ivory tower', the school grounds, and the VLE each promote a separation of learning and learners from other social worlds. Even in apprenticeship settings, the duties of the apprentice may be separated from those of the master, perhaps by type of task, tools that can be used, or responsibilities that can be assumed. Text, the mainstay of education in both verbal and written forms, creates another separation; a symbolic remove from the flux of day-to-day experience, however informal or formal the experience (e.g. a chance encounter on a street compared to a taught, timetabled class). Yet, because e-learning must be both text and space, formal class and informal encounter, the degrees of removal – we could say 'abstraction', but only in the sense of being pulled away from 'direct' experience rather than in ethereal degrees of generalization – are greater for e-learning than conventional learning, and the dependence on symbolic systems of representation and communication is greater. Whereas communication theorists might talk about how interaction is 'mediated' between two parties (through language, media, etc.), consideration of e-learning scenarios makes us think about the *distance* between learners. The greater the physical distance (in other words, the likelihood that the two learners would never meet face-to-face), the more dependent are the learners on the computer interface. Verbal language and the other modes we have discussed so far in this chapter, have to do more work as a result.

Another aspect of interface work, and work through computer interfaces, is evident in the management of frames, first of the screen itself and then of frames within that overall frame. Also, online, there is a more obvious, more conscious *interrelation* of modes than is the case in everyday formal and informal experience (it is no surprise that the rise of the study of multimodality in the 1990s coincided with the prevalence of computer screens). This plays out in two ways: separate windows leading to specific applications that each sustain a single mode, for example as we cycle between word processor, spreadsheet, search engine, and drawing packages; and single windows that present multiple modes, for example in an online newspaper with text, still images, videos, blog commentary opportunities, or in a VLE. In either case, the screen gives us the first access into further symbolic worlds. But the very nature of frames within frames of symbolic representation also provides a territory for learning. The mental management and interrelating of frames is an effort, and one that, done successfully, provides a coherent world view. If each frame separates out ('boxes') a particular section of information, the art of learning is to make connections between the boxes.

Let us summarize this dense argument so far. First, we are focusing on multimodal discourses in relation to e-learning because we think that (a) the terms 'literacy' or 'literacies', though a convenient shorthand, do not fully account for the range of modes of communication used in e-learning, and (b) the social frames that operate in face-to-face encounters are replaced by symbolic frames and a range of discourses (word, icon, image, etc.) in e-learning. Second, although digitization and multimodality are often seen as related to each other, they are not synonymous and thus we wish to retain separate trajectories for each of them. Digitization has made possible the coding, encoding, decoding (and re-coding) of text that has given rise to e-learning, and as such is the subject of this entire book; multimodality is addressed particularly in the present chapter because the focus is on how e-learning is *communicated*. We are giving our attention here to the stained glass window rather than looking through a transparent window to the field of e-learning. In short, attention is given to the *how* rather than to the *what*. Third, we see e-learning as highly framed learning spaces, both in terms of interface design and engagement by the learner. This suggests an underpinning to e-learning theory that derives from sociology as well as from the visual and performing arts, an area explored in depth by Andrews (2010) in *Re-framing Literacy*.

Implications for the Learner

This discussion of frames and the interpretive work to be done to learn from and through them can be taken further to consider the implications for the learner. It is not just the designer of the interface who has to do more to bring out the learning elements in a virtual environment and to make them more explicit, more accessible, more interpretable by a learner than the conventional teacher and classroom; the interface also offers more layers of symbolic representation for the learner to interpret. The learner still needs to make the most of what is offered by the virtual learning environment, and by the range of signs and sources of information and knowledge available through offline channels: libraries, online resources, television, film, etc.

In a conventional learning situation, the teacher plays a major role in making those tissues of connections and transformational links apparent, demonstrating them to the learner and thus in a sense doing the connection work for the learner. However, in e-learning, due to the distributed nature of participation, the onus falls much more on the learner to make such connections. One could argue that in an e-learning situation, rather like the solitary scholar working at a desk and exploring his or her own thoughts, the possibilities for intellectual connection are greater. Certainly, there is no shortage of information that is waiting, inert, for a learner to access it, combine it with existing knowledge, and make something new that we could characterize as learning. *Composition* of this sort is at the heart of the learning process. But to say one kind of learning has more *potential* than another is dangerous territory. We are not arguing in this book that e-learning is better than conventional learning; rather, that it is different.

Implications for Society

As Kress and Pachler (2007) discuss, the presence and increasing pervasiveness of ICTs and connectivity, and the notions of e-learning and m-learning (normally denoting mobile learning) are entering society as arguments about societal transformation. While mobile learning in itself is not the principal focus of the present chapter (or of the book; see instead Pachler, 2007; Pachler et al., 2009), the range covered in the Kress and Pachler chapter is highly relevant to the argument of the present book. 'Mobility' is seen as one particular manifestation of the impact of digital technologies which 'hold out the promise of unlimited access to educational commodities and of the consumer-learner's sovereignty of choice' (Kress and Pachler, 2007: 9) in a 'fast capitalist' market (Gee et al., 1996). The characteristics and effective use of new digital technologies 'revolve around a combination of technology- and user-related factors' (Kress and Pachler, 2007: 12) and include: flexibility and portability; multifunctionality and technical convergence; nonlinearity; interactivity and communicative potential; and multimodal representation. Through the combination of new digital technologies, mobility and multimodality, learners can take charge of the direction, scope and depth of their learning, contributing to it more actively (at least in the manipulation and re-framing of signs) than would be the case in a conventional, teacher-directed classroom.

Kress (2009) further elaborates on mobility in a chapter on the social semiotics of convergent mobile devices, that is, those that provide single platform mobility, connectivity, social networking and work production. While his particular focus is on third generation mobile phones ('smartphones'), his general points have considerable application to e-learning. Working from a principle that 'the social is prior' (2009: 184) – that social interaction determines communication and the means of communication, more than the other way round – Kress develops the point that social conditions are fast-changing and fluid, even unstable and provisional. In such a climate, rhetorical considerations become essential as each communication situation requires a renewed assessment of power relations, the function of the communicative act, and the media and modes available to make the communication.

The main point to draw from these works is that the processes described are not bound at the level of the individual reader and their interface. Instead, development in multimodality and mode, and the continuing development of new discourses happens across all levels of society.

A Reciprocal, Co-evolutionary Model of Literacy Development and Learning

It was consideration of the relationship between literacy development and new forms of technology that led us to a model that showed a reciprocal, co-evolutionary relationship between the two. What we had first thought to be relevant only to literacy turned out to be relevant to learning more widely, and to have implications for our understanding of e-learning development.

As noted in Chapter 3, in Andrews and Haythornthwaite (2007) we posited a model for the relationship between the development of new technologies on the one hand, and literacy and learning on the other. This model, which we do not discuss fully here but replicate in Figure 4.4 below, needs further explication in the light of the present book. Its genesis was helped by discussions with biology professor Angela Douglas, who suggested that the relationship between the development of new technologies on the one hand, and literacy learning on the other, was not *symbiotic* (as we had imagined) because symbiosis suggested

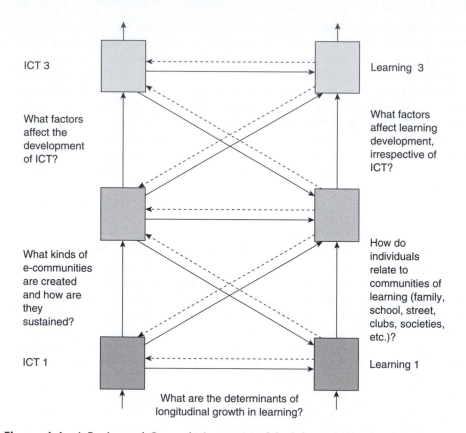

ICT 3

Learning 3

What factors affect the development of ICT?

What factors affect learning development, irrespective of ICT?

What kinds of e-communities are created and how are they sustained?

How do individuals relate to communities of learning (family, school, street, clubs, societies, etc.)?

ICT 1

Learning 1

What are the determinants of longitudinal growth in learning?

Figure 4.4   A Reciprocal Co-evolutionary Model of the Relationship between Information and Communication Technologies (ICT) and Learning

the maintenance of a static relationship. Rather, the changing nature of both parties in the equation in a dynamic system suggested another term from biology: *reciprocal co-evolution*. (Other uses of biological metaphors are discussed in Chapter 8 in relation to *e-learning ecologies*.)

Taking this model now to address learning rather than just literacy, moves us away from a causal one-way connection between learning and technology, putting learning and technological advancement as taking place alongside each other. The relationship is not merely symbiotic and static, it is instead co-evolutionary as each element affects and changes the other. Residual effects are noticeable too, in the sense of time-lags in the development of either phenomenon. That is to say, advances in learning practices could make way for new technologies, just as advances in new media could engender new forms of learning, new kinds of learning networks, and so on – and sometimes reciprocal development takes time to catch up.

Behind our model is the assumption that the process of learning is not the same from one decade to another, from one generation to another, but rather that the dynamics of learning, and its particular visible presentation at any time, are affected by the social and technological nexus. This is very much in keeping with Engeström's (2009) formulation of *expansive learning*, where understanding of an 'object' (that which is being studied or learned about) forms at the nexus of a set of elements in an activity system that includes mediating artifacts as well as constituents of the local context. The assumption about continuous and mutually influential change, in turn, has allowed us to see that e-learning is different from conventional learning because of its tight coupling with technology, and thus requires a new theory of learning.

What would a move from literacy and literacies to socially situated discourses mean for such a model? We believe our original model could accommodate such a shift with ease. To re-state the model succinctly: as the patterns, media and modes of social and political discourse change, so too do the means via which we learn. These means are intimately (reciprocally) related to the development of new forms of technology, particularly information and communication technologies. The coming together of forms of representation in multimodal formats; the convergence of media in third and fourth generation phones; the continued evolution of portable and handheld devices; the ubiquity of possibilities for learning, all suggest that the landscape of learning is changing. The result is that not only how knowledge is communicated, but also how social networks attend to, validate, store and make available that knowledge, is changing. The implications for practice are discussed throughout the present book, but especially in Chapters 6 and 8 where we address learning communities and ecologies of e-learning. The implications for research are considered in Chapter 12.

Developing a New 'Language' for E-learning

A new approach to learning that sees 21st-century discourses as part of the fabric of learning, mediated by electronic means of communication, requires a new 'language' – or, in our preferred term, a new set of discourses. We mean more here than a vocabulary or a set of technical terms that describe the field (a 'diction' or less positively, a 'jargon'). Rather, by 'set of discourses' we mean the very means via which we are able to describe, discuss and move forward in the field: a common language. We have already set out some of the terms of this brave new world. Not all the terms, or the shifts in alignment we have proposed, will stick. The test will be usage. But in addition to the key terms already mooted – transformation, discourse, communities, networks, modes and media, reciprocal co-evolution – what other terms and accompanying perspectives will be useful in charting the territory?

Learner Agency

Learner agency implies learner control of their experience. It includes the ideas of self-directed learning in how and what is learned, the pedagogy of self-directed learning (Hase and Kenyon, 2000), and student ownership of the learning path.

It is an expected way for adults to learn, as well as for expert groups to explore new knowledge (Bransford et al., 1999; Scardamalia and Bereiter, 1996). In educational systems, school administrators, designers of curricula and, most keenly, arbiters of the assessment and accreditation of learning, like governments, are wary of learner agency because it is unpredictable and often hard to measure. It happens at the interface of formal and informal contexts for learning; it is hard to capture because the particular spiritual, intellectual, emotional and/or practical moment of learning is complex. Assessment systems like 'assessment for learning' or 'personal learning plans' are attempts to capture this fast-moving process. Generally, however, they become unwieldy, attempting to measure the stable after the horse has bolted. At worst they can constrain learning by assuming that it can only happen within the confines of the already charted pathways. Learner agency, on the other hand, gives learners power to move in the directions the learner feels are necessary; to explore uncharted territory; to go over the same ground if required. We would argue strongly for learner agency in e-learning environments. Such agency can be designed in by those who create material, programs and environments for e-learning; but as technologies develop, we refer also to the e-learner having more power and more responsibility for the way in which their learning moves and develops (see also Chapter 9 on ubiquitous learning).

Participatory Culture

The rise in demotic (sometimes democratic) participation via e-learning has been a hallmark of the last few years. Whereas in a pre-Web 2.0 world, design and production of information for learning environments was handed to the learner by the software and course designer, in a participatory model there is space and facility for the learner to determine the direction of the journey. They may contribute to the material that is studied; suggest new avenues for exploration; make visible new connections between existing elements or bodies of information. Mash-ups, re-mixes, combinations of material in different modes and via different media are all part of the possibilities that a participatory culture affords. At the same time, it raises issues of copyright and appropriate use of materials, of the authority of the teacher, and of the nature of the learning community. These and other issues relating to participatory culture are explored in more depth in Chapter 5.

Peer Production

Related to participatory culture and the notion that a map of learning can be created by a group of learners, is the practice of peer production. Although we have emphasized so far in the book that e-learning tends to give the learner more autonomy and choice, and therefore power over the process of learning, we must recognize that peer production is also made possible in ways that were previously unimagined. For example, a website of images and music could be created by three individuals or three groups of individuals each working in a different part of the world. The creation of a shared platform means that work could be produced synchronously and/or asynchronously. Parts of a production can be overlain: for example, a rhythm track can be overlaid by a melodic track and then overlaid by lyrics (see Chapter 12 for an exemplary case by Domingo (2010) of such collaboration and peer production in the Filipino community in London). Such collaborative production raises questions about how such production and learning are assessed. There is already much experience in the assessment of joint work, for example in drama, musical production and other forms of cultural activity, where the individual contribution is distilled from the collective piece; or, in a different environment, in the way in which co-authors of a research paper can agree on the respective contributions of each individual. However, questions still remain on the acceptance of *collaborative* work products, for example those where ideas are pooled in such a way that no particular contribution can be tagged to a particular contributor.

Framing and Re-framing

We have argued that e-learning interfaces are more highly and more obviously framed than conventional learning situations (although further analysis of conventional situations would reveal a high but different kind of sociological, institutional and political framing). The framing in e-learning is conscious, explicit and visible. A disadvantage of virtual learning environments is that this frame is not easily broken. But, this is not the case for free-form e-learning, where the frames can be selected, created or re-created by the learner. Framing allows a particular shape to the design of the learning in question, and control over the parameters of that frame. *Re*-framing, on the other hand, is a way of acknowledging pedagogic patterning in learning, and the power of looking at phenomena through a different frame, with a different set of questions, values and assumptions. Andrews (2010) provides an extended exploration of framing and re-framing in relation to literacy, using perspectives from sociology and the visual and performing arts. One of the key points about framing and re-framing is that they sit easily alongside multimodality. While framing delimits and sets a line within which attention is focused, multimodality is more about what goes inside the frame, and what – by implication – is left outside.

Summary

These four aspects of e-learning – learner agency, participatory culture, peer production and framing/re-framing – help define the priorities of the field of e-learning. They are related in that they all imply active learning on the part of the e-learner. Elsewhere in the book we emphasize the motivational dimension of e-learning: how one has to be motivated in order to join discussion groups, contribute to wikis, and manage and make sense of the received information. Participatory cultures and peer production follow from such commitment because the learner is seen as a maker of knowledge and knowledge connections, not just a passive recipient of existing patterns of knowledge. Finally, the acts of framing and re-framing relate to the above processes in that not only do e-learners manage their own learning, but they also actively frame it and re-frame knowledge that has been packaged by others.

Conclusion

As we conclude, we are aware of the long road yet to follow to explore fully the nature of e-learning. This dynamic process challenges learning conventions through the potential self-direction of learners, new learning spaces that remix attention and the remove from daily life, multimodal reading and production, and societal trends in connectivity and mobility. We have argued that the new literacies and new discourses associated with e-learning are best seen as a new type of social, interactional dynamic. We find 'discourses' is a better term than 'literacy' or 'literacies' because it links such communication to the wider political 'discourses' of a discipline, and addresses and embraces modes beyond the verbal, and the way the immediate dialogic potential approximates speech rather than writing. Nevertheless, we still use the term 'literacy' or 'literacies' at times in the book as these terms are current in discussion about communication and e-learning practices. To avoid cumbersome terms (that are sometimes more accurate) like 'communicational competence' we have in this chapter tried to sharpen the tools of the argument by suggesting that the terms 'literacy' and 'literacies' disguise the fact that what we are talking about are the multimodal *discourses* of the field: both in the local sense of communicational exchanges, and in the wider sense of an emerging 'vocabulary' that can help us define and explore the field more capably.

Further Reading 📖

Andrews, R. and Haythornthwaite, C. (2007). 'Introduction to e-learning research', in R. Andrews and C. Haythornthwaite (Eds.), *The Sage Handbook of E-learning Research.* London: Sage. pp. 1–52.

Kress, G. and Pachler, N. (2007). 'Thinking about the "m" in mobile learning', in N. Pachler (Ed.), *Mobile Learning: Towards a Research Agenda.* London: Institute of Education, Work-based Learning for Education Professionals Centre. pp. 7–32.

Laurillard, D. (2007). 'Pedagogical forms for mobile learning: Framing research questions', in N. Pachler (Ed.), *Mobile Learning: Towards a Research Agenda.* London: Institute of Education, Work-based Learning for Education Professionals Centre. pp. 153–75.

New London Group (2000). 'A pedagogy of multiliteracies: Designing social futures', in B. Cope and M. Kalantzis (Eds.), *Multiliteracies: Literacy Learning and the Design of Social Futures.* London: Routledge. pp. 9–37. (An earlier version appeared in 1996 in the *Harvard Educational Review*, 66(1): 60–92.)

5

Participatory Cultures

Introduction

The idea that students need to take control of their learning pervades many progressive approaches to learning such as active learning, learner-centered learning, self-directed learning (Hase and Kenyon, 2000), and entrepreneurial learning (Senges et al., 2008). It also encompasses approaches that focus on how to motivate learners, capture their natural interest and curiosity, and use materials relevant to a learner's experience and needs, such as situated learning, apprenticeship models of learning and recognition of indigenous knowledge (e.g. Gee, 2003; Senges et al., 2008). However, it isn't until we come to e-learning, that is, learning on and with web-based methods and information, that the novice learner has the potential to be freed from authorities who control the content, method and delivery of information. As new online practices are developed, and new areas of interest emerge, the contemporary e-learner is always deriving new methods for learning, from surfing the web, to developing game-playing rules, to constructing discussion in an online forum. They can be learning on their own, but are just as likely to be learning in concert with other novices as individuals come together to form communities of practice and inquiry.

Perhaps this description is somewhat utopic, with its pro-innovation bias toward new ways of working and learning online, and an ideal of egalitarian learning. Yet, the reality is that we have many more and different options for learning, literally at hand on the computer and via the web. The new found freedoms are being extolled in discussions of virtual communities, online communities of interest, health and social support groups, blogs and blogging communities, and multi-player games, as well as open source environments for computer programming, open access for research dissemination, and crowd-sourcing for a range of knowledge productions (e.g. Wikipedia, mapping, citizen journalism). Participation in these forums takes many forms. At the instrumental end of participation, computer cycles may be donated by signing up for applications that make use of idle time on individual computers (e.g. see the Berkeley Open Infrastructure for Network Computing at http://boinc.berkeley. edu/). At a more personal end of participation, social networking sites provide the platform for getting to know others, participating in social disclosure and group engagement (for a scholarly review of social networking, see boyd and Ellison, 2007; for more on youth and new media, see Ito et al., 2009).

For education and learning, participation in an information culture is having profound effects on who creates, controls and retrieves knowledge. Data, information or knowledge may be added as crowdsourced human judgements of the meaning of images (e.g. NASA clickworkers project to identify craters on images of the moon), as tags that classify the content of online resources (e.g. folk taxonomies or 'folksonomies', Mathes, 2004), as new entries, updates or corrections to online wiki-based collections (e.g. Wikipedia), as original postings or commentaries on blogs (e.g. Slashdot), and as contributions to institutional repositories (e.g. the US Association of Research Libraries' Scholarly Publishing and Academic Resources Coalition, SPARC). Web pages, websites, and web communities constitute an online complex for posting, retrieval and discussion. Topics can capture the interest of few or many, with purposes relating to careers and work, information and learning, social support and socializing, and leisure, recreation and play. Activity may stay entirely in the online realm or spill over into real-time, real-world engagement.

These technologies and their social constructions form the basis of the emerging participatory culture. As will be discussed below, technological developments in computing applications and infrastructure reveal an evolution of the web from an expert-only arena for information circulation, to a worldwide bulletin board for posting, to a wealth of spaces for collaborative knowledge and play-based community formation. This evolution has been accompanied by a hidden, steady accretion in skills associated with working and learning with others through computer media. Although the growth has been steady, it is only with the recent, massive expansion of contributory behaviors associated with Web 2.0 tools that attention has turned to considering the participatory literacies (or 'discourses', see Chapter 4) that individuals – particularly young learners – need to acquire to be part of this online culture.

This chapter looks at the development of the web and the contributory practices that lead to today's *participatory culture*. Before reviewing the history of technology development, we highlight the participatory education perspective of *collaborative learning*, which has developed in parallel with web and ICT development, and which provides an important theoretical lens through which we can view participatory culture from a learning perspective.

From Collaborative Learning to Participatory Culture
One of the major changes in institutional settings that has occurred with the move to online education has been the adjustment from teacher-centric to

student-centric learning. The major theoretical and practical approach adopted for teaching online has been that of *collaborative learning*. As a pedagogy, collaborative learning aims to engage learners in active construction of knowledge through exploration of ideas in peer-to-peer communication (Bruffee, 1993; Dede, 1990; Garrison and Anderson, 2003; Harasim et al., 1995; Koschmann, 1996; Miyake, 2007). While supporting scaffolding for younger or more naïve users, collaborative learning, and its technological counterpart, computer supported collaborative learning (CSCL), stresses the building of a 'community of inquiry where students are fully engaged in collaboratively constructing meaningful and worthwhile knowledge' (Garrison, 2005, n.p.). Collaborative learning advocates a transition of the teaching role from authority and disseminator of information to facilitator of knowledge acquisition. It draws on the way experts learn as they extend understanding and co-construct new knowledge (Bransford et al., 1999; Sawyer, 2006; Scardamalia and Bereiter, 1996).

As a framework for design, CL is the foundation for the field and technologies associated with CSCL. However, CL has also been adopted because the overwhelming quantity of conversation exhibited in online forums has driven the need for a new kind of class management. When everyone can contribute simultaneously, at anytime, from anywhere, and in response to anyone, the amount of text can increase dramatically. Moreover, since conversations no longer unfold in a single stream of real-time talk on one topic at a time, the number of conversational threads also increases. Collaborative learning has become a key answer to the 'problem' of keeping up with such online conversations. By design or default, authority has been ceded to students to manage their learning and learning discussions. While many are content with the new setup, as Lea (2005) points out, a management solution for overload is not a pedagogical solution, and there is still room to examine more seriously whether this turn to CL is a convenience for class management or a truly pedagogically sound decision:

> We need to have a better understanding of how different environments might afford different forms of participation and, in the case of on-line learning, ask questions about the ways in which such spaces are institutionally constructed rather than rely on the benign interpretation offered by collaborative learning paradigms and the repositioning of the tutor as facilitator. (Lea, 2005: 193)

Collaborative learning may also be seen as a wider response to contemporary learning needs. With rapid change in knowledge base and technologies, and the extension of learning well beyond traditional school attendance ages, learners are no longer just 'students', nor are they 'lifelong learners' in the sense of returning to formal education to update skills or develop new competencies. These both exist, but the contemporary digital citizen is also a continuous e-learner, dipping into the web for short-term information needs, evaluating across multiple sources for long-term needs, engaging with work through proprietary databases and knowledge management systems, and determining strategic directions in concert with colleagues both online and offline. Collaborative learning is now as much a movement in knowledge practices as an idea for higher education or the realm of research collaborations. As a theoretical framework, CL provides a very important foundation for discussions of the participatory aspects of contemporary online activity.

Technologies of Participation

Computing technologies have come a long way from the programmer controlled environments of the 1960s, and the expert-only use of the 1980s. It would have been hard to imagine then the current landscape of open source software, wiki encyclopediae, collaborative tagging, home pages, and blogs and commentaries. A number of transitions have occurred along the way, including major advances in programming languages and techniques, responsiveness in systems design, and the increasing ability of non-experts to manipulate computing technologies and online content.

The rise of non-computing experts on the Internet is the focus of this chapter. The new technical ease and speed of widespread information capture and exchange are driving qualitative change in how we communicate and learn. The technical side entails the combination of applications, devices and infrastructures. The *applications* include blogging (Blogspot, Wordpress) and microblogging software (Twitter), social networking sites (Facebook, MySpace, Orkut, LinkedIn), and music, photo and video sharing sites (LastFM, Flickr, YouTube); the *devices* are those that allow contribution from anywhere, anytime, such as mobile and smart phones, laptops and the multiple fixed devices that provide Internet access in schools, libraries and Internet cafés; and the *infrastructures* are the electrical, phone, microwave, cable and wireless telecommunications hardware and exchange protocols that keep devices and communication channels in operation. Together, these technologies provide a platform for rapid, widespread information exchange in the form of text, audio and/or video, for work, learning, socializing or play. Of particular interest in this chapter is how the development of new technical platforms has created and brought forward a social culture of participation.

Together, we might call this combination of computer applications and social practices the *technologies of participation*. As we write, new practices are emerging every day about what, when and how to talk about, disseminate and upload information of relevance to co-workers, friends and families. An important aspect of the latest wave of social media and ubiquitous computing is how participation crosses the domains of work, home and school. Such connection both blurs the lines of engagement for personal fulfillment, social interaction and career advancement, and blends the practices from one domain to another. In looking at what is ahead, it is not just the application or device that matters, but also how it is adopted and adapted by individuals, pairs, groups, communities and crowds to create new practices of information capture, storage and forwarding. Moreover, it is not just posting that matters. New participatory practices go beyond broadcast of information to include reflection and attention to the postings of others, for example commenting on others' contributions, tagging uploaded items for better retrieval, and engaging in continuing dialogue and discussion about the jointly produced end product. This attention to others and its visible representation online is the essence of the new participatory culture.

Learning and the learning environment are currently being radically changed by the outcome of these developments, and in particular by the transition from using the Internet for retrieval to using it for production. As we write, crowds of contributors are establishing and reinforcing new norms of participatory practice. While still nascent, these practices are rapidly finding their way into formal learning. Students entering formal learning are bringing practices learned in other settings, such as in social networking sites, Twitter, and online games and communities. Similarly, teachers and administrators, also aware of, and often well-versed in, using these technologies from their own research or interest communities, bring these practices into the teaching realm.

Yet, from an overall view, educational preparation for this new wave of behavior is not keeping pace with the change in behavior itself. Jenkins (Jenkins et al., 2006) has been a major advocate for the need to accept and plan for the challenges associated with this change, specifically addressing the case of education. In the paper, *Confronting the Challenges of Participatory Culture: Media Education for the 21st Century*, Jenkins and colleagues call for education about new media to be included in new curricula, but also for the use and integration of participatory media in the education system. In particular, he highlights the need for new ideas of literacy for participation, including learning how to be a good participatory citizen.

To set the scene for the new participatory practices, we start with a brief history of IT development, describing the transitions from pre-Internet development to Web 1.0 to Web 2.0, and the shift from consumption to production. This history is presented because, as described in more detail below, attitudes, uses and design of technology still range across these forms, with each being present in current technology options as well as in use for learning. As described in Chapter 10, new rounds of technology appear as waves which not only wash up on the shore, but also interact with each other to diminish or augment effects. One outcome of such an effect can be that progress of technology and social implementation are out of synch. While we normally assume this to be exhibited as resistance to a new technology, the case by Leaning (Case 5.1) highlights issues in the other direction as readiness to adopt was out of synch with technology capabilities. Later sections delve into the transformations and literacies associated with bringing participatory cultures into learning.

CASE 5.1: WEB 2.0 INTENTIONS MEET WEB 1.0 TECHNOLOGY

Marcus Leaning, Winchester University, UK

I inherited a first-year course in teaching academic writing when I joined the University of Winchester in 2009. Being interested and a keen advocate of e-learning I wanted to use the University's e-learning platform (called the Learning Network) to encourage the students to write. For the most part the Learning Network was used by teaching staff as a repository for materials and was not used in any generative sense, students downloaded texts and submitted work but did not actually 'work' on the system. I wanted to move the students onto working and actually using the system for learning and teaching activities rather than just as a file transfer medium.

My big plan was that students should keep a blog on the Learning Network recounting their learning practices and experiences. After some considerable trouble with the system (it did not permit a course blog for the students, only a personal one, and some of the students were keeping these independently of the course; I toyed with using an external blog but then ran into the problem that the University's filter denied access to certain blogs on campus), I finally found a tool on the system I could use.

I asked the students to make a number of entries, one of which would be a 1000 word examination of their own experiences of learning (part of the course concerned examining different approaches to learning and teaching), this would be corrected by the tutor for writing errors but not graded. The students would then write a response to the corrections and detail the various strategies they would use to improve their written work. The rationale for using the Learning Network for the blog was that I wanted the students to have a 'sand pit' in which they could practise their writing without a formal grade being given.

Unfortunately it all went a bit wrong.

The interface for the students to write proved to be extremely 'clunky', far less user friendly than a word processor or even a normal blog tool. This was even worse for the tutors who were to do corrections online; it took about seven mouse actions to insert text of a different colour, some-thing needed to correct grammar, and the network would freeze or lag for a few seconds on a regular basis. This may not sound much but when making a large number of changes to a large number of texts it was infuriating. The worst bit, however, was occasionally the system would 'time out' when trying to save and all corrections would be lost.

All the tutors on the course reported their frustration with the exper-iment and one ended up printing out the student work and correcting in pen, which sort of defeated the point of working online. We came to the conclusion that we could use the Learning Network to exchange files but it had such a heavy cost in terms of time we couldn't use it for much else. This was a great disappointment to me as up to that point I'd been a bit of an evangelist for it all.

As an afterword, fortunately the degree has since been rewritten and we were able to develop a new course that uses WordPress blogs to deliver the course – a far more successful approach.

Dr Marcus Leaning is Senior Lecturer and Programme Leader for Media Studies at the University of Winchester.

Brief History of IT Development

The focus in this chapter is on the more recent participatory developments associated with new media, supported through what Tim O'Reilly named Web 2.0 technologies (O'Reilly, 2005; O'Reilly and Battelle, 2009). However, as a still diffusing form of technology, earlier forms of information and communication technology currently co-exist with leading-edge technologies. Here we take a brief look at pre-Internet, Web 1.0 and Web 2.0 development to gain a comprehensive view of the landscape of contemporary computing in education and learning. Because they co-exist, in considering these phases, it is perhaps best to think of them as a range of *approaches to technology* or *genres of computing* rather than a sequential history of development. The recap of historical development is relevant because educators and learners bring to the participatory realm attitudes and practices learned on earlier platforms. Moreover, many of these forms of computing exist, and will continue to exist, in parallel with the latest new media (see also Chapter 10 regarding delayed use and digital lag regarding the uptake of Internet technologies).

For those not engaged in computer systems development, the number 2.0 can be a bit of a mystery. It originates from numbering traditions in software development. A software product comes together first in an *alpha* version, suitable for in-house testing. This is followed be a *beta* version that is ready to be released to key clients to show the system and for testing in actual use. When this version passes quality assurance, it is first released as Version 1.0. Typically, versions 1.1., 1.2 and so on contain fixes for known problems and may include efficiency upgrades. A change to a version 2.0 indicates significant change in functionality – and that is what Web 2.0 signifies over Web 1.0, and what O'Reilly and colleagues meant when they coined the term. Web 2.0 systems have been described as in a state of *perpetual beta* (O'Reilly, 2005), and discussed in more depth in Neff and Stark (2004) as *permanently beta*. With this systems view, there is no fixed, final version that gets delivered, but instead a constantly evaluated, upgraded and corrected version that leads again to the next *beta* version.

IT to CMC: The Pre-Internet Stage

Early information technology applications were designed to *automate* routine tasks and paper-based office functions. Use was primarily for in-house management of data entry, reporting and analysis. Electronic data processing systems relied on pre-defined forms and reports that often were just online replicas of earlier paper forms. Experts were needed to write these programs, and in-house data processing departments created templates for data inquiries and reports. Soon, however, more flexibility was introduced for report design and generation. End-user computing allowed users to query databases directly, and to create and generate their own reports. At the same time automated systems were developed to capture data at source. Today these systems still exist in transaction processing and management information systems. Equivalents in educational institutions are the centralized systems that allow course registration, payment of fees, and management of internal information. In their emphasis on automation, the near equivalents in teaching and learning are independent tutoring systems, and packaged training courses. 'Learning objects' also follow ideas of automation; such re-usable units become defined by common attributes, including content and educational level. The definition of standard attributes and the classification of each object according to these attributes (i.e. the *metadata* about the learning object) provide data for automated selection and combination to serve desired purposes.

A second revolution in IT came with the development of operating systems that allowed users to share time and run multiple programs on a single computer. These *time-sharing* systems propelled a transition from sequential, batch processing to simultaneous processing of multiple programs for multiple users. This advance provided the base on which communication systems could operate, and email, file-sharing, and even early forms of chat soon emerged for in-house communication. These systems allowed more unstructured means of communicating and transferring data, complementing the more strictly defined entries associated with data forms.

In education, email is commonplace as an administrative tool, meeting organizer, and information dissemination route. It is an essential part of the academic landscape for communication among peers in research groups and disciplinary interest groups. However, it is really only quite recently – from the mid- to late 1990s – that higher education institutions have provided email accounts for all students as part of their enrollment rather than by special request, and even more recently that email communication has become an expected communication channel between teachers and students.

Internet and Web 1.0

As means of connecting to time-sharing systems expanded from dedicated in-house networks to remote connection over telephone lines via computer modems, the adoption and practice of communicating via computer spread widely. Not only email communications, but also file-sharing became important parts of daily work. It was the need for better file-sharing systems that led to the development of hyperlink protocols that evolved into what we know as the World Wide Web. The web operates by files embedding tags in a markup language such as HTML or the newer XML that tell a web browser how to display and link to other sites. A URL indicates the address where the file can be found, and may include an extension (.html, .exe, .pdf, .docx) that instructs the web browser what to do with the file that is retrieved. Pages written in HTML or XML are interpreted into screen displays by web browsers; other kinds of files, for example word processing or slide presentations, are passed on to be displayed by other programs.

Web 1.0 was made possible by the combination of the Internet and the web. The Internet is the computer backbone that provides the network through which requests for retrieval are processed and pages retrieved. The web and the Internet are distinguished by the Internet being the network connecting the computers on which these files reside, and the web being the instructions and interfaces for this kind of file sharing. The combination of the web's hyperlinking of documents, and the Internet's computer networks set the scene for easier definition and retrieval of individual files, now formatted as web pages. The age of Web 1.0 – which got its name and number only in reaction to the later naming of Web 2.0 – ushered in a great wave of posting to the web.

Web 1.0 was all about having a *web presence*, with personal and professional web pages, information posted to the web, and search engines to find and retrieve these pages. While posting personal work to the web required some expertise when the web first appeared, for example needing to know HTML and how to post a web page, systems have since been developed that make creating simple pages as easy as using a word processor. Blogging tools in particular have made it very easy to take electronic text and place it online. Managing major sites, however, can require greater skills. The role of webmaster has emerged as an individual who creates and manages websites and is well versed in site architecture, mark-up languages, site and page design, and web accessibility issues (e.g. for people with disabilities, see http://www.w3.org/TR/WCAG10/).

Web 1.0 applications are characterized by *serial contributions*, for example of email messages, bulletin board postings, web pages, online resources, podcasts. They show a Web 1.0 over a pre-Internet form where they are accessible over the web and interpretable to web browsers by means of common protocols, rather than limited to proprietary networks and proprietary protocols. Online chat, Twitter and texting also fit a serial style, and thus might be classified as Web 1.0 mode applications, even if the short turnaround time lends them more of a 2.0 feel.

Web 2.0
While Web 1.0 has been about being seen, Web 2.0 is about being seen with and by others, and becoming part of a conversation and community. The focus is on *participation* in blogs, commentaries, wikis, Twitter, and YouTube, with broad access, contribution, retrieval, rating, classifying and evaluating. Web 2.0 operates on simultaneous updating, shared production, and a final product

that is greater than the sum of the parts. A prime example of this mode is the wiki, where each update repositions and recreates the whole. Web 2.0 applications create a larger, sometimes unexpected whole from individual contributions, for example ramifying networks of connections via social networking sites, new norms of participation in online collaborations, co-constructed places and spaces in Second Life, and worlds with new rules and norms of behavior, as in multi-player games.

Although beyond the scope of discussion here, those involved in web development are looking ahead to the next phase of development. The near future looks likely to continue and more deeply embed the social aspects of Web 2.0, with extended and extensive use of collaborative spaces and social networking sites (e.g. Ning, Google Wave), growing practices of joint production (as in Wikipedia), and contribution from local sources on local events (e.g. as in citizen journalism and photoblogging). At present, Web 3.0 efforts center on the idea of *convergence*, with new semantic techniques solving retrieval problems by meaning rather than specific words and spellings, and with posting and searching integrated across different application platforms (e.g. a single posting being simultaneously updated to Flickr, Facebook, or other personal or institutional sites).

Participatory Media

Participatory media include a range of technologies that allow contribution to ongoing online conversations. While almost synonymous with Web 2.0, we cast the net wider here to encompass not just the latest forms of media, nor those only in action over the world wide web, but all that allow participation. This catches all current communication mechanisms from email, listservs and bulletin boards to blogs (e.g. Digg), music sites (e.g. Last.fm), video (e.g. YouTube), social networking sites (e.g. Facebook), wikis (e.g. Wikipedia) and micro-blogging (e.g. Twitter). The definition is deliberately broad to highlight the continuity of the social practice involved. The essential component of any participatory medium is precisely that individuals should be able to participate, regardless of whether participation is limited to members of a community of interest or open to an unmoderated horde, whether contributions address content, practice, augmentations, or evaluations in text, audio or video. Each contribution adds to the conversation, whether it stays within the proprietary walls of an intranet or is published to the web, managed through older listserv technologies or the latest in social networking sites, or furthers the interests of products of scholars, hobbyists, or commercial enterprises.

That said, there are indeed distinct *genres of contribution*, from the memo-inspired genre of email, to the personal diary-inspired genre of many blogs (Herring et al., 2004, 2006b). Some genres are more attuned to multiple player participation. Scholarly and news bloggers expect comments while diary bloggers may not; posters to social support lists on bulletin boards expect direct and personal responses, while those on informational lists may not. Some sites expect participation that is in keeping with the norms of the online community (e.g. as outlined in their FAQ listings) and the identification of contributors, while others expect new, anonymous contributions. As with all technologies, the combination of social use and technical affordance can affect the extent to which any of these mechanisms are participatory (as discussed in Chapter 7).

Among all the possible details of new media and their effects, there are two main constellations of features of these technologies that stand out in considering what is changing in online conversation and e-learning: anyone, anywhere, anytime contribution; and the conversational nature of participation.

Anyone, Anywhere, Anytime

The first constellation of effects relates to the way social media and the Internet combine to draw contributions from *anyone, anywhere, anytime*. The greatest transformative effect is likely to be felt when *anyone* can contribute since this allows pooling of ideas, experiences, and corrections from around the globe. As Raymond stated about open source, 'given enough eyeballs, all bugs are shallow' (Raymond, 1998, online). In the same manner for e-learning, given enough contributors, the range of opinions and experiences will be more varied, resource lists more complete, and omissions and errors more quickly corrected. When contributions can come from *anywhere*, the diversity of local norms, experiences, cultures and communities can add variety and depth to information and understanding, even if sometimes accompanied by disagreement or conflict. *Anytime* contribution is somewhat bound up with *anywhere* as people in different time zones enter conversations at different times of our day or night. However, transformative effects within time zones are equally important as teachers and students come to asynchronous classes at various times of their work day and work week, and juggle that participation with full-time work and home lives. The 'third shift' of e-learning (Kramarae, 2001) is no longer just a night shift. It pervades the day as educational and learning conversations weave into the fabric of our daily lives.

Conversational Participation

The second constellation of features about social media relate to the way engaging in a participatory culture requires reflective, attentive and (at least) dyadic interaction. Conversations mean 'trying ideas out in the world' (Cook and Brown, 1999), in this case the world of other learners, and the community of inquiry. Two characteristics of current online conversations aid academic interests: (1) the *text-based* nature of most e-learning; and (2) the way the contributory effort leaves a *persistent record*, accessible to current and future participants.

Text-based

Written text remains key to contemporary notions of literacy, and is a mainstay of online communication, even in the face of increasing attention to audio, video and multi-media production. As texts, however, online conversations sit somewhere between formal writing and talking – they are written, but spontaneous;

ephemeral, yet preserved. Texts written in email persist on servers, potentially retrievable as documents that can be used in legal cases (e.g. in the Enron case, Diesner and Carley, 2005); conversations about class topics remain visible in online discussion boards, and can be used to grade what might otherwise be informal chat; and records of updates to wikis are retained in history pages, documenting the progression of how a text is created. New media both inherit and create genres of textual communication. Email inherited its header design (To, From, Subject Line) from paper-based memos, but is now influenced by text conversations in other media, for example, short message text (SMS) conventions from mobile phones (for more on literacy and technology co-evolution, see Andrews and Haythornthwaite, 2007, and this volume, Chapter 4).

While tensions can emerge in formal e-learning contexts between off-topic conversation and on-topic academic discourse, an often overlooked, but key point about participatory media is that *every* post to a participatory forum is a contribution to ongoing production. The use and reactions to on- and off-topic, social, instrumental, emotional, supportive or admonishing postings shape the norms of the group, and define their being (see also Chapter 6). Learning, knowledge, joint products and practices emerge from interaction, participation, and reflection in a conversational exchange. As individuals add to, elaborate, comment on and question others' contributions, the visible stream of their questioning and others' responses to them become important contributors to the content and the social definition of the space. The character of the environment is revealed in the way online places provide a safe space for new members to stay on topic or happily drift to new definitions, use formal writing conventions or mix with informal conventions, and/or deal with their trolls, jokers, and dominant voices. Knowing the character of the environment provides norms to follow, making it easier for participants to understand how to behave in their new e-learning world, and thus easing tensions about what is right or wrong to do in these spaces (Bregman and Haythornthwaite, 2003).

Persistent

Added to these new norms of participatory, textual conversation is a shift from transient to *persistent conversations* (as named by Tom Erickson and Susan Herring, e.g. Erickson, 1999). This shift has important outcomes in education since it turns spontaneous interaction such as classroom questions and answers into permanent records. This sets up the potential for misreading what these records are, and confusion over whether these records are textual submissions for grading or exploratory conversations for learning. Approaches to online teaching that have chosen to use these records for evaluation and grading put an increased burden on students to perform for grading in exchanges that might otherwise be opportunities for exploration in a 'safe space' for asking 'dumb questions' (Bruffee, 1993); and it leaves a distributed, online student with no forum where contribution is free from evaluation.

Grading online conversations also puts an increased burden on teachers. It can take a considerable amount of time to accomplish such evaluation, including time to define the procedures (rubrics) for grading (e.g. Liu, 2007, which reports on grading from instructors of 50 online courses). Such definitions may need to address comparability between online and offline versions of the same course. Moreover, online conversational contributions need to be evaluated in a way that can stand the test of re-evaluation. After all, the record persists as accessible not only for students and teachers, but also for those who might evaluate the evaluators. Preservation of these online conversations may then become necessary as a matter of student and employee records. Developing preservation practices for online education is an activity that has, to now, been left to systems designers. It may soon become an educator's area of concern.

Educational Spaces: 1.0 and 2.0

In education, web presence is most evident in static institutional and individual professional home pages, and the currently typical e-learning setup of closed communities with serially produced content and text (e.g. asynchronous bulletin boards). It is also evident in education-based information sources, from online posting of course syllabi and meeting times, to academic papers posted on institutional repositories. Web pages provide a means to advertise to potential students and faculty, and provide details on current research, teaching and programs; online portals provide access to course syllabi, schedules, electronic catalogs and online journals; and standalone tutorials provide training in a variety of areas (e.g. ethics, research methods, educational technologies).

Among Web 1.0 initiatives, the implementation of digital libraries and the adoption and provision of access to electronic resources is a change that has had a profound effect on academia, and is one that has been implemented at the institutional level (libraries, universities) in concert with publishers, vendors and academics. The move to open access for academic materials, started and led by initiatives in educational institutions, is also affecting how we think about information. Open access journals, e-journals, e-books, and institutional repositories have created a *web presence for documents* that is having far reaching effects on information access and use (see below).

Where web features remain in use only as delivery mechanisms, for example in presenting course notes or distributing slides, they exemplify a Web 1.0 rather than a 2.0 mode for education and learning. What characterizes Web 2.0 mode of use is the ability of many individuals to contribute, whether they add small or large contributions or whether these are later modified or deleted by others. In education, Web 2.0 style use is currently quite limited. There is some use of wikis, some of Second Life, and some distribution and interaction via mobiles and Twitter, but widespread adoption in educational settings has yet to occur. While most, if not all, higher education institutions maintain a web presence, few go to the extent of creating institution-wide student or alumni online communities, and few use the kind of blogging and commentaries found in contemporary news sites. However, many smaller applications of just these types appear, implemented by research groups, student groups and individual faculty and students. While less centralized than found in the for-profit sector, the basic toolkit of participatory media is in use in many varied forms within educational institutions.

Adopting Web 2.0 practices in education is going to be difficult because institutional as well as teacher and learner practices are at odds with blended participation and melded work products. Traditions of individual learning and grading are at odds with the idea of collaborative projects, particularly of large-scale joint projects and projects where no one individual's contribution can be untangled from the whole. The privacy of individual records, and particularly of grades, is at odds with peer and group evaluation of student work (but see Swan et al., 2006). The teacher as authority, single speaker and content manager is at odds with open contribution to the direction of learning. As with many kinds of changes to organizational and work practices, as important as any technical aspect is recognition and attention to social aspects – not just in the sense of socializing, but also in how existing institutional, disciplinary and educational practices limit adoption of new ways of learning *in the service of education* (borrowing the idea of design 'in the service of learning' as used by Barab et al., 2004).

While Web 2.0 is a contemporary mode of interaction, the origins can be found in many earlier online developments. In education, world-wide participation inherits from habits of interactive discussion that began in email (Hiltz and Turoff, 1978), academic listservs (e.g. Sudweeks et al., 1998), and asynchronous learning networks (e.g. Harasim et al., 1995; Harrison and Stephen, 1996; Hiltz, 1994; Hiltz et al., 2007). In workplaces, email, group decision support systems, distributed computing, shared databases, knowledge management systems, and online communities of practice contribute to contemporary practices. On the web, online support groups, virtual communities, virtual worlds, and multiplayer online games lay an equal foundation for Web 2.0 practices. While some are new – such as social networking sites – others have been present for many years. For example, virtual worlds began as MUDs and MOOs, and other text-only forms of communities for play and social interaction (e.g. arts.rec.soaps discussion lists on soap operas, Baym 1995, 2000; Electropolis virtual world, Reid, 1991), work support (e.g. BlueSky, Kendall, 2002), and learning (e.g. MooseCrossing, Bruckman, 1997).

What is new about current technologies is that they bring into institutions and organizations a suite of practices that originate in open, web-based interaction. For example, a work group may use public Twitter channels on mobile phones to stay in touch while located anywhere, anytime. A student may query the web inside or outside class to find resources related to learning. Habits from gaming, texting, and peer interaction find their way into class communication and contributory behaviors.

We can look to the habits of younger generations to predict what will enter the classroom in the future (Brown, 2000; Livingstone, 2010; Tapscott, 1998). Kingsley and Wankel (2009) note that, while there are still relatively few people over 20 years of age registered in virtual worlds (they report 156 million 11–14 year olds, 33 million 15–20 year olds and 16 million over 20 years of age across nine of these worlds),

> the younger teen generation is growing up with VWs (such as *Penguin Club, Habbo, Gaia*) as an integral part of their social and online lives. Within five years, this generation will be seeking placements at universities and in companies, and it will be as natural for them to turn to VWs as it is for older people today to seek information in the Internet. (Kingsley and Wankel, 2009: 2)

Each new generation that is 'growing up digital' is also growing up with the latest of the digital technologies, from instant messaging to texting, online research, social networking, Twitter, and virtual worlds. As noted above, the result is an array of generations of technologies and technology users, each at different stages of adoption and familiarity with these platforms. (For recent work on the virtual world Second Life and learning, see Hunsinger and Krotoski, 2010; Oliver and Carr, 2009; Scopes, 2009, 2010).

While outside influences have always had an effect on educational practice, the boundaries between in-class and out-of-class practice are far more permeable than before (see Box 5.1; see also Chapter 8). For example, instead of classrooms creating a segregated environment insulated from outside influences, students now meeting in physical classrooms are often simultaneously operating laptops with connections to the Internet. Whether in the service of the class or for personal interaction, the boundary between in-class and out-of-class is transcended by this online connection.

The permeability of this boundary is perceived by some as a challenge to the sanctity of the classroom. Interruptions from outside (email, web surfing, friends), or even from across the classroom (backchannel whispering), distract attention from lessons and instructors; sources from outside (web pages, blogs) challenge the authority of materials selected for reading; new means of evaluation (online ratings, page rank, commentaries on blogs) challenge existing systems of peer review in determining the value of texts. Common across all these concerns is a recognition of a shift in where authority resides and who retains, cedes or assumes authority and control in the learning process. The next section discusses these changes, focusing on the way participation changes who learns from whom, who represents intellectual authority, and who creates authoritative content.

BOX 5.1: LAPTOPS IN THE CLASSROOM

As universities have increasingly promoted the use of personal laptop computers, and implemented wireless computing across physical campuses, the same features that promote easy access to learning resources also have the effect of

(Continued)

(Continued)

allowing easy access to personal resources during classes. The laptop as distraction has been tied to negative outcomes on student learning (e.g. Fried, 2008; Hembrooke and Gay, 2003). As David Cole at Georgetown University in the US put it: 'This is like putting on every student's desk, when you walk into class, five different magazines, several television shows, some shopping opportunities and a phone, and saying, "Look, if your mind wanders, feel free to pick any of these up and go with it"' (quoted in de Vise, 2010).

Responses have included banning laptops from class, and implementing ways of turning off Internet or email access during class. It is not just the laptops but also mobile phones that add to distraction, as texting and using the web features of a phone can happen during class.

While such devices are obvious in the physical classroom, they are invisible in the online class. Students can easily be engaged in carrying on conversations with other students, for example via online chat, during class. Other distractions also hound the at-home or at-work learners, such as family, co-workers or personal tasks. Students have reported doing laundry, eating dinner and managing children while 'in class' online. They also have reported a lot of 'whispering' via online chat channels that parallel the class chat session but are not visible to the class as a whole – although they assure us these were for clarification of lecture material (Haythornthwaite et al., 2000).

It is not all bad news for technology in the classroom or for backchannels. While communication technologies may distract, 'clicker' technologies can engage. Clickers are in-class tools that allow students to select answers from questions crafted by the teacher to engage students in the class content (http://www.classroomclickers.com/). The online equivalent is voting systems available in many VLEs. Not only are many finding these tools important for gauging understanding during lectures, others find they help those more reluctant to participate in class to join in. For example, James L. Ellenson, at North Carolina Central University finds these tools important for reducing stigmas associated with class participation, and particularly notes the importance of this for reaching minority students (Miller, 2010). Such comments are reminiscent of first reactions to computer-mediated communication, that is, that the anonymity and reduced social cues of CMC made for more egalitarian contribution of ideas. Similarly, the asynchronous nature of online discussions has been described as important in online education because the lack of turn taking makes it possible for more students to participate.

Changes in Authority and Contribution

The various features and changes discussed above, and in previous chapters, combine to affect who contributes and who attends to contributions, who determines conversation or course content, and what resources are brought into discussions. This is creating changes in relationships with experts, with documents, among learners, and with local communities, each of which has direct effects on e-learning.

Change in Relationships with Experts

Perhaps the most discussed change in e-learning settings is the way participatory technology challenges the role of experts. When anyone can contribute content, comment on work, and rate contributions, control of knowledge is taken out of the hands of appointed authorities and given into the hands of everyone, everywhere. This is a daunting change that affects those whose identities are expressed in the specialization of knowing how to collect, filter and disseminate knowledge. It challenges the authority formerly held by publishers and presses, journalists and news media, academics and peer-review journals, librarians and library collections, and teachers and educational institutions. In each case, online initiatives give rise to parallel systems for information and learning, from open posting on the web, to newsblogs to virtual universities. These initiatives also drive change. In a bid to maintain or regain control, institutions appropriate participatory practices: newspapers go online and provide their own blogging environments; libraries maintain digital collections; university libraries create institutional repositories; and universities create e-learning programs. What progressive leaders in these areas have acknowledged and acted on is the need to modify practices to accommodate participatory trends in a way that facilitates a new kind of collaboration between experts and novices. This is an equal challenge for e-learning in formal classes and across all aspects of teaching and learning.

In e-learning, teachers are often concerned about the erosion of authority and control formerly maintained in the classroom. Authority can be lost when online sources are consulted inside or outside class. Where these contradict in-class teaching, they challenge the teacher as the authoritative voice on a subject, method, or choice of study materials. Similarly, a change in format from lecture to asynchronous discussion challenges authoritative control over how class interaction unfolds. Face-to-face traditional lectures allow only for questions to be asked sequentially in real time, with questions directed to and answered by the lecturer. Online, the sequenced, controlled process gives way to content, questions and answers initiated and supplied by students that further stimulate student questions and answers. This can take discussions in unplanned for directions, wandering from course content, requiring teachers to corral speakers back onto relevant topics.

Research and experience with computer-mediated communication (CMC) adds to our understanding of how authority can be eroded online. Since its first appearance, people have observed how CMC levels the playing field by removing cues to status formerly available and visible through dress, seating arrangement, and interactions among members of the audience. While some cues to status have been reintroduced in CMC, for example in email signatures, or may be evident in writing style and language use, written online exchanges remain a way to obscure personal features. To remain visible, or to show roles and authority, online participants must take deliberate action to identify themselves and reveal aspects of themselves that legitimate their claim. Although much of the worry about this has come from instructors, it is interesting to note that as more adults take on online learning, they also need to establish their credentials. Their life experience or current position of status outside the classroom is important for signaling the legitimacy of their contribution. Given the ability to write their own profiles, attach signatures to messages, and add information about themselves to postings, adult online students may actually have more ways and opportunities to signal status and experience that in traditional physical classrooms. Thus, in keeping with much that can be said about participatory culture, all participants are learning and acquiring new skills, including those relating to the practice of self-presentation.

Change in Relationships with Learners

As noted earlier, in learning and education, we find some advance preparation for these kinds of transitions from the area of collaborative learning, with its emphasis on peer-to-peer communication and a less rigid view of the teacher as authority. Collaborative learning has been well received in online education, led by work in the area of computer-supported collaborative learning (e.g. Koschmann, 1996; Koschmann et al., 2002; Miyake, 2007). The appeal of collaborative learning for e-learning stems from the realization that when students can and are contributing at anytime of the day or night, there is no boundary to class discussion time. Single instructors cannot monitor and be on top of conversations that run seven days a week, 24 hours a day, and thus many teachers turn to designing classes for self-sustaining online interaction with intermittent intervention.

Collaborative learning is well suited to adult learning as it acknowledges the autonomy and capabilities of self-directed learners. But, its appeal and applicability is wider than just for adults, and wider than just for formal learning settings. With the general trends toward participation, it is not just adults who are autonomous learners but the many individuals who partake in open source projects, online forums, virtual communities, online gaming, and creative production in online writing, art and videos. Collaborative learning is not just about autonomous individuals gaining knowledge for themselves. In these learning collectives, groups of learners create the critical mass for collaborative learning. Participatory learners are autonomous in the sense that they take on the responsibility to learn for themselves, but also *to learn with others*. In open forums, this may include determining what content is to be addressed by the group, in contrast to formal education where content is more likely to be set by educators.

This changes both the role of the learner, and the relationships among learners. As teachers embrace participatory and collaborative learning practices, learners are increasingly challenged to be active and engaged in the enactment of learning.

At a time when we are all increasingly distracted by social media – email, blogs, Facebook, Twitter – we ask learners to be increasingly, and visibly, engaged via these media. Instead of attending a lecture in a large hall, or, more remotely, listening to an online lecture at a time and place of their own choosing, students are asked to join bulletin boards, with instructions to post, respond and discuss points with other students throughout the length of the entire course. Independent work on reading and writing is converted to *interdependent* work, with opinions expressed and responded to online, and writing becoming conversational discussion. Teachers still prepare syllabi and determine course conduct, but their role becomes one of managing the production of visible interaction among the members of class. As teachers step back from their position as 'sage on the stage' and settle into the facilitating role as 'guide on the side' (King, 1993), learners are asked to step up to the stage, and indeed to populate and become the dramatis personae on the stage.

At present, the heavy emphasis on changes to teaching practice, and to overcoming resistance to change by teachers, has overshadowed the very real changes to the roles and work of learners. This may be a reason why many programs begin with graduate education. Motivated, advanced and adult learners are willing and able to take on the greater engagement role that is emerging as an essential component of successful online learning. Their greater academic or life experience provides a natural addition to classroom discussion, ranging from personal stories of life and work, to skills in computing, project management and information management, to interdisciplinary knowledge. As e-learning – in the sense of this kind of expanded cooperative, CMC-supported conversation – continues to trickle down from graduate education to undergraduate and younger, and as it bubbles up from young learners already conversant with contemporary communication and collaborative habits, the potential is there for a full transformation of what it means to teach and learn in the age of Web 2.0 and participatory media.

Change in Teaching Materials

A relatively new issue is also arising relating to ownership of materials produced in association with online learning. Teachers are rapidly building up sets of personally created and produced materials for online courses. These materials create an immediate and potentially lasting record of their teaching. Lecture notes that may formerly have remained only in the hands of the teacher are now posted online, and possibly also with a recorded copy of the lecture. Materials collected and created to extend the class – digitizations, slides, drawn diagrams, simulations – can easily be copied and reused by others. Whole courses can be downloaded, transferred or copied from course management systems.

These materials hold value for three constituencies. First, they have value to the teacher who created them and for whom they serve as material for future iterations of the course, evidence of their teaching effort, and, potentially, as ideas that form the basis of academic publications. Second, they have value to the institutions for whom the course was taught. If the teacher is considered to be acting as a course designer, then the agreement to pass on materials to tutors or instructors may be clear. But, this convention differs across universities. The agreement with a teacher who designs and delivers the course themselves may be more problematic, particularly if this individual is on contract and not a faculty member of the institution. Third, these materials have value to students. Where teacher-created materials are used instead of a textbook, what lifetime of access can they expect? Once a course is over, how long do they have to re-view course materials? This also applies to their own materials, including the essays submitted online within a course management system, and the persistent conversations in course discussion boards.

When developed as an employee, student, or on contract, who holds the intellectual property rights to these materials? While creative commons licensing can help articulate an individual's desired copyright for openly available content, an agreement around 'work for hire' needs to serve the interests of both the employer and employee. Similarly, an employed faculty member may be required or strongly encouraged as part of their contract to share courseware, for example as might be done through open courseware initiatives (e.g. MIT's OpenCourseWare project: http://ocw.mit.edu/OcwWeb/web/home/home/index.htm; see also Case 5.2). However, the itinerant scholar, adjunct professor or graduate teaching assistant may not find this sharing in their interest. As policies are developed around online course development and delivery, both administrators and teachers will become more versed in the issues related to future uses of their intellectual property derived from syllabi, associated materials *and* online conversations.

CASE 5.2: OPEN ACCESS WITH THE FEDERICA SYSTEM

Rosanna de Rosa, University of Naples Federico II, Italy

The Italian University 'Federico II', besides being one of the oldest Italian universities, is, with its nearly 100,000 registered members, greatly attractive to all southern Italian students. The percentage of outstanding students is high, yet the capacity of the city and the university facilities are very limited: the university dormitories fail to meet demand, various university buildings are located throughout the area and are sometimes very distant from central services (administration, libraries, computers, etc.), and classroom seats are available for less than 50% of enrolled students. To reduce the impact of these problems, many e-learning programs have flourished in different faculties. However, while these separate initiatives have played a key role in raising awareness of the importance of e-learning, the lack of a common platform, and the experimental nature of a lot of these initiatives, has made widespread adoption of e-learning extremely difficult.

Federica (www.federica.unina.it) is an initiative systematically and organically structured that was brought online in 2007, supported by FESR (ERDF) funds of the European Commission and managed by the Federico II University Information Services Center. In the framework of the Italian university system, Federica is the only e-learning platform that is completely open access. It is also designed to facilitate access using a very simple interface. The navigation between different faculties, courses, classes and materials available proceeds through an identical logical and graphic format that ensures homogeneity and coherence for all the materials and guarantees equal access for all students.

The choice of this open access system was made on the basis that separate platforms with restricted access intimidate students who consider these initiatives as a limit for their freedom, and leave teachers with no opportunity to compare the quality and quantity of the content across courses, nor to learn from other teachers. By contrast, an open access model empowers both students and teachers, improving internal cooperation and collaboration, and enabling the creation of joint projects, integrated courses, translated courses, etc. Finally, open access provides countless functions supporting the operation of this very large university, such as: orientation for students; lifelong learning and education for professionals unable to attend the university; learning support for foreign students; internal communication to create a common university culture; and external institutional communication to improve the overall image of the university.

After three years of use, Federica supports over 250,000 visits per month, an average of 8,000 unique visitors per day from 192 different countries. These numbers are clearly related to the fact that Federica ensures an immediate control of all stages of content production and navigation, which is crucial for users with low knowledge of network technologies. The methods of iconographic representation of the academic content and cognitive organization scheme of the teaching materials, designed on the base of students' common level skills, allow easy and immediate interaction with the lessons. In addition to these developments Federica presents some specific functions (e.g. Living Library, Campus3D) connecting the university courseware units with cultural offerings available on the web, and effecting integration into the educational paths of both primary and secondary scientific sources, experimental research data, and academic production. As a lecturer at the University of Naples Federico II, who has used the platform and followed its development, I believe Federica has inaugurated a new paradigm of web-learning that supports the combination of orienting and teaching with a strong connection to web resources in an open and inclusive environment.

Rosanna De Rosa is an Assistant Professor at the University of Naples Federico II, Italy.

Change in Relationship with Information

The change in teaching materials is one part of a more general trend in an overall change in our relationship with information. The general trend toward placing information online, building and consulting crowdsourced encyclopediae, and searching and retrieving from the web combine to affect where, when and from whom we find information. Formerly, we depended on publishers and peer review to judge and edit material before it was publicly available, and on libraries to select works of the right character for their collections (young adult, popular fiction, academic, specialized). In the past, we could also expect these works to contain within them a stable corpus of references. However, even with these gatekeepers, information is now released and re-updated so rapidly that tracing information back to its source becomes an issue. Note, for example, this disclaimer, taken from the front matter of a physical copy of the *Handbook of the Learning Sciences* (Sawyer, 2006).

> Cambridge University Press has no responsibility for the persistence or accuracy of URLs for external or third-party Internet Web sites referred to in this publication and does not guarantee that any content on such Web sites is, or will remain, accurate or appropriate.

Thus, while we increasingly act as the judge of material we retrieve online, for academic purposes, we also increasingly act as its steward and the keeper of its reliability and provenance (e.g. 'Retrieved on [date]'). Further, we also gain knowledge about the forms and genres of online publications so we can distinguish peer-reviewed from self-published materials, and personal opinion from academic research.

Such information literacy skills, exercised by each individual at every information turn, is becoming a given in the age of the Internet. As the ALA Presidential Committee on Information Literacy put it in 1989:

> Information literacy is a survival skill in the Information Age. Instead of drowning in the abundance of information that floods their lives, information literate people know how to find, evaluate, and use information effectively to solve a particular problem or make a decision – whether the information they select comes from a computer, a book, a government agency, a film, or any number of other possible resources. (Retrieved 20 April 2010 from: http://www.ala.org/ala/mgrps/divs/acrl/publications/whitepapers/presidential.cfm)

While at the time of the ALA report, there was no World Wide Web, the articulation of this as a survival skill still holds. Yet, a number of changes have occurred. Until recently, librarians could play a key role in teaching and aiding in information retrieval and information education at the point of access to materials, that is, in the library, even if librarians have never held that these one-shot, just-in-time teaching opportunities were adequate. Now, however, the library itself is online through catalogs and electronic references, and the 'collection' includes all that is available on the web. One effect of this is to cast information literacy as a lifelong learning skill, as in the formulation of competencies associated with the 2005 Alexandria Proclamation on Information Literacy and Lifelong Learning (Box 5.2). These updated competencies include aspects of multi-cultural information literacy, economic impact, and technology-independent critical evaluation skills.

BOX 5.2: THE ALEXANDRIA PROCLAMATION ON INFORMATION LITERACY AND LIFELONG LEARNING

Information literacy

- comprises the competencies to recognize information needs and to locate, evaluate, apply and create information within cultural and social contexts;
- is crucial to the competitive advantage of individuals, enterprises (especially small and medium enterprises), regions and nations;
- provides the key to effective access, use and creation of content to support economic development, education, health and human services, and all other aspects of contemporary societies, and thereby provides the vital foundation for fulfilling the goals of the Millennium Declaration and the World Summit on the Information Society; and
- extends beyond current technologies to encompass learning, critical thinking and interpretative skills across professional boundaries and empowers individuals and communities.

Adopted in Alexandria, Egypt at the Bibliotheca Alexandrina on 9 November 2005 by the International Federation of Library Associations. (Retrieved 10 February 2010 from: http://archive.ifla.org/III/wsis/BeaconInfSoc.html)

What is needed for information literacy? Many lists are available that help define this, such as: the seven pillars of information literacy from the Society of College, National and University Libraries in the UK; competency standards from the Association for College Research Libraries in the US; and the six core standards from the Australian and New Zealand Institute for Information Literacy (see Boxes 5.3, 5.4 and 5.5). In general, we can summarize these as addressing the identification of an information *need*, the ability to *locate* information and to *evaluate* the information located, and to *apply* that information appropriately.

BOX 5.3: INFORMATION LITERACY: SOCIETY OF COLLEGE, NATIONAL AND UNIVERSITY LIBRARIES (UK)

Seven Pillars of Information Literacy

Pillar 1. The ability to recognise a need for information.

Pillar 2. The ability to distinguish ways in which the information 'gap' may be addressed.

Pillar 3. The ability to construct strategies for locating information.

Pillar 4. The ability to locate and access information.

Pillar 5. The ability to compare and evaluate information obtained from different sources.

Pillar 6. The ability to organise, apply and communicate information to others in ways appropriate.

Pillar 7. The ability to synthesise and build upon existing information, contributing to the creation of new knowledge.

Originally published 2008. (Retrieved 12 February 2010 from: http://www.sconul.ac.uk/groups/information_literacy/headline_skills.html)

BOX 5.4: INFORMATION LITERACY: ASSOCIATION OF COLLEGE AND RESEARCH LIBRARIES (US)

Information Literacy Competency Standards for Higher Education

The information literate student:

- determines the nature and extent of the information needed.
- accesses needed information effectively and efficiently.
- individually or as a member of a group, uses information effectively to accomplish a specific purpose.
- understands many of the economic, legal, and social issues surrounding the use of information and accesses and uses information ethically and legally.

Originally published 2000. (Retrieved 12 February 2010 from: http://www.ala.org/ala/mgrps/divs/acrl/standards/informationliteracycompetency.cfm#ilhed)

BOX 5.5: INFORMATION LITERACY: AUSTRALIAN AND NEW ZEALAND INSTITUTE FOR INFORMATION LITERACY

Six Core Standards

[There are six] core standards which underpin information literacy acquisition, understanding and application by an individual. These standards identify that the information literate person:

- recognises the need for information and determines the nature and extent of the information needed
- finds needed information effectively and efficiently
- critically evaluates information and the information seeking process
- manages information collected or generated
- applies prior and new information to construct new concepts or create new understandings
- uses information with understanding and acknowledges cultural, ethical, economic, legal, and social issues surrounding the use of information.

Bundy, 2004. (Retrieved 12 February 2010 from: http://www.library.unisa.edu.au/infoskills/infolit/infolit-2nd-edition.pdf)

Perhaps most open to interpretation in these lists is what it means to use information appropriately. Contemporary literacy involves a shift in what constitutes information and how it is used, and thus what information literacy means. Here is a prescient telling by the 1989 ALA committee of what an 'information age school' would look like when information literacy is used as a central theme. Most notable in this description is the way the learner is described as a comprehensive information seeker and user operating in the model of collaborative learning and readily attuned to a world of self-directed learning. (See also Senges et al., 2008, for a contemporary educational implementation that very much resembles this projected view.)

BOX 5.6: AN INFORMATION AGE SCHOOL, ALA PRESIDENTIAL COMMITTEE ON INFORMATION LITERACY

An Information Age School

An increased emphasis on information literacy and resource-based learning would manifest itself in a variety of ways at both the academic and school

(Continued)

(Continued)

levels, depending upon the role and mission of the individual institution and the information environment of its community. However, the following description of what a school might be like if information literacy were a central, not a peripheral, concern reveals some of the possibilities. (While focused on K-12, outcomes could be quite similar at the college level.)

The school would be more interactive, because students, pursuing questions of personal interest, would be interacting with other students, with teachers, with a vast array of information resources, and the community at large to a far greater degree than they presently do today. One would expect to find every student engaged in at least one open-ended, long-term quest for an answer to a serious social, scientific, aesthetic, or political problem. Students' quests would involve not only searching print, electronic, and video data, but also interviewing people inside and outside of school. As a result, learning would be more self-initiated. There would be more reading of original sources and more extended writing. Both students and teachers would be familiar with the intellectual and emotional demands of asking productive questions, gathering data of all kinds, reducing and synthesizing information, and analyzing, interpreting, and evaluating information in all its forms. In such an environment, teachers would be coaching and guiding students more and lecturing less. They would have long since discovered that the classroom computer, with its access to the libraries and databases of the world, is a better source of facts than they could ever hope to be. They would have come to see that their major importance lies in their capacity to arouse curiosity and guide it to a satisfactory conclusion, to ask the right questions at the right time, to stir debate and serious discussion, and to be models themselves of thoughtful inquiry.

Original publication, 1989. (Retrieved 20 April 2010 from: http://www.ala.org/ala/mgrps/divs/acrl/publications/whitepapers/presidential.cfm)

Participatory Literacies

While online retrieval is making information literacy skills an essential part of what it means to be literate in today's information world, a new and forthcoming literacy addresses the growing practice of contributing online content in the service of community and communal products. These new *participatory literacies* (or perhaps, in keeping with discussions in Chapter 4, *participatory discourses*) include basic fluency with the technologies of collaborative production, from the wide-ranging crowdsourcing initiatives to more personal virtual communities, and from individual applications such as email and social networking to appropriate combination of media and platforms (e.g. social networking + microblogging + digital repositories). Until recently, effecting a participatory environment has meant cobbling together a loose affiliation of tools to connect groups of known membership, for example using a combination of email communication, web pages, shared databases, and digital libraries.

Efforts to bring separate platforms together can be traced to the idea of *web portals* which provided single entry to multiple resources, and the development of research *collaboratories* described as centers without walls (Wulf, 1989).

E-learning environments share great similarities to collaboratories, with participants brought together in common space where social and informational resources for learning are present. Contemporary participation extends beyond known members, and, in many cases, is deliberately designed to support the social intention of increasing memberships, for example in crowdsourcing and social networking applications. Yet, still to a great degree, participation in learning environments entails known others using a variety of means that suit the group as a whole, and which, through repeated use, become part of the character and definition of the group.

Conclusion

The turn to participatory culture is driving change across the range of communication and learning behaviors associated with work, education and play. This chapter has outlined some of the themes relating to this new culture that specifically affect learning, with attention to where online represents a Web 1.0 attention to online presence and posting of static materials, to a Web 2.0 attention to participation with others. Changes to a Web 2.0 participatory culture include general shifts in authority, such as changes in the role of teachers in relation to students, and students in relation to each other. Collaborative, participatory practices modify the role of teachers from that of a single authoritative voice to one of expert guide, a move that is in keeping with ideas of apprenticeship into a community of practice (Lave and Wenger, 1991; Wenger, 1998), and cognitive apprenticeship into the practices of learning, knowledge and academic work (Collins, 2006; Goodyear, 1998). However, students are also newly confronted with the responsibility of engaging with other students, building joint knowledge and the community of practice. While attention in e-learning has been given to leading and guiding teachers in new online practices, far less has been done in preparing students for their new role, and this is an area that will need attention in the transition to participatory culture.

Also emerging are differences in our approach to and use of information. As relevant, up-to-the-minute information is increasingly found online, there is a greater acceptance of information acquired from non-peer reviewed, non-publisher approved sites, such as web pages, blogs, wikis and online journals. Parallel to this acceptance is an increased need to learn and practice information evaluation skills. As well as retrieval skills, participatory practices also include a range of literacies relating to postings in the context of education, including an understanding of privacy, ownership and copyright, affecting whether it is appropriate to ask students to post assignments to the web or add comments to a blog, what may be used and reused, and who owns materials created for teaching.

Finally, participatory culture entails a range of literacies and discourses relating to collaborative practices, from knowing how to work with others, online, and at a distance, to understanding responsibilities associated with participatory efforts, including offering and articulating ideas, pooling resources, and engaging in the creation of a collaborative whole. We continue this discussion in the next chapters.

Further Reading

Dirckinck-Holmfeld, L. and Jones, C. (2009). 'Issues and concepts in networked learning: Analysis and the future of networked learning', in L. Dirckinck-Holmfield, C. Jones and B. Lindström (Eds.), *Analysing Networked Learning Practices in Higher Education and Continuing Professional Development.* Rotterdam: Sense Publishers.

Haythornthwaite, C. (2009). 'Participatory transformations', in B. Cope and M. Kalantzis (Eds.), *Ubiquitous Learning.* Champaign, IL: University of Illinois Press. pp. 31–48.

Jenkins, H., with Clinton, K., Purushotma, R., Robinson, A. J. and Weigel, M. (2006). *Confronting the Challenges of Participatory Culture: Media Education for the 21st Century.* Chicago, IL: MacArthur Foundation. Available online at: http://digitallearning.macfound.org/atf/cf/%7B7E45C7E0-A3E0-4B89-AC9C-E807E1B0AE4E%7D/JENKINS_WHITE_PAPER.PDF.

Rheingold, H. (2003). *Smart Mobs: The Next Social Revolution.* New York: Perseus Books. See also the accompanying blog at: http://www.smartmobs.com/

Virkus, S. (2003). 'Information literacy in Europe: A literature review', *Information Research*, 8(4). Available online at: http://informationr.net/ir/8-4/paper159.html

Learning Communities

Introduction

Chapter 5, Participatory Cultures, outlined new trends in learning, partly driven by the rise of social media. These new approaches emphasize collaboration over delivery of education, and recast the role of learner from a recipient of pre-determined information to a joint creator of information and learning contexts. This emphasis on collaboration leads us to consider how to create the conditions that support pooling and co-construction of knowledge and resources, and thus to a concern about how to initiate, sustain and manage successful communities of learners, co-workers and knowledge creators. In online contexts, there has been an equal concern with how community can be sustained based only on lean computer-mediated communication. Much research and debate have surrounded the notion of *virtual community*, first questioning whether community can be used at all as a label for a non-geographically based collective, and later coming more to terms with an interpersonal, relational definition of community rather than one based on common geographical location.

In addressing e-learning, we combine attention to the process of collaboration among participants with its practice in a virtual environment. In doing so, we follow a dual focus on understanding the mechanics of collaboration as well as the emergent characteristics of online community. Together these help in understanding the social and technical design goals for creating and sustaining online learning communities. This chapter explores the relational underpinnings of collaboration and community that make it possible to create vibrant learning environments online, and how this plays out in e-learning environments.

Defining and Locating Community

Attention to the online learning community will provide the main focus of this chapter, yet there are other ways in which 'community' plays out in e-learning that will be returned to throughout the chapter. These include the nature of the local and embedding community, the online community, and the epistemic community of practice.

Local and Embedding Community

A long-standing role of education is to educate citizens to be functioning, contributing members of their community. Educational systems enculturate individuals into their local (geographical) culture (Bourdieu, 1986; Crook, 2002). They promote recognition and adherence to appropriate community conduct, teach skills and values for future contribution to the community, and bestow status associated with learning and educational attainment. Thus, education and educational systems, including e-learning systems, are always concerned and interacting with the *embedding societal and local community*.

Online Community

With distributed learners, the question of what is meant by the embedding society or the *local* context can be problematic. Discussing context in relation to e-learning grapples with the way students come together in one class while distributed across regional, national and international boundaries, with attendant differences in cultural experience, attitudes and future work prospects. Similarly, what constitutes the embedding education environment can be problematic as students join common online classes but enroll from different institutions. E-learners also join their own community, the one constituted in cyberspace, where they create norms for their 'cyber-local' *online community* that are different from any geographically local set of norms.

Epistemic Communities of Practice

Communities with norms of conduct, memberships, and distinct practices exist around the disciplines and professions that create and enact the knowledge being learned (Haythornthwaite, 2006b; Haythornthwaite et al., 2006; Knorr-Cetina, 1999). These communities maintain certification, accreditation, and publication practices that determine proper conduct within the discipline or profession. Networks of colleagues are known and continuously visible to each other, supporting *invisible colleges* of like-minded researchers and academics, and recognition of what it means to be an expert (Crane, 1972). Learning to belong to one of these *communities of practice* (Lave and Wenger, 1991; Wenger, 1998) involves learning about the community and its norms, including its tolerance or promotion of online and e-learning practices.

With these nuances of the idea of community in mind, we begin the discussion of learning communities by asking: Why does community matter?

Why Collaboration and Community?

E-learning is becoming bound up with ideas of collaboration and community, but what is it that these two ideas bring with them? What is to be gained by designing and implementing collaborative work and learning, and building e-learning communities? The answers lie in the intellectual and human bene- fits of collaborative activity, a form of organizing that pervades and supports human activities. Designing for collaboration combines attention to work and work goals with the affiliative needs of those who work together to achieve these goals. Community also entails affiliative needs, but combines this with attention to the development and maintenance of norms, standards and iden- tity associated with local and embedding social groups. Members of well estab- lished communities can expect consistency in interpersonal behaviors as people follow group norms. This reduces the evaluation work that needs to be done in vetting others and their contributions, and increases trust in others' commitments. (A review of these concepts is beyond the scope of this chapter, but see Argyle, 1991; Burt, 2000; Haythornthwaite, 2006a, 2007b; Koschmann, 1996; Wellman, 1999).

Group work and *communal action* bring more minds to bear on a problem, potentially increasing the value of group effort. Investment in social relation- ships within the group builds trust among members and commitment to joint goals. Such groups provide access to people who are both willing and moti- vated to share resources, and who are more likely to provide social support that strengthens in-group connections. Individuals can benefit with a greater sense of well-being and happiness, as well as access to a network of resources, both material and personal. Getting to know others in a work group allows indi- viduals, and the network as a whole, to build *transactive memory*, that is, cogni- tive social structures of 'who knows what' (Hollingshead et al., 2002; Moreland, 1999; Wegner, 1987). Such knowledge facilitates group work, and makes it easier to reconstitute groups in the future as needed (Nardi et al., 2000, 2002). Communities benefit from the *social capital* that resides in the network and which increases the stability and longevity of communities as individuals come and go (e.g. Argyle, 1991; Bruckman and Jensen, 2002; Hagar and Haythornthwaite, 2005; Haines et al., 1996; Haythornthwaite, 2006a, 2008; Lin, 2001; McGrath, 1984; Putnam, 2000; Walker et al., 1994).

Collaborative learning returns benefits from group interaction similar to those for group work, including wider exposure to new knowledge, active construc- tion of knowledge, enhanced problem articulation, and information and knowledge shared among participants (Bruffee, 1993; Dede, 1990; Harasim et al., 1995; Koschmann, 1996). The transactive memory that develops helps indi- viduals be aware of who has what kind of expertise, such as knowledge about other disciplines, professional practices, or cultures. Communal interaction and 'being there with others' satisfy human needs for affiliation, increasing satisfaction with collective activities. Attention to e-learning as a collaborative, cooperative community holds the promise of more satisfied, supportive and active learners, committed to the group's learning goals. It also holds the promise of a network richer in information and support resources, potentially more ready and able to act as the sounding board for new ideas, and more likely to persist in the face of turnover in members.

Until the advent of the Internet, these collaborative and communal benefits have been treated as closely tied to local, face-to-face interaction. When online interaction began, it brought with it the fear that such benefits would be lost in a move to the reduced-cues, computer-mediated environment. Although this perception still persists, in general we find that community (in computer-rich societies) is now maintained through a mix of both on- and offline interaction with local and distance friends, family and colleagues. Attention has turned from rejection of the Internet to its integration in everyday life and offline practice (Haythornthwaite and Kendall, 2010; Wellman and Haythornthwaite, 2002). In a comparable move for e-learning, attention has shifted from wholly online learning to forms of blended learning that integrate online activity with face-to-face class meetings. However, whether for blended or fully online e-learning, what underpins collaboration and community remains the same. Although we will tend to focus here on fully online learning, what works for the all-online experience should also hold well for any blended learning community.

A major response to fears about the loss of communication cues and their impact on interpersonal and communal relations has been to attend to recreating *social presence*, that is, the sense of being there that is inherent in physical co-location (Garrison and Anderson, 2003; Short et al., 1976). Promoting social presence has been shown to lead to greater group cohesiveness and higher levels of critical thinking (Aviv et al., 2003; Polhemus et al., 2001; Swan 2001). Addressing social presence for e-learning has been elaborated as a primary area for attention by Garrison and Anderson (2003), who also stress the equal need for *teacher presence* and *cognitive presence*. However, like Garrison and Anderson, many have found that attending to presence alone is insufficient to create an active community. Creating a community requires attention to the basis of community, that is, what it is that constitutes interactions and group goals. The idea of a *community of practice*, as outlined by Lave and Wenger (1991) and Wenger (1998), has had an important influence on understanding learning and work-based knowledge sharing. This perspective more clearly articulates that communities are based on common practice rather than common location, enacted through mutual engagement, engagement in a joint enterprise, and a shared repertoire (e.g. of routines, vocabulary and concepts).

To see an e-learning environment as a community of practice requires shifting attention from the content of the class to the group behaviors involved in being in the class and participating with others (see Case 6.1). This is an important shift that is often overlooked in considering how to teach online. E-learning environments are increasingly evident as communities of practice and as such are complex social as well as learning environments (e.g. Cuthell, 2008; Haythornthwaite et al., 2000). (For more on building online communities, see Kim, 2000; Preece, 2000; and specifically on online learning communities, see Barab et al., 2004; Palloff and Pratt, 1999; Renninger and Shumar, 2002).

CASE 6.1: DEVELOPING AN ONLINE COMMUNITY OF PRACTICE FOR PRINCIPAL LEADERSHIP DEVELOPMENT

Juel Chouinard, McGill University, Québec, Canada

Beginning in February 2009, 12 principals from elementary and secondary schools in Québec, Canada, representing four English school boards located in remote, rural, and semi-rural areas, came together in an online group to inquire into practices for building leadership capacity among teachers. My purpose was first, cooperatively to facilitate the principals in developing an online community of practice (CoP) for leadership practice inquiry; and second, to support them in examining their leadership capacity-building practices. Synchronous and asynchronous, verbal and Internet communications made up our ways of exchanging and discussing. We used one-to-one and focus group conference telephone calls, a listserv, and an Internet classroom. For the first five months, the communications were primarily via conference telephone as the verbal communications built confidence and ease of use of the online technologies.

Five telephone conferences were conducted between February and June with an average of six participants. These provided an opportunity for connections to develop between the principals as they identified common concerns around their practices with teachers of building trust and relationships. This concern was especially evident from the questions and inquiry reflections of the four newer principals. To facilitate using online communications, since there was no face-to-face contact, the principals' reflections and inquiry questions were either scaffolded to other principals' similar practices or connecting these back to a principal's earlier, related listserv posting.

My one-to-one conversations with the principals partly served the purpose of drawing attention to other principals who were dealing with similar daily topics such as managing response to the HINI flow virus or implementing a positive behavior program. I facilitated by drawing attention, suggesting questions, and highlighting similar experiences to support principals in connecting with another principal on the listserv. Related to scaffolding, remarks were made to draw together or connect principals' practices, especially in the case of connecting an

(Continued)

(Continued)

experienced principal with a relatively new one. Again, I began in the one-to-one conversations by briefly describing a principal's practice to create resonance between contexts and practices. Then, I suggested questions that could be asked to facilitate decisions about using the practice. Finally, I identified some of the resources I was aware of and suggested not only asking for the resources but asking how the resources were used. I let principals know that if asked I would send back notes, which some principals used as a basis for asking more specific questions about practices, processes, and resources on the listserv. To complete the process of connecting principals, I did some advance one-to-one emailing to the experienced principals alerting them to some of the questions that might appear on the listserv. This facilitation practice, which at first seemed artificial, led to a turning point in July, when two principals facilitated a listserv exchange and led a conference telephone focus group on the framing and process of one-to-one teacher conversations. This turning point experience has continued strengthening the development of the online CoP as scaffolding principal remarks and connecting principals according to leadership practices is increasingly becoming a facilitation role and responsibility shared among the principals.

Juel Chouinard is a Doctoral Candidate, McGill University, and Pedagogical Consultant, Littoral School Board, Québec, Canada.

We turn next to exploring the concept of community and its basis for understanding the constitution of community online.

The Concept of Community

In order to understand how to design, build, or work with a learning community it is important to understand what perspective we have on community. In doing so, we aim to understand what signifies community when unbundled from dependence on co-location, and, perhaps more significantly, when unbundled from our taken-for-granted ideas about community. In approaching online community, the aim is not to determine whether offline is better or worse than online as a way of working, communicating or maintaining community, but rather to consider how best to create the social and learning setting you want, with the tools and contexts at hand. In other words, *if* online, distributed, asynchronous learning is the way you are reaching learners, *what is the best* configuration of social and technical considerations that builds the best online learning community for that situation?

Where is Community Held?

If we consider the *geographic* community, such as a neighborhood, village, town, or city, what can be identified that signifies community? It may be the local gathering places, the agoras, 'third spaces' ('third' after work and home), and 'great good places' such as cafés, community centers, or beauty parlors where people interact (Oldenburg, 1989). Or it may be in the representations of community in local landmarks, such as statues, art installations, parks, buildings, streets and storefronts. If these are the vital parts of a community, *and you have to do the best you can to create a community online*, then the aim is to create online interaction spaces and representations of community. Gathering places for conversation translate easily into online chat rooms, discussion boards, social networking sites, and even into Twitter feeds; and symbols of community translate into web pages, e-learning portals, and the 'streets and avenues' of the VLE.

Community can also be held in the head and heart as *imagined communities* (Anderson, 1991). They may be held in the image you have of your last geographic home, perhaps in another country, perhaps in an earlier time. Ideas of community may be based on an imagined pastoral ideal that no longer exists, and perhaps never did (King et al., Tönnies, 1887; Wellman, 1999), or were thought to have been lost in urban jungles, but instead may be found in local neighborhood action (Wellman, 1979). Imagined communities take on another level altogether online as cyberworlds create new means of interaction and self-presentation (Turkle, 1995). Computer-mediated communication in general has augmented the ability to maintain invisible colleges and communities of interest, particularly when such interests are sparsely distributed around the world (Sproull and Kiesler, 1991). Communities of interest can exist tied to disciplinary and professional knowledge, but also by common interest in geographical spaces (Budhathoki, 2010) or 'serious leisure' pursuits (Stebbins, 2006).

Common across these communities is the way the joint focus, and practices in support of that focus, are set by community members. Norms, rules, conventions, specialized language, and laws are enacted and reinforced by use, enforced by sanction, and modified through continual and mutual adjustment (Clark and Brennan, 1991; Contractor and Eisenberg, 1990; Miller, 1994; Poole and DeSanctis, 1990). Online we also develop norms, but new ones, for example in how we 'talk' online in a manner that sits somewhere between writing and speech, and in our adoption of CMC as a means of communicating (Baron, 2008; Crystal, 2001; Erickson, 1999; Herring, 2002).

Within communities, the emergence and recognition of roles is a key indicator that social structures are forming that support communal action through division of labor and development of specialized expertise. Roles emerge that allow distinctions between expert and novice, and leaders and followers, and also identify those who are the jokers or social support providers (e.g. Haythornthwaite, 2001).

As conditions change, new roles emerge, such as that of the technological guru or gatekeeper (Allen, 1977), or online wizards and trolls. Older roles re-emerge as experienced online community members distinguish themselves from new-bies by sanctioning behaviors and controlling group focus (Smith et al., 1996; Sudweeks et al., 1998). In e-learning communities, new roles can be designed or emerge. For example, in the Mirandanet online community of teachers, recognition structures are designed into the operation of the community by assignment of visible roles and status to users who contribute particular kinds of content (Preston, 2008); elsewhere roles emerge, as in the role of 'learner-leaders' in an online learning community (Montague, 2006).

In general, most of what we call community is maintained by continuous observation, modification, and adherence to norms of behavior. Although the mechanisms across a whole society may be complicated, our more local experience of community depends on interactions and exchanges with others. Viewing community as enacted through interaction and exchange fits with a social network perspective on community (Haythornthwaite, 2007b, 2008; Wellman, 1979, 1999; Wellman et al., 2002). Such a view originates from studies that found that, separate from geographically based ties, individuals maintain their own *personal communities* with both close and long-distance contacts. Work places and neighborhoods provide face-to-face contact, but phone, car and air travel maintain ties to distant friends and relatives (Wellman et al., 1988). From there it is not much of a step to add online connection as a means of maintaining social ties, bringing us up to the idea of online community (Wellman et al., 1996).

A social network view provides a means of separating *what* people do with each other from the physical or cyber-geography *where* they do it. It provides a way to view community as the net result of interactions among a set of people instead of something bounded by home location or online enrollment status. It lets us question whether the collective that is a housing development, campus dormitory, or online class is indeed a neighborhood, learning, or online learning community.

Two major concepts underpin a social network view of community. First is the concept of *ties*, and second, the idea of *social capital* (also discussed in Chapter 2). Ties are the connections between people in networks. These can be based on very minimal activity, such as between people who met once at a party or neighbors who live far down the street from each other; and they can be based on a range of work or social activities of varying types and significance to the pair. The former, minimal activity ties are referred to as *weak ties*, and the latter, multi-threaded attachments are referred to as *strong ties*. A wealth of social network literature reveals that, compared to those who are strongly tied, weak tie pairs engage in fewer, less intimate exchanges, share fewer types of information and support, are less likely to reciprocate in exchanges, and use fewer media to communicate. By contrast, those in strong ties engage more frequently with each other, in more different kinds of exchanges, and include emotional as well as instrumental content in those exchanges. Strong ties show a higher level of intimacy and self-disclosure, reciprocity in exchanges, and the use of more media. Weak ties are maintained with the people we refer to as acquaintances, and other casual contacts in a class, school, workplace or neighborhood. Stronger ties include people we call friends and close friends, colleagues and co-workers. Family ties are a little different since our kinship tie does not change with the activities we engage in. Yet, we can also distinguish among family members according to which ones are close because of joint activity rather than just because of a kinship tie.

The significance of ties is that we tend to be quite similar – in activities, taste, circles of friends, life aspirations, socio-economic status – to those with whom we share strong ties (known as 'homophily'). And we tend to be more different from those with whom we share a weak tie. The result is that our weak ties provide us with access to information different from that accessible through our own tight network of friends. This *strength of weak ties* (Granovetter, 1973) provides the basis for *bridging social capital* (Putnam, 2000) that connects otherwise disconnected others to bring new information and resources into a community. The catch is that our weak tie contacts are less motivated and less obliged to share what they have with us. The *strength of strong ties* (Krackhardt, 1992) is the attachment, concern, and interest in helping that comes from close tie contact. This forms the basis of *bonding social capital* (Putnam, 2000), and the enduring, multi-threaded connections that sustain and stabilize community (Burt, 2000; Lin 2001, 2008).

The strengths of both weak and strong ties are important for sustaining a long-term community. Too insular a group, one that hears only from its own members, each of whom agrees with and views the world from the same standpoint, can create communities that are unprepared for change, and that lack sufficient knowledge of outside activities to deal with challenges and to make good use of new opportunities (Cohen and Levinthal, 1990; Rogers, 1995). With too few strong ties, communities rely too heavily on particular individuals to maintain ties, undermining the long-term stability of the community. When such central players leave, the community has no structural base for continuity and can fail (Bruckman and Jensen, 2002). Technologies can be used to advantage to build weak tie networks, thereby increasing access to others with information (Constant et al., 1996; Haythornthwaite, 2002a). However, these ties need to be balanced with strong ties in order to connect to those committed to doing more than just sharing information, but also to accomplishing joint goals and completing projects (Haythornthwaite, 2002b). (For a longer treatment of social networks and online community, see Haythornthwaite, 2007b).

One of the interesting aspects of educational environments as collaborations and potentially as communities, is that, within the short timeframe of a course (a year, a semester, even just a weekend), the process of close interaction has been started, sustained, and wrapped up. We will return to later stages below, but here we take a moment to discuss the start-up phase from a social network perspective.

One key aspect of many classes is that the participants who join online classes often do not know each other beforehand. For e-learners, the online environment is the primary and often only structure through which they meet, learn to work together, and create the kind of social ties necessary for collaboration and community. This *latent tie structure* lays the foundation for how and with whom ties are initiated (Haythornthwaite, 2002a). Only those with access can form ties, and ties can only be first initiated through the means made possible through this structure. Thus, it is at this stage that the teacher, instructor, or designer has the biggest role in initiating practices. As the person with the authority and role of connecting learners, the teacher (or designer) controls the start-up phase, which happens through the technology and social activities chosen or designed by them and becomes the means by which latent ties (inactive) are activated into weak ties, and perhaps from there to strong ties. It is akin to pushing a snowball over the crest of a hill. It's been packed and shaped, and now it is set rolling to pick up more snow on its way downhill.

While not all learners in all networks will become strongly tied – and indeed it may be beyond the ability of an authority to influence truly strong-tie formation given variations in personalities, lifestage, goals, etc. – attention to the power of the authority to get the ball rolling and start ties forming is highly important for recognizing this vital stage in time-limited groups. While many teachers will spend time concentrating on how to get the course content going, there is also a need to get the desired e-community going. This, we suggest, is another part of the reason that the nature of e-learning is close to but different from conventional learning, with the distributed, asynchronous and technology dimensions adding another layer of transformation to learning practices.

Creating an E-learning Community

Reviewing these conceptions of community reveals how much a personal perspective can determine what is focused on when creating rather than experiencing community, and when designing for collaboration rather than analyzing it. When management initiatives began deliberate efforts to build communities of practice as part of a general trend in knowledge management, there were misgivings that community was not something that could be created by formula, but instead needed to develop organically. To some extent this reaction comes from a prioritization of the term 'community' to refer only to the imagined ideal which is somehow expected to work all on its own, without initiation, tension and resolution. But, when we are considering deliberately constructed collectives – classes, degree programs, work groups – we need to temper the idea of a 'real' community with the requirements and realities of time-limited cooperative and collaborative endeavors. It is important to acknowledge that along with the ongoing development of organic, self-organizing communities, there are specific interventions that can help enact local groups, whether for civic engagement, work production, learning or recreation.

A complication for e-learning is that, by contrast to conventions for behavior in face-to-face classes, norms for the embedding e-learning context are not as long-standing and widely understood as they are for the embedding school, lecture, seminar or workshop contexts. Neither as yet are there expected sets of online learning practices – and there may never be. As discussed in earlier chapters, the tie between learning and technology suggests that e-learning may always be bound up with the idea of continuously emergent, perpetual beta, practices. Again, we suggest that this is indeed part of the nature of e-learning.

The result is that we are developing in-class practice in tandem with changes in embedding technology, and in dialogue with e-learning practices that are emerging daily. Norms about online communication, online teaching and learning practices, and the kinds of e-learning communities being created have all been developing over the last few decades. Such norms emerge from a background of offline learning conventions and expectations, but are changing with each new technology addition, and as new teaching approaches develop. Because of its newness, to date, e-learning communities have been far more volatile communities of practice than their face-to-face counterparts. E-learners have been called on to adopt and mutually adjust their behaviors with each new wave of technology and online teaching practice. Despite rapid technological change across all learning settings, adjustments for online learning have been more visible and disruptive than for those in face-to-face settings. While e-learning is still in this emergent phase, we can continue to expect such online communities of practice to face the considerable challenge of learning how to be distributed, online, communities of learning at the same time as grappling with teaching and learning for today's class in this context.

Where does this leave us as we face creating new and ongoing learning communities? Are we left waiting for community to emerge, or can we actually take steps toward creating and maintaining such communities? Our premise is that the features of community are highly relevant for all learning settings, and that applying what we know about communities can provide important benefits for individuals as well as groups and communities as a whole. Learners are always in the vulnerable state of needing to acquire knowledge from others. To ask and to give such knowledge requires a trusting relationship and a supportive community. Learners need the 'safe space' where they can ask for help without risk to their reputation or position (Bruffee, 1993). On the other side, knowledge providers (other learners, or teachers) need to know that their efforts are worthwhile, and time spent is not wasted time. Such trust is fostered through continued interaction and exchange and through the network of connections that constitute and sustain the community.

Community in an Online Masters Degree Program

To take a closer view of e-learning community building, we look at the results of some studies of an online graduate degree program that were conducted by

Haythornthwaite and colleagues. This section summarizes the results of research studies and observations of this program that relate to the experiences of learners, teachers and program directors in creating, working in and sustaining this online learning community.

An in-depth investigation into the sense of community perceived by students in the program was conducted in 1998–99. The year-long study involved four interviews with each of 17 students at regular intervals over the year. The focus of these interviews was on how students managed in the program, where they gained support, and whether they perceived that they belonged to a community. Conducted at a time when many were highly skeptical of community of any type being possible online, we felt it was important to get the learners' view of their experience. The study provided important insights into how students were experiencing and coping with this 'brave new world' of e-learning (Haythornthwaite et al., 2000; Hearne and Nielsen, 2004). Further examinations of learner experiences have continued since, as well as extensive attention to new developments in the program and student experience (for a compilation of studies, see Haythornthwaite and Kazmer, 2004a; other studies include Bregman and Haythornthwaite, 2003; Kazmer, 2000, 2007a; Montague, 2006; a bibliography of studies is available online at http://www.lis.illinois.edu/academics/leep/leep-bib).

When these students were asked whether they perceived their e-learning environment to be a community, the answer was an emphatic 'yes'. Interviews revealed that a major contribution to the sense of community came from the social bonds formed and maintained online between learners in the program. While the program included some on-campus components (a two-week on-campus orientation and initial course work, and an on-campus week each semester where students attended one day for each course they were taking), these distributed students were faced with a situation where offline was the add-on to online rather than the other way round. As such, their human contact was almost all computer mediated. This experience was strange to them, requiring them to get used to new ways of 'talking' online that often left them, as they reported, 'wondering if what I was posting sounded okay'. They found that being 'present' online required them to be 'more purposeful … more strategic' in making and maintaining contacts. While the experience was strange to them, it was even stranger to those not involved; those 'on the outside' couldn't understand the students' 'different kind of world'. Thus, students found themselves looking for support from members of the online community, reinforcing the differences they perceived between their experience and that of others.

Social bonds were created and maintained in several ways. Cohorts of students who began the program together shared the face-to-face on-campus class and took their first online class together. This early bonding experience provided them with connections to others with whom they then communicated online. When first at a distance, these ties sustained them through the early strangeness of the online experience. Continued interaction in class, in program-wide student discussion boards, and in on-campus visits helped to reinforce these bonds throughout the program.

Study of this program has also shown how being part of this e-learning community followed a series of stages: *joining* the community; *maintaining presence* in the community; and *disengaging* from the community. Attention to joining stresses the importance of getting participants oriented to the learning environment, but also draws attention to what makes it difficult and strange for new online participants. While much attention is paid to the technological basis of e-learning, reports from students showed that not knowing *what* to post was a psychological barrier that needed to be addressed (Bregman and Haythornthwaite, 2003). Other stages were also important: attending to learner presence does not stop at initiation, but persists as the distance relationship makes it easier to 'fade back' over time. Finally, after all this work to get students to be functioning and highly participative members with a strong sense of community, an unexpected finding was the sense of loss that occurred as students suddenly found themselves both graduated and out of a community. These experiences show that managing the exit process and student *disengagement* from the online community are important in supporting students as they go off to related professions, (re-)form bonds back in the home environments, and tell others about their online experiences (Kazmer, 2002, 2007b).

Shared experiences have been important for forming communal bonds within and across cohorts. One such experience has been a compelling tale of the power of a story told to incoming cohorts of students by the professor who teaches the first course they take. As described in Hearne and Nielsen (2004) this telling became a major contributor to group memory as it provided an emotional shared experience for the cohort. Another incident related by Hearne and Nielsen again highlights group memory. The incident happened as a group of students were using the private 'whisper' function of the online chat feature to discuss what they were drinking – or wished they were – when one student posted to the entire class 'Brass Monkey. It's sold in all the best bodegas in New York'. With this slip of the fingers, he coined the term 'brass monkey' for any inadvertent public posting. The term was used for a number of years by students in the program as the name for an inadvertent public posting of a privately intended comment. Although this term has faded with time, new forms of expression are continuously emerging in this community, not least of which are many short message text usages imported from texting and other CMC.

Over the years, stories such as these have created common experiences and a shared history among instructors and students. Norms of communication have developed, supported in part by a growing, shared understanding among instructors from the Graduate School of Library and Information Science at the University of Illinois, Urbana-Champaign, of how to conduct classes which lead to a more common experience across classes. As a whole, the online program has become a stable community that withstands the comings and goings of members, both instructors and students.

Promoting a Community

How do we use what we know about community to promote a socially sustainable e-learning collective, one that participants might even refer to as a community? Three concepts help in focusing on the answer to this question: acceptance of 'community' as an ideal and a continued work-in-progress; attention to a shared, dual focus on both content and community; and promotion of the relational basis of community and online community.

Imagined Ideal and a Work-in-Progress

A start to answering the question of how to enact a community is to come to terms with the knowledge that 'community' is always an imagined ideal. As such, efforts to create or sustain community entail development of a process rather than a finished result, with the community itself a work-in-progress, with a continuously emergent repertoire of rules, norms, roles and behaviors. As described in Chapter 2 and elsewhere in this book, a key element of current practice and discourse is that they are continuously emergent. Acknowledging the emergent nature of community gets around the idea of a formula to apply to create community, and turns attention instead to following communal processes of participation, collaboration, respectful exchange, sanctioning of undesirable behaviors, and maintenance of focus on community goals.

Shared, Dual Focus on Content and Community

Second, to initiate and sustain a community requires understanding its focus and working on ways to expedite cooperative and collaborative effort in support of that focus. In e-learning, shared community focus entails attention to both the subject matter *and* its teaching and learning. Learning becomes the motivator for participation and commitment. Learning communities also enact their own way of learning as part of their repertoire. Content can be taught or learned in many ways, from personal tutoring to on-campus lecture halls to online interaction. In each case, how the 'practice of learning' progresses is identified, adopted, and enacted through instruction, compliance with requirements, and the way achievement of learning is recognized (e.g. prizes, degrees, certificates). At the same time, the community enacts a practice around *how to be a learning group*, that is, how to participate and show commitment, and to whom (discussed further in Chapter 11). In every community, and every group, members learn rules of behavior and norms of discourse; they learn about others in the community and build tacit and explicit directories of who knows what, and who does what. This knowledge, combined with attention to the shared focus, builds cognitive structures about the composition of the network as well as about its boundaries. E-learners also share in the adoption of online practices: they learn how to establish individual and communal identity online, to communicate via computer-mediated communication, and to get the measure of other members to the point of trust and commitment to group goals.

Relational Basis for Community

Third, we can work with the knowledge that communities are created and sustained through interactions between people. This entails both a research and a practical component. On the research side, there is still more to know about what it is that people do in learning communities that promotes participation and commitment to others, and results in a sense of community. Such interactions form the basis of social networks, and thus we can also ask what impact different configurations of interaction will have on learning (Haythornthwaite, 2002b; Haythornthwaite and deLaat, forthcoming). On the practice side, we need to know how to enact this online. Knowing the stages of communal and relationship development provides direction on what interventions are required and when. Such intervention starts with attention to the latent tie structures on which ties have the opportunity to form, carries on through the maintenance phase of interaction when engagement may weaken as e-learners fade back, and continues through the exit stage and the work of disengaging learners from their e-learning community as they re-align to professional and personal communities.

Conclusion

Creating and supporting e-learning communities requires attention to how people interact and form social bonds. As such, research on community, collaboration, groups and online communities all provide an underpinning for understanding the dynamic and emergent aspect of e-learning practice. To date, we find that the newness, distributed participation, asynchronicity and computer-mediation of the online environment and the time-limited characteristic of most formal learning courses and programs demands greater and more deliberate attention to participant interaction than face-to-face learning environments. Distributed learners do not have the opportunities for out-of-class, informal interaction that face-to-face learners have. They can't run into each other in the halls or coffee shop; students may not even share classes with the other students as they go through a part-time program one class at a time. On the formal side, students may understand how to receive or retrieve material but not know how to act as a contributor or collaborative participant in the community. The benefits, however, make it worth giving the e-learning community such attention. Outcomes for both time-limited, formal classes and more open, web-based learning communities include greater individual satisfaction with the collective process and a network of people to grow and learn with, while the community gains with longer-term stability sustained across the full membership of the network, plus internal knowledge and resources to support future communal action.

Further Reading

Barab, S. A., Kling, R. and Gray, J. H. (Eds.) (2004). *Designing for Virtual Communities in the Service of Learning*. New York: Cambridge University Press.

Haythornthwaite, C. (2007). 'Social networks and online community', in A. Joinson, K. McKenna, U. Reips and T. Postmes (Eds.), *Oxford Handbook of Internet Psychology*. Oxford, UK: Oxford University Press. pp. 121–36.

Haythornthwaite, C. and Kazmer, M. M. (Eds.) (2004). *Learning, Culture and Community in Online Education: Research and Practice*. New York: Peter Lang.

Palloff, R. M. and Pratt, K. (1999). *Building Learning Communities in Cyberspace*. San Francisco, CA: Jossey-Bass.

Preece, J. (2000). *Online Communities: Designing Usability and Supporting Sociability*. New York: John Wiley and Sons.

Renninger, A. and Shumar, W. (Eds.) (2002). *Building Virtual Communities: Learning and Change in Cyberspace*. Cambridge, UK: Cambridge University Press.

Sociotechnical Perspectives

Introduction

Every time we approach the computer to teach or learn we enter a space that co-mingles the social and technical. We want to work on a project together, and so we arrange meetings using online calendars and email, share data by formatting entries to central repositories, write drafts of papers using word processing software, and stay aware of others through a social networking site or Twitter. Each time we reach for the mouse, keyboard or mobile device, we enter a technology-mediated interaction with colleagues, work teams, friends, family and community.

Some of our choices about technologies are unconscious, often because of such long-standing use that we don't even see the technology in place (Bruce and Hogan, 1998). That has been the case for meeting people through the 'mediation' of a building, such as a place of work or learning. Yet, building design has a great influence on who meets whom, where, and how often (e.g. Swales, 1998). Lounges, water coolers, coffee rooms, cafeterias provide an informal space for serendipitous interaction with colleagues, class and meeting rooms a formal place, and offices a personal space. Yet it is the social convention of common drinking and eating times that increases the likelihood that people will meet at specific locations. The combination of the technical (e.g., the cafeteria) with the social (common lunch hours) sets the scene for encounters. It sets their likely formality, regularity and topic of discussion, as well as who is likely to be there. A regular faculty, support staff or research meeting sets the scene for where colleagues meet, and a physical or virtual classroom for where teachers and students meet.

Other choices about technology are more deliberate. For example, we may decide to use the phone rather than email because we want immediate interactivity and we know the other person does not read or respond to email regularly. We make conscious decisions about social arrangements, for example, by setting up meetings, workshops or conferences that bring a set of people together who otherwise would not overlap in time and space. Online means of contact, such as synchronous office hours or class meeting times, make more obvious use of a technology to promote contact. But, contact would not happen among participants unless the social structure of an office hour or class existed to bring them together in the common, online space.

While the technology of a building has become almost invisible when planning work or teaching, other technologies can range from slight background visibility to glaringly obvious. Videoconferencing, for example, is more or less obvious depending on the quality of the connection and equipment. To use a high-quality connection that conveys image and voice in a way that is almost like 'being there' can require meeting at a location distinct from normal meeting spaces, perhaps not even owned or operated by the institution itself. Operators take charge of connecting sites around the globe at bandwidths and processing speeds that make real-time interactions seem natural, that is, recapturing the feel of a face-to-face meeting, and thus rendering the technology almost invisible.

By contrast, video connections that present low-grade images, limit the range of view, or have connections that drop and must be restarted, keep the technology in the foreground as something that needs constant monitoring. Participants in such gatherings have to learn how to work effectively with and around these technological idiosyncrasies. Together, group members negotiate and reinforce a mutually agreeable way of communicating that optimizes their joint effort and work practice (Clark and Brennan, 1991; Poole and DeSanctis, 1990). In a research group one of the authors belonged to, members spent considerable effort learning about technology foibles and negotiating communication practices through various iterations of videoconferencing and audio-conferencing systems. We became familiar with dropped connections, frozen images, and the remoteness of colleagues connecting from five coast-to-coast locations across the US, sometimes from mobile phones while on the road. Over time, we learned to poll remote members to be sure they were still with us, and used this opportunity to create a space in the conversation for input from those not visible to the larger, co-located group. Overall, we learned how to manage remote, multi-point, technology-based (it is hard to reflect on these meetings and call them 'technology-enabled'!) conversations, with the attendant tasks of paying attention to those not visible in the room (for more on this, see Haythornthwaite et al., 2006).

Looking back on this experience brings to the forefront how much we had to learn about communicating in this new environment. Whereas 'how to communicate' had been taken for granted when we first worked as a co-located team, once distributed, 'how to communicate' became an ongoing concern and often a barrier to getting our work done. E-learning is no less affected by this need to learn to communicate. When teachers or learners first approach e-learning, every feature of the practice and of the technology is new and strange, and every aspect needs monitoring. The technology in many cases seems more a barrier to getting the job of teaching done than a facilitator of new practices.

This alone would be enough to explain the trepidation and increased effort that new e-learners experience, but they actually take on more than just using media. E-learners also take on a new social domain where the traditional ideas of time-delimited, single-speaker lectures followed by sequential audience questions give way to multi-way conversations, anytime and anyone contribution, and the emerging role of teacher as learning facilitator. While not all environments billed as 'e-learning' will implement a model of egalitarian, collaborative learning and knowledge building, no matter what the pedagogical or technological implementation, by being online, social interaction will be different from the equivalent in face-to-face classes, and new social conventions will be associated with question asking and answering, conversation, collaboration, assignment management, and class conduct.

The Sociotechnical Perspective

This chapter provides a framing for approaching the changes in social practices arising around the use of technologies in e-learning. In discussing these trends, we consider implementation, use and evolution of practices from a *sociotechnical perspective*, that is, with attention to the way technologies are used in association with social requirements of work, or in this case, of teaching and learning. The aim of a sociotechnical perspective is both to understand what determines the present configurations of social and technical systems, and to optimize the balance between the social and technical for the task at hand. It is useful as a way to prepare for discontinuities in practice, as well as a way to analyze results of technology implementations.

While the sociotechnical perspective helps in making informed design decisions at the level of accomplishing local tasks, it also draws our attention to the larger contextual influences which affect work and technology use. For instance, choices made about what technologies to use, in what way, and for what social outcomes may be constrained by outside influences such as: the already made, institutional choice of virtual learning environment (VLE)/ learning management system (LMS); readiness of faculty and students for online education; availability of high speed connectivity in the communities where students live; individual and institutional financial constraints for purchase of computer hardware and software; time constraints on implementation and training in the use of new technologies; synchronization with efforts across regions or institutional units; and the need to maintain competitiveness with comparable institutions.

In addressing the domains in which e-learning is situated, we follow a *social informatics perspective*, that is, the *'interdisciplinary study of the design, uses, and consequences of ICTs that takes into account their interaction with institutional and cultural contexts'* (Kling et al., 2005: 6, italics in original). Social informatics has emerged from over 25 years of studies of information and communication technology. It draws our attention to how technologies work in practice and in context, and adds consideration of influences beyond workplace or institutional settings. Dutton (2008) presents a social informatics perspective as an 'ecology of games' that provides a way of addressing interacting elements of social, technical and political elements:

> [T]he term 'game' [is used] to indicate an arena of competition and coopera-
> tion structured by a set of rules and assumptions about how to act to achieve
> a particular set of objectives, and an 'ecology of games' is seen as a larger
> system of action composed of two or more separate but interdependent
> games (Dutton, 1992). Defined in this way, the idea of an ecology of games
> helps to reveal the dynamics of technical, social, and policy choices shaping
> the development of a technology. Aspects of an ecology of games – games,
> rules, strategies, and players – offer a 'grammar' for describing the system of
> action shaping technological change. As a framework for analysis, it over-
> comes major limitations of single-inventor notions and adds new insights to
> understanding computerization as a social movement. (Dutton, 2008: 502)

This is particularly relevant for e-learning as Internet applications and use drive changes in learning and knowledge practices across society as a whole, and require policy choices in response. (See also Dutton, 1992; Dutton et al., 2004 for an application of the ecology of games to a university-wide e-learning implementation; for more on ecological views, see Chapter 8.)

Extending the principles of social informatics to e-learning logically leads to the idea of *educational informatics*, which Levy and colleagues have defined as 'the study of the application of digital technologies and techniques to the use and communication of information in learning and education' (Levy et al., 2003: 299). Levy and colleagues describe two main concerns of educational informatics:

> First, research in educational informatics seeks to understand the effects on
> people of using digital information (re)sources, services, systems, environ-
> ments and communications media for learning and education. It examines
> the issues and problems that arise from their practice and how these relate
> to factors such as educational and professional context, communication and
> information practices, psychological and cognitive variables, and ICT design
> and use. Second, it seeks to contribute to the development of practical
> knowledge that is relevant to diverse forms of ICT-supported learning. (Levy
> et al., 2003: 299)

In some descriptions, educational informatics is more attuned to technical aspects, for example to the metadata of learning objects (e.g. Ford, 2008). Since our interest here is on the intersection of the social and technical, and the embeddedness of e-learning in larger contexts, we will refer to our discussion as covering the *social informatics of e-learning* (see also Andrews and Haythornthwaite, 2007b; Haythornthwaite, 2006d).

The following sections address e-learning configurations of the social and the technical. First, we review briefly what sociotechnical and social informatics studies have shown about the impact of computers in the workplace and discuss the parallels in e-learning implementation. Then, we address the mix at the instructor and learner level to look at how the social and technical can be, and have been used together to support desired outcomes. Third, we look at the larger context of the adoption of e-learning practices and systems, including the way e-learning is built on existing institutional practices, and also how it is supported and influenced by new online ways of learning outside institutional contexts.

Reviewing Social Processes and Technology

Research on work and organizations has been examining the relation between social processes and ICTs for many years. This builds on a foundation of studies on workplace interventions that include the time and motion studies by Taylor (1911), the wiring room group behavior studies by Roethlisberger and Dickson (1939) and the longwall miners studies by Trist and Bamford and the Tavistock group (1951). These studies identified the importance of context on the presentation of *technology-in-use* and recognized that similar technologies can take dissimilar forms depending on the social, political, and institutional contexts in which they are implemented (Carroll, 2002; Coakes et al., 2000; Huysman and Wulf, 2005; Nunamaker et al., 2009). When computing entered the workplace, the sociotechnical perspective became an important approach for understanding the changes happening in work practices.

Automate and Informate

The kinds of impacts observed in response to early computing systems persist today in contemporary uses and presentations of ICT, including e-learning. Perhaps most notably, Zuboff (1988) observed that *when computers automate, they informate.* This is one of the key transformative effects of computerization. The acts of entering data, communicating, capturing transactions, or retrieving information, cash or e-tickets, each stores not just the data but also the attendant transaction information. This provides a record of who did what, where, when, and with whom, and thus form the basis for monitoring human activity. Data capture is also increasingly passive, requiring no direct act by those observed, for example in the myriad closed circuit television (CCTV) cameras that dot major cities (a news report in 2007 indicated 10,524 cameras in 32 London boroughs, Davenport, 2007; see also Schneier, 2009; for more on surveillance, see Lyon, 2007).

The technologies in common use for e-learning also informate: every email, bulletin board posting, online chat message, assignment submission, grading commentary, etc., is stored, identified with a unique user, known to come from a particular computer address, etc. As Berge (1997: 15) noted, '[an] interesting line of research involves the fact that computer conferencing programs can produce complete transcripts of all interactions they have mediated. These transcripts are a rich data source'.

The persistent texts provide an unprecedented record of all the conversations that happen over the length of a course. These remain available for review for grading and student evaluation; they also remain available for administrator evaluation of teachers, should anyone care to look. A caveat is that use of data summations will be more likely than close readings, reducing the nuance of in-class interaction to the lean representation given in statistics on posting frequency, length, and timing. As Hrastinski (2009) points out, use of such measures alone equates e-learning with 'talking or writing', and fails to capture aspects of learning such as abstract conceptualization and reflective observation. However, more sophisticated extractions are possible, from close readings to automated text analysis, extraction of social network connections and sentiment analysis (Gruzd, 2009; Gruzd and Haythornthwaite, forthcoming; McCalla, 2004). Along these lines, a newly forming research area addressing 'learning analytics' is developing with the aim of examining capturable data for understanding and enhancement of e-learning design and practice (see Siemens, 2010).

Interconnectivity

A second major transformation has been the development of interconnectivity between systems, which has made electronic data interchange from remote transaction to centralized analysis a reality. Interconnectivity is an essential component in building systems that can operate across a wide geographic domain. All data exchange depends on adherence to a limited set of fixed, agreed-upon formats. Internet connections and the attendant data format standards (e.g. XML) are a major way of sharing and connecting data. In e-learning, Learning Objects Metadata (LOM) standards are designed to formalize the definition of units of instruction and learning so they can be shared across systems.

Although local systems can be defined and refined by individuals (e.g. Marty, 2005), large-scale, remotely defined systems can create an infrastructure that then drives work practices and limits their options for interaction. As Oliver (2005b) states:

> Metadata may be described as having the potential to transform ('redeem') higher education, but such descriptions are problematic. They form part of a wider struggle to legitimate the role of educational metadata, a struggle that pits its potential against educational diversity and complexity. (2005b: 84)

Moreover, it is often the case that designers of the technologies and standards operate at a remove from actual users of these systems. Users may exercise their own control by resisting use of such systems (Rogers, 1995), particularly where the practice is markedly different from their current work practices. Such resistance can also be seen in responses to e-learning. Separation between the goals and work practices of designers of e-learning systems and the teachers and students who enact their use can lead to false expectations about control of outcomes from the overall implementation. Jones (2005), for example, discusses how e-learning may be misidentified as confined by the boundaries of educational institutions when instead influences spill over from and into other realms of life. This is certainly the case as the Internet enters the classroom (see also Chapter 5). Design and implementation can also have a political and power dimension, raising some up in status and lowering others (e.g. see Markus, 1983; Markus and Bjorn-Andersen, 1987). Again, from Oliver (2005b):

> Metadata has located itself as part of a wider discourse in which higher education is re-conceived as a market economy. As part of this discourse, it contributes to a politicised process of re-defining the role of academics, marginalising them in the learning and teaching process. (2005b: 84)

Flexibility

In computing, early data processing systems were strictly data-field oriented. These *prescriptive systems* permitted entries only from pre-defined lists of options. Such systems were not well suited for exceptions and informal interaction. These prescriptive systems became balanced by more *permissive* systems as systems were 'reinvented' to meet local use and needs (Galegher et al., 1990; Rice and Rogers, 1980; Rogers et al., 1977). New systems then evolved to include more permissive features, from open memo fields within data forms to accompanying computer-mediated communication. Permissive systems are more interpretively (or interpretatively) flexible (Bijker, 1995; Orlikowski, 1992), that is, more tailorable by and for the user, and thus able to result in more varied and reinvented local presentations. This trend to flexibility continues and becomes part of e-learning. As discussed in earlier chapters, the increasing role of the learner becomes a feature of e-learning. Open source software, open courseware, mash-ups, and social media add to the options learners have to create and interpret computing environments to meet their needs and identities.

Task-Technology Fit

Throughout these developments there has been a long-held goal of finding the best *task–technology fit* between how work is organized and the types of transformations required to convert inputs into outputs (Daft and Lengel, 1986; Lawrence and Lorsch, 1967; Perrow, 1970; Thompson, 1967; Trevino et al., 1990). *Technological determinists* view changes – for better or worse – as the inevitable outcome of technology, with human activity shaped by the technologies that are available or imposed on them. Thus, the goal is to design the perfect technology. *Social determinists* see humans as directing outcomes, for example through strategies such as non-use or more complicated appropriations of the technology to local contexts (Danziger et al., 1982; Rice and

Rogers, 1980; Rogers, 1995; Rogers et al., 1977). Thus, the goal is to choose and design technology according to human needs. Increased attention to users of computer systems has led to a range of new approaches starting with the ideas of *participatory design* or *user-centered computing* (see the papers in Suchman, 1995), as well as new fields such as *computer-supported cooperative work,* and *computer-supported collaborative learning*, that focus on collaborative practices.

However, no system, no matter how well defined ahead of time from a technical or human task perspective, can predict all uses in all places. To do so assumes an all-knowing observer, and stable and identifiable social and technical conditions. Instead, the combination and forms of technologies and tasks will vary both when initiated, and over time, as multiple adjustments are made to both technical and social practices. Designers and users need to be cognizant of the changing domain in which they are working. Instead of looking for specific, long-term ways of 'fitting' the social with the technical, more permissive and flexible approaches are needed, and here too that flexibility refers to both the social and technical.

Newer perspectives recognize and work with the *emergent and co-evolutionary* nature of such sociotechnical mixes. From this view, each new round of practice influences the next instantiation of technology design and use, which in turn affects the next round of practice (Andrews and Haythornthwaite (2007); Bruce, 2010; see also, Chapter 4). The result is a view that sees technology, in the manner of John Dewey's notion of *pragmatic technologies* (Hickman, 1992), as a theory to be tested against the reality of the practice. In Dewey's view a technology is the embodiment of the state of the art at the time of its creation:

> A tool is in this sense a theory, a proposal, a recommended method or course of action. It is only a proposal and not a solution per se because it must be tested against the problematic material for the sake of which it has been created or selected. (Hickman, 1992: 21)

Just as knowledge needs to be tried out and modified through interaction with the 'facilities and frustrations' of the world (Cook and Brown, 1999: 389), so too technologies, as embodiments of knowledge, become amenable to change when confronted with real-world use. As a theory, a proposal, the technology is amenable to change. On-campus, face-to-face teaching can and does give way to online teaching, and the latter, in turn, modifies the former. Thus, technologies can be seen as both *antecedent* and *consequent* to use, and users as able to both adopt and adapt technologies to their needs (Bruce, 2003).

While some technologies are socially agreed upon ways of doing things, such as rules and procedures in organizations, others are more solid physical artifacts, such as university campuses, computers, electron microscopes, or particle accelerators. The more social the technology, and the more flexible and amendable, the more quickly cycles of change and presentation are likely to take place. Current computing technologies respond in this way, particularly those managed through open source development, with additions and local user needs addressed on an ad hoc and just-in-time basis. The idea of *agile computing* captures this kind of development, characterized by nimbleness, improvisation, and a balance of flexibility and structure (Highsmith, 2002).

While directed at programmers, the agile approach is equally important for the users of such systems. Computer-savvy users are already being agile when they bring features of various programs and online resources together in *mash-ups*. Computer-literate users exhibit agility as they adopt a variety of media and applications into their daily use. E-learning also exhibits agility – in open source systems such as Moodle, local appropriations of LMS features for teaching and learning, and mash-ups that bring non-standard technologies or inventive uses into learning. One such inventive use is described in Case 7.1, in which a spreadsheet is brought in to demonstrate probabilities in a 'live' fashion.

CASE 7.1: THROWING THE VIRTUAL DICE: SPREADSHEETS FOR MODELLING FROM FIRST PRINCIPLES

Chris Bissell, Open University, UK

A few years ago my kids' school ran a fundraising event at the Bedford River Festival (UK), where you could roll eight dice to try to win a prize. The highest score at the end of the weekend would get a new bicycle. I rolled 42 with my first throw on the Saturday morning, so I was naturally interested in how likely it was that someone would beat me over the next two days – there would probably be several hundred competitors.

Now, the classic approach to questions like this (if you study probability theory or combinatorics) is to list the number of different ways there are to score a particular total. In this case, there's only one way to score the maximum, 48 – straight sixes:

6 6 6 6 6 6 6 6

There are eight ways to score 47:

5 6 6 6 6 6 6 6
6 5 6 6 6 6 6 6
6 6 5 6 6 6 6 6
6 6 6 5 6 6 6 6
6 6 6 6 5 6 6 6
6 6 6 6 6 5 6 6
6 6 6 6 6 6 5 6
6 6 6 6 6 6 6 5

(Continued)

(Continued)

... and lots of ways of rolling 46 – these, for example (and there are many more):

```
4 6 6 6 6 6 6 6
6 4 6 6 6 6 6 6
6 6 4 6 6 6 6 6
6 6 6 4 6 6 6 6
6 6 6 6 4 6 6 6
6 6 6 6 6 4 6 6
6 6 6 6 6 6 4 6
6 6 6 6 6 6 6 4

5 5 6 6 6 6 6 6
5 6 5 6 6 6 6 6
5 6 6 5 6 6 6 6
5 6 6 6 5 6 6 6
5 6 6 6 6 5 6 6
5 6 6 6 6 6 5 6
5 6 6 6 6 6 6 5
```

Now, the math of all this is well known, and the approach leads to a general formula for working out the probability of any particular total, which I couldn't remember. I didn't have a suitable math book at home, and gave up trying to work it out from first principles! It was beginning to look far too difficult for a Saturday evening ...

But I began wondering about the possibility of using a computer. I'd become very interested in the use of spreadsheets for modelling in general, and in particular, the way spreadsheets enable you to build modelling assumptions directly into the spreadsheet. Spreadsheets for me had become a sort of automated design tablet, where you could have data, mathematical formulas, graphics, interaction, notes to yourself or others, and dynamic displays – all on a comparatively simple, single platform.

So I set up a spreadsheet simulation to model throwing the dice, and to tot up the occurrences of particular totals. When you recalculate the spreadsheet shown in the figure [7.1] a random number between 1 and 6 is entered into the first eight columns of row three. The total is totted up at cell I3. Then, in an area of the spreadsheet not shown in the figure, you keep a tally of every time a particular total is scored – from an 8 (the lowest possible) right up to 48 (the highest). If you run this spreadsheet a great many times (6,000 in my example), you get a pretty good idea of how likely it is for any particular score to be rolled, which you can plot as the height of the column for a particular score. You have to run it a lot of times because, like me, the spreadsheet could 'roll' 42 – or even 48 – on the first run. You can see

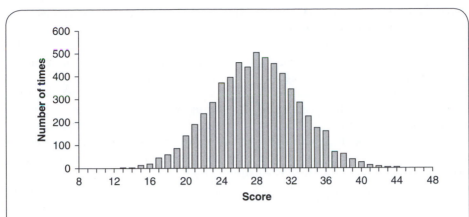

Figure 7.1

from the figure that scoring 42 was pretty unlikely; one in a thousand or so (but you'd have to run the simulation for far more than 6,000 throws to get an accurate estimate of the probability).

So why is this case study significant? Basically because it shows what you can do with a pretty generic application package (the spreadsheet) – using it in a way far from the purposes for which it was designed. You build your modelling assumptions directly into the spreadsheet formulas, and don't need much formal math. Don't get me wrong, you do need to have a certain competence in building the spreadsheet, and understand the meanings of formulas – but it can be a lot easier, much more pedagogically effective and instructive, as well as a lot more fun than the conventional math. (Oh, and yes, I did win the bike!)

Chris Bissell is Professor of Telematics in the Information & Communication Technologies Group, Open University, UK.

This co-evolving, emergent and agile view of systems provides the background for approaching the social and technical aspects of e-learning practices. Moving forward to an actual technology-in-use involves a balancing of the social and technical, with additions and deletions from either side according to how the two act together at any particular time. But more than that, it means moving on from the notion of 'fit' to an image of the social and the technical as reagents in a dynamic chemical process. Depending on what is mixed, the results can be satisfying, disappointing or even explosive!

Managing the Social and Technical Mix in E-learning

In blending the social and technical, whether slowly with established systems, or more nimbly using agile approaches, the key is to consider the technology affordances in relation to the desired outcomes. Chapter One introduced the concept of affordances of technology, that is, what a technology permits or allows by virtue of its design. One of the main observations about new media is that they convey fewer social cues than face-to-face means of communication. When such new media are used to support teaching and learning, the first challenge is to recognize that the missing cues matter, that is, it is not just business as usual on a different medium. The second challenge is to recognize that the lack of cues can be used as a way to change the mode of teaching and learning, that is, that teaching can now include more varied and managed ways of proceeding. Thus, we can approach decisions about what cues to reintroduce, or what features to design into e-learning, based on what matches the instructional and learning aims, and then monitor and adjust as the e-learning progresses.

Such an approach does not have to mean only trying to recreate the face-to-face experience or the physical classroom, for example by using videoconferencing or creating a virtual classroom in Second Life. It can mean a studied choice of what works best for teacher and students given their technology, independence, available time, work schedules, etc., as well as the nature of the material to be learned, as can be seen in Case 7.2. In practical terms, technical choices usually mean selecting among the alternatives available through the institution, that is, using the forms of communication and information management provided through the VLE/LMS and/or other widely available media. Of course, more specialized applications are available, such as educational technologies that provide simulations of scientific processes or virtual world environments. While these will not be dealt with in depth here, choosing to use them also entails a choice about how to reintroduce what can happen locally (e.g. in a laboratory), with the requirement of reaching distributed, online students. Simulations even offer the possibility to do things not possible in a lab, allowing e-learning to extend beyond the classroom in new ways.

CASE 7.2: PROMOTING COLLABORATIVE LEARNING AND INDIVIDUAL ACCOMPLISHMENTS

Paul F. Marty, Florida State University, USA

I have been teaching students about Museum Informatics (the socio-technical interactions between people, information and technology in museums) every year since 2001, first at the University of Illinois and then at Florida State University. While the course was originally developed for and taught in face-to-face classrooms (with students completing hands-on projects in computer labs under instructor supervision), I took the course entirely online in 2004. The shift to a fully online teaching platform necessitated a new approach to the hands-on work that had previously been accomplished in face-to-face computer labs.

Attempts to replicate the lab environment through short weekly individual assignments – where students were asked to explore and write about their experiences using different museum systems or technologies, all available online – were ultimately unsuccessful, primarily because there was little opportunity for collaboration among students. After experimenting with various research and project-based assignments, I identified four topics that were not only integral to the study of museum informatics, but also ideally suited for a collaborative, online learning environment.

Each topic centers around a suite of collaborative systems and online tools, supported by recommended readings and discussion topics. Students work together to share ideas and lessons learned online, spending three to four weeks on each topic, but with each student individually responsible for completing the following four projects:

Collections Management. To understand how museums use collections management systems to manage digital information about their collections, students use open source systems such as Omeka (http://omeka.org/) to create object records using metadata standards such as Cataloging Cultural Objects (http://www.vrafoundation.org/ccoweb/).

Digital Exhibits. To examine how museums reach their visitors through interactive, digital exhibits, students use multimedia authoring tools such as Pachyderm (http://pachyderm.nmc.org/) to create online exhibits, including animations, images, text and multimedia files.

Social Computing. To explore how museums involve visitors in the collection process, students use bookmarking systems on museum websites such as ArtsConnectEd (http://artsconnected.org/) to develop their own personal digital collections of favorite artifacts, annotating their collections with comments, and sharing their collections with others online.

Virtual Worlds. To learn how museums use multi-user virtual environments such as Second Life (http://secondlife.com/) to reach new audiences, students use the School's island in Second Life to design and develop their own virtual exhibits, creating 3D objects and environments using Second Life's integrated development tools.

This approach has succeeded in leveraging the online environment by encouraging collaborative learning while supporting individual work. Students start the course by contributing their object records to a common database, helping each other learn how to apply metadata standards effectively. Students finish the course with their avatars working side by side in Second Life, learning from each other how to develop 3D exhibits, and in the process, what constitutes an effective multi-user virtual environment. The successful migration of this class online underscores the importance of selecting e-learning tools that promote collaborative learning and individual accomplishments.

Paul F. Marty is Associate Professor, School of Library and Information Studies, College of Communication and Information, Florida State University, USA.

Balancing the Social and Technical

The following presents two examples that illustrate balancing the social and technical for two e-learning concerns: anonymity and boundaries.

Confronting Anonymity

Perhaps the most daunting part of any transition from offline to online is the lack of cues about individuals in the class. There are many reasons for trying to re-establish individuality. Being known gives individuals a sense of belonging to the class, and it lets them know about individual histories and backgrounds of others in the class. As they get to know others, and what they and others can do, individual students are more able to judge their own place in the class, perhaps gaining confidence in their skills and perhaps learning who to go to for particular kinds of information. Teachers can tailor their teaching to the background knowledge and interests of class members and follow the progress of individuals as the class unfolds. Individual identification can build trust among participants and increase their commitment to each other and to the learning tasks, encouraging contribution to dialogue and collaborative learning (see also Case 1.1 in Chapter 1).

There are also reasons for maintaining anonymity. Idea generation may be more successful when no names are given with the contribution, and hence no public embarrassment for a silly idea. New users may not know how to post, and some initial anonymity may provide an experimentation space for learning how to contribute appropriately. This 'free zone' may be particularly important in settings where discussion content is graded.

In either case – whether for identity or anonymity – there are ways to balance the social with the technical. To take a socio-technical perspective does not mean determining hard and fast rules on what to do to create a particular outcome, but focuses instead on what attributes of the technologies are most likely to support the desired outcomes. It is at this point that the instructor holds most influence over what kind of a learning environment they will model, create and use for the course.

In a formal educational setting, the instructor has a major role in establishing protocols for interaction, for example setting participation practices, such as whether students will post publicly or privately, as independent contributions or in dialogue with others; whether discussion is assessed toward class credit, and if so on what criteria; and whether projects are group or individually based. However, choices can be constrained by local technical considerations, such as whether real-time technologies are available for synchronous chat sessions with students, or local social norms, such as how much of a final grade can be based on participation. With these caveats in mind, an instructor might choose from some of the suggestions below to encourage getting to know and sustain attention to others in the class.

Disclosure of Personal Information

Personal information can enhance the perception of others as complete people. This can be conveyed through personal pages where individuals can display information about themselves and their outside class activities, asking for an introduction when first posting to discussion, or opening a discussion area just for personal introductions. An instructor can initiate and model desired behaviors. For example, they can: maintain a personal page that describes their personal interests and models what a student might post; use informal language in online discussion to encourage conversation rather than academic writing; respond to postings in a way that opens discussion for others to continue, for example by leaving questions to be answered. If the ideal is that students learn from each other, then work can be posted publicly to the class, and students can be engaged in commenting or adding to others' work. To promote knowing who is in the class, the instructor can refer to class members by name so a sense of individuals and their contributions is created. The instructor can request that personal names be used to identify posters rather than email or network identities, and real pictures used instead of character icons, or the family pet, as identifiers.

Interactive Discussion

Discussion practices can be set that require participation on a regular basis, sometimes including the requirement not only to make an original contribution, but also to read and comment on others' contributions. As discussion expands, it often becomes difficult to see the contributor trees for the conversation forest – something we are much more aware of in face-to-face classes. Regularly consulting contribution statistics – something not available for face-to-face classes – can help sort out who is involved in the conversation and who is not. Following up with reminders and incentives can help bring in the peripheral members. Asynchronous discussion is well suited for distributed learners, but 'being there with others' is a tried and true way to increase the sense of *social presence* (Garrison and Anderson, 2003; Heeter, 1992). The immediacy and presence with others during synchronous lectures or chat sessions provides a social boost that many crave, and that helps compensate for the distributed educational environment (Haythornthwaite et al., 2000; Bregman and Haythornthwaite, 2003).

Many of these options make ordinary good sense, and are fairly obvious when presented. But, the newness of the online environment, both for instructors and students, can sometimes overwhelm our good sense as each way of presenting, contributing, and giving feedback is new. Working out new ways of getting teaching done, as well as evaluating how that is going, is the *invisible work* (Star and Strauss, 1999) of e-learning. Such work in improving class assignments is seen in Case 7.3.

CASE 7.3: MEANINGFUL ENGAGEMENT

Michele M. Kazmer, Florida State University, USA

I have taught the required class on Information Organization at the Florida State University School of Library & Information Studies online since 2002. One assignment requires students to write about current problems in subject access (i.e. how the subject of an item such as a book, video, or image is chosen and represented so that others can search for and retrieve it effectively through a database or search engine). In recent semesters this assignment required students to write about social tagging and how tags develop into folksonomies. The assignment requires students to use and cite a substantial amount of the appropriate research literature in their papers, but each semester students had difficulty performing a thorough literature search *and* incorporating a sufficient number of references into their papers.

I thought about how to improve the students' performance in a *meaningful* way; I didn't want to ask them to submit bibliographies to me two weeks ahead of time, and the assignment already included a grade penalty for inadequate use of the literature. In the end, I radically reconceptualized the assignment so it *integrates use* of social media as part of the process. Now, students perform their literature searches first, and as a class they collaboratively contribute the citations to a shared online bibliography. As students share citations to materials *about* tagging, folksonomy, etc., they add tags to the citations, thus creating their own folksonomy. Then they write a paper analyzing their use of the tagged collection and the resulting folksonomy, comparing it with their analysis of a 'naturally-occurring' tagged collection and folksonomy found online. While writing the paper, they support their arguments using literature that was contributed to their shared bibliography. No work (theirs or mine!) goes to waste, and because they *use* the collaborative bibliography to support another task (writing the paper), they really get a feel for what it's like to use it (not just examine it).

Michelle M. Kazmer is Associate Professor, School of Library and Information Studies, College of Communication and Information, Florida State University.

Setting Boundaries

The second example is about managing boundaries. As the Internet reaches into all hours of our lives and e-learning moves into work and home spaces, an issue that faces both teachers and students is setting boundaries for class participation. For example, teachers can find themselves caught in a cycle of rapid posting and response with 20–30 distributed students that ends up stretching their engagement into evenings and weekends. At the same time, since no one can 'see' an online class in operation, and no students are visible, it may be hard for colleagues and administrators to see that work hours are already filled. Managing an online class can get squeezed out of a daily schedule by competing calls on time from those in the face-to-face setting. At the other end of the day, the presence of a laptop in the kitchen, or the absence of the e-learner from the kitchen, can make engagement in online courses all too obviously an invasion of home space.

The office space and the social organization of workplaces has acted as a well-established and recognized boundary to contact hours, as well as established conventions for signaling availability, for example an open office door or established office hours. Online, however, there are no such conventional boundaries. These have to be set by instructors. For example, instructors can use synchronous office hours to manage contact hours and interruptions. And they can give notice up front on what expectations students can have for response time, including days of the week when they will not be attending to online discussions.

At home, students may be newly integrating office space into home space, as well as home study habits into communal time and spaces. E-learners can be faced with setting boundaries *for* learning, for example so they can have space to attend synchronous class sessions or time to attend to asynchronous discussion, as well as boundaries *from* learning, for example so that there is time for the people in their lives (Kazmer, 2000). Again, with no conventional boundaries to signal when a home learner is 'at work' versus 'at leisure' (since these days, in both cases, this may mean a person absorbed in activity on the computer), deliberate attention must be paid to establishing new conventions: a closed bedroom door, a separate learning space, a formal hand-off of childcare duties. Negotiations may also be necessary around home spaces, including space for the computer, and times when the e-learner is 'in class'.

The many domains of activity students are engaged in can leave them 'juggling multiple social worlds' such as those of work, home and school (Jones, 2005; Haythornthwaite and Kazmer, 2002; Salaff, 2002). Since students may be unaware of these kinds of adjustments, it can be important information for program organizers and teachers to convey to their students. Also, by teachers stating up front what their weekly schedule will be, this will also model that kind of scheduling behavior, as well as giving the e-learners a clearer idea of interaction times with the teacher and other learners.

Conclusion

In this chapter we have discussed how adopting e-learning is more than designing or selecting the ideal technology. Neither is it a search for the best 'fit' between a technical design or choice and the desired social outcome. It is instead an active process of continuously balancing the social and the technical in the *service of learning* (Barab et al., 2004). Both the technology and its proposed use in context are theories to be tested in relation to the subject matter, student body, institution and societal context. As such, the hypothesis about use may be accepted or rejected, and if the latter, then the theory is ready to be modified before further use. As a new way of teaching and learning, e-learning participants have to be ready to pay attention to the way learning is proceeding. Already we can see that teachers need to pay attention to new technologies. Students equally face changes. In interviews with students, we have heard how they need to make a deliberate effort to remain 'present' and visible in the online environment (Haythornthwaite et al., 2000). As e-learning evolves to a more collaborative learning style, students are again faced with change. Students are required to take an active role and responsibility for sustaining discussion and working with others, while the teacher pays attention in their new role as facilitator.

The sociotechnical and social informatics perspectives provide an important framework for preparing for and analyzing e-learning practices. This chapter has focused more on the sociotechnical mix, considering examples at the level of teachers and learners. The discussion of sociotechnical effects is continued in the next chapter, where discussion of e-learning ecologies brings us into contact with wider spheres of education and learning affected by and affecting ICTs.

Further Reading

Garrison, D. R. and Anderson, T. (2003). *E-learning in the 21st Century: A Framework for Research and Practice*. New York: RoutledgeFalmer.

Jones, C. (2005). 'Nobody knows you're a dog: What amounts to context in networked learning?', in R. Land and S. Bayne (Eds.), *Education in Cyberspace*. London: Routledge. pp. 105–16.

Kling, R., Rosenbaum, H. and Sawyer, S. (2005). *Understanding and Communicating Social Informatics*. Medford, NJ: Information Today.

8

E-learning Ecologies

Introduction

Online initiatives are changing not only the way we teach and learn but who we learn with, where, and when. E-learning has left the classroom, and in doing so also leaves the sequestered space that comes with the face-to-face classroom or the campus library. E-learning happens in the workplace, at home, and on the road; in the (former) leisure spaces of coffee shops and hotels, and the learning spaces of public as well as academic libraries. E-learning has also left the campus, and with it the idea that higher education is completed at a certain age and produces graduates who go on to gain all future learning on the job. The content of interest also changes, from pursuit of an academic discipline to just-in-time learning on scholarly, work or leisure activities. In leaving the campus, e-learning joins the world, connecting adult learners across the globe, pooling and sharing resources through interpersonal exchanges as well as shared repositories. Each of these changes puts the e-learner in a new mix of people, technologies and content, managing within a new *ecology* of resources, instruction and education. As formal learning leaves its niche of the school, university or workplace, an ecology metaphor is particularly apt for giving attention to the way resources flow across boundaries, creating new places and spaces for different species of learners and different kinds of learning activity.

The ecology metaphor has been used in various ways to address human organizational systems (Morgan, 2007; Scott, 1992). It came into favor as a way to think about information technology through the work of Davenport (1997) and Nardi and O'Day (1999). These authors leveraged the metaphor to discuss *information ecologies*, which Nardi and O'Day define as 'a system of people, practices, values and technologies in a particular local environment' (1999: 49). An information ecology view arose as a response to silo-oriented views of information and its management; it directs attention to how information does (or could) flow through organizations, and the ecological base of people, technologies and social practices relevant to this flow. The relevance of information flow is well described in Brown and Duguid (2000) which refers to the 'social life' of information. Others also adopt an ecological view of technology. Dutton (1992, 2008) uses an 'ecology of games' metaphor to consider overlapping but separate competitive and cooperative systems that operate like games with rules, strategies and players affecting social, technical and political elements of environments (discussed in Chapter 7). Girard and Stark (2007, and see below) refer to 'digital ecologies' of online and offline assemblies of communications around a single theme. Goodyear (1998) suggests an 'ergonomics of learning environments' that draws on the ecology metaphor to turn attention to the relationship between learners and their environment and to address e-learning design with a view to the actual versus idealized view of what a learner's work entails.

Applying an ecology metaphor to e-learning provides a way of talking about the many elements that make up an e-learning enterprise, and the way these interconnect (Sandars and Haythornthwaite, 2007). The metaphor is useful for balancing the identification of central concerns with ones that may at first seem to be peripheral. For example, while focusing on the technological construction of a VLE, an ecological perspective adds consideration of the technical sophistication of students, the readiness of instructors, the availability of high speed connectivity at remote locations, and the educational systems that feed in students to an e-learning environment. It leads us to consider boundary conditions, such as the meeting of school and home when e-learners go online in a family setting, and the meeting of school and work when e-learners are being considered for employment.

Another interpretation of 'ecology' in the e-learning area considers the view from the individual e-learner's perspective. Such a view is presented by McCalla (2004) and Luckin (2008, 2010) who each describe an approach to facilitating learning that is based on technology support for individual behavior. McCalla describes an 'I-Help' system (Tang and McCalla, 2003) that captures both learner characteristics and episodic information such as annotations made about the learning object – in this case a research paper. Data clustering and data mining techniques are seen as the way to make sense of this combination of data to find patterns that can then help this learner or other learners. Luckin's (2008, 2010) learner-centric 'ecology of resources' has a similar focus on the individual in their eco-system. She describes both a school 'HOMEWORK' computer system and a multi-channel 'VeSEL' project for rural education in Kenya. The ecology of resources approach focuses on the learner at the center of their ecology of the subject they are learning, its epistemic community, the local social and physical environments, and the human, textual (online and offline) and equipment resources that are used for information access. As from other ecological perspectives, these authors and the systems they describe capture the complex of activity that defines learning, including retrieving and fitting that knowledge to local circumstances.

The aim in referring to ecologies is not to prove an ecology exists in a biological sense, but to use the metaphor to open up understanding of a complex phenomenon (Morgan, 2007) through ideas such as: a *diversity of species*, each in competition for different resources, and acting differently on those resources; a *diversity of niches* with different local resources and species; *border* zones where different niches and species meet; and *populations* of species that rise and fall in concert with each other, or die off and are succeeded by other species. The ecology metaphor provides conventions for naming local regions: *environment*, to name the place in which organisms live, and the attributes of that place; *ecosystem*, to identify the set of organisms that dwell and interact in an environment; *habitat* to identify the place an organism inhabits in an environment, and *niche* for the combination of function, place and organism within an environment. Species within the environment can be *generalists*, able to function and survive within a wide range of conditions, or *specialists*, adapted only to particular niches. Some species are *producers*, adding to an ecosystem, for example as plants convert sunlight into energy for growth, some are *predators*, and some are their *prey*. Organisms may also live in *symbiotic* relationships, taking, giving or sharing resources. Or, they may be in the more complex and emergent relationship of *reciprocal co-evolution*, a concept we have already adopted to refer to the relationship between learning and technology (see Chapter 4, this volume, and Andrews and Haythornthwaite, 2007).

An ecological view lets us follow different aspects of the e-learning enterprise, from administration to student experience, information production and consumption, educational systems, and the connection between them. Each aspect provides a different image around which we can frame the issue of e-learning, whether for the purpose of implementing a program, teaching a class, or learning. As asked in Haythornthwaite and Kazmer (2004b):

> When you set out to build and operate an online program – aiming to provide quality education for students who cannot, or choose not to, move to an on-campus facility – what kind of a problem is it? Who are you gonna call to fix it?
>
> Is it a technical problem? – in which case you call on computer software designers, implementers, vendors, and operators. Is it an institutional problem? – in which case you negotiate with educational administrators, education boards, etc. Is it an administrative problem? … It's always an educational problem, so how do you learn to teach online? … But is it an information problem? Should the focus be on how to deliver information across space and time, including library materials, lectures, course notes? … [M]aybe it's a workplace problem … a recruitment and retention problem … a student experience problem. (2004b: xv)

E-learning is, of course, all these 'problems', and the purview of each of these stakeholders. As exemplified in this quotation, a range of roles is associated with e-learning. Table 8.1 lists various kinds of perspectives we can take on e-learning, along with the people or jobs most associated with that perspective and the kinds of tasks involved. While already long, this list is by no means

Table 8.1 Perspectives on E-learning

Perspective	People	Tasks
Technical	Designers, programmers	Creating and implementing systems
Institutional	Education administration, boards	Selecting systems
Administrative	Faculty, office and support staff, visiting teachers	Managing an online enterprise
Educational	Teachers	Learning how to teach online
Pedagogical	Researchers	Deriving theories about e-learning
Informational	Librarians, teachers	Delivery of content and materials
Communication	Participants	Learning how to 'talk' online
Financial	Administrators, politicians, students	Making ends meet
Student life	Student communities, alumni	Learning how to learn online
Work life	Employers	Evaluating graduates
Material	Laboratories, libraries	Bringing people and materials together

exhaustive. However, it does demonstrate the range and diversity of species and niches associated with the e-learning ecology – educational, technical, social and more – each of which provides a different perspective on the enterprise as a whole.

While one's personal perspective will be bound up with the particular job to perform, a comprehensive view of e-learning needs to consider all roles – teacher, student, administrator, programmer and employer. It is here that the ecological view helps as it encourages thinking of e-learning as a system of interconnected people and settings, each with a piece to offer and a responsibility in the whole. An equally important aspect of an ecological view is that it lets us see how the system we are focusing on, such as an e-learning program, sits within larger ecological systems that supply inputs to our programs and receive outputs from them. For example, a university level e-learning program sits within a larger educational system that starts from primary schools and extends to graduate programs; and even this educational system sits within other systems of politics, government and society.

Ecologies are not bound by specific quantities and processes that can be predefined. Instead, they moderate to achieve a balance among the elements that sustain the system. Continuous modification and adjustment create a structure that remains stable over time even as individual constituents enter and leave the system. The ecology is maintained through a 'balance found in motion, not stillness', based on 'the stable participation of an interconnecting group of people and their tools and practices' (Nardi and O'Day, 1999; see also Robins, 2002, 2004). As discussed in Chapter 6, communities that become stable in this way gain social capital (Lin, 2001), that is, resources and access to them maintained through networks of interpersonal motivations and obligations (see also Chapter 2).

While flexibility in the face of change is important for maintaining the balance of an ecology, human ecological systems can also be proactive in effecting change in the embedding environment. For example, educational institutions have lobbied government and professional organizations for accreditation and acceptance of online programs, allowing them to create new niches to serve different students and regions. Thus, an educational ecosystem (e.g. higher education) may itself be an active agent in the larger embedding environment and ecology of games.

One further aspect of ecologies is important to consider as we look at e-learning systems. An ecology can be thought of as a complex arrangement of parts, each with strong interrelationships and dependencies, where a change in one part can quickly affect another and then all parts of the system. This *tight coupling* is often the goal of designed systems, where the aim is to increase efficiency by reducing redundancies and delays in processing. By contrast with tight coupling, there are systems that exhibit *loose coupling*. Weick (1976) identified how many systems operate with a loose coupling between those who perform the work and those who supervise or set goals. His particular example was of the loose coupling in educational organizations, in particular between the goals of administrators and the actions of teachers in the classroom. The work that teachers, police, social workers and librarians undertake, and any other job that entails authorizing a professional to operate without constant supervision, exhibits loose coupling. In a tightly coupled system, changes in one item or part of the system directly affect another, but with loose coupling the change does not *directly* affect other items or the system. Thus, the actions of a teacher in the classroom do not immediately affect the work of other teachers, nor of the school or university. However, the actions of many teachers, over time, certainly do affect the operation of the educational institution. Similarly, the actions of many students and scholars moving to use and create online resources creates indirect, or delayed changes in educational practice. Again, this reiterates our model of reciprocal co-evolution, but here situating the outcomes as also indirectly affected by general societal or species population trends.

Often when organizing work, or designing programs, attention is given only to the strongly tied, tightly coupled aspects of the system. In such cases, all the mechanics are in place, but the 'softer' components of identity, attitudes, and social relationships are forgotten. The *invisible work* (Star and Strauss, 1999) of advising students, providing social support, learning to use new technologies, learning to teach online, maintaining home offices, and more, can easily be overlooked in focusing on establishing online learning programs.

(For an illuminating case study that describes the specification of the invisible social support work of nurses, see Timmermans et al., 1998.) Also invisible is the social interaction happening on the side in a face-to-face class, that then needs to be designed into an online class (see Chapter 6). Early computing initiatives often suffered from this oversight, as systems designed to process information created unexpected consequences on power structures within work organization and on the social life of workers (e.g. Zuboff, 1988).

In loosely coupled systems, individuals performing their job are also enacting the identity of their profession. The 'softer' ideas of representing the profession, maintaining professional conduct, and dealing with others in a professional manner affect both the local system and the professional system to which they belong. Two ecologies – games – overlap. In education, the ecology of the school or university overlaps with the ecology of the discipline or profession. Major failures of e-learning initiatives have resulted from inattention to this kind of duality and to the ecologies of different stakeholders (see below).

We turn now to the e-learning ecology, first taking an overall view to consider the landscape of actors, niches and boundaries, and then considering the view from the perspective of the individual in their 'personal ecology'.

The Ecology of the E-learning Environment

Using the idea of ecologies as a base, and particularly information ecologies, we can look at e-learning with attention to the key elements of species, niches, localities and technologies. In discussing these we draw attention to the inter-connecting system of 'people, practices, values and technologies', as well as the embedding environment in which the overall e-learning system operates.

Species

The 'species' seem fairly easy to list – teachers, students, administrators, support staff. But is there a keystone species, one 'whose presence is crucial to the survival of the ecology' (Nardi and O'Day, 1999: 53)? Nardi and O'Day suggest this keystone species may be 'often unofficial, unrecognized, and seemingly peripheral to the most obvious productive functions of the workplace' (1999: 54). But, whose presence is crucial? In keeping with Nardi and O'Day's observation, it seems the crucial species is the student. No e-learning endeavor has much purpose without its students. We have evidence for this in a number of examples of e-learning. Learning communities often arise online without anyone in the teacher function. Fellow learners in health support groups provide each other with scientific and experiential information (Smedberg, 2008), and members of online writing groups like Livejournal provide each other with critiques and commentaries on stories (Rebaza, 2009). Online universities fail when enrollment is insufficient to sustain the operation. This was the case for the

UKeU, a wholly online university in the UK that operated only from 2000 to 2003. According to Garrett (2004), among the reasons for the failure of the UKeU was its use of a US rather than a UK model of higher education. The initiative failed to understand the ecology and cultural meaning of a higher education degree within the context of its UK embedding culture, thereby failing to attract and keep its keystone species.

Species interact in their local habitat, and interconnect with people and practices from other niches. For example, teachers and learners interact regularly, synchronously or asynchronously, within the habitat of the online class. Outside class, these species also interact regularly with librarians and the library habitat, including the online spaces. When everything is running fine, the work of some species is invisible. Technology specialists for example are invisible until a technology fails. Then their role becomes highly visible, and unfamiliar people and practices are brought into a formerly stable environment. Similarly, invisible practices make relatively seamless connections between teachers and students and the administrative operations of enrollment, fee payment and collection, and awarding of grades and degrees.

Each of these operations shows the overlap of species in the larger institutional habitat. While day-to-day teaching need not be concerned with these layers, administratively e-learning includes all these overlapping habitats and niches. It also includes consideration of the competition for resources. E-learning as an enterprise competes for resources with on-campus programs from the same institution, but also offers that institution a way to compete with outside programs in both traditional and online schools and universities. Symbiotic relationships can also exist, for example, where online programs add access to courses not available locally, such as advanced secondary school courses (e.g. Advanced Placement [AP] courses in the US that let students petition out of an introductory university class), or where courses are shared across specialized programs (e.g. the Web-based Information Science Education [WISE] program that shares access to online Masters degree courses among cooperating library and information science programs).

Beyond the institutional level, e-learning fits within larger regional spheres of educational practice and accreditation, and the overall setting of the embedding society. Thus, e-learning ecologies are also affected by decisions at the level of educational and government policy-makers, as well as by attitudes of businesses and professions regarding the validity of online education.

Niches
What niches exist? A very visible niche is the class. Joint interaction between teachers and students builds the intimate niche of the class with its local social and pedagogical conventions. Online programs occupy niches, sometimes uniquely filling an otherwise uncovered content area or reaching an otherwise

underserved population (e.g. extension programs, workplace learners). E-learning as a whole fills a niche in the learning and education environment. It occupies the cyberspace portion of the environment, where online educators and learners interact.

Other kinds of e-learning niches exist outside educational institutions, such as in online discussion groups and communities. These may be openly available sites or private sites for knowledge management and sharing in organizations. As these new online species develop, they compete with established offline species: online sites are already competing with established print publishers for the information niches of newspapers, encyclopediae, dictionaries, journals, magazines and books; online universities compete with traditional educational institutions; and online information competes with that published, reviewed and collected through established publishers, professional societies and libraries (for more on this, see Haythornthwaite, forthcoming; Willinsky, 2005). At present, the prestige of the degree is sustaining the value of learning through accredited institutions and reducing competition from online learning communities. But it is clear that the nature of accredited institutions as a species is changing, not only to include all-online institutions, but also to fit all online and blended online options into the traditional mix (e.g. see the statistics on the growth of online and blended options in the US in the Sloan Consortium reports, such as Allen and Seaman, 2010). Conventions for cooperation and collaboration are still emerging for the more open sites for information sharing (encyclopediae such as Wikipedia, video sharing as in YouTube, blogging and contribution rating as in Slashdot or Digg). The rules of competition – for example, why post to this site rather than another, why comment or rate in this venue rather than another – are currently emerging, as are models for long-term 'persistent structures' of these new information, participation and learning enterprises (Benkler, 2006; Haythornthwaite, 2009a; Raymond, 1999; see also this volume, Chapter 5).

Border Conflicts

Different interests meet at the *borders* of niches and can sometimes result in conflicts. In e-learning, conflicts have arisen over the validity of online education, accreditation of online programs, acceptance of online teaching and learning by teachers and students, employer acceptance of online graduates, and acceptance of online materials as valid knowledge sources. Interests outside or inside educational institutions may be involved. Outside agencies may control their borders by disallowing credit for online courses or programs. For example, the American Bar Association (2010) is maintaining its boundaries against online education. As of April 2010, their Standard 306 on Distance Education states:

> (d) A law school shall not grant a student more than four credit hours in any term, nor more than a total of 12 credit hours, toward the J.D. degree for courses qualifying under this Standard.

(e) No student shall enroll in courses qualifying for credit under this Standard until that student has completed instruction equivalent to 28 credit hours toward the J.D. degree.

(f) No credit otherwise may be given toward the J.D. degree for any distance education course.

Within institutions, disputes can play out when administration ideas about e-learning meet faculty ideas of education and governance. Often the conflict is about e-learning as a means to increase revenue versus e-learning as a way to increase educational opportunities. Such conflict is demonstrated in a quotation with reference to a failed attempt to create a fully online campus for a major US university:

> 'While it made economic sense to take course content from top-flight professors and hire outsiders to deliver it for less than half the price, it did not make pedagogical sense in the eyes of the faculty,' Burbules said. 'Teaching is not a delivery system, and I think most faculty were just not interested in giving up their course content to be "delivered" by adjuncts with whom they might have little to no contact,' he said. '... You can't divorce the syllabus from the delivery.' (*Inside Higher Education*, 3 September 2009)

Over time, some species and some niches disappear. Particular interests can lose control as jobs evolve and change character, as may become the case for resistance to e-learning as it expands into more and more aspects of higher education and daily life. In this way *species populations rise and fall*, with some species declining in numbers and being *succeeded* by other species. In e-learning, we have been seeing the rise of online programs and the online university, two new organizational populations that have been challenging the evening and distance education niches of traditional programs, leading the traditional venue to modify and adapt in the face of changes and new competition in their environment.

Locality

One issue that stands out in trying to grasp the idea of the ecology for e-learning is the concept of locality. In this locality, '[t]he local participants in each setting – librarians, office workers, small business owners – construct the identities of their technologies through the rhythms and patterns of their use.' (Nardi and O'Day, 1999: 55). What does 'local' mean in the context of e-learning? What is the e-learner's 'local' environment? As discussed in previous chapters, when students are distributed, their experience of 'local' can differ from each other and from that of the teacher. While this has been the case for distance students before e-learning, a major difference is in the creation of a cyber-locality for e-learning. (For more on how research on distance education can inform e-learning, see Thompson, 2007).

The habitat for the e-learner is the online world, organized around the prime locality of the e-learning community (or VLE), and the online environs for foraging for information. We have already covered in Chapter 6 how the online space can become a functional community with routines, roles and conventions; here we look at how this online environment sits within various other ecologies, affecting both institutions and individual e-learners.

Some examples show the impact of a multiplex notion of 'local' for e-learning. The first example pertains to acquiring information resources. Libraries remote from the enrolling institution are beginning to experience the impact of their institutionally remote, but geographically local e-learners. Pedagogical requirements for use of online resources have the unexpected consequence of distributing responsibility to public access points, for example public and university libraries at locations local to the students. Such institutions act as nests for the distributed learning 'cuckoos' (Searing, personal communication). Libraries end up carrying the load for readings and assignments set at educational institutions *remote* from their own site and clientele, with consequent impacts on inter-library agreements and collection development (see also, Searing, 2004).

Second, as adult students, distributed e-learners are often taking classes while embedded in the workplace, and always while embedded in their local community. Resources for internships, interviews, and data gathering are all now remote to the degree granting institution, but local to the student, potentially crossing regional and national boundaries, laws or other conventions (e.g. in university and regional human subject review conventions for research data collection). Kazmer (2007a) has found that beneficial effects emerge from the dual locality of *community-embedded learners*. Their simultaneous presence online *and* in geographically local communities provides benefits as remote knowledge is brought into the workplace or community, while the online learners benefit by being able to apply their newly acquired knowledge to situations of importance to their lives. In cyber-local e-learning classes, students benefit by hearing about multiple experiences from diverse locations (Montague, 2006). (For more on this, see Chapter 9.)

As another example, consider the learner who is embedded in a contemporary on-campus class. In the mid-2000s, universities were vying for status to be among the 'most wired' campuses. Many institutions began promoting or even requiring the use of laptop computers for class. In 2005, Indiana State University became the first US public university to require undergraduate students to have notebook computers, with the requirement to go into effect in fall 2007 (Indiana State University, 2005). More recently, however, the blend of online life with classroom life has run amuck. Learners are simultaneously operating in in-class and distributed communities to the point of distraction. In efforts to manage boundaries between online and in-class worlds, lecturers are beginning to add explicit instructions about attention management to their classes, including banning the use of laptops, and wired campuses are introducing ways to turn off web access during classes (de Vise, 2010; Fang, 2009; see also Box 5.1 in Chapter 5). While in-class distractions can be annoying, other kinds of cross-border interaction can have a serendipitously positive effect, as Case 8.1 demonstrates.

CASE 8.1: THE SERENDIPITOUS LIFE OF FACEBOOK INFORMATION

Gale Parchoma, Lancaster University, UK

This case does not begin with a known problem. It does not contain a planned solution. It does, however, illustrate the power of social media to distribute teaching and learning resources.

During a pre-conference day in Aalborg, Denmark a number of delegates from the 7th International Conference on Networked Learning toured the Lindholm Høje Viking burial site, which had been used from AD 400 to AD 1000. Among the graves, information plaques display detailed drawings and archaeological information from the 1952–1958 site excavation. As I toured the site, I took photos of the graves and the information plaques.

With the single intention of sharing my experience with my daughters in Canada, I posted my photos on Facebook. Within the hour I received an email message from my niece in Singapore. As my niece does not have access to Facebook at the elementary school where she teaches, she asked if I could email her copies of the photos she had indicated she liked so that she could use them as resources for a unit on ancient civilizations.

Over dinner with conference delegates the following evening, I related this story. A colleague commented that her daughter was also studying ancient civilizations in her elementary history class in Manchester, UK. Would I mind if she downloaded the photos from my Facebook album for her daughter's project? I told her I would be delighted to have my photos contribute. The next request came from Caroline Haythornthwaite, co-author of this text. Would I write this case for her and Richard Andrews' forthcoming book?

The following morning, I received an email thank-you note from the children in Singapore, noting they 'couldn't believe [the Vikings] buried the guy with his dog'.

Gale Parchoma is Lecturer in the e-Research and Technology Enhanced Learning doctoral program, Department of Educational Research, Lancaster University, UK.

Technology

E-learning is bound up with and inseparable from the idea of a technological platform. At the class level, teachers and students come in close contact with technology as their tool for interaction with all its limitations or facilitations; in the information ecology, online retrieval and interaction form the basis of a distributed knowledge base. Part tool and part habitat, ICTs serve as both the means and place where e-learning survives. As outlined in previous chapters, practices emerge from the conventions of use and the affordances of technologies. Technologies are not the driver of ecologies, but create an underpinning for how these ecologies unfold.

More detailed analysis of the complex of technology and practice is found in the ideas of activity theory (Engeström, 2009; Engeström et al., 1999; Nardi, 1996; Russell, 2002). Engeström's now classic approach grapples with the multiple influences on learning and sense making in communal activity, including the influences of the mediating artifacts of tools and technologies. A major aspect of his perspective is that interaction among the elements of the activity system creates new configurations and new understandings of local conditions. Knowledge and understanding of what an 'object' is in an activity system – that is, the end result of a set of interacting elements but also the moving target that is created by the continuous interaction of elements – emerges from the interaction of the activity system elements, which are the mediating artifact, subject, rules, community, and division of labor. While the diagrams present a static view, activity systems are meant to be seen as dynamic; they grow and evolve with every nudge and contradiction between elements, and every subjective interpretation of these interactions. Over time, activity systems are shaped and re-shaped, with meanings and activities reconsidered repeatedly.

Individual, active engagement in these dynamic changes creates the conditions for expansive learning, where individuals can learn to be something that has never existed before (such as being an e-learner).

> In some cases, this escalates into collaborative envisioning and a deliberate collective change effort. An expansive transformation is accomplished when the object and motive of the activity are reconceptualized to embrace a radically wider horizon of possibilities than in the previous mode of the activity. (Engeström, 2009: 57)

Such a transformation is evident in the emerging attitudes, meanings and instantiations of e-learning systems and practices. Institutions, employers, professional organizations, teachers and learners are all in the process of modifying their understanding of what e-learning means. While it is beyond the scope of this chapter to discuss activity theory in more detail, it is useful to think of it as a more detailed specification of ecological ideas. Activity theory captures the way that what we need to know and how we view a problem is affected and promoted by environmental influences: communal, cultural, historical and technological.

A number of other writers also draw our attention to the role of technology in activity systems and networks, and the continuously emergent nature of current practices. Theory and research on social construction of reality (Berger and Luckmann, 1966), social shaping of technology (MacKenzie and Wajcman, 1999; Pinch and Bijker, 1984), sociotechnical systems (Fulk and Steinfield, 1990), and social informatics (Kling, 1999) all point to the way use enacts and re-enacts social structures. Of particular interest in relation to information and knowledge ecologies (Star, 1995) is the perspective of actor-networks (Latour, 1987) which places the technology as an actor in the network of interacting elements – essentially assigning technology the role of a species within the ecology. Research from this perspective shows how knowledge production systems are often formed around an essential piece of equipment – an electron microscope, a particular cell-preparation process, or a Hadron collider. These pieces of equipment represent substantial financial investment but also substantial intellectual commitment to particular ways of doing things.

Physical settings also become technologies in this way, shaping who meets whom, where, and how work gets done. People meet and work in laboratories, learning to work with others in the lab and with the particular set of equipment and procedures present there (Knorr-Cetina, 1999). Buildings can constrain or facilitate interaction among people according to office and open space arrangements in buildings (Heerwagen et al., 2004; Swales, 1998). Buildings can also create sequestered spaces for learning and study, for example in schools and libraries (Crook, 2002). Systems of knowledge and learning emerge around these physical artifacts of equipment and space in ways that maintain the ecology of the participants and their practices. (See also Lemke and van Helden, 2009; and Hewling, 2009, on technology as 'cultural player'.)

While technologies can constrain practices, technologies are also instantiations of practices (Bruce and Hogan, 1998). In e-learning, key practices involve lectures, assignments, tests and grades, each of which can be seen instantiated into features of VLEs. Practices also include the educational and scholarly conventions around methods, writing conventions, statistics, etc. As Crook (2002: 164) states, '[F]ormal learning must involve engagement with disciplinary material, but that engagement is structured by the formats and rituals of the institutional experience: expositions, texts, annotations, discourse genres, roles, social relations, and so on'. Sociotechnical constructs for instructional delivery, assessment and academic production all form part of the scholarly ecology, each potentially disruptable by new online and e-based practices.

Emergent technology combinations are appearing more frequently, both deliberately in programming 'mash-ups', and more spontaneously as people adopt multiple forms of online and offline communication and information technologies to achieve their desired outcomes (Haythornthwaite, 2005a). Girard and Stark (2007) refer to this combination of means of communication as forming *digital ecologies*. In following community memorialization efforts in New York city after 9/11, Girard and Stark (2007) found a transformation of formerly face-to-face public assemblies to *sociotechnical assemblies*:

> [M]any public assemblies involve a mix of physical and virtual forms. From a face-to-face meeting, announced by photocopied posters affixed to the bulletin boards of local schools, groceries, and beauty shops, someone produces minutes that are disseminated by email and posted on a website with links later pointing to it from another site. Assemblies are recombinant technologies of masking tape and digital servers. Accordingly, in place of studying new digital technologies per se, or engaging in yet another comparison of online and offline forms ... we attend to *digital ecologies*. (Girard and Stark, 2007: 150–1)

In keeping with Latour, Girard and Stark incorporate 'not only people but also cultural and material artifacts into our network analysis' (2007: 152).

> Doing so expands and enriches our conception of 'the social.' Cognition is socially distributed across persons and tools. As Roy Pea (1993) writes in a study of distributed intelligence in the field of education ...: '[M]ind rarely works alone. The intelligence revealed through these practices [is] distributed – across minds, persons, and the symbolic and physical environments, both natural and artificial' (47). (Girard and Stark, 2007: 152)

Such digital ecologies also play out at the personal level. Studies by Haythornthwaite and Wellman (1998), and Haythornthwaite (2001, 2002a) found that strongly tied pairs use more media to communicate with each other than weakly tied pairs (referred to as *media multiplexity*). Moreover, the way media were added to a pair's repertoire followed a common pattern within groups. In the e-learning classes examined (e.g. Haythornthwaite, 2002a), this meant that the medium chosen by the instructor as the main communication channel for the class (e.g. bulletin boards, chat) became the only medium through which weakly tied pairs communicated, and the only way in which they could get to know each other. This finding shows that the technological choices instructors or program administrators make about media use can have a profound effect on who gets to know whom in an e-learning class. In effect, the instructor is creating the (cyber-)building in which people will meet, and hence this decision is an important one for class interaction (for more on this, see Haythornthwaite, 2002b, 2005a; see also Chapter 7).

Before leaving the discussion of technologies, one final aspect should also be noted: the invisibility of technology infrastructures (Star, 1999; Star and Bowker, 2002). Buildings, routine practices, laboratories, libraries, and technological infrastructures of electricity, computers, broadband and wireless connectivity are often so taken for granted that their roles in the ecology are overlooked. They become obvious again in e-learning when distributed students do not have access to the same campus-based resources as other students, from books to health services, and high-end computers to broadband connection (see also Chapter 10 on issues relating to the digital divide and e-inclusion). Moreover, what is truly invisible are the technologies that institutions *might* have, such as the latest in telecommunications, graphics capabilities, virtual worlds, immersive technologies, or haptic technologies. These future grounds for e-learning sit at the periphery of current practice, but need to be on the radar as potential new practices. Monitoring the outside environment for potential innovations increases the 'absorptive capacity' of organizations and institutions (Cohen and Levinthal, 1990), helping them to compete in their niche by evaluating and adopting appropriate new technologies as they appear.

Personal Ecologies

So far we have looked at ecologies from an overall perspective. Often this view fails to resonate with the on-the-ground experiences of teachers and students. To get a better feel for the reality of daily experience in e-learning, we can look at ecologies from a personal perspective. Taking a personal view provides an understanding of the load that an individual has in their online class or in their daily and e-learning life and gives a better understanding of likely personal motivations, initiatives and responses to e-learning demands. For example, studies of personal networks across four online classes (14–23 members; Haythornthwaite, 2000) showed that students maintained an average of three strong ties with others with whom they communicated daily, three intermediate strength ties with whom they communicated two to three times weekly, and four weak to intermediate strength ties with whom they communicated weekly. Beyond that, students were just 'other members of the class' communicated with on an infrequent basis if at all outside synchronous class time. Although these classes were relatively small, it gives an idea of the communication load with classmates. Add to this the load of communication in other spheres and we can see how much of an individual's time and attention is given to the class within the e-learning program, and the program within their daily life. Building up those layers provides a good view of student load. Similar profiles could be built regarding teachers' e-learning lives to gauge the impact of learning to operate in the online environment. In both student and teacher cases, communication load has a direct impact on the economics of attention (Goldhaber, 1997; see this volume, Chapter 9) that operates in the learning process.

Individuals in the Information Age
A personal view accords with a number of depictions of the individual in the information age that suggest a reconfiguration of social relations around online activity, with new technologies changing social interaction through new meeting places and communication spaces (online communities; Twitter), meanings of association (e.g. in the meaning associated with a 'friend' tie on a social network site; boyd and Ellison, 2007), and the relational basis of ties (e.g. in more diverse, but single threaded associations in multiple online worlds). Castells (2001: 128) argues that 'a new system of social relationships centered on the individual' is emerging, in which the individual creates his or her own individualized communities in a society which emphasizes the individual.

Wellman (2001) has described this as *networked individualism*, with the individual in charge of their personal universe of contacts spread across different contexts and roles (see also Wellman et al., 2003). Such personal communities can spread around the globe, leading to dual attention to both the global and local community, a phenomenon that Hampton and Wellman have termed *glocalization* (Hampton, 2001, 2010; Hampton and Wellman, 2003; Wellman, 2002).

Although individual distributed networks have existed for a long time, supported through letters and phone calls, and travel by car and plane (Wellman, 1979, 1999), the Internet in particular has been cited as supporting (and creating) such individualized sociability (Castells, 2001; Wellman, 2002; Wellman et al., 1996, 2003). Reports are divided over whether the consequences are positive or negative for individuals and their local contacts. Some describe the Internet as taking people away from local, interpersonal, and face-to-face interaction and as having negative effects on individuals' well-being (e.g. Kraut et al., 1998; Nie, 2001, but see also Kraut et al., 2002). By contrast, others praise the connectivity the Internet affords, and describe how this increases individual well-being (e.g. LaRose et al., 2001). (For a review of these two positions, see Haythornthwaite and Wellman, 2002.) In general, current thinking supports a view that online complements and extends offline, with new balances being found between uses of these two interaction platforms (Haythornthwaite and Kendall, 2010).

E-learning and Personal Worlds

Although the research referred to above does not address e-learning *per se*, the implications are that e-learners sit at the center of their universe, rotating and participating in multiple social worlds. Unlike on-campus learners who come to class and interact as directed by the instructor, e-learners may be quite different, coming on and off line at times and places of their own choosing, and participating according to different motivations than traditional students. However, a view of e-learner-centered control needs to be balanced with the likely realities of other calls on an e-learner's attention. The e-learner may not be at the control center of their own universe, but is just as likely at the beck and call of many ecologies (home, work and school) and people (spouses, children, employers, teachers), each with their own demands on time, energy and engagement. Support or opposition from these competing ecologies determine to a large extent whether the student finds the online program manageable (Kazmer and Haythornthwaite, 2001). (See also Chapter 9 in the section on the learner and the economics of attention, p 176.)

Kramarae (2001) describes e-learning as the third shift in the day on top of work and home. Kazmer and Haythornthwaite (2001) describe it slightly differently, referring to juggling multiple *social worlds* (Clarke, 1991; Strauss, 1978) that include work, home and school, but also voluntary and leisure worlds.

While Kramarae's image implies a separation across the day for each world, the social worlds idea captures the way these worlds intertwine. E-learners rotate attention between these worlds, particularly when they interweave online time for school with at work or at home activities. As online activity increasingly mingles with daily activity, we continue to juggle these social worlds, for example as email, Twitter and blog feeds bring news from different worlds and move our attention through multiple social worlds.

While the e-learner may not be independent of local demands, they may, however, exercise more control in the learning context. The more that individuals become used to being in command of their own cyberlife, the more they may want to pick and choose what, when, and from whom they learn. They may create for themselves a personal 'ecology of resources' (Luckin, 2008) that connects people and objects in support of a particular learning context. This may be akin to a personal activity system within which they gather resources to create a framework for continual personal interpretation of an object of study. Many personal websites appear to fulfill this kind of user-centered role, with reference lists, blogs and commentaries, and links to other sites and others with attention to the same object. This may increase participation and self-directed learning, but may also have the impact of leading learners away from institution-based programs. The many learning opportunities rapidly appearing on the Internet may provide just the venue for a society of e-learners (Senges et al., 2008). We continue this discussion in Chapter 9 on ubiquitous learning.

Conclusion

This chapter has outlined the ecology metaphor, suggesting ways this can be applied to e-learning contexts as a way to view overall e-learning environments. Ecological concepts such as key species, niches and localities, plus the added dimension of technology, allow exploration of how individuals and e-learning enterprises compete for space and resources in collective and personal interactions. Ecological views, as well as ideas from activity theory, actor-network theory, and the social construction of technology and practice, focus attention on the cyclical and emergent nature of human activity, including e-learning (see also Chapter 2). As a new niche in the education environment, e-learning entities – programs, teachers, learners, stakeholders – are experiencing, in Engeström's terms, expansive learning and an expansive transformation of collective and individual understanding. The ecology of e-learning is being formed as we write this book, and is driven and expanded by each new use and trend in learning and knowledge creation, dissemination and retrieval. E-learning is currently a rapidly expanding concept and field that we can expect to keep on growing and shifting over the coming years as we continue to move forward with developing the ecology of the Internet and Internet-based learning.

Further Reading 📖

Brown, J. S. and Duguid, P. (2000). *The Social Life of Information.* Boston, MA: Harvard University Press.

Luckin, R. (2010). *Re-designing Learning Contexts: Technology-rich, Learner-centred Ecologies.* Abingdon, UK: Routledge.

Nardi, B. and O'Day, V. (1999). *Information Ecologies: Using Technology with Heart.* Cambridge, MA: MIT Press.

Ubiquitous Learning, Ubiquitous Learners

Introduction

The idea of *ubiquitous learning* (Cope and Kalantzis, 2009) takes it cue from *ubiquitous computing* (often called 'ubicomp'), a computing presence that is continuously available and synchronized with daily life, and more noted by its absence that its presence (Weiser, 1991). The ubiquity of the computing platform marks a stage of routinization of innovation when presence and use in everyday life is taken for granted. Yet all is not static. Ubicomp is still enlarging its domain, with computing colonizing new arenas of life. Emerging uses include the ubiquitous communication channels of social media, and the pervasive image capture through webcams, digital cameras, cell phones and closed circuit television. Ubiquity also pertains to ideas of 'lifelogging', that is, the chronicling of daily life through wearable computing and digitization (e.g. MyLifeInBits: Gemmell et al., 2006; see also Bell and Gemmell, 2007), although less sophisticated devices such as digital cameras, Facebook postings and microblog 'tweets' also provide a chronicle of daily action and thought. New analysis techniques facilitate the further use of the ubiquitous computer traces we leave on a daily basis, for example for facial recognition, and data mining that analyzes consumer behavior and trends in online conversation. Print resources are rapidly being digitized and thus becoming ubiquitously available, for example the Google Books Project, and the British Library newspaper digitization project (King, 2005). We talk of wired and cyber-cities (Graham, 2004) that provide ubiquitous network infrastructures for connecting to the web, and remote computing that provides awareness of activities at distant and distributed locations or in places we cannot physically reach (Hinds and Kiesler, 2002).

These computing infrastructures and applications provide an increasing wealth of automated features, communication opportunities, and knowledge and learning possibilities (as in Case 9.1). Ubiquitous computing infrastructures are embedded and invisible. Use is achieved seamlessly and feels natural, and we only 'see' the infrastructure when it fails (also in Case 9.1). Such failures point out where infrastructures are as yet incomplete, and provide awareness of our dependence and synergy with these invisible, yet ubiquitous structures (Star, 2002; Star and Bowker, 2002).

CASE 9.1: UBIQUITOUS COMPUTING

Caroline Haythornthwaite, University of Illinois at Urbana Champaign, USA

As I write this chapter on ubiquitous learning I am in an airport (3 June 2010) waiting on a delayed plane. I have complimentary access to the web using the free facilities at my local airport. My portable laptop contains software for text editing and storing files, and my personal files necessary to work on this chapter. It seems perfectly natural to have all these electronic capabilities at hand. I also have my cell phone listed with the airlines for notification of the updates on the (inevitable) further delays. I am even beginning to be aware of the frequent fliers among my fellow travelers as their cell phones ring about the same time as mine. I am connected at every turn and can gain information on flights via the web, even re-book online.

Of course, such ease of access is not available everywhere and when it is not available we notice it is missing. At a recent conference in Denmark, quite a few of us turned up with the wrong electrical plugs for Europe, and were unable to power our laptops. At this and other conferences, we have found that the typical hotel computing infrastructure is designed to support casual hotel-wide use or to support the official speakers only. The systems are quickly overwhelmed and fail when a conference of networked learners arrive and audience members want connection during presentations to blog and tweet about what they are hearing.

At the time of this case, **Caroline Haythornthwaite** was Professor, Graduate School of Library and Information Science, University of Illinois at Urbana-Champaign, and Leverhulme Trust Visiting Professor at the Institute of Education, University of London.

It is through the (near) ubiquitous computing infrastructures that we arrive at ubiquitous learning: retrieving, evaluating and/or contributing data, instructions, information and knowledge in concert with crowds or communities of similarly interested participants. Ubiquitous learning is possible because of the many forms of computing that pervade daily life. Of particular relevance are the applications that support the production, location and consumption of knowledge such as programs that support easy website creation, content contribution (e.g. blogging), collaborative production (e.g. wikis), online conversation (social media), and information retrieval (search engines). The combined technical infrastructure of the Internet (as the hardware and telecommunications) and the web (as the interlinked set of file sharing protocols), and the software and file management applications (such as blogging applications that simplify website design and posting to the web) have put computing power in the hands of individual users and made engaging with these sites so simple even a child can do it (although sometimes *only* a child can do it).

While Internet access on its own is insufficient to say that learning is happening, it opens up the possibility of learning anywhere, anytime. As practices of learning online become part of everyday life as well as contemporary education, learning leaves the classroom. Consideration of ubiquitous learning grapples with the emerging reality of *learning anywhere*: in classrooms, online spaces, at work, on the road, in the coffee shop, at home. Sometimes the ad hoc, ubiquitous learning is in a recognized learning space such as a classroom, library, workshop or conference; at other times it is a makeshift learning space, for example squeezed into bedroom spaces, at kitchen tables, in hotel rooms. Or, as in the example given in Chapter 4 of people searching the web using a mobile phone while traveling on a train, the learning space may be both literally and technologically mobile. The result is that learning is not just anywhere, but also *anytime*: morning, noon or night; separate from other activities or in conjunction and/or conflict with other activities, for example work, home, vacation.

When IT is adopted in keeping with the intention of the designer, it is considered a *faithful appropriation*, which contrasts with an *ironic appropriation* (Poole and DeSanctis, 1990). Similarly, we can refer to faithful appropriations of ubiquitous learning, such as surfing the web for information for class while in class, or ironic appropriations, such surfing the web for personal reasons while in class. Going one step further, we can see that with ubiquitous learning it is not just the class setting that is affected. Appropriation can be ironic when learning for work or school happens while at home. Crossing boundaries is made easier with new technologies. While the expansion of support for learning onto mobile platforms makes it easier to learn anywhere, anytime, it equally increases the places and times when, appropriately or not, individuals will learn. (For more on mobility, mobile technologies and learning, that is, *m-learning*, see Pachler, 2007; Pachler et al., 2009; Sharples et al., 2007; Vavoula et al., 2009.)

Becoming a Ubiquitous E-learner

With the idea of ubiquity comes a general expectation of availability, seamless integration, and a perception of the ubiquitous activity as normal and natural. This is the future of ubiquitous learning. But, for each new learner, early experiences are hardly natural and seamless; they are instead quite awkward, anxiety producing, and in Bayne's (2008, 2010) terminology, 'uncanny': '[T]he familiar being rendered unfamiliar, a blurring of the boundary between the animate and the inanimate, the living and the dead, the embodied and the disembodied, the present and the past or absent' (Bayne, 2010: 5). Bayne (2008) writes that the uncanny is perhaps more disturbing than the totally new. Old ways of learning hover as ghosts, and perceptions of the self are unbalanced by the doppelganger of one's own typed text, recorded voice, or avatar.

As Bayne describes, for learning, perhaps the most relevant aspect of uncanniness is that it creates intellectual uncertainty, particularly as it blurs the boundary between fantasy and reality. In e-learning, as in discussions of computer-mediated communication in general, the blurring of this boundary gives rise to many warnings about online life: online will be the realm of play and chat rather than serious work; it will create addictions to fantasy worlds, lead youth to distorted views of friendship relationships and take people away from 'real life'. Indeed, many of the additions to CMC practices can be seen as ways to re-root online (fantasy) life into a real-life context: adding signatures to email to signify real life roles; adding security features to ensure the identity of online participants; and establishing firewalls to prevent exposure to extra-organizational contact and content.

Yet it is through play, disruption, and intellectual uncertainty that we move forward in our learning:

> [R]ecent thinking in higher education teaching … stresses the place of the troublesome, the anxiety-inducing, the strange and the liminal (Bayne 2008). Meyer and Land (2005) describe the notion of the 'threshold concept', a grappling with 'troublesome' areas of the curriculum (Perkins 1999, 2005) which prompts a 'transformation' in the student, a 'reconstruction of subjectivity' (Meyer and Land 2005, 7). (Bayne, 2010: 6)

The uncanny thus appears to be our stock in trade for learning, and doubly so for e-learning where both the knowledge and the setting take on troublesome forms: 'in working online as teachers and learners, we are working in 'destabilized' classrooms, engaging in spaces and practices which are disquieting, disorienting, strange, anxiety-inducing, uncanny' (Bayne, 2010: 6). Uncanniness also extends well beyond the classroom setting. Unsettling aspects of e-learning are exhibited in the openness of the web, where we learn on our own, unguided by a teaching authority. Learning how to be a 'canny' self-guided e-learner entails becoming comfortable with the nuances of this new learning platform.

The following sections continue the exploration of what it means to become an e-learner. Attention is given to learning in and for courses, but also to the individual as an independent web-based, ubiquitous e-learner. While e-learning inside and outside formal educational settings can be approached separately, it is our view that they rapidly become variants along a single scale. Hence, in discussing ubiquitous learning, we approach e-learning as encompassing learning on and through the web for personal, educational and/or communal purposes, and including the concomitant learning that entails becoming a fluent collaborative, entrepreneurial and engaged e-learner.

The remainder of the chapter discusses what it means to be a ubiquitous, personal or educational online learner. Sections are loosely organized around the *who, what, where* and *when* of becoming and being ubiquitous learners and e-learners. The discussion begins by addressing *who* falls into the category of ubiquitous learner, and then engages with the range of knowledge such learners acquire on the way to being fluent ubiquitous e-learners.

Who Is a Ubiquitous E-learner?

In addressing ubiquitous learning, the image is of a *willing learner*, motivated to acquire knowledge in pursuit of personal and/or formal educational interests. The e-learner is a *purposive information gatherer*, highly, or even overly, goal-oriented, with the maturity to sustain an enduring interest in the problem being addressed. He or she also *transforms* what is found and uses it to change the pattern of knowledge and understanding with which he/she started the search. The assumption is that this is an adult learner, with attendant maturity in behavior, attitudes, interpersonal relationships and work habits. However, where younger learners follow the pattern of willing learning and purposive engagement, the view of them also as e-learners will pertain. Moreover, the habits of younger learners, particularly in digital learning, are habits that are rapidly entering the adult population and/or being adopted simultaneously across all ages. Hence these worlds are not that far apart, and need not be rigorously distinguished by age. (For more on children and young adults and their learning and Internet use, see Ito et al., 2009; Livingstone, 2010.)

In keeping with what has been discussed in earlier chapters, the (imagined) e-learners we find online in group forums or formal educational settings are *collaborative learners*, working with peers to explore new areas of knowledge, guided by the expertise of facilitators and/or other learners, and in turn offering what guidance or input they can from their own knowledge, experience or information gathering. They are engaged in the collaborative process as much as in the learning process, motivated by personal need or co-orientation to an area of interest or problem to be solved. They are like open source contributors in being motivated by a 'personal but shared need' (Raymond, 1998, 1999), whether that is to create free software, make freely available all texts on a subject, or mobilize a social movement.

Considering e-learners as following the style of adult learners encourages a shift away from pedagogies predicated on a teacher and a student to those better suited to adults and to collaborative processes. Andragogy – adult pedagogy – portrays the learner as independent and self-directed, internally rather than externally motivated, with learning tied to personal experience, intended to be applied to current problem-centered needs. Since its introduction by Knowles (1968), there has been a recognition that this kind of problem-centered, independent learner can be of any age, and that many adults at certain stages of their learning still do better with a teacher-centered pedagogy (for a review, see Merriam, 2001).

To some extent, andragogy, as a pedagogical approach rather than a theory on how adults learn, can be a useful approach to apply to the practice of teaching. However, the attention to 'problems to be solved' may not be sufficient to address the process of learning for pleasure, whether through educational institutions or social groups. Lifelong learners, hobby learners, game players, and particularly young learners, seek and become proficient in areas seemingly unrelated to education and serious learning (e.g. learning about health or safety issues), yet vital to their growth as individuals and to their personal identities. Although it is beyond the scope of this current work to explore this in detail, it appears that much of what the Internet has done is make these many kinds of learning more visible, thereby increasing the range of what is learned, why, and with whom on the platform of the Internet. As we continue to discuss ubiquitous learning, this wider realm of human growth and learning is always present (for more, see Cope and Kalantzis, 2009; Ito et al., 2009).

Highly relevant in the digital age is the way adults form information collections that support their learning. While individuals have long been creating libraries of physical texts around professional or personal interests, the resources of the web extend the variety of forms that go into such collections (electronic journal articles, blogs, online news, email messages), as well as the rapidity of additions. While some will organize these resources in formal digital library configurations, others manage through an array of applications (word processing, photo management), locations (desktop, laptop, mobile, flash drive, institutional subscriptions to online content, centralized depositories for interpersonal file sharing), and location references (e.g. URL bookmarks). On an individual, group and even institutional and societal level, the configuration of such collections each forms an ecology of resources. The ubiquitous learner, when operating as the independent, self-directed learner described in the andragogy image, creates a *learner-generated context* (Luckin, 2008; Luckin et al., 2007).

As we consider ubiquitous learning, the image of the web-surfer actively mining the web for information to address an immediate need sounds like the andragogic, self-directed learner. But when production is added, and particularly production in the presence of and in concert with others, e-learning begins to look more like learning by experts as they co-create new knowledge (Bransford et al., 1999; Scardamalia and Bereiter, 1996). As productive co-learners, they negotiate through the equivocal information environment, defining their joint learning focus, purpose of inquiry, method of research and production, and shared identity around their knowledge problem.

However, when co-learners operate as online, distributed, e-learners, it is not just knowledge that they co-create. E-learners also engage in co-construction of the meaning and configuration of the use of these technologies. E-learners have in common with all users of technologies that they are constantly engaged in processes of adaptive structuration, mutual negotiation and reciprocal evolution – with each other and with the technologies – around ways of working, socializing and learning (Andrews and Haythornthwaite, 2007b; DeSanctis and Poole, 1994; Haythornthwaite et al., 2006). In concert with the particular setting, emergent configurations of technologies-in-use appear, complete with individual and group understandings of the meaning of use of particular ICTs for particular purposes within the local activity system (Engeström, 2009). The end result may be strict rules of media use, or a wide-ranging free-for-all use of multiple platforms, or resistance and discontinuance of the use of particular platforms (Rogers, 1995). But again, all is not static. The activity system is always and continuously in negotiation. In e-learning settings in particular such evolution of practice is quite visible, coming in waves with the arrival of each new online interaction option (discussion boards to VLEs to social media to Second Life), and because of the disciplinary effort to understand how to use technologies for teaching and learning.

Our first observation about becoming an e-learner and ubiquitous learner is that personal motivation drives the learner forward. Adult, self-motivated learners seek out information and connections proactively, acting as entrepreneurs in their own learning enterprise (Senges et al., 2008). In this way, they become more than students waiting on the wisdom of teachers, but instead whole people with interests, experiences, and skills who engage in local and cyberlocal communities. They are motivated enough to seek people and information to answer immediate questions, and to sustain inquiry in a way that enhances their knowledge and understanding. This may seem utopic, but this is precisely what the ubiquitous learner does. They search the web for facts to answer questions, read news online to follow community activity, and join online groups and communities to engage with others on topics of interest. We may construe the role of e-learning education to be not only to provide a technical and intellectual scaffolding for a new learner to gain command of course content, but also to build the confidence and literacy that allows an on-course e-learner to become a sophisticated ubiquitous learner.

What Does a Ubiquitous Learner Learn?

Ubiquitous learners come with many different kinds of motives for learning. The learning addressed here may include information seeking, online engagement and learning for:

- academic certification, for example while enrolled in institutions of higher education, training colleges, or other schools
- work, whether by apprenticeships, acculturation or formal training
- home, including information on health or child care (e.g. Leimeister et al., 2008; Mallen et al., 2005; Miyata, 2002; Rice and Katz, 2001; Smedberg, 2008)
- leisure, including recreational browsing, but also *serious leisure* (Fulton and Vondracek, 2009; Stebbins, 2006, 2009), and *lifelong learning* (Jones and Symon, 2001) which can include *learning for its own sake.*

As well as the subject to be learned, being ubiquitous learners also entails two major issues. One major issue is learning how to grapple with finding, managing and selecting information among the increasing number and types of publications found online, from peer reviewed academic studies to opinion pieces and personal stories, plus access to sources not openly available online, such as many academic journals. This is a problem shared in all educational contexts whether online or off (see Chapter 12 for discussion of information literacy).

The second issue is that collaborative, participatory, community-oriented e-learning requires learning about co-constructing engagement with others through technology. This includes learning about online group and communal norms, the history and practices of groups, workplaces, disciplines, institutions and organizations, and technologies and their collective use. Learning around this cluster of norms, practices and technologies has yet to receive adequate attention in the e-learning field, and yet it pervades the literature addressing what makes groups successful (or not) at working online, at a distance, and in a collaborative manner (Haythornthwaite, 2006a; Orlikowski, 2002). For example, studies have examined the development of practices related to distributed teams in globalized companies (Orlikowski, 2002) and computer-supported collaborations (Haythornthwaite et al., 2006; see also the papers in Haythornthwaite, 2005b). The work involves learning to combine new work practices with new technology use, building what Resnick (2002) has called *sociotechnical capital* (an analog to social capital). This kind of capital is created and sustained in a group's ability to function, manage and prosper through information and communication technologies (ICTs) (for a paper using this concept in e-learning, see Kazmer, 2006).

The process involved is one of *learning 'to be' an e-learner*, a ubiquitous learner, a member of a distributed, collaborative group, or online learning community, that is, to become a member of the socio-cultural practice associated with this new community (Brown and Duguid, 2001; Wenger, 1998). The end result is that participants come to a sense of self as an accomplished, literate, natural, online learner. They have mastered the technical requirements, experienced the pros and cons of online conversation, learned with others, created joint products with others, and found and used online resources. They have been received by others as belonging to the class of actors who are e-learners, and are treated as a member of that class. They have acquired sufficient fluency in a suite of sociotechnical, literate practices that they can now confidently apply these across multiple contexts and multiple media.

In examining how an individual comes *to be* a member of their group and acquires an identity in keeping with the group, we follow seminal works in sociology about the enculturation of individuals into marginal and mainstream cultures. These include 'Becoming a marijuana smoker' (Becker, 1953), and *Boys in White: Student Culture in Medical School* (Becker et al., 1961). From education, we follow work that has described the way the constraints of the physical class-room and school inculcate specific norms of social behavior as well as norms about how learning is done (e.g. see chapters by Lankshear, Peters and Knobel; Crook; and Cornford and Pollock in Lea and Nicoll, 2002). Similar work can also be found in the area of the social studies of science, notably Latour's *Science in Action* (1987), and Knorr-Cetina's *Epistemic Cultures* (1999).

Learning *To Be* in a Sociotechnical Landscape

What are the literate and learning practices that ubiquitous learners have to acquire? What do we have to learn to be distributed groups, collaborative learners and participatory citizens?

Emergent Practices

One of the more difficult aspects of new learning environments has been the newness of practices for online teaching or learning. These have emerged by planning and experimentation over the 15 or so years of e-learning. This has meant that participants – teachers and learners – have engaged in a mutual process of negotiation around the form of online learning. Even as these for-mal practices are solidifying – particularly in the emerging standardized design of VLEs – new resources, applications, and social media continue to push the need for negotiation around use in online learning contexts.

The *procedural knowledge* around e-learning, that is, knowing how to go about a task (in contrast with *declarative knowledge*, knowing that something is true or false) remains in a state of flux. It is again the *perpetual beta* state discussed in Chapter 5. What this means for an e-learner or ubiquitous learner is that one of the skills they accrue entails learning to operate under conditions of change.

A useful way to approach this is to consider Perrow's (1970) distinction between problems of *uncertainty* and those of *equivocality*. He outlined these in the context of dimensions of information processing and knowledge in relation to the kind of inputs coming into the decision-making process. *Uncertainty* is a condition where the rules to make decisions are known, even if complex (e.g. in engineering) and the decision-making task is one of acquiring information to solve the problem. With *equivocality*, the rules are not known, and even the question of what information will support the decision is not known. The task then becomes one of determining the question – often through negotiation with others – in order to agree on what information to consider for action and decision making (e.g. in research and development).

If we apply this idea to *educational practice*, we can see that for the traditional *face-to-face classroom*, with its set time for meeting together, no disturbance from outside, fixed library resources, and well established assessment methods (exams, essays), there is *little equivocality* in what is expected of teachers and students. Enter now the *online* realm, with no set time to meet, discussions that run without teacher supervision, students learning from students, resources sourced from any location (from library to news to blogs to Twitter). There is *equivocality* in how to run, assess and engage with *learning in the service of formal education*, and equivocality in the assessment of the authority of sources. As discussed in Chapter 5, information literacy is an ever-increasingly important form of knowledge for contemporary e-learners precisely because of the equivocality involved in judging sources.

Situated Practices

Addressing the learning environment, and the way we learn to function within the norms and practices of the group, takes us out of the area of learning as an individual cognitive process to address communal processes. The theoretical perspectives informing this include those on apprenticeship (including cognitive apprenticeship, Collins, 2006) and communities of practice (Barton and Tusting, 2005; Lave and Wenger, 1991; Wenger, 1998), distributed cognition, activity systems and expansive learning (e.g. Engeström, 2009; Engeström and Middleton, 1996), and situated cognition (Brown et al., 1989); for a review in the context of e-learning, see Mayes and de Freitas (2006). Individuals in these contexts negotiate their identity in relation to, and sometimes in resistance to, the community and context in which they find themselves. In learning communities, identity formation can pertain to various aspects of alignment with the community. For example, in a study by Hughes (2010), identity formation in a learning context involved negotiation around social (relationships within the group), operational (group practice) and knowledge (what is studied and how) aspects of the learning group. These common ideas of behavior being constructed in conjunction with many aspects of local conditions are brought together by Greeno (2006) as representing a *situative perspective*:

> The defining characteristic of a situative approach is that instead of focusing on individual learners, the main focus of analysis is on *activity systems*: complex social organizations containing learners, teachers, curriculum materials, software tools, and the physical environment. (Greeno, 2006: 79)

A few examples show the way situated practices play out in learning communities. These examples highlight three aspects of online learning communities: the attention to group processes; the development of roles and levels of expertise within the group; and application to outside locations. The latter is a surprising, and hugely pleasing result – that the supposed isolation and seclusion of online interaction can actually spill out into geo-local settings. (As well as in the references noted below, these accounts are also collected in Haythornthwaite et al., 2007).

The first example is Mirandanet, an online community promoting the use of technology in education. Preston's evaluation of the community (Preston, 2008) emphasizes the way practices around 'braided texts' define the community (see Box 9.1 for a comment on the repeated use of fabric-related metaphors). Preston identifies three stages that teaching professionals in Mirandanet (http://www.mirandanet.ac.uk/) adopt and practice in their professional, online learning. In the first stage, members create a braided text online that supports diversity and a range of opinions. At this stage roles evolve as some members spontaneously emerge as *e-facilitators* who help to shape the argument, provide interim summaries and influence the direction of the discussion. *Braiders* appear who re-interpret the online debate in different styles for different audiences, for example creating newsletters for their local communities and reports for their local school senior management. *Accomplished fellows* take the initiative to set up working parties to explore a subject in more depth. At this point the participants become active professionals, using collaborative knowledge to build new theories and policies that will impact their profession in the longer term.

BOX 9.1: THREADS AND PATCHES

As an aside, it is interesting to note how many times ideas of fabrication come into play in describing e-learning. It is common to talk of online discussions in terms of the *threads* of conversations, and, of course, of *weaving the web* (Berners-Lee, 1999). In this book we have referred to 21st-century discourses as part of the *fabric* of learning, and the internalization and then externalization of signs as both *weaving* and creating the *fabric* that is the learning community.

Some *braid*. Jenkins (2004) describes the blending of chat and audio lecture as *braided conversations* that emerge from the combination of the visible chat contributions by students and instructor, and the audio channel available to the instructor. Preston (2008) describes *braiders* whose role in an e-community is in re-interpreting the online debate for different audiences.

Others work with the cloth. Writing instructors grapple with whether *patchwriting* is a legitimate first form of understanding and production or a form of plagiarism (Howard, 2009). Ryberg (2007) appeals to *patchworking* as a metaphor of adaptive learning, which supports 'processes of continuously assembling and reorganising multiple patches and pieces into provisional patchworks, which are then made into a "final", new patchwork' (Ryberg and Dirckinck-Holmfeld, 2008: 145). For Ryberg, it is the patchwork process that

(Continued)

(Continued)

matters as the site of learning. In keeping with efforts to understand learning in productive, participatory, ubiquitous settings, these ideas of how the integrative process is used to transform understanding seem highly relevant to the ideas of e-learning presented in this book.

Another example comes from an online degree program. Montague (2006) identifies how students take on the role of *learner-leaders*. These active participants engage in an emergent and iterative process of leading and learning by sharing information, experiences and opinions. They bring experiences to the learning community but also take their online learning and apply it in their embedding community. Montague's learner-leader model emphasizes the leadership role in such contexts, both inside the learning community and outside as students lead new directions in their local communities as a result of their learning experiences. Students take their learning and enthusiasm and let it 'rub off on others' and 'light a fire' outside the online environment. Students exhibit the kind of confidence and transference one hopes to be the result of learning in any context, and the simultaneous embedding in the online *and* geo-local community makes it possible to apply the learning immediately rather than waiting for graduation.

A third example further articulates the way the knowledge and experience of online learners provides synergistic connection with their local community. Kazmer (2007a) suggests *community-embedded learning* as both an effect of distributed learning, and as a model for online learning. Her research showed five major types of knowledge transfer occurring around e-learning: from community to the classmates and the online learning community; from the course to the learner's workplace; from the course to the learner's home community; from one community to another; and from one institution of higher learning to another through e-learning contacts.

Knowledge Structures

These examples also illustrate the kind of learning that goes on in groups that is seemingly unrelated to the content of the learning. Implicit in work team, group, or community engagement is learning about the knowledge structures in these social networks. This includes learning about roles, positions and relationships (what niches can be filled, how these place people in the network, and how people interact who occupy these relative positions), who knows who within the network (cognitive social structure), who knows what (transactive memory; Hollingshead, et al., 2002; Moreland, 1999; Wegner, 1987), and who knows who knows what (Monge and Contractor, 2003). The presence of and adherence to structural relations reduces the overhead of managing in-group settings and increases trust in interpersonal contracts (Burt, 2000). When procedures are known, the problem of what to do becomes one of uncertainty, solvable by application of rules. As noted, this is often not the case in newly formed and emergent online learning groups. Negotiation around what to learn, how to learn it and how to communicate can often overwhelm individuals and the group effort. We might consider existing procedures to be part of the social capital of mature groups, a goal to achieve for consistent action.

Learning *To Be* a Distributed Group

While the thrust of attention to learning settings is around the acquisition of knowledge relating to a particular domain or community of practice, technology-mediated groups face a corollary learning challenge – that of *learning to be a distributed group*. One of the key aspects of learning to be a distributed group is that it has been (and perhaps always will be) marked by equivocality. What is the best way to organize distributed work? How do we, and indeed, should we, cede control from central authorities to distributed participants? How should an array of technologies be used to support the local setting and learning community?

We can approach this challenge as another knowledge problem. In keeping with the idea of ubiquitous learners as willing, purposive learners, acting like experts in breaking new ground, the adoption of an ICT-based, distributed interaction platform can be seen as no different than learning at the edge of established knowledge. *What ICTs have created*, because of their newness and the ability to break established rules, *is a set of learning conditions that match those of experts working jointly to create new knowledge*. What we see in the turning point from face-to-face to online (and also from online back to face-to-face in blended learning) is a widely, mutually negotiated, and emergent definition of what it means *to be* an online group, learning community, and online learner. Definitions of the types of tools to be used emerge just as do definitions of the questions to be asked for exploring knowledge. Group use of tools is tried and revised in a process Poole and DeSanctis (1990) refer to as *adaptive structuration*.

Management theory refers to instances of 'unfreezing' of practices while they are revisited and revised, usually in response to changes in the market or business environment (e.g. in developments in science, laws, technologies). Once revamped, the systems *refreeze* (establishing again decision-making conditions based on uncertainty rather than equivocality). However, in keeping with what has been discussed above, the current expansion of technology, knowledge and group practices sets up conditions for a long continuation of an 'unfrozen' and amenable state. Refreezing is then a poor or unsustainable option, and knowledge and practices need to or just do remain in a state of *perpetual beta* (see Chapter 5). One such condition is the current changing landscape of knowledge and technology. Another is changes in attention to cross-cultural matters. For example, Haythornthwaite, Lunsford, Kazmer, Robins and Nazarova (2003) studied a group that was building a repository of culturally appropriate materials for children. The group came to a way of *keeping their particular knowledge problem open* by creating guidelines for evaluating each new piece within a thoughtful context of appropriateness, rather than determining rules on what constituted appropriateness. This group learned to manage appropriateness as a continuously open problem, rather than one that was amenable to freezing. (For more on cross-cultural issues and e-learning, see Chapter 11.)

Freezing and unfreezing also happen in knowledge, as tacit knowledge becomes explicit and is instantiated into rules and practices. And, it happens to technology as current ideas of how things work are instantiated into machines, equipment and computer applications. From Latour (1987), we learn that technologies limit the kinds of questions asked, that is, the questions have to fit the investment in technological infrastructures; and from Weick (1990) that decision-making algorithms embedded in computer programs are rarely reviewed. But, as discussed in Chapter 7, from Dewey (Hickman, 1992) we learn that even seemingly fixed items such as technologies are themselves only theories to be tested and thus are amenable to evaluation in practice and modification. Until the appearance of online learning, the technology of the classroom had been a 'resourceful constraint' (Cornford and Pollock, 2002), and one frozen for a long time. What these new perspectives suggest is to look again at the classroom as a technology and consider how it will or should be opened up and re-examined for use in the digital age.

Learning to be a distributed group, and to be a member of a distributed group, entails bridging a number of 'divides' (Haythornthwaite, 2006b) and the adoption of a number of new practices. There are three important *divides* or *distances* to bridge for collaborative practice: *cognitive distance* (e.g. in discipline, traditions, expertise), *distance in practices* (e.g. commitment to sharing, familiarity with teamwork, and reward structures), and *physical distance*. Relating to these are three major practices to attend to: *technology* use, including both social and technical aspects, and use across multiple platforms that blend to meet the task needs of the group; *co-construction of practices* around technology use; and *active participation*. The latter is important for overcoming the potential invisibility of online participants (Haythornthwaite et al., 2000, 2006), and to sustain a critical mass of participants in communal construction (for an example of a failure because of lack of community-wide participation, see Bruckman and Jensen, 2002). Further, it involves picking practices from a *continuously evolving state of knowledge, and technology*, a problem elegantly captured by Bruce (2010) in the title of his paper about an evolving research group, which he describes as 'Building an Airplane in the Air'.

Learning *To Be* Anywhere, Anytime

With the move from face-to-face to online learning, we trade meeting in set places and at set times, with the teacher and all students in synchronous attendance, for anytime, anywhere connection, divided attention and presence, and asynchronous engagement with content and others. While this is a trend affecting interaction for work and social engagement in general, formal learning has formerly been a retreat from such engagement, keeping the different social worlds separate. Ubiquitous connection to all social worlds (home, work, school, leisure), channeled through the same gateways (one email address, one mobile phone), pools all our interactions into one interface (or set of mutually interconnected interfaces). Email from home can sit next to bank statements that sit next to details of work assignments. As we mix more worlds online we manage the load by breaking down the barriers between them, for example by forwarding email from various worlds to one combined address. This has the resulting effect of having worlds intrude outside their 'proper' domain, either of time (work emails and updates on weekends) or of domain (family messages received mid-work meeting).

The Internet, combined with a growing infrastructure of wireless connectivity and the ubiquitous presence of mobile devices in many countries, provides the technical basis for learning anywhere. A few statistics show how prevalent this is likely to be. Data from 2009 from the International Telecommunications Union (2009) show mobile phone subscriptions in undeveloped countries as high as 57.9 per 100 inhabitants. Even with the likelihood that richer citizens may own more than one phone, this still puts a mobile phone as most likely present among local community, family or colleagues. In developed countries the number is much higher at 115.3 per 100 inhabitants. Across regions, the high is 118.6 in Europe, and the low 31.5 for Africa; and for specific countries: China 55.51, Japan 90.37, India 43.83, the US 94.83, and the UK 136.55. (For more on the impact of mobile phones on society and social relations, see Ling, 2004, 2008; for more on mobiles, mobility, and learning, see Pachler, 2007; Pachler, et al., 2009; Sharples et al., 2007; Vavoula et al., 2009.)

The widespread availability of online access, and thus to both Internet resources and other people, also has a co-evolutionary impact on expectations and use. The 'always on' netizen will expect 24/7 access and rapid turnaround in information gathering and communications (for a view of university student life as the 'always on' and 'wired life', see Baron, 2008). This drives anytime and anywhere expectations about availability of friends and co-workers, and of information resources, both human (teachers, co-workers) and digital (web resources, digital libraries, online databases, directories), as well as technical infrastructures (institutional computing systems).

In distributed learning, by definition, the learner sits in a different place from the learning setting. They may enter a common cyberspace, but they are situated in a different physical place. Conflicts can arise in the attention learners can give to the learning experience while simultaneously juggling home or work worlds. Distributed students and teleworkers can be managing child care at the same time as working, and must struggle to maintain boundaries around their learning space (e.g. the computer in the bedroom) or working time. For example, children at home have difficulty understanding that a parent is still 'at work' or 'in class' even though physically present at home (Haythornthwaite and Kazmer, 2002; Salaff, 2002; see also Chapter 3 regarding Strauss' (1978) social worlds theory).

The juggling metaphor is highly apt for how at-home learners and workers manage. It captures what Kazmer and Haythornthwaite (2001) heard as the emerging lifestyle of distance learners who added learning not just as a third shift after work and home (Kramarae, 2001) but as another *stream of continuous attention*. They used the quotation below from Levine (1998) to illustrate the process of maintaining attention to multiple foci, and the need to 'cope gracefully' with multiple demands. It remains a fitting description of the lifestyle of the contemporary e-learner and e-worker.

> Enrico Rastelli, the most legendary juggler of the twentieth century ... stands, ostrichlike, on one leg, with a large ball balanced on the top of each foot, one on his bent knee, one in each hand, and one on top of his head. A stick extends from his mouth, and a ball perches on the end of the stick, balancing yet another stick, which is balancing yet another ball. The juggler looks like a human house of cards ... It isn't simply that jugglers can do things that other people can't, I thought, but that jugglers are a peculiarly apt embodiment of the human effort to cope gracefully with more demands, from more directions, than one person can reasonably be expected to manage. (Levine, 1998: 76)

The Ubiquitous Learner and the Economics of Attention

In the previous section we mentioned the notion of a 'continuous stream of attention'. In many ways, such a prospect is a nightmare: not to be able to stop or control the stream of attention, nor to be able to 'switch off' at times and direct one's attention to lighter, seeming ephemeral concerns. At other times we might wish to focus on particular topics, objects, people or concerns in depth. We tend to associate learning with in-depth kinds of attention; with concentration, absorption, focus, a process of problematization and clarification.

While conventional learning situations grant the teacher in the classroom the opportunity and responsibility to capture and direct the attention of the learner, this role is always compromised in e-learning. To an extent, the design of a VLE and of a particular program, course or module, is determined by the course designer and teacher. Most obviously, such direction is manifest in the resources made available, the assignments set, the deadlines and channels of communication that are laid out (the networks, the accessibility, the power or not to add material to the site). But there is a greater degree of freedom for e-learners (than for the conventional classroom-bound learner) who can direct attention as and when (and from where) they want. They can also use whichever media and modes of communication best suit, and are available, at a particular moment. So, for example, a learner can *read* a verbal text and *look at* some images in combination, then *phone and speak/listen, write an email, make a blog entry, write a note on paper*, move around the room and cogitate, be inspired to sit down and compose a long response, work on a multimodal response, etc. This freedom of media and mode, and of timing and place, is a crucial and distinctive aspect of e-learning. It allows the learner's own rhythms of study and attention to determine the pace and timing of a response. It also allows him or her to choose which medium/media and mode(s) of communication best suit the moment and his or her learning preferences.

Why is the economics of attention and communication important? In a world where there are many demands on our attention, the question of *where* we devote our attention, for how long, and with what degree of concentration is intimately connected with our capacity to learn. We can flit from topic to topic, from short text to short text, and learn little other than the superficial; or we can engage more deeply, for sustained periods of time and concentration, and learn more deeply. (For more on the wider implications of a move from an industrial economy to an 'attention economy' see Goldhaber, 1997, 2006, Davenport and Beck, 2001, and Lanham, 2006a, 2006b, who approach the problem respectively from economic, business and rhetorical perspectives.)

Behind both the economies of attention and communication are issues of autonomy and individual operation in a fast capitalist, kaleidoscopic world. 'Fast capitalism' is shorthand for the complex of industrial and post-industrial work activities, many of them in service industries where human interaction is at a premium; it is a phenomenon that is globalized. For learning to be effective in such a world of fast capitalist and shifting networks (Gee et al., 1996), then it must be (a) up to speed, and (b) responsive, that is, able to extract, select and evaluate from the moving panorama and to freeze the action in order to gauge and assess the patterns that offer themselves.

Moreover, the literacy – skills, competencies, fluency with new discourses – required for an attention economy are different than in industrial economies. They include knowing how to pick out relevant information from a data stream, to search and select the right resources, to forward and draw group attention to resources (e.g. serve as an information source, sink or conduit in a network), to use and reuse information appropriately (e.g. use in keeping with copyright, and assigning a more open, creative commons licensing to products), and knowing when and how to participate.

Finally, we come back to the prospect of a world in which we are continually online, ever available to work colleagues, always (potentially) learning, always open to a stream of information (even if resistant to a continuous stream of attention). How do we maintain equilibrium in such a world? This question is one we can only raise here, but it is one we assert as important, given that equilibrium, whether in terms of work–life balance or in terms of the balance between mind, soul and body, is essential to continued and sustained progress in learning.

Conclusion

Ubiquity connotes seamless, ever-present, natural and taken-for-granted resources. For ubiquitous learning, such resourcing draws our attention to the infrastructures that support online connectivity, and the applications and educational materials that sustain a learning enterprise. Beyond educational institutions, e-learning becomes ubiquitous as habits of searching, retrieving and learning with others online become routine, and lead into co-construction of knowledge domains and authentic participation in these domains.

In contemporary e-learning and ubiquitous learning, we are faced with an open learning field that not only challenges notions of instruction-based pedagogy, but actively bypasses it. New developments need to lead to new discussion and development of perspectives addressing sociotechnical theories of learning, social construction theories of learning, virtual community theories of learning, and theories about actor roles in digital learning.

Ubiquitous learning calls for attention to learner or community-directed knowledge content, while also raising questions about how knowledge will be shared, pooled, owned and assessed, who will take on the responsibility for directing learning, and what trust there will be in learning relations. This potentially leads to theories about the ubiquitous e-learner: how does an individual *become* an e-learner; how do motivation, leadership, ownership of the learning process, responsibility, commitment and trust play into what it means *to be* a digital learner? These considerations also suggest further inquiry into relational theories, such as new definitions and explorations of teacher–student relationships for e-learning, learner–teacher–technology relationships, community learning relationships, and community and knowledge relationships. Ubiquitous learning practices cut across all ages, and open up questions about styles of online learning that will be learned and persist as the young become adults, workplace learners, and collaborative and community-building ubiquitous e-learners.

Further Reading

Cope, B. and Kalantzis, M. (Eds.) (2009). *Ubiquitous Learning*. Champaign, IL: University of Illinois Press.

Goldhaber, M. H. (1997). 'The attention economy and the net', *First Monday*, 2(4). Available online at: http://firstmonday.org/htbin/cgiwrap/bin/ojs/index.php/fm/article/view/519/440/

Ito, M., Baumer, S., Bittanti, M., boyd, d., Cody, R., Herr-Stephenson, B., Horst, H. A., Lange, P. G., Mahendran, D., Martinez, K. Z., Pascoe, C. J., Perkel, E., Robinson, L., Sims, C. and Tripp, L. with A. Judd, M. Finn, A. Law, A. Manion, S. Mitnick, D. Scholssberg and S. Yardi (2009). *Hanging Out, Messing Around, and Geeking Out: Kids Living and Learning with New Media*. Cambridge, MA: MIT Press.

Ling, R. (2008). *New Tech, New Ties: How Mobile Communication is Reshaping Social Cohesion*. Cambridge, MA: MIT Press.

10

E-inclusion and Exclusion

Introduction

It is fitting that we follow a chapter on ubiquity with one that considers limits to ubiquity. The e-learning and ubiquitous learning revolution described so far draws a picture of near continuous use and easy facility with a computer and the Internet. Access may be accomplished on multiple devices, or on portable personal devices, but the individual is never far from their communication portal. With seamless integration into everyday life, managing the activities of searching, learning and communicating via the web is easy and swift. With adequate infrastructure, materials and contacts are where they are needed, when they are needed. New applications and devices are acquired on a just-in-time basis, and learning to use them is integrated into daily tasks. This is the utopia of learning environments, and very closely describes the acquisition, uptake and use patterns of affluent young users. Their luxury is not just the money to buy new devices, but also the time to learn them and the circle of friends to learn with and with whom they can initiate a critical mass of participation for such things as multi-player games, social networking sites and social media.

For most users in developed countries, the reality of access may be somewhat less ubiquitous than just described, but not to the point of breaking the model. Time to sit down at a computer for learning may be constrained by desktop rather than mobile computers, local area rather than wireless network access, shared or public use of computers, or shared attention to other tasks for work or home. But e-learning for education or pleasure can still be fit into the techno-logical and social infrastructure that is generally supported through educational and technical infrastructure in institutions and countries.

That e-learning *can* be fit into the schedule does not, however, mean that it is easily fit into that structure. Constraints exist in the availability of high-speed telecommunications links, local expertise, attitudes to the online environment, the cost of equipment, and charges for mobile phone and broadband services. E-learning may not have entered the community, and potential learners are then not aware of possibilities for online courses and qualification. The courses that are offered may be at a level or on topics that do not reflect the interests or needs of local communities, or are associated with educational pathways that have entry requirements that cannot be met by members of certain communities (e.g. graduate degrees). Further, the standard technology devices and interfaces may be impossible, or very difficult, to use without specific modification for those with visual or motor impairments.

If we take as a given that access and use of the Internet are precursors to adoption of e-learning, and the more widespread use of information for ubiquitous learning through the web, then concerns for e-learning inclusion or exclusion can expect to be predicated on socio-economic and regional trends related to Internet adoption. This is the focus of this chapter. In this we are fully aware that we are leaving out major potential areas of inclusion and exclusion, particularly relating to disability. Limitations due to physical disability, for example, are a major area of concern, best covered at present in interface design and human–computer interaction development work in computing. Equally important is the interaction of learning disability with e-learning, an area in need of research. (For more on accessibility and disability, see Caldwell et al., 2008, regarding World Wide Web Consortium (WC3) accessibility guidelines, Seale, 2006 and Ellis and Kent, forthcoming.)

The issue of 'access' – or lack of it – has been discussed widely as a *digital divide*. Yet, as computing has become more integrated with everyday life, the idea of a digital divide signifying differential *access* to computers has been modified first to recognize differences in facility with *use* of computers – in awareness, motivation, experience, facility with learning, and opportunity for learning – and next to what the Internet provides for engagement of different kinds of racial and ethnic communities and identities. As discussed next, the idea of a digital divide that can be bridged through the provision of some sort of physical access or social initiation has given way to more nuanced views of choices and a spectrum of engagement with the digital world.

Digital Divide

The term *digital divide* became popular after the publications of the US National Telecommunications and Information Administration (NTIA) reports such as *Falling Through the Net: Defining the Digital Divide* (NTIA, 1999) and *Falling Through the Net: Toward Digital Inclusion* (NTIA, 2000). The term refers to the division between those with and without access to computers and the Internet, and the resultant impact this has on inclusion or exclusion in the activities and benefits of the information age. In general, this has meant the divide within affluent countries. However, there is also an important global divide between countries where computing and the Internet are widely available and supported versus areas where they are not. This is sometimes referred to as the *global digital divide*. This is an extensive and growing area for research and policy and is not addressed in detail here (but see Chapter 11 on cross-cultural issues in e-learning). For more on worldwide aspects of the Internet, see the activities and reports associated with the United Nations World Summit on the Information Society (WSIS http://www.itu.int/wsis/basic/index.html), and initiatives in the area of the Information and Communication Technology for Development (sometimes shortened to ICT4D; e.g. see Rizvi, 2009).

Reasons for concern about the digital divide first centered on work and how those without computer skills would be excluded from opportunities in jobs from high-end computing to the increasing number of jobs that required basic computer skills for office and factory tasks (word processing, spreadsheets, email, computer-assisted design and computer-assisted manufacturing). The focus on Internet access as part of the digital divide followed on from many years of looking at adoption of computing, notably measured by home ownership of computers. For example, the US Census Bureau began asking about computer ownership and use in 1984, with questions about Internet use beginning in 1997 (e.g., see Kominski and Newburger, 1999). During the 1990s, a large number of initiatives and studies addressed distribution of computers to low income areas, training in computer use, deployment of wide-scale Internet access, and the integration of the Internet into work as well as economic and social life (e.g. Bishop et al., 2004; Cohill and Kavanaugh, 2000; Katz and Rice, 2002; Keeble and Loader, 2001; Loader and Keeble, 2004; Mehra et al., 2004; Schuler, 1996; Selfe and Hawisher, 2004; Wellman and Haythornthwaite, 2002).

Contemporary studies and critiques have widened the scope of interest beyond the physical hardware of the computer. Reports and analyses include attention to:

- adoption of mobile devices, notably cell/mobile phones (Ling, 2004, 2008; Madden and Rainie, 2010; Rainie and Keeter, 2006)
- Internet access via high speed connection (rather than the slower and now fading use of dial-up services; Horrigan, 2010)
- attitudes to Internet use (Commission of the European Communities (CEC), 2005; Dutton, et al., 2009; Lenhart, et al., 2003)
- effect of years of use (Eastin and LaRose, 2000; Nie and Erbring, 2000)
- fluency and skill in online searching (Hargittai and Shafer, 2006)
- kinds of information retrieved (Dutton et al., 2009; Howard and Jones, 2003; Pew, 2009b)
- 'proxy use', when one person accesses the Internet on behalf of another (Dutton et al., 2009; Hagar, 2005; Haythornthwaite et al., 2000; Horrigan, 2010; Lenhart et al., 2003)
- differences in use in urban versus rural settings (Gilbert et al., 2008; Hagar, 2005; Stern and Wellman, 2010).

Recent work extends critique to consider whose knowledge and identity are represented online, including how information online follows socio-economic lines (Crutcher and Zook, 2009; Zook, 2009), the presentation of gender (Herring, et al., 2006a), race and racially charged subjects online (Brock, 2005, 2007; Kolko, et al., 2000; Nakamura, in press, a), how search engine results portray particular populations (Noble, in press), and how standard, so-called generic, templates for presentation online limit the expression of personal race, gender and ethnic character (Noble, in press). Along with consideration of information use by individuals, research and thought extends to the support of inquiry by communities (Bruce and Bishop, 2008; Merkel et al., 2005), and use of the Internet for support of groups with specialized ability/disability (e.g. http://www.gimpgirl.com/; Ospina et al., 2008).

These newer areas of attention highlight a need for critical analyses that address the intersection of technology, education and learning with attention to power, politics and the nuances of race, ethnicity, gender and ability/disability. This provides a new lens for looking at e-learning. At present, the forms of e-learning being established are being driven and operated by elite use and users, that is, those with access to high-speed Internet, high-end computers, new software, and mobile access, living in regions where such services are available and affordable. As e-learning evolves, it becomes possible to see new initiatives begun and promoted by individuals, communities, hobbyists, and more (e.g. see the projects in Senges et al., 2008). We need to ask what is the pedagogy of the oppressed (Freire, 1970/2003) in the age of online pedagogy?

This list of multiple lines of discussion about digital inclusion and exclusion show how far the discussion has come from counts of computer ownership. Successfully assuming a digital lifestyle – one that provides a well-rounded background for adoption of e-learning – now entails the adoption of a bundle of related technologies, both technical and social. Technically, beyond the computing device, the savvy e-learner adopts Internet access, most likely high-speed, most likely at home, quite often wireless, and increasingly on a mobile device. They have probably long since adopted the use of email and standard word processing, spreadsheet, and presentation software; they now move on to adopt the use of Internet search engines and social media, install and use specialized applications, download and evaluate information content, and, increasingly, they post content online. Finally, they adopt the practices of e-learning: searching for just-in-time information; reading news online; using online databases; participating in online communities; contacting others; and judging the appropriateness and reliability of information sources.

This chapter can barely touch on the extensive literature relating to digital inclusion and exclusion, including the nuances of technical and social adoptions of technology. Instead, we pick a few topics to provide a grounding for further reading on the topic. We begin with a closer look at the notion of 'divide', following some of the statistics on the topic, and explore further the views that frame the larger meaning of digital inequality today and its potential impact on e-learning (for a more in-depth treatment, see Haythornthwaite, 2007a).

Digital Spectrum

Although the term 'digital divide' persists, it is now more generally recognized as a *digital spectrum* of access and use (Lenhart and Horrigan, 2003; Warschauer, 2003). Both formal e-learners and self-guided ubiquitous learners are thus drawn from a spectrum of personal digital capability that is affected by local telecommunications structures as well as political and personal desires. Among potential learners are the majority of people who have access to and use the Internet from home or elsewhere. As shown in Tables 10.1 and 10.2, penetration rates for Internet use differ greatly by region. At the same time, some of the less connected regions around the globe nevertheless represent a very large population. Asia, for example, with 20 percent penetration connects 764.4 million users, compared to North America, where the 76.2 percent penetration connects 259.6 million users. Thus, statistics on percentage of use may give a false idea of the quantity of learners engaged or potentially engaged online.

Table 10.1   Access to the Internet from Home

Country/Region	Home Access	Sources
US	74% (65% through broadband)	Horrigan, 2010; Pew, 2009a
UK	70% (96% through broadband)	Office for National Statistics, 2009; Oxford Internet Surveys (Dutton et al., 2009)
EU (27 countries)	65% (all forms of access)	Eurostat (2010)
Europe	Less than 40%: Bulgaria, Romania and Greece Over 80%: Netherlands, Iceland, Denmark, Norway, Luxembourg	Eurostat (2010) (data were not available for all countries)

Table 10.2   World Internet Statistics

Region	Internet Use (%)
Africa	8.7
Asia	20.1
Europe	53.0
Middle East	28.8
North America	76.2
Latin America/Caribbean	31.9
Oceania/Australia	60.8
World	26.6

Note: Retrieved June 25, 2010 from: http://www.Internetworldstats.com/stats.htm.
This site aggregates data aggregated from multiple surveys; data presented are those from 31 December 2009.

Access from home rather than school or work can be particularly important for e-learning. It provides school-age children with access to resources outside school hours, and extended time to gain familiarity with Internet use for school and non-school tasks. It is important for adult learners as the home is likely to be a prime location for the after-work and after-child care hours of e-learning. Access at home follows socio-economic lines. Statistics from the early 2000s showed clear differences in home versus school access for US school-age children (age 2–17) by race and income: 46 percent of those in households with incomes less than $40,000 US had Internet access at home, compared to 78 percent with incomes of $40,000–74,999, and 86 percent with incomes of $75,000 US or greater; 73 percent of white children had access at home compared to 35 percent of African-American children (Parsad and Jones, 2005). More recent statistics on Internet use and home broadband adoption by minorities in the US continues to follow socio-economic lines. Those with higher incomes (over $50,000 US) and/or higher education (college-educated) are more likely to use the Internet regularly than those with lower incomes ($20,000–50,000 US) or without college education. For example, in the higher income group 91 percent of African-Americans, 89 percent of Hispanics regularly used the Internet, compared to 75 percent in each group in the lower income group. (For more details, see the report on national minority broadband adoption by Gant et al., 2010.)

Non-Users

While 74–78% are online from somewhere, this leaves a segment of 22–26% of adults who are non-users and not reachable at present for e-learning. Understanding what keeps people away from the Internet may help shed light on what causes resistance to this new space for information and learning. Of the non-users, some want to be online, but because of remote location, local telecommunications infrastructures, or the inability to afford up-to-date computers, are constrained in their use. At the same time, others are living in information and IT-rich environments, yet opt to forgo online interaction, or limit their use. While access at work and school have become common, the same spectrum now exists for home with the broadband access speeds suitable for today's use. Horrigan (2010) describes two categories of those willing but not yet using high bandwidth Internet at home: *digital hopefuls*, for whom cost and digital literacy are cited as barriers (8% of US adults); and *near converts* (10%) who are comfortable with computing but for whom cost is a major barrier. Horrigan also described two categories of non-interested, non-users: the *digitally uncomfortable* who lack skills to be online and have a 'tepid' attitude to being online (7% of US adults); and the *digitally distant* who do not see the point of being online (10% of the general US population).

Although there are no equivalant data on hand, it is quite likely that similar attitudes will be found for the adoption of e-learning. The classifications do tend to fit the patterns found for adoption of innovations in general. As Rogers (1995) found in multiple studies of adoption of innovations, early adopters tend to be more cosmopolitan, more connected with others, and with higher socio-economic and educational attainment; late adopters are less well connected and are more likely to discontinue using an innovation. A caveat is that rhetoric about innovations tends to view adoption from the stance of a pro-innovation bias. This view sees the late adopters as resistant 'laggards' in the use of technology, implying some fault in their evaluation and capabilities. A different perspective might explore further whether the particular innovation affords for such potential users the 'relative advantage' that is so key to making a positive adoption decision, and if not, why not.

While non-users of the Internet were formerly considered as those resistant to technology or beyond its reach due to cost, location, awareness or knowledge, and for whom an intervention of some sort would get them online, this sector of the Internet population has now been recognized as a persistent part of the information landscape, with a significant portion having decided not to engage with technology and/or the Internet. For example, a 2008 Pew survey of non-users in the US (27% of adult Americans at the time), found reasons for not using the Internet included: no interest (33%), no access (12%), too difficult or frustrating (9%), too expensive (7%), and a waste of time (7%) (Jobbins and Lenhart, 2008). In a UK study of children, Livingstone (Livingstone and Bober, 2005) found that 3 percent of the children studied made no use of the Internet (compared to 22% of their parents) and 13 percent were considered low users (among the remainder of the children 41% were daily users and 43% weekly users). Of the low and non-users, reasons for non-use included: no access (47%), no interest (25%), lack of knowledge in how to use it (15%), and lack of time (14%).

Although interest and intention may play a role, the statistics on adoption and use still show that non-use is highly related to socio-economics. In the US, as of December 2009, use is comparable across adult men and women (74% of each), and close by race (White, 76%; African-American, 79%; Hispanic, 64%). However, the proportion online is markedly different across age, income and education (see Table 10.3; Pew, 2009a). Only 38 percent of those 65 years of age and older are online, 60 percent of those in the lowest income bracket, and 39 percent of those with the least formal education. In the UK, Dutton, Helsper and Gerber (2009) report that 97 percent of people in the highest income category used the Internet compared to 38 percent in the lowest income category. Large differences were also found by education level: 93 percent of those with university education used the Internet compared to 49 percent of those with 'basic education' (up to secondary/high school). Moreover, they note that between 2007 and 2009, the gap between these groups had increased from 35 to 44 percent. Livingstone (2006) also noted sizeable differences by socio-economic status: 88 percent of children described as in middle-class homes have access to the Internet at home compared to 66 percent of those described as in working-class homes.

An interesting comment in Livingstone's (2006) report is that there were more access points to the Internet in middle-class homes than in working-class

Table 10.3   Percentage Who Use the Internet in the US, as of December 2009

		%		%		%		%
Gender	Men	74	Women	74				
Race	White	76	African-American	70	Hispanic	64		
Age	18–29	93	30–49	81	50–64	70	65+	38
Income (US$ in thousands)	< $30	60	$30–50	76	$50–75	83	> $75	94
Education	< High School	39	High School	63	Some college	87	College +	94
Community type	Urban	74	Suburban	77	Rural	79		

Source: Pew Internet and American Life (December, 2009). Who's online: Demographics of Internet use. Retrieved 23 July 2010 from: http://www.pewinternet.org/Static-Pages/Trend-Data/Whos-Online.aspx

homes. This makes it more likely that members of the household will be able to use the Internet when they want, without waiting for others to free up use of the computer. Since access to the Internet is a vital part of e-learning, those with such access can be expected to be able to fit online use more easily into their schedule, perhaps studying or surfing while others are also engaged in the same kind of activity.

Delayed Use

Current thinking goes a step further in adding nuance to the spectrum of access by recognizing that issues of difference are not solved by supplying a missing technical, social or educational device or instruction. Most evident is that with current, still rapidly emerging hardware and applications, even after supplying devices or applications, the next wave of innovation puts this population again behind the curve. Terms such as *delayed use* and *digital lag* are used to refer to this idea of slower adoption. A report by the Commission of European Communities (CEC, 2005) sums up this phenomenon well. The report identified three patterns of Internet uptake evident in the traditional categories of the digital divide: a *temporary* pattern, with groups catching up to forerunners in the medium term; a pattern of *ever evolving delays*, with groups catching up in the very long term, but lagging behind with every new innovation; and a pattern of continuing *delay and exclusion*, with considerable delay between social groups, and some groups never catching up. As Rice (2002) points out, delayed use is impoverished use, which itself can be a significant source of social inequality and unequal participation in IT use and the information environment to which it provides access. It also means that, as discussed in Chapter 5, different genres of technology may be prevalent across potential e-learners by region and income. Further, as discussed below, delayed use in a participatory culture also means a lag before presentation of a particular culture's ideas, heritage, language and goals appear on the web.

However, even the more nuanced characterization of the digital divide as a *spectrum* or characterized by various stages of delay continues to treat 'the digital' as one unitary assemblage to be learned, acquired and practiced. But, as discussed in earlier chapters, current technology landscapes include a wide range of technology to choose from, some of which will be local to the specific work or learning environment and others that are more universally available. Being up to date with digital technology is now more complicated than owning a computer and using it to find resources. What has to be adopted to remain current – or operational – is more varied. Being on the right side of the divide becomes a process of both continuous adoption *and* continuous discontinuance. Keeping up at the leading edge means always approaching a moving target that is composed of the latest, newly emerging technologies. Keeping up at the trailing end means always being at least one step ahead of the discontinuance of technologies. A prime example at the leading edge is the adoption of smartphones and m-learning; and an example at the lagging end is moving on from dial-up connection through phone lines to a home broadband connection. Resistance to change, or difficulty in changing, now plays out in the mode of access to the Internet. A 2008 Pew study (Jobbins and Lenhart, 2008) of non-users in the US (27% of adult Americans at the time), found reasons for not using the Internet included: no interest (33%), no access (12%), too difficult or frustrating (9%), too expensive (7%), and a waste of time (7%).

Delayed Use and E-learning

Delayed use, as well as use that is markedly behind current technologies, can be a major issue for e-learning. As IT-rich environments such as universities plan and implement e-learning programs that require the latest in high speed processors, particularly for graphics applications, they risk leaving behind those without the latest technologies. As Johnson and colleagues (2004: 116) noted: '[s]ince the colleges are using distance learning to attract nontraditional students, their decision to design their distance learning courses around the lowest common denominator is probably an appropriate choice'. However, as they also note, '[w]hat is lacking in these technologies is the ability to incorporate multimedia and real-time exchange of information among individuals or groups within a course' (Johnson, et al., 2004: 116). Accommodating, or over-accommodating, the low-end users may work against some of the key benefits of e-learning that should be made available to such users, that is, interactivity with peers, real-time exchanges, simulations, use of virtual worlds, as well as training in the more technically sophisticated areas of computer use.

Thus, it is not that high-end applications should not be developed; indeed, learning and using the latest technology is part of the benefit of e-learning (Haythornthwaite et al., 2000). Nonetheless, it is important to maintain awareness of the implications of who can participate, and who is likely to be ready to participate, and balance this with technology choices and support. Every upgrade in equipment and telecommunications requirements, every change in technology, is an added barrier to remote, economically disadvantaged, and/or disabled e-learners, as well as those less familiar or comfortable with adopting new technologies.

Another aspect to consider is that while educational institutions may manage the technology sophistication necessary to operate within their VLE, wider learning on and from the web may require the latest technologies. Downloading documents, running videos, and operating programs found on the web may require up-to-date technology, high speed access, and the ability to install programs. The latter in particular is often not possible unless the individual owns and/or has administrator control of their computer, something often resisted in workplace settings. Thus, even within a wider context of e-learning, we may see a divide between in-class and out-of-class information access, and between formal e-learning where technology requirements can be minimized and informal e-learning where such control is not possible.

Waves of Technology

Other images are useful for understanding further aspects of access and use. Zook (2009) for example, borrowing from Crampton (2004), chooses the image of waves on a beach: 'One comes in, we figure it out, and the next one's already coming in' (Zook, 2009: 29–30). Waves also interact with each other, and in keeping with the ideas of reciprocal co-evolutionary development (Chapter 4), one wave can diminish or augment another. Moreover, as noted throughout this book, uses and effects have both technological and social dimensions. In a fine example of this, Crutcher and Zook (2009) describe how the newly configured representation of space being created online is reproducing and augmenting socio-economic conditions found in physical places. To extend (or perhaps mangle) the metaphor, the wave of technological innovation washes back onto the existing shores of socio-economic difference. In their analysis, Crutcher and Zook looked at the relatively new contributory feature of the Internet in which content can be tagged to physical locations, using global positioning data – geographic coordinates that are easily obtainable on a handheld GPS device. This capability is now inherent in many mobile phones, and the whole idea of using GPS location is the foundation of the popular sport of geocaching (e.g. www.geocaching.com). After Hurricane Katrina, a website appeared (Scipionus.com; the site is no longer operating) that allowed individuals to tag New Orleans map locations with local information, for example on water or wind damage (see also Singel, 2005). Crutcher and Zook (2009) found that the information posted in cyberspace about physical places in New Orleans followed socio-economic trends: more information was available online for areas of higher affluence than for poorer areas. Zook (2009) found similar trends in cities around the world, with a particularly higher quantity of postings in rich city centers. This does not seem an issue until we consider the impact on what this means for the representation of cities and their citizens: low income, non-computer using areas and demographics become unrepresented on the web, and hence invisible in the so-called egalitarian representation of the world online.

This non-uniform contribution to the web highlights some essential new trends in the digital divide (or spectrum or landscape). From being a hardware access and use divide, it is becoming an information divide (or spectrum or landscape) played out online. As Castells predicted in the *Internet Galaxy* (as cited in Zook, 2009), it is in the *consequences* of the technology – computers, telecommunication infrastructures, the Internet – that the digital divide is formed. In our discussions of ubiquitous learning, we have not gone into depth about the kinds of information that are online except to highlight the digital/information literacy that is needed to evaluate sources. But here we can see that digital exclusion can play out in the absence of participants who speak for and represent different regions, cultures and knowledge domains. While earlier concerns about the digital divide addressed exclusion as a lack of access to already posted resources, focusing on the importance of retrieval of resources (a Web 1.0 model), contemporary concerns need to turn to who can and does contribute information to the Internet, and thus who is instrumental in creating a critical mass of resources, opinion and conversation online (a Web 2.0 model).

Concern about and study of the representation of different knowledge domains and community oriented information is wrapped into the emerging area of *community informatics* which has a major focus on how information technology can be used to support marginalized communities and their interests (Bishop and Bruce, 2005; Gurstein, 2000; Schuler, 1996; see also Chapter 11). Online contribution and representation are also increasingly part of the agenda in the field of geography which is also having an influence on community informatics work. The simplification of programs that support geographic information systems (GIS), combined with the growth of systems and practices of voluntary geographic information (VGI) and platforms such as Google Earth and Open Street Map, have greatly expanded ways to tag information to geographic places (Budhathoki et al., 2008; Goodchild, 2007; Haklay and Weber, 2008). Again, the concern is about who contributes, controls and has access to information about local places, and thus the landscape of information available for those searching and learning via the Internet (e.g. Dodge and Kitchen, 2001, 2005; Dodge and Perkins, 2009).

Conclusion

The concept of the digital divide, including all its contemporary nuances, sensitizes us to the way different people of different economic situations and racial, ethnic, gender and disability identities, approach the potential of the Internet. As e-learning as well as more general learning via the Internet progresses, the pressures on Internet access and use stand as a precursor to the ability to promote educational programs and ubiquitous learning. As long as trends of Internet access and use, information technology adoption, and information representation are differentiated by income, education, occupation, age, race, ethnicity, region, and ability/disability, so too is e-learning. While there is no quick fix to digital difference and inequality, just as there is no clear definition of the dividing line between digitally thriving and failing to thrive, perhaps the best we can draw from this discussion is that the digital divide (spectrum, landscape) is something to keep continually in view in planning and promoting e-learning.

Further Reading

Caldwell, B., Cooper, M., Reid, L. G. and Vanderheiden, G. (Eds.) (2008). *Web Content Accessibility Guidelines (WCAG) 2.0.* W3C; 11 December. Available online at: http://www.w3.org/TR/WCAG20/

Dutton, W. H., Helsper, E. J. and Gerber, M. M. (2009). *The Internet in Britain 2009.* Oxford: Oxford Internet Institute.

Haythornthwaite, C. (2007). 'Digital divide and e-learning', in R. Andrews and C. Haythornthwaite (Eds.), *The Sage Handbook of E-learning Research.* London: Sage. pp. 97–118.

Seale, J. (2009). *Digital Inclusion: A Research Briefing by the Technology Enhanced Learning Phase of the Teaching and Learning Research Programme.* Available online at: http://www.tlrp.org/tel/digital_inclusion_writing/

Selwyn, N. and Facer, K. (2007). *Beyond the Digital Divide: Rethinking Digital Inclusion for the 21st Century.* Futurelab. Available online at: http://www.futurelab.org.uk/resources/documents/opening_education/Digital_Divide.pdf

Warschauer, M. (2003) *Technology and Social Inclusion.* Cambridge, MA: MIT Press.

11

Cross-cultural Issues

Introduction

One of the taken-for-granted considerations of e-learning is that learners are *distributed*. As discussed in previous chapters, distributions can be physical with remote learners embedded in their own local context and community with consequent distance in geography, time, setting, and, as we discuss in this chapter, *culture*. Many nuances on the concept of culture are possible. Whether face-to-face and/or online, contemporary learning settings, particularly in higher education, manage with a mix of students, all of whom are distinctive, ethnically, nationally, geographically and culturally.

In discussing culture, we use a liberal, multi-faceted and global perspective on the meaning and interpretation of the term. Nationality, ethnicity and culture are not treated as a single unified aspect of individual identity, coincident with geographical nation-state or national origin. On the contrary, identities in the 21st century are complex and hybrid: people are born in one country, migrate to another, marry into a third, and pick up languages and cultural contexts as they go. A student may be of US/UK parentage, born in China, with a British passport, domiciled in Saudi Arabia, studying in France and bilingual in English and Spanish (a real case). Another (equally real) case is a student of Chinese nationality (born in China, Chinese passport holder), married to a French/ Algerian, living and studying in England and multilingual in English, Mandarin and French. Each of these students might be taking a hybrid, mixed-mode e-learning course from a UK, US, EU or Australian university. These two real examples indicate how complex 21st-century identities are, and the error that can be made in simplistically considering culture to be synonymous with nationality and with ethnicity.

Such complexities and differences between students are, of course, balanced by commonalities. Entry to an e-learning course is most likely controlled by a language proficiency requirement (say in English) and a certain level of academic achievement and performance. Motivation and a desire to learn from this particular program will be another unifying factor, as is the entry into e-learning as a culture of its own. But this chapter addresses the different nature of national, social and pedagogical practices in order to promote understanding of the cross-cultural issues that are *exaggerated* in an e-learning context. They are exaggerated because the a-physical lack of proximity in e-learning is more dependent on verbal and two-dimensional visual communication (images, either still or moving, but not sculptural, plus sound) and thus more open to misinterpretation and misunderstanding because communication lacks the three-dimensionality of physical communication and the gestures, local context and other cues that aid mutual understanding.

Distance is not as just a matter of the transactional distance as suggested in Moore's (1997) theory (see Chapter 3), nor it is merely geographical; it is also cultural. We are concerned in the present chapter not so much with Moore's three variables of dialogue, program structure and learner autonomy (these are generic to any consideration of 'distance learning') but rather with geographical and cultural issues as they pertain to e-learning.

Issues Arising From Cultural Diversity

Many issues arise from cultural diversity, and – as has been suggested above – these issues tend to be highlighted or exaggerated by e-learning because other channels of communication normally available in face-to-face communication are denied. The following sections cover some major ways culture plays out in e-learning environments, both when students from multiple countries are involved, and when identity with particular social groups is involved.

Learning Cultures

With international participation in e-learning environments there are many opportunities for differences in national and/or cultural expectations about traditional learning to be carried over into e-learning. One key difference is in the deferring to the teacher that is characteristic of many Confucian-heritage education systems. Such respect can sometimes be misinterpreted as passivity; and challenges to teacher authority in these systems are likely to take place outside the classroom rather than within it, for example in individual conversations. The perception of passivity is not confined to Eastern classrooms (if we can make a rather simplistic distinction between East and West): it is also common in Western classrooms and can mask intense concentration and absorption of what is going on in the class, or laziness and non-involvement. Possibly related to engagement or non-engagement, and deferring or not deferring to the teacher, is the question of argumentation, in speech and in writing. This capability is seen as essential in school and higher education (Andrews, 2009b) and yet is not always taught as a necessary skill for success.

In e-learning environments, passivity and argumentation are two issues that go to the heart of learning cultures. We have seen elsewhere in the book that motivation and active learning are essential in e-learning: you cannot drift along in an e-learning class in ways that might be possible (if undesirable) in a face-to-face classroom. But the more interesting problem is argumentation: as a skill, the ability to argue requires the marshalling of evidence; the generation of propositions/claims; the explication of the assumptions and values underpinning your argument; the taking of stances; and a willingness to question received assumptions. E-learning environments *can* militate against argumentation because of the overriding sequential and hierarchical logic of arguments (see Chapter 1). The computer screen tends to present a two-dimensional interface so that hierarchies and sequences are 'replaced' by arrays of text, image (and potentially sound) in a spatial relationship to each other. While such a different e-learning culture is not anathemic to argument as we know it, the new culture requires a change in what counts as argument: in how we make connections between points, in the sustainability of arguments, in the marshalling of evidence that is both verbal and visual in nature.

The points above suggest that e-learning is a new culture of learning: one that requires self-motivation within a range of networked communities; that generates new forms of argument; that requires cultural sensitivity via a 'reading between the lines'; and that is able to understand and practice new forms of data-gathering, alignment and presentation. Teachers and course designers who try to impose formal and well-established patterns on the development of e-learning are likely to find these patterns increasingly at odds with ubiquitous e-learning trends.

Learning Styles

Within countries, different learning styles have been attributed to different subgroups within the dominant culture. Cheong and Martin (2009) cite Mestre's (2006) notion that in the US, African-American students tend to prefer experiential learning and minimal structure; and Native Americans and Latino/Latinas prefer social and relational learning. 'All three groups tend to be field-dependent learners whereas Asian Americans and white males tend to be field-independent' (Cheong and Martin, 2009: 83). While such generalizations may prove useful, they are also exclusive. What about Caucasian women? Asian men and women? The truth is that learning styles and preferences are affected by a number of factors, including gender, socio-economic status, character and genetic wiring as well as national and cultural differences. As with face-to-face conventional learning, students appear to be happiest when there is a range of learning approaches available and they can choose when to deploy such different learning approaches according to their own learning needs and rhythms. The dangers of generalizations about large ethnic groups are that not only are the ethnic groups themselves diverse and hybrid; but that learning styles and preferences within an individual can vary from occasion to occasion, from day to day or from hour to hour. The lessons emerging from such a range of preferences is that flexibility is key; and one of the flexibilities afforded by asynchronous e-learning is that it allows learners to work when, for how long and where they choose. The design of e-learning courses and programs, then, is one which should take into consideration a range of different learning styles and preferences.

Institutional Cultures

Another cross-cultural factor becomes evident in how the particular institution operates in which the e-learning experience takes place. In general, we can characterize institutional culture as operating on a spectrum from highly bureaucratic to learning-focused, from product and grade-oriented to process-oriented, and with a weak or strong culture of teacher involvement in student progress. An online Masters-level course in research methods at the Institute of Education, University of London, for example, operates in the following way. There are optional face-to-face meetings at the beginning and end of the 12-week course (referred to at the Institute of Education as a module). These tend to be well attended by students who are within travelling distance and provide a sense of physical as well as electronic community. Those who are not able to travel are offered video links to the face-to-face meeting. Each week of the course is devoted to a different topic of research methodology or methods, with short (500-word) assignments expected each week. These assignments act as attendance markers, but they are also responded to individually and collectively by the course leader. The course also has discussion spaces where students can initiate and respond to each others' questions; each student has posting rights, which is important for such a community to build on. The community as a whole operates largely on trust, though there are simple rules of etiquette, and the course leader mediates the conversations if necessary. Such program design makes the most of the community of learning that is created for the course: all students can have access to and learn from each other as well as from the course leader and other tutors. The cross-cultural issues at play in this particular group entail differences in academic expectation and style of study. Full-time students are surprised to find themselves in a largely 'distance' program when they are attending an institution full-time; all students are grappling with both the content of the course and the style in which it is taught. The problems, then, are to do with epistemological and pedagogical assumptions and approaches.

Marginalization

What happens if a student or set of students is marginalized for cultural or other reasons? Becoming peripheral in a group could be a result of class, ethnicity, gender, disability or another factor. In e-learning, it can often be because of postings.

In an online context, such exclusion could be a result of a feeling of inadequacy or inexperience with the technology. In e-learning, exclusion can often result from unfamiliarity with the norms of online discourse or from inappropriate behavior, either inadvertent or deliberate, as in the case of online trolls. Disruption can be an extremely difficult matter to deal with in any class, but as described in Case 11.1, the institutional structures to deal with issues may be out of the purview of the institution hosting the program.

CASE 11.1: DEALING WITH STUDENT PROBLEMS AT A DISTANCE

Anonymous, from a university in the USA

As we encounter more people in our distance programs, the more different kinds of students and student issues we're likely to face. A case offered to the authors reported on the problem of a highly disruptive adult student whose problem was not just a matter of classroom socialization, but was instead the way the student's particular mental health problem was enacted in the online context. The problem was first manifested in rude and repeated emails to the course instructors, then by extraordinarily excessive postings to asynchronous discussion (about 10 times the number of posts of other students), and finally developing into hostile postings to other students. Needless to say, the other members of the class, and the instructors, needed a resolution.

Traditional attempts to communicate with the student to discontinue the behavior went nowhere. In dealing with this case, the instructors became aware of the gap between university services designed for full-time, on-campus, young adult (17–21) learners, and for mature, adult learners. On-campus student, health, and legal services – counselling centers, academic conduct offices, departmental personnel, the legal office – had little experience with either distant, mature students, or with online learning contexts. Suggestions made on how to deal with discussion problems failed to understand the way online teaching is organized, for example, that barring a student from online communication (discussion, chat, email) would require blocking the student's access to the entire coursespace (webCT). To block a student from the course as a whole then comes up against student rights issues in their access to resources, and ability to complete the coursework. In this case, as for most distance or part-time programs, health care services are not part of the package associated with student enrollment. Thus, without student cooperation, no documentation of illness is available to activate other course completion or withdrawal options. The best

(Continued)

(Continued)

that can be done in these cases is to offer campus-based services as a contact for referral to local assistance.

This case highlights the weak university policies for distance learning: how to provide distance learners with services and what their rights are to services that mimic students who live or come on campus; how to consider the experience of fellow learners who find themselves in a class with a disruptive presence; and how to help distance teachers deal with cases of disruptive student behavior while still providing a supportive e-learning environment for all their students.

As with face-to-face teaching, it is normally the responsibility of the teacher to address under- or over-participation. While the case noted above is an issue of over-participation, most attention in online contexts and e-learning has been paid to increasing and understanding motivation and participation (e.g. Budhathoki, 2010; Haythornthwaite, 2006a; Hrastinski, 2006; Hughes, 2010). Recommendations and practices developed by instructors include requiring contributions be made each week; linking one person to another as partners in dialogic exchanges (these partners can be outside as well as inside the group); or by one-to-one discussion with the teacher.

Linguistic lack of confidence can be a factor in preventing a student from participating fully in online and offline exchanges, particularly when the language of the course is not a language with which they are completely comfortable. Because e-learning puts a great deal of emphasis on written contributions, there needs to be strong language and academic literacy support for students registered in courses in any institution, whether that student has already met the language proficiency requirements or not. As academic literacy is more than being competent in the language of instruction, but also includes understanding and using the discourses of academia and of the particular discipline studied, there needs to be support for such literacy. With regard to literacy, we should note that *The European Journal of Open, Distance and E-learning* (EURODL; http://www.eurodl.org/), as a state-of-the-art online journal in the field, includes frequent articles about a range of issues in e-learning, not so much about cross-cultural questions but about community-building. See, for example, Soylu (2009) and Arenas et al. (2010) on the achievements, problems and possibilities of building e-learning communities in specific cultural environments. These are cross-cultural in the sense that they include issues of bi- or multi-lingualism, as well as issues about learning styles, community-building and many of the other issues we have mentioned above. Another example is the *Journal of E-learning and Education* – http://eleed.campussource.de/ – where the very bilingual nature of the e-journal offers cross-cultural perspectives on policy, practices and research in the field. See also Danet and Herring (2007) for more on the multilingual Internet.

The most successful universities in terms of cross-cultural recruitment appear to be those that make linguistic and other support part of the fabric of the scholarly community, rather than an expensive add-on. While one celebrated feature of computer-mediated communication has been that cultural identities and differences can be 'hidden' – particularly if there is no visual dimension to the communication – where such differences matter to identity, self-presentation, development of learning, writing and conversational skills, ignoring such differences means failing to come to terms with the learning to be done and the composition of this online learning community. Developing a community requires a deeper engagement with identities, and acknowledgement and celebration of differences – as well as moving toward intercultural exchange and understanding.

Case 11.2 provides an exemplary case on this topic, developing both the 'problem' of diversity, and the steps necessary to open up the diversity black box. The case demonstrates how one particular school of communication at Arizona State University in the US has created a class to address cross-cultural issues. The case discusses teaching cross-cultural sensitivity. Note in this case 'that students in [the] department [in question] are predominantly white, middle class and have limited knowledge and experience with members of other cultures'. It's not really about the issues of dealing with a multi-cultural class. As such it is more about preparing students for an e-learning world, with multiple cultures. In many ways, taking students beyond a safe comfort-zone of co-learning with a homogenous cultural group is more important than dealing with mixed groups of students, face-to-face and/or online. It is not suggested, however, that online learning courses can compensate for limited experience in encountering other ethnicities and cultures, but what is interesting about this case is that this is exactly what the program at Arizona State University tries to do. We should also note here that homogeneity is usually an *apparent* characteristic of such a group, rather than reality: in any group of students, there will be heterogeneity and diversity. Understanding the balance between homogeneity and heterogeneity is essential in cross-cultural understanding.

CASE 11.2: BRIDGING PARTICIPATION DIVIDES IN E-LEARNING: THE CASE OF AN INTERCULTURAL COMMUNICATION CLASS

Pauline Hope Cheong and Judith N. Martin, Arizona State University, USA

Intercultural communication pedagogy as a field has traditionally focused on the face-to-face domain, with an emphasis on understanding differences between cultures as manifest in traits, nationality-based

(Continued)

(Continued)

dissimilarities and stereotypes. Yet, in light of the increasing mediation of everyday life in contemporary wired contexts, a significant portion of communication, including intercultural communication, takes place online. Together with the rising demand for online courses, we have undertaken the task of establishing an intercultural communication class online with a face-to-face option at Arizona State University. The Hugh Downs School of Human Communication serves about 3,000 undergraduates, and the course has been offered in multiple classes each semester (enrolled to maximum capacity of 30 students per class) since the fall of 2006 (see Cheong and Martin, 2009).

Beyond issues associated with the primary digital divide, that is, that some students cannot access their online class materials due to lack of or inadequate electronic access, we face the challenge of bridging secondary digital divides in our classes. Key secondary digital divides in this case concern the participation gaps that are associated with students' attitudes and motivations to engage in online pedagogy, particularly with some of the sensitive and mentally provoking material associated with the course. Although Arizona State University is the largest public university in the United States, with sizeable numbers of students of different local and international backgrounds, we have found that students in our department are predominantly white, middle class and have limited knowledge and experience with members of other cultures, including differences and similarities they share with other students of a different race and/or ethnicity.

Solution (a) Experiential Activities

To supplement learning from textual materials, we designed experiential activities for students to gain intercultural experience and develop critical thinking skills. These activities include field projects that require students to think about their own intercultural background and experiences by interviewing their older siblings, parents and grandparents, as well as engaging in online interviews and correspondences with students from another country (whom we have set up in advance) to complete class assignments. In an assignment on the topic of stereotypes, students experientially explore the role of nonverbal communication in prejudicial thinking. Using Breeze Plug-in technology, they close their eyes and listen to an online audio recording of their instructor telling them to imagine a US student and Japanese student interacting in front of the student union. Then they are asked to open their eyes and describe the US student very specifically (how tall, what color eyes, hair, appearance, clothing, etc.) in a written paragraph. They then look at their description and are asked to write about who they did NOT see as US American (e.g. Latino/a, disabled person, old person, heavy person?) and then write about and later post their ideas on the class discussion board about the implications of intercultural interactions (e.g., if we only 'see' certain people as 'Americans' what does that say about how we interact with people we meet?).

Solution (b) Evaluation Modification

We have purposefully revised our course evaluation to encourage honest and open discussions among students interacting online. The course assessment is structured so that students earn credit/no credit points for the discussion section of the course. In order to receive credit, the students must: (1) post messages on different days during the unit, so that a discussion takes place and it is not just every student posting two messages on the last day of the unit; (2) address the questions listed in the assignment; (3) demonstrate that they have completed a prior activity, if required; (4) make a substantive contribution that moves the discussion forward (they can't just say 'I agree'); and (5) be respectful of others in their postings. On the syllabus, it is stated that:

> Some of the topics we cover in this course can lead to emotionally intense discussions. One of the goals of the course is to help us become more aware of how people from different backgrounds think and experience life. This learning cannot occur when people feel threatened or defensive. If postings are deemed by me to be hostile or demeaning to others, the message will be removed and the sender will not receive credit.

As instructors, we monitor all online discussions closely, and also keep office hours online and offline to encourage students to give us feedback on their experiences and share any problems they have with the class.

Pauline Hope Cheong is Associate Professor, and **Judith N. Martin** is Professor, in New Media and Intercultural Communication at the Hugh Downs School of Communication, Arizona State University, USA.

E-learning Across the Globe

While cross-cultural issues are evident when access and use of information and communication technologies are relatively similar, for example in comparing between the UK, US and South Korea, they are further exaggerated when the differences between access and use are greater. Issues emerge that go deeper into the politics and economics of the specific countries involved. In many developed countries, we can assume that high speed broadband, the ubiquity of computers and hand-held devices, and a general facility with these devices exists within the country's infrastructure, even if not available or used locally.

For example, many assume that all parts of the US are well linked by the latest in information technologies and infrastructures. Yet the vast geographical distances often belie that image as carriers need time and incentive to install cell phone towers, broadband and wireless facilities in remote regions. However, as a country, the US is continuously aware of the need to work toward universal, equitable access to online resources and practices, and hence as a country holds expertise in this area. In developing countries, such country-level familiarity and infrastructure may not be the case. Moreover, for e-learning in education, awareness and intentions include collaborations between institutional providers and government infrastructures.

A case where institutional intention and the realities of e-learning have not been fully matched is that of the African Virtual University (AVU), established in 1996, and discussed in Rizvi (2009). Although much in the way of resources has been provided by the World Bank and other funders, there remain questions as to whether e-learning has been integrated into the economic, social and pedagogical practices of the continent. As in any continent or indeed any country, there is huge variation in digital access and use; but there are major shortcomings in the split between course content and 'delivery':

> [T]he AVU educational model appears to be based on a fundamental distinction between the development of the course content and its delivery. The course content is developed by international academics who are not themselves involved in teaching it and who often have little knowledge of the African context. It is left up to the tutors at the local learning centers to communicate the significance of the content to local students. While this cultural translation always involves processes of interpretation – appropriate and active negotiation of content on the part of the tutors and students – the fact remains that this pedagogic model embodies an assumption of unmediated reception of content that is often assumed to be culturally neutral. But as a number of recent learning theorists in the socio-cultural tradition have pointed out, this is a fundamentally misguided view of how knowledge is acquired. The contexts of content design and its delivery cannot be so easily separated, and education is most effective when learners are not only consumers of knowledge, but also its active creators. (Rizvi, 2009: 115–16)

Cultures (not only those of sub-Saharan Africa) which depend heavily on course content being created elsewhere, and which thus subscribe to a transmission model of education in which textbooks – or their equivalent in e-learning – provide a basis for learning, may well have problems in adapting to community-based aspects of contemporary e-learning, *even though community is a key part of learning in traditional formats*. What is implied by a discussion of communities in e-learning is that becoming a good e-learner is partly about being able to move between different kinds of communities with technical ease and with social familiarity and confidence. Moreover, mismatches between what faculty perceive as their role in teaching and learning, and administration's desires to implement e-learning can occur over this precise point of the separation of course creation and delivery, and have led to the failure of programs elsewhere (see the section on 'border conflicts' in Chapter 8).

We have suggested elsewhere (e.g. Andrews and Haythornthwaite, 2007) that in the digital, e-learning and multimodal age, learning is an *effect of communities* (adapting Rogoff's (1992) notion that 'learning is an effect of community'): not only the various communities we operate in (including electronic ones) but also the relations between these communities. Becoming an e-learner means being able to navigate between the various communities, and being an active co-creator of knowledge in at least some of these communities. Also, as suggested earlier in this book, the community learner is very much like an expert learner, working with others to create the new questions and directions of inquiry (see Chapter 6). The implication is that becoming a good e-learner in a world of various cultures means being able to understand and adapt to different learning cultures, and specifically to the different ways in which e-communities mediate with real-world communities in specific contexts. Moreover, with the increasing mix of cultures, and the unexpected combinations that can occur, it is yet more important for learners in a global world to be ready to jointly understand and dynamically set their criteria for interaction.

One example of a project in Africa in which adaptation of technologies to the local contexts was particularly sensitive is reported in Leach, Ahmed, Makalima and Power (2005). It was one of a number of such projects run by the Open University (UK) in collaboration with African partners (e.g. Dladla and Moon, 2002; Leach and Moon, 2002). The project in question was called The Digital Education Enhancement Project (DEEP), and focused on the ways in which information and communication technologies (ICT) could improve access to and quality of teacher education in the global south. The specific sites for the research were Egypt and the Eastern Cape Province of South Africa; 12 primary schools were included in the study, with two teachers from each school. Teachers worked in pairs ...

> to implement and evaluate a short, curriculum-focused, school-based professional development program, using a range of new technologies including hand-held computers. Activities focused on the teaching of literacy, numeracy and science. ICT was used in some significant ways in schools as a whole, as well as [in] many of the communities in which project teachers lived and worked. (Leach et al., 2005: vii)

It can be seen, then, that the linking of electronic and real-world communities was well managed in this particular program. All project teachers in both contexts quickly developed confidence in using desktop/laptop and hand-held computers for a range of purposes; they developed basic computer skills relatively easily, and the majority learnt to use digital software tools and other peripherals in a short timeframe. Where technical support was thin on the ground, teachers worked collaboratively to solve problems.

In general, the project's success can be attributed to the appropriate deployment of technologies; the embedding of the activities into the curricular, educational and pedagogic practices of the local communities; and the high quality professional support that the network of teachers provided for each, and that was also offered by the project coordinators in the UK and Africa. One of the key success factors in the case of the DEEP project appeared to be mobilizing the communities involved (see the report for a more detailed account of key success factors). In terms of cross-cultural issues and practices, then, the essential approach seems to be to identify the commonalities in the first instance, and then to work in some depth to acknowledge the particular circumstances that distinguish different cultures and contexts.

Such cross-cultural listening is a key element in success in other areas dealing with communities and IT, notably in collaborations between the 'IT-rich' implementors and the 'IT-poor' local participants. The growing area of *community informatics* (Bishop and Bruce, 2005; Gurstein, 2001; Haythornthwaite and Kendall, 2010; Schuler, 1996) is particularly concerned with this kind of outsider implementation effort. The idea of *participatory action research* has come to the fore as way to work with an IT-poor community to implement the kind of IT initiative that makes sense for the local community (Merkel et al., 2005; Stoecker, 2005a, 2005b). Learning to 'talk across difference' applies as much to situations within countries as across countries, and is an important skill for understanding differences in knowledge across race, ethnicity and income (Flowers, 2003; Gutiérrez et al., 2000; and Case 11.2 by Cheong and Martin).

These projects and initiatives again challenge the simplistic notion of the digital divide. We have already noted that it is important to re-conceptualize the 'digital divide' as a *spectrum* of access and use. Once the spectrum is identified, the task is to work out how differences in provision and use can be bridged or minimized. Leach and Moon (2002) suggest that the simplistic notions of the digital divide reinforce the developed versus developing countries distinction. However, they also acknowledge that, at least at the time of their writing, '95% of the world's computers are in the North; forty-nine countries have fewer than one telephone for every 100 people and at a global level, 80% of the world's population still lacks the most basic telecommunication facilities and resources' (2002: 8). The figures for 2010 were somewhat different in nature, but give an indication of the continued gap between developing countries and the 'developed' world: 750 million of the 1.25 billion adults in low and middle-income countries had mobile phone coverage but do not own a handset. The difference between urban and rural settings is marked, not only in a country like the UK where broadband speeds are greater in the city than in the country, in general; but also in India where, in 2010, of the 9 million broadband subscribers, 95 percent lived in the major cities.

One aspect of the digital divide or spectrum that has yet to be mentioned is that of gender. Although there is huge variation across the world in women's access to mobile phone technologies, it was still the case in 2010 that there were 300 million fewer female subscribers than male subscribers worldwide; that a woman was 21 percent less likely to own a phone than a man in low- and middle-income countries (23% in Africa, 24% in the Middle East, and 37% in South Asia); and that women in rural areas and lower income brackets stood to benefit the most from closing the gender gap in terms of ownership and use of mobile phones (see GSM world, 2010). Cross-cultural issues, therefore, must take into account gender divides in the access and use of mobile phone tech- nologies in e-learning as well as in day-to-day communication, community- building and global awareness.

Case 11.3 by Choi looks at e-learning practice in higher education in South Korea, with specific focus on the use of hybrid and blended learning approaches to second language learning and testing. It provides an example of problems encountered in a highly developed country: one which scores highly in PISA tables in literacy and numeracy at school level, and where investment in new technologies in higher education is considerable. Such investment and success still generates pedagogical problems that need to be addressed.

CASE 11.3: BLENDING E-ELEMENTS INTO PEDAGOGY: E-LEARNING PRACTICE IN KOREAN HIGHER EDUCATION

Sun-young Choi, Institute of Education, London

Various manifestations of networked environments and their advanced technology applications have been widely utilized in the field of educa- tion in South Korea. The government has also made sustained efforts towards constructing the foundation for the digitization of Korean uni- versity education and has given substantial support to higher education institutes, so that the individual universities have been able to set up e-transformation of their programs and systems. The keen interest of South Korea in the virtual, and in e-learning implementation has affected policy-making in educational institutes, launching the Comprehensive University Informatization Plan (e-Campus Vision 2007) and leading to the '2006–2015 u-Korea IT839' project which aims to 'develop techno- logical strategies to lay the foundation for u-Korea' (see Korean Educational Development Institute, 2007; Latchem and Jung, 2009).

In line with such policy, a number of universities have started to inte- grate e-learning courses with their traditional curriculum. Throughout this expansion of e-learning practices, blended learning courses began to gain attention in order to enable a combination of the best features of the traditional classroom learning with those of online-based e-learning, thereby minimizing the emerging problems of purely online-oriented

(Continued)

(Continued)

e-learning courses. In the context of these current practices in South Korea, the researcher has explored the perceived influence of a university hybrid EFL course in an attempt to understand both the 202 students' and four teachers' perceptions of a series of factors arising from their use of the target course.

Despite a number of studies that have been dedicated to the investigation of language learners' perceptions of online courses, to date there have been very few studies looking at the blended/hybrid EFL learning curricula. It also becomes an issue to examine how this new model brings technology and e-learning elements into the conventional classroom and how the users and instructors can achieve a balanced program so as to enhance language learning performance. In this respect, it was assumed that the exploration of the learners' and the teachers' experiences and perceptions might lead the researcher to attempt a portrayal of the particular educational research problems faced at present.

Five criteria to determine the perceived influences of the blended/hybrid course were initially constructed in designing the research instruments so that the researcher could sharpen focus on the research problem. The five criteria were: (1) influential factors/phenomena; (2) self-motivation in the online learning environment; (3) strong and weak points of the blended course; (4) the proportion of online element perceived to be the optimum in the blended course; and (5) the part played by multimodality in e-learning environments. In order to find a specific set of influential factors and the pedagogical benefits and drawbacks stemming from the blended learning curriculum, a pilot study was undertaken on the basis of a review of relevant literature. Following piloting, a 70-item questionnaire survey was designed which met the five criteria.

This study consisted of three phases of methodological approach: (1) an understanding of EFL students' perceptions of hybrid instruction and their blended learning experiences, by means of a questionnaire survey; (2) a more in-depth investigation through structured interviews with students and semi-structured interviews with teachers; and (3) multimodal analysis of the online learning environment displayed in the computer interface. The questionnaire was used to achieve a wider understanding of students' perceptions of blended learning experiences, while the interviews and the multimodal analysis of the e-learning environment were carried out in order to investigate the in-depth nature of perceptions and the e-learners' specific learning context.

In particular, the target blended/hybrid EFL course involved measurement of students' language improvement throughout the course, addressing the aspects of actual language proficiency improvement on the basis of the course exams. In addition, multimodal traits residing in e-learning environments were taken into account by looking into the function of images and the resources used for representation. The interview instrument was also partially used to probe into the students' awareness of the multimodal aspects of the course.

Sun-young Choi is a doctoral candidate at the Institute of Education, University of London.

Potential Problems with Cross-Cultural Approaches to E-learning

Much of what has been discussed so far in this chapter has looked at the positive side of cross-cultural e-learning. Ess (2009), however, describes further cultural differences that learning initiatives have failed to acknowledge. His examples are from cross-national cultural differences. He suggests, for example, that 'white' educational views of individual learning and of book learning have been applied to cultures where learning is more oral and collective (e.g. for indigenous South Africans, and Maori people in New Zealand). There is a danger that systems and practices designed in one country will be imposed, inappropriately, in another country.

As far as e-learning goes, Ess highlights the potential problem of hegemony. If power in e-learning design, adoption and dissemination is in the hands of a few 'Western' countries, then the irony is that what is seen as a 'global solution' to learning may well impose upon cultures an inappropriate model of learning. Issues of individualism versus collectivism; uncertainty avoidance; masculinity/femininity; long-term versus short-term orientation; and power distance (see Hofstede, 1983, 2001 and www.geert-hofstede.com/), all bear upon the difficulties that may be encountered when mismatches between expectations, *mores* and other aspects of cultures are evident. We can add to this that if Western institutions' e-learning programs become dominant, then also, arguably, Western ideas of content and what is granted the status of advanced learning will also become dominant.

The polemicization of the debate about cross-cultural dimensions to e-learning tends to separate parts of the world from each other, to exaggerate differences, and to reduce debate to simplistic dualism. It is important to bear in mind that not only are there cultural differences between existing, supposedly 'static' cultures, but that also cultures are changing, and that e-learning, with its marrying of different forms into new hybrids, and its bringing together of different people and their backgrounds from around the world, can act as a force for convergence and inclusion. As ever, and to continue the dialectic, the question is whether that convergence is of high quality, reflects the different cultural qualities, and moves people forward into new forms of identity and engagement with learning.

Such discussion opens up the question as to whether e-learning itself is trying to instantiate a different kind of learning culture, one that is more oral and 'noisy' (Ess, 2009: 21). We think it is too early to tell whether such a culture is, in fact, developing; and if it is, whether it will be suitable in all learning contexts. There are important implications for acceptance of e-learning packages and implementation, particularly in developing countries where the infrastructure to support such forms of learning may not be available.

Further Reading

Australian Institute for Social Research (2006). *The Digital Divide: Barriers to E-learning*. Final Report for Digital Bridge Unit, Science, Technology and Innovation Directorate, Adelaide: The Department for Further Education, Employment, Science and Technology (DFEEST). Available online at: http://www.umic.pt/images/stories/publicacoes/barriers_ digitaldivide.pdf

Leach, J., Ahmed, A., Makalima, S. and Power, T. (2005). *DEEP IMPACT: An Investigation of the Use of Information and Communication Technologies for Teacher Education in the Global South*. London: Department for International Development (DFID). Available online at: http://www.open.ac.uk/deep/Public/web/publications/core.html

Olaniran, B. A. (Ed.) (2009). *Cases on Successful E-learning Practices in the Developed and Developing World: Methods for Global Information Economy*. Hershey, PA: IGI Global.

van Dijk, J. (2005). *The Deepening Divide: Inequality in the Information Society*. Thousand Oaks, CA: Sage.

12

Researching E-learning

Introduction

As the chapters in this book have stressed, e-learning is a multi-faceted phenom-enon. It comprises intertwined social and technical dimensions that can be viewed for effects at individual, group and communal levels. Effects are more than pedagogical. As e-learning leaves the classroom and is found anywhere, anytime and with anyone, for education, work and leisure, it becomes woven into the fabric of everyday life and thus becomes a social and sociological concern. As an educational intervention, it changes patterns of long-standing relation-ships of authority and knowledge. In combination with trends to open source, open access, and participatory culture, the role of authoritative sources is changing (Haythornthwaite, 2009b; Jenkins et al., 2006; Willinsky, 2005). This includes the often-cited change of the teacher from 'sage on the stage' to 'guide on the side'. But it also includes changes in learning units as a whole, for exam-ple, when online groups form and define their own direction of learning, and learning by individuals as they take more active roles as entrepreneurial learners, seeking out and creating their own learning agenda and acting in support of fellow learners. Technology developments hurtle us forward into new learning paradigms: learning with others around the globe as we find those interested in our (narrow) area of interest; and contributing to knowledge resources through online participation, for example in crowd or community-sourced sites sup-ported through wikis, blogs, blog commentaries or ratings, and email lists (Benkler, 2006; Haythornthwaite, 2009a; Ito et al., 2009 ; Jenkins et al., 2006).

The contemporary rapid change in knowledge base, and the subsequent need for lifelong learning in support of, and alongside work and career, spur the need for adult learning platforms that are manageable by the full-time worker. E-learning has become that platform, taking evening classes and library use online, in the growing number of online learning courses, programs and support mechanisms. Such change further drives e-learning innovation as design and use of online learning environments, mobile learning, and online resources become integrated into what it means to teach and learn online, and computer-mediated synchronous and asynchronous participation, with distributed others, become essential to what it means to be an e-learner.

The research agenda is thus wide open for e-learning, from pedagogical concerns with how to provide the best teaching practice and the best learning environment, to management and administrative concerns about how to implement and support online programs, to social, psychological and sociological concerns about group learning processes, quality of life, and internet-supported trends in information seeking, retrieval and use. Disciplines and research traditions that provide background literature that support research in e-learning thus draw from a wide range: education, management, psychology, sociology, communications, library science, information science, social studies of science, social studies of technology and computer science.

Such scope in turn suggests a wide range of methodologies and methods for researching e-learning: quantitative and qualitative data analysis, controlled and field experiments, participant observation and ethnography, statistical modeling, textual analysis, design studies, longitudinal study, meta-analysis, and more. An even wider range of methods can be used, some of which have been generated by more available electronic facilities: obtrusive or unobtrusive observation; interviews with individuals or focus groups with e-learning participants; online questionnaires and surveys; automated data collection; and data mining. Various units and levels of analysis can be addressed: individual perceptions, recollections, attitudes or usage patterns; relational data on interactions among learners; characteristics of different program level initiatives; societal impact in short- or long-term educational or career outcomes. Results from these studies may be used immediately to adjust practice in local programs, form theoretical foundations for future study, form the basis of policy recommendations, or provide better insight into how e-learning is affecting individuals and changing learning in society.

Our earlier collection of research perspectives, *The SAGE Handbook of E-learning Research* (Andrews and Haythornthwaite, 2007) was an attempt to help researchers and research students navigate the new territory of e-learning. E-learning research is spread across the many fields that provide input from a theoretical perspective as well as the many fields that implement e-learning programs for their own use. This mêlée has made it hard to locate sources that bring together these different disciplinary approaches. The *Handbook* was an attempt to rectify that, with chapters by prominent e-learning researchers addressing theory, policy, linguistic dimensions and design as groundwork for future research and support for new and emerging e-learning researchers. The *Handbook* was also a response to the needs of new e-learning researchers, particularly students, who were finding that the tried-and-tested routes for research, as well as the formats for presenting research for examination, were increasingly unsuitable for the kinds of research that were actually taking place.

Here at the end of this current book, we wish to re-visit the question of researching e-learning. While e-learning as an educational practice is increasing its reach daily, many of the themes that characterized early responses to the field still remain: themes of resistance to change, fear of the commodification of learning, and views of online learning as a way to save money and increase revenues. Yet, as outlined in the chapters of this book, the reach of e-learning as a learning practice now has ramifications beyond the educational institution. This opens up new areas of research, while also putting a different cast on the original concerns. For example, resistance to change in an organizational context implies a change imposed by authorities from above. Yet e-learning practices are now as likely to be pushed from below, as students bring internet-savvy practices into educational institutions, and from outside, as institutions are pushed to offer online access both on- and off-campus to remain competitive but also to remain up-to-date with current trends in online communication and information use. Thus, research questions about 'old' concerns need to be revised in the light of contemporary influences.

In the current chapter, we suggest a framing for approaching e-learning research. This is not a listing of research questions nor an outline of a research agenda. Instead we aim to clarify the dimensions of research areas for e-learning. To this end, we distinguish between research *about* e-learning and research *for* e-learning, with the former addressing e-learning as a social and pedagogical phenomenon, and the latter addressing design and practice in support of e-learning programs and processes. We begin by addressing how to start e-learning research, with particular attention to the elusive 'research question'. The central section of the chapter looks at new forms of research in the digital age, and is followed by a section on becoming an e-learning researcher. Finally, we turn to the research areas in the field that we think are in need of research: a prospectus for e-learning research.

Getting Started in E-learning Research

Forming research questions is an essential part of any research project, and yet one of the most difficult. Research questions capture the nature of the problem to be addressed, and form the basis on which approaches and methods will be determined. They represent a high level of inquiry that situates the research project in an area of literature and previous study, while also providing the staging from which more specific research questions and hypotheses are formed that define the scope of a particular study. To specify a question requires knowledge of the area in order to understand the kinds of questions already being asked. A research question may emerge as a gap in existing studies, for example a particular problem may not have been addressed with other than mainstream populations, opening up an area of research on children, seniors, disabled, low income, or rural populations. A question may emerge by bringing a perspective from another field into a home field – for example applying management theory in an educational context, or (e-)learning theory in a management context – or theories of games and play from developmental psychology to e-learning.

In general, framing a research question entails a process of first identifying the larger area of interest such as design of e-learning systems, class interaction in e-learning, teaching in a multi-cultural online context, alumni relations for distributed learners, or policy for cross-institutional and international programs. From there, it is necessary to narrow the scope to a specific population and context to formulate specific research questions such as: What is the most appropriate social and technical configuration for getting new e-learners talking online? This can then be taken into the decision about a method for the research. This particular question could be addressed in an experimental procedure, and/or in a balanced design that tries different configurations and assesses outcomes of quantity and/or quality of interaction. It could also be addressed by interviews with e-learners asking what helped them begin and continue to talk online. While the larger research questions point to the field of inquiry, specific questions form the basis of a research project. However, a number of research studies may be (and most likely are) necessary to fully address a research area. Thus, the scope of research and the number of individual projects will differ with the different time constraints for undergraduate or graduate students pursuing theses and dissertations, academic researchers pursuing tenure and academic reputation, and e-learning practitioners, administrators or community activists aiming to implement and adjust local practices. A final point to note is that research questions are guides. In many cases as research progresses, particularly over the course of a longer research agenda, different questions will emerge. It can even be the case that the end result of a research project is a more precise research question that serves as the basis for future work.

In the introduction to *The SAGE Handbook of E-learning Research* (2007), we posited a relationship between new information and communication technologies and learning that embraced causal research designs, but went further. The model we proposed saw the relationship as reciprocal and co-evolutionary (see pp. 33–41 in the *Handbook*, and Chapter 4 of this book for a summary of the model). Such a relationship requires a new approach to research: one that is more ecological (see Chapter 7 of the present book) and which recognizes that just as new technologies influence the nature and environments of learning, new kinds of learning (characterized by changing forms of social and community networking) influence the development of new technologies. Not only is the relationship reciprocal and co-evolutionary, it also is partly residual in the sense that not all reciprocity is simultaneous: influences of technological advances may exhibit a residual or time-delayed influence on certain aspects of learning and teaching practice. For example, the effects of asynchronous communication enabled by applications such as email, discussion boards, etc. were not immediately felt in learning contexts. Yet, now the asynchronicity of discussion boards is the mainstay of contemporary e-learning practice. The residual, delayed effects of wikis and virtual worlds are yet to be felt, but they are beginning to show influence at the edges of e-learning practice. Equally, new forms of learning and teaching may take time to filter through to technological change. One example is the way new learning practices acquired by use of online technologies have washed back onto on-campus practice in the form of 'blended learning'. Our model, then, describes a web of reciprocal interaction between new technologies and learning that is built over time with increasing filaments of connection between old and new practices.

Such complexity cannot easily be accounted for in simple causal research designs. In this we caution against a model of e-learning that can be tested by looking at the impact on learning of a technological intervention in the teaching or learning environment. It is not sufficient to look only at the way '*x*' has an effect on '*y*' in the area of e-learning research, as was much of the emphasis in early studies of whether online learning was 'as good as' offline learning (see the 'no significant difference' studies at http://www.nosignificantdifference. org/; Russell, 2001). While it is possible to consider controlled or field experiments of e-learning practice (e.g. Varvel, 2010), where students can interact on- or off-line across groups, given the widespread use of online applications for learning, communication and recreation it is difficult to assert the independence of the separate conditions or 'on-' versus 'off-'line. Similarly, it may be difficult to isolate the impact of the use of a new technology when students come with, and continue to gain, different experience with technology and with its use in learning settings during the experimental period. Problems also exist in defining learning outcomes. As described throughout this book, outcomes of e-learning can entail learning to work with groups online or to communicate through technology, each of which is (we argue) a legitimate outcome for e-learning, but which are also factors that can facilitate or constrain learning of knowledge content. In short, since e-learning entails a complex of social, technical, political dimensions, and more, it is not one simple phenomenon. Thus, it is a challenge to define precisely what comprises the e-learning condition or to create and operationalize a definition that has a real-world corollary.

Thus, for *e-learning research*, rather than for research on technology in education, we see that the kinds of questions to be addressed need to capture more of the evolving, contextual practices surrounding this increasingly societal-wide way of learning. Rather than research questions like 'What is the effect of [a new form of information and communication technology] on learning?' or 'Does the provision of a high degree of new technologies in the classroom increase learning outcomes?', *at this stage in the evolution of research in the field*, different questions need to be asked.

We are in a stage when the parameters of e-learning research are being defined; the complex relationships between learning and new technologies are beginning to be taken into account, and differences in access, use and the political, social and pedagogical contexts for e-learning are coming to the fore (as discussed in Chapter 11). Larger research questions in e-learning address substantive issues by asking questions such as the following:

- What is the societal impact of the increased use of online resources for learning and knowledge?
- What are the impacts on the educational system of certification of knowledge with regard to new online learning initiatives?
- What is the meaning and place of university certifications and degrees in the age of ubiquitous learning?
- How are knowledge sources vetted and authenticated in the digital age?
- How can e-learning be used to increase educational, economic, career and equal opportunities for remote or marginalized sectors of society?
- How does technology affect how, what, where and with whom we learn?
- How can e-learning, and participation in an e-learning society, increase global understanding?
- What are the implications of the 'economics of attention' for e-learning practices?
- What is the nature of the digital divide/spectrum now, and how might it develop? What can be done about it?

From these large questions, we can move on to more local and specific ones such as the following. Given the new and potentially unexpected outcomes, it is worth phrasing many of these questions as not just 'what' is happening, but more openly as 'how' is this change affecting particular actors, settings, relationships, etc.

- What are the social and pedagogical conditions that best support the use of whiteboards (smart boards) in primary (elementary) school classrooms?, or, How is whiteboard use affecting social and pedagogical conditions in the classroom?
- What are the economics of supplying every child with a laptop or handheld device in the school system of any one country, and what are the implications for lesson design? How does – if it does – the presence of laptops or handhelds in the classroom affect learning in [a particular setting]?
- What are the advantages and disadvantages of [a particular piece of software] when used with autistic children in a special needs school for the teaching of drama?, or, How has the implementation of [this particular piece of software] affected relations between teacher and students, and/or among students?

While such questions might seem too precise, too specific, or even addressed too narrowly to one setting or technology, they are the kinds of questions that research (and particularly individual research students) can address. They represent a necessary adjustment to transform the high-level, large questions into a manageable research project level, so that the research community can begin gathering studies to inform and ultimately address the higher-level policy and educational interests.

It will be clear from these examples that the tenor of our approach is to situate technologies within their social, political, economic and pedagogical contexts.

We do not see new technologies as a panacea for educational problems, nor (more broadly) as the answer to social ills and/or inefficiencies. Rather, we see technologies as embedded in human and social development; as means to a communicative end rather than as 'interventions' in a research design. That is why we think that research questions need to be teased out that investigate the relationship of new information and communication technologies to learning.

E-learning Research Dimensions

We now turn to discuss the differences between research *about* e-learning and research *for* e-learning. There has always been an inherent tension and confusion around what is involved in e-learning and hence what the goals are for research in the area. Research and writing under the heading of e-learning have addressed: technology in education from stand-alone tutoring systems to current VLEs; practical tips on how to teach online; reports of how implementations of online programs have unfolded; discussion of the future of the institution of higher education in the age of the Internet; studies of e-learner experience, and group and community processes in online learning environments; studies of 'networked learning' (Dirckinck-Holmfeld et al., 2009; Steeples and Jones, 2002); surveys of the spread of online learning initiatives (e.g. Sloan Consortium reports: Allen and Seaman, 2010); and studies in the theory (e.g. Parnell, forthcoming) and methodologies (Vavoula et al., 2009) of e-learning. Policy reports outline intentions from government level for the future of e-learning and the infrastructures that support e-learning (for the UK see Joint Information Systems Committee (JISC) reports; for Europe, see European Commission reports and EU e-learning papers; for the US, see National Science Foundation Task Force on Cyberlearning 2008; see also Mayadas et al., 2009; Watson et al., 2009).

As well as these areas, there is work that directly or indirectly addresses learning in groups and with technology, such as theory and research on communities of practice (Lave and Wenger, 1991; Rogoff, 1992; Wenger, 1998), expansive learning (Engeström, 2009), and organizational learning (Argote et al., 2003; Brown and Duguid, 1991). Goals of research and inquiry include successful implementation strategies at the local, institutional and international levels; satisfactory learner experience; greater and more inclusive reach for education, and theoretical understanding of new pedagogies, technology support group processes, and societal impacts. In teasing out research for theoretical and for practical perspectives we make the distinction between research *about* e-learning, and research *for* e-learning.

Research *about* and *for* E-learning

Most academic e-learning research fits under the heading of research *about* e-learning, examining e-learning as a social and pedagogical phenomenon.

Most socially inspired research will be *about* e-learning rather than *for* it. Research about e-learning is a valid and popular activity. It is almost always *ex post facto* research; that is, it is research that traces activity after the event, attempting to read pattern into activity that has already happened. The aim is to understand more fully the processes and activities of e-learning. A good example of such research is Choi's blended/hybrid learning project described as a case in Chapter 11 (Case 11.3). The aim of that project was to determine student perceptions of asynchronous online approaches to second language learning in English, in the Korean higher education context. Methods used included student questionnaire and interviews, teacher interviews, direct observation, and analysis of the particular software designed for second language learning and multimodal document analysis. The results of the research tell us about the nature and perceptions of such an e-learning approach in Korea, and may be generalizable to other countries. There will be *implications* for the future design of software programs, as well as for policy, practice and further research, but these will not be taken as far as a model for such design, let alone guidelines for the design or improvement of existing designs themselves.

Research *for* e-learning is different. It is part of the design process, and thus has a more practical end. It asks questions like: What is the best way to design 'in the service of learning'(Barab, et al., 2004)? What are the best available existing designs for e-learning software [in a particular field or on a particular topic]? How can I best compare two emerging designs to see which one is the more efficient and fit-for-purpose? Under what circumstances would a particular design work well, and what are its advantages and disadvantages? In other words, whereas research *about* e-learning aims to *understand* it better in social and pedagogical terms, research *for* e-learning aims to help improve its social, pedagogical and technical design.

Let us take the example of a virtual learning environment, Blackboard Academic (see Figure 4.2 in Chapter 4). The particular affordances of Blackboard Academic are well known. It allows institutions to register and induct students into a specific culture of e-learning that mirrors, in many ways, conventional learning approaches and procedures. Its off-the-shelf framework suits many institutions and programs or courses, but not all. So research is possible into what its affordances are, and where it has shortcomings. Such research can take the form of an *evaluation* of Blackboard Academic as a virtual learning environment, and thus lead the researcher to use again the more conventional approaches listed above in researching *about* e-learning. Comparisons can be made with other commercial VLEs, or with web-based, freely accessible VLEs like Moodle. Where the research leads toward suggested improvements in the design, and where that research is implemented in the use of Blackboard or its design at source, then it becomes research *for* e-learning.

There are other fundamental ways in which research in the e-learning field can act as research *for* e-learning. Although this kind of research might be characterized as applied research, it can start as blue sky research (i.e. thinking without barriers). For example, a focus group could be set up to brainstorm and subsequently prioritize the elements and qualities that a fit-for-purpose virtual learning environment might possess. Some important new directions in design work advocate the inclusion of the intended learners of the system, particularly when learning systems are designed to support regional or minority groups, yet are designed and delivered by more remote or mainstream providers. Participatory action research methods in particular form the basis of this approach (e.g. Bishop and Bruce, 2005; Stoecker, 2005a).

The results of such requirements gathering could be fed into the design process, so that a number of alternative proto-designs might be created. These again can be evaluated and tested by stakeholders, focus groups or other groups or individuals. The process of trial and re-trial, a form of testing the robustness and appropriateness of an emerging design, can be used to develop the product that will emerge from the process. At a later stage, as the product reaches the point of being scaled up to meet the demands of a wider audience, larger constituencies can be used for field trials. The model behind such research for e-learning is fundamentally a market-research and design model, the aim of which is to test and develop products for use. The premise behind such a model is that products can be improved to meet the demands of the market. With rapid change, however, there is caution about taking on such market models with the idea that there is one best way to implement an e-learning system. As discussed in earlier chapters, the 'perpetual beta' status of many information technology implementations suggests the need for continuous evaluation of design, as the entry of new technologies and practices, and the residual effects from earlier changes, affect and interact with literacy and learning practice, and continuously change the dynamic of local implementations. Thus, we move from ideas of one-off design to a continuous process of design in the service of learning (for more on design for e-learning, see Barab et al., 2004).

Such discussion of the *approaches* taken by e-learning research leads us to further questions about the changing *nature and format* of research itself in the digital age.

New Forms of Research Formats in the Digital Age

Why is there a need for new thinking about the nature and format of advanced research work? Specifically, what is it that we don't yet know in research about or for e-learning? What kinds of research would enable us to fill these gaps? Is there, indeed, a future for research in an environment that is changing rapidly in terms of the pace at which research is conducted and presented, especially when informing policy formulation? A burgeoning interest in e-learning and new theoretical interests in the effects of digitization and awareness of *multimodality* has raised interest in how knowledge is formed and presented (Kress, 2003, 2009). Increasingly, the conventional printed and bound word-based thesis or dissertation is inappropriate and/or anachronous for much advanced research. Not only are students pushing for change, but supervisors, supervisors' colleagues (who are on academic approval and upgrade panels), internal and external examiners and administrators of the doctoral process in universities need to be apprised of changes in the field. Web and digital-based submission at doctoral level, for example, has implications not only for the way the dissertation is developed and composed, it also has implications for the way it is read (see Andrews et al., 2011).

For example, it is possible to imagine a dissertation on the subject of complexity theory and e-learning design that is both *about* and *for* e-learning. First, the research underpinning such a dissertation might want to explore various theories of learning from a complexity theory perspective – which will assume there is no single explanatory theory, that multiple perspectives are necessary to explain the act of learning, that e-learning adds yet another complicating dimension to the challenge of the research, and that conventional, sequential argumentation is not appropriate to the structure of the emerging thesis. Furthermore, when it comes to design issues, the researcher may decide to include moving image as well as words, still images and three-dimensional models, diagrams or computer programs in the thesis to demonstrate the e-learning designs. A consequence of these deliberations may be that the conventional, printed thesis is not appropriate to represent and convey the research. Instead, the material lends itself to interactive website presentation, affording the opportunity to include sections of verbal text (as in a conventional thesis), image banks, moving image/video, kinetic model designs, or the running of a software program.

The structure of such a thesis would not be sequential (although a sequence for reading could be suggested); rather, the website would offer a variety of routes through the material, each starting at a different window on the home page. In every respect other than conventional, sequential argumentation, the criteria for a successful thesis could be met: criticality, scholarship, full referencing, innovation and originality, a contribution to knowledge, coherence and 'suitability for publication'. There is no reason why argumentation could not be included, in visual and/or verbal form, as part of the website as a whole. A different order of argumentation would also be offered by the totality of the submission: one which was driven by choreographic rules of composition and arrangement, rather than by rules of sequence and logic. Assessment of such submissions represents a new area of both practice and research.

There is, it must be acknowledged, resistance to the idea of multimodal/digital theses, and a question mark as to whether paper-based dissertations will become obsolete – though, in some universities, they already are. The central European tradition, based on rational humanism, suggests words and print are the principal medium via which arguments are made and tested; that e-learning is no different from learning, except as far as the 'conditions' for learning go; and that images (still or moving) and other modes of communication are peripheral and subsidiary to the verbal construct. And yet, undergraduate, graduate and research students are pressing for new forms of representation of knowledge, and specifically of the dissertation/thesis, the means by which their contribution to new knowledge is examined.

Often the arbiters of whether new forms of knowledge can be approved are the universities themselves. Their regulations and guidance for the conduct, shape and examination of dissertations and theses need to be under frequent review to make sure that students are not disadvantaged by working in new areas of research that require new forms of expression.

Becoming an E-Researcher

An e-researcher both examines and uses the opportunities afforded by contemporary information and communication technologies to accomplish research. As many areas embrace the digital as part of their research practice, so too can the area of e-learning. For our discussion here, we consider two aspects of e-research. One sense portrays an e-researcher as using all the tools available to become a network-based, collaborative and participatory researcher operating in the research field. This accords with much of what we have described of how we expect e-learners to operate, that is, as experts breaking new ground, as contributors in research communities, and as entrepreneurs making and using opportunities for their research. It also means retrieving and evaluating research literature from various sources, and using Internet communication technologies for research, interaction with others, collaboration and publication.

The second sense is of a researcher who uses *e-research* techniques to effect their research, for example through automated data collection, data mining, computer analysis of texts, and use of new technology tools and devices. E-research is a new and growing research area and research practice. There are new centers emerging devoted to e-research. A few of these in the UK are:

- Oxford e-Research Centre (www.oerc.ox.ac.uk)
- Oxford Internet Institute (www.oii.ox.ac.uk)
- National Centre for e-Social Science (www.ncess.ac.uk)
- Centre for e-Research at King's College London (www.kcl.ac.uk/iss/cerch/)
- Joint Information Systems Committee (JISC) (http://www.jisc.ac.uk/whatwedo/programs/eresearch.aspx)

E-research extends to science, social science and humanities. Depending on the country, these are known as cyberinfrastructure, e-science, e-social science and digital humanities. (For more on this area, see American Council of Learned Societies, 2006; Anderson and Kanuka, 2010; Atkins et al, 2003; Hine, 2006; Jankowski 2009; Schroeder and Fry, 2007).

These resources and centers provide support for e-researchers in finding their way through the e-research landscape. But *becoming* an e-researcher can be given an extra dimension by considering the activities as part of an e-learning framework, as in the present book, where the focus is not on e-research as a technical or networking facility but as a means of investigating e-learning practices. E-learning on the one hand, and e-research on the other, have operated to date largely as though they are separate and unconnected. Our proposal is that – like research, teaching and learning in a more general sense – both e-learning and e-research benefit from a closer association.

Becoming an e-researcher is like becoming an e-learner in that it requires a predilection for e-communication as well as the technical skills to develop in the field. For example, two distributed authors co-writing a book (e.g., as in the case of the present book) might create a common text on a file-sharing site for building up their draft chapters and bibliography; someone enrolled in an e-learning course or program may open a file to record their own critical reflections on their learning process; and research teams will operate with col-laboratories that contain digital libraries, data repositories and facilities for joint writing.

E-researchers commit notes and records to electronic documents rather than, or in preference to committing them to paper. It follows, logically, theoretically and even pragmatically that the final product of their research might be published and broadcast electronically, rather than in print. It may also follow philosoph-ically, as ideas of open source and open access lead e-researchers to post their work publicly online. One way of doing this is to publish via a creative commons license (Lessig, 2006; see http://creativecommons.org/). Creative commons was founded in 2001, with its first license being issued in 2002. It provides a legal mechanism for authors and creators to make their works available freely in the public domain, without fear of losing ownership or intellectual property rights to what they post. By 2008, there were 130 million licensed works, with special sections of the enterprise devoted to open and free educational material. Examples of organizations that use creative commons licenses are Al Jazeera, Flickr, Google and MIT OpenCourseware, all part of the larger Open Access movement for making knowledge available freely to a wide audience (Willinsky, 2005). The creative commons movement reflects a principle of freely available and open material, accessible via the Internet, and a resource to which writers/composers can contribute as well as access. The major breakthrough has been that contributors can use creative commons licensing to indicate how permissive they want to be in the use of their postings, choosing from completely re-usable and modifiable by anyone to attribution and non-commercial use only.

Using e-research as a way to conduct research entails using the emerging digital tools in the research process. Data can be collected from transaction records (e.g. in online discussion lists, blogs and comments), defined for automated collection (e.g. in collecting page view statistics, or posting behavior), via online means (surveys, email interviews), or data mined from available resources. Research may also be conducted on and through new devices, such as video cameras, mobile phones or GPS devices. Jones and Healing (2010), for example, used video cam-eras as diary tools for capturing student experiences at times of the day triggered by a mobile phone alert. Bruce (2008) used technologies such as GIS/GPS geospa-tial tools, video, podcasts and the Internet to engage youth in community action through community asset mapping and community journalism.

Future Research

What are the areas that we see as relevant for future research on e-learning? We characterize these under the following headings: learning theories; community-based studies; learning environments and ecologies; research methodologies and methods; and non-institutional research. Some of these headings have provided elements in the structure for the present book, and are thus those that we think are salient in the field at present, and for future research.

Learning Theories

As we have discussed in Chapters 2 and 3 of the present book, e-learning needs to build on conventional theories of learning by developing new dimensions: principally these are related to community-based practices (learning as an effect of communities and the navigation of their interconnections by learners), transformation, and emergence. Research projects usually need to define their theoretical foundations, yet much research to date in the field has been un- or under-theorized. We suggest that any e-learning research project, whether it is about e-learning or for e-learning, needs to define its theoretical framework. Such broad framework-setting allows for clear discussion of the constituent terms, for clarity in understanding the limitations/parameters of the research, and crucially for gauging whether progress has been made in the research. Such theoretical underpinning is important whether the research is empirical or not (see also Mayes and de Freitas, 2006).

Community-based Studies

Building on Chapter 6, in which we addressed learning communities and learning networks – and on the notion that learning is an effect of communities that we operate in, *and* the borders, boundaries and interconnections between them (see also Chapter 7) – one area for future research is exactly this area. One of the most telling contributions to research in the nature of communities and learning is Heath (1983), an ethnographic study of the development of communication styles and attitudes toward learning in two contrasted communities: one of these communities is characterized as less socio-economically advantaged than the other, but with closer social ties, more implicit forms of communication and a stronger sense of community. Such a study needs to be undertaken comparing e-communities with 'real world' communities – or communities in which e-learning and day-to-day activity (not mediated by e-learning) interact. In a point we will make throughout this section, such ethnographic studies are valuable in the field of e-learning research because, by contrast with the many single class, single teacher accounts about e-learning, they allow deep and thorough analysis of the various aspects of e-learning as embedded in communities – in particular how e-communities (e.g. discussion groups online, co-participants in an e-learning course or program, subscribers to a common e-cause) interface and interact with real-world connections. There are few such studies to date. Most research has focused on large-scale statistical surveys or self-reported descriptions of e-learning discoveries and innovations with little analysis or critical perspective.

Learning Environments and Ecologies

In Chapters 6 and 7 we looked at learning communities/networks, and at e-learning ecologies. Dutton et al. (2004) provide an example of a case study that explores the learning ecology of a virtual learning environment in a higher education institution. As the abstract declares,

> [T]his paper describes a case study of the introduction into a university of a widely diffused e-learning platform: an enterprise-wide virtual learning environment. The study suggests a variety of patterns and themes tied to the social dynamics of this innovation. These highlight variations across instructors in how the technology was employed, which illuminate the complex ecology surrounding its implementation and use. This offers insights into the faltering development of e-learning in higher education, and learning more generally. (2004: 131)

Learning environments and ecologies explore the *social dynamics* of innovation: for example what happens to social patterning when a new VLE is introduced. Such dynamics are far-reaching and include: library provision; the role of librarians; different roles for teachers and online tutors; administrative support for such e-learning innovation; student-to-teacher interaction and student-to-student interaction; and the submission and examination of student work. It follows that, given the emerging state of e-learning research, case studies are excellent ways of describing and evaluating such ecologies. Because, as in any ecological chain or cycle, changes in one part can affect other parts of the ecology, it is hard to examine with an organic, rounded, inclusive case study approach. At the same time, we need to build on case studies to generate and improve theory, and to make generalizations that can be tested with larger groups.

Research Methodologies and Methods

Is it possible and desirable to carry on researching e-learning via the conventional methodologies and methods? In terms of methodologies, most *ex post facto* research looks out of date by the time it has been published: the worlds of e-learning, new technologies and new social practices have moved on. So how can research come up to speed with developments in e-learning? There is a dilemma for research here: it wishes to describe, explain and find patterns in social practices. At the same time, in the field of e-learning, new practices are developing and outrunning research. First, we suggest that *research* in the field becomes faster. That does not mean it is of lower quality or is less rigorous. Rather, that it moves alongside developments in e-learning by using some of the approaches that e-learning itself uses: rapid surveying of samples with electronic tools, based on well-piloted questionnaires; online interviewing via video and/or audio, with interview files being saved and stored electronically rather than being 'transcribed'; and observation via video and the saving of clips of footage that can be stored, arrayed and compared easily. Texts can also be captured and analyzed automatically. This is a potentially powerful tool for e-learning analysis given the amount of text produced and available for analysis for signs of learning or other outcomes (Gruzd, 2009; Gruzd and Haythornthwaite, forthcoming).

Such an approach requires facility with the tools of e-research, but it also assumes a methodological framework that is *kaleidoscopic* in the collection and analysis of mixed-mode data. The kaleidoscopic approach in itself creates a frame around the researched area: it is a frame that both delimits the research and also provides a means through which the research can be disseminated. If such an approach seems too quick-fix and potentially superficial, consider the alternative, conventional approach: fast-moving, complex social activity is recorded and transcribed into verbal print. The transcription itself may enable analysis, bringing critical frames to bear; but, on the other hand, it may transmute the data in its effort to abstract it and to find patterns within it. The advantage of a quicker, kaleidoscopic approach is that practice can be held up for reflection, analysis and examination *closer to its source* than in conventional approaches.

In terms of methods, these remain secondary technical issues in the conduct of research. It is not so much the methods themselves (typically, questionnaire, interview, observation, document analysis, think-aloud protocols and other forms of self-report) but the way in which the methods are conducted which can be transformed. For example, Google analytics can record and analyze visits to a website: not only the number and source of such visits, but their duration and whether they are 'returners' or new visitors. (For an interesting analysis of trends derived from Google searches, see Google flutrends; http://www.google.org/flutrends/about/how.html.) These are examples of instantaneous data that can provide one perspective on the social phenomenon of e-learning. Another is the very simple practice of using email for in-depth interview, rather than undertake an interview orally (e.g. via Skype which is a useful tool in this regard, especially for long-distance interviews), questions can be sent in advance, by email, to a respondent who replies in kind. Once he or she has replied, further probing and follow-up can take place to increase the depth of the interview. In such an approach, there is no need for transcription: it takes place as part of the written interview exchange itself. (For a comparison of interview methods, see Kazmer and Xie, 2008.)

Research methodologies and methods adapt to different environments and to changes in technology. There is no reason why they could not continue to adapt to come up to speed with changes in e-learning practices themselves, and also be available in formats for showing to respondents and to audiences for the research, so that changes to practice, if required, can take place without long waits for research reports.

Non-institutional Research

Because learning and e-learning can take place anywhere (see Cope and Kalantzis, 2009), in informal as well as in formal, institutional settings, research needs to be able to explore and investigate practices outside formal education. At the risk of coining yet another term in the field, *ubiquitous research*, which has been undertaken throughout history as fieldwork, ethnographic and anthropological studies, socially situated research and other forms of 'real-world' research, needs to be fleet of foot, adaptable to circumstances and systematic. Hand-held devices like digital audio recording equipment and third or fourth generation mobile devices that can take still and moving images, record sound, enable note-making and have wireless connectivity are ideal for capturing data and evidence in non-institutional settings. A case study on exactly this sort of research follows. The case describes ongoing research in a non-institutional setting: in this case, the digital productions of Filipino-British youth in Hounslow, west London.

CASE 12.1: MIGRATORY PRACTICES IN E-COMMUNITIES AND E-LEARNING RESEARCH

Myrrh M. Domingo, New York University, USA

Given the vast movement of people and ideas in our global and digital world, language and literacies research must increasingly attend to the migrating practices occurring across diverse social contexts, including that of e-communities and e-learning. My ethnography of Filipino British youth in London – the 'Pinoys' – speaks directly to this shift. They challenged prescriptive approaches to literacy learning as they shaped and were shaped by multimodal texts and digital technologies in their everyday lives (Cope and Kalantzis, 2000; Kress and van Leeuwen, 2001; New London Group, 1996). Contrary to the stillness that comes with viewing literacy as a fixed skills set, my work with the Pinoys focused on their *migrating literacies* – a term that I use to describe their merging rather than distilling of their linguistic diversity, cultural knowledge, and social identities – across contexts. Documenting such migratory patterns is essential given that digital technologies and global migrations increasingly enable such fluid movements to be a part of daily life in most urban settings (Alvermann, 2008; Appadurai, 1996; Banks, 2008; Kirkland, 2009; Suarez-Orozco, 2007). Understanding how youth – like the Pinoys – navigate social contexts is critical as current research demonstrates that students must develop multilingual and cross-cultural competencies to manage diverse networks of relationships in our global and digital world (Hull, et al., 2009; Jayakumar, 2008; Lam, 2006).

Because the Pinoys were constantly *crossing* multiple social contexts (Rampton, 1995), it was problematic to study their everyday practices of languages and literacies as rooted only in the place-based structures that they frequented. The scope of my research necessitated that I display the ways in which the Pinoys merged their linguistic diversity and cultural knowledge, or their *migrating literacies*, to attend to the competing discourses of their social worlds. While ethnographic methods can provide insight into everyday practices of languages and literacies as situated in social interaction, these lived realities in online contexts remain a relatively new ethnographic domain in language and literacy studies. To this end, my participant observations and interviews spanned both the world navigable by the body and the world mediated online. In addition, the literacy artifacts I collected were often 'noisy and moving', and could not be captured for line-by-line transcription like most static and monochromatic texts.

My data collection and analyses methods required that I also partake in migratory practices to make meaning of the Pinoys' distinctive ways with words. I physically traveled with them across social contexts and participated in their online communities. Further, to visibly document their engagement of language and literacies in e-learning environments necessitated that I expand beyond traditional ethnographies of language and literacy research. Though my research builds upon this tradition, I also drew from ethnographies of media to enhance my understanding of culture from rooted-space orientations to more fluid configurations (Condry, 2006; Dornfeld, 1998). This ethnographic approach enabled me to make meaning of the data collected beyond *Third Space* (Bhabha, 2004) literacy conceptualizations, whereby in-school practices and out-of-school practices overlap to create an intermediary space. Rather, the migratory approach I employed opened new possibilities for studying additional everyday learning spaces in the lives of the Pinoys (e.g. composing music on a mobile phone while riding public transportation or listening to a podcast while walking to school). Studying these migratory learning spaces made it possible to display how the Pinoys, their ideas, and their 'noisy and moving' texts were crossing discourses of schools, homes, communities and workplaces.

Myrrh M. Domingo, is a doctoral candidate at the Steinhardt School of Culture, Education and Human Development, New York University.

From Research *about* E-learning to Research *for* E-learning

Earlier in this chapter we distinguished between research *about* e-learning, as in the case study above, and research *for* e-learning. Research about e-learning is valuable because it helps to identify pattern in the field; it can evaluate; it provides historical background; and it links e-learning to the history of learning. Crucially, it can frame and re-frame discourses in the field so that contexts, problems and solutions can be clearly defined, as in Myrrh Domingo's case study (Case 12.1) – whether they are economic, social, political, cultural and/or pedagogic.

But the pace of change in e-learning, not only in technological change but in the ecologies and social dynamics of the field, requires a different kind of research. It is our contention that, increasingly, research *for* e-learning will need to stand alongside research *about* e-learning. The reason for this is that the market demands that development and research run hand-in-hand, or preferably that research runs ahead of, not behind, development. Consequently, research that contributes to the design and development of new products, new networks, new forms of e-learning, will be highly valued. Such research is not all geared toward product development in the commercial marketplace. Much of it is concerned with improving systems, designing new learning interfaces, and providing better network facilities and possibilities. The crucial link is that between the research itself and its transfer to real-world application, including making available digitally borne and digitally recorded dissertations and theses to a wider community via the web as soon as they are approved, edited and ready for publication (see Andrews et al., 2011 for a number of chapters on this topic).

Even published research *about* e-learning can contain, as is the convention, implications for practice, policy and further research in its conclusions. All too often, however, these concluding statements are hypothetical. It would be good to see *models* of future practice and design included in theses and dissertations, and sharper definition of the key questions that need to be asked. Also useful will be discussion of how methodology and methods can be improved and exploited in the pursuit of knowledge about and for e-learning, and specific guidelines for the formation of policy and practice.

Conclusions

We come not to a single conclusion to a wide and fast-changing field, but to a number of interim conclusions about e-learning theory and practice.

First, we wish to reiterate that e-learning needs a new theory of learning. Even though theories of learning in the 1980s and 1990s took a turn to the social, there is still a strong residual body of learning theory that sees it as located in cognition or brain science. While it is quite proper that a balance is maintained in psycho-social approaches to learning, there are dimensions of e-learning that do not seem well served by conventional learning theory. Two of these are: the notion that learning is an effect of communities and the inter-relationship of those communities; and that learning is transformational at the individual, social and political levels. In particular, we think that the networked dimension of e-learning has been underestimated by theory.

Second, new discourses are emerging around e-learning that need to be reviewed, used, applied and tested in everyday and in academic use. If we see bodies of knowledge as being transformed by the interaction *between* people, and also at the *interconnections* between different electronic and real-world communities, then the discourses that both embody and carry those transformations will change. Just as there is a reciprocal relationship between new technologies and learning, so too the relationship between new discourses and new practices is reciprocal: at times social action runs ahead of terminology, at other times, language and other forms of (multimodal) communication create a reified world which can itself determine the formation of ideas and new products, because these terms are the tools we think with.

A third conclusion is that we wish to emphasize the social over the technological. Just as 'the social is prior' in communication studies (and yet, as in the previous paragraph, the technological can at times break new ground and take the lead in the relationship), so too we approach e-learning from a social point of view rather than from a technicist one. The social view is less prone to over-exaggeration and flushes of excitement about new technologies. Early 1990s publications, for example, contained grand hopes that the Internet would 'democratize' society, free up information access for all users, simplify and make more efficient business transactions, revolutionize academic study and generally act as a panacea for many social ills. To an extent, such changes have happened and we fully acknowledge that writing at the start of the second decade of the 21st century, we are dependent on such changes. But new technologies find their place in an economy of means of communication, just as the wax cylinder of the 1890s became the vinyl record and transmuted into CD technology, and as the printed book continues to have a place in everyday life, despite e-book advances.

Fourth, we have emphasized the importance of an ecological understanding of the operation of e-learning in society and within learning and learning-management systems. E-learning is not an off-the-shelf option that can be used discretely in situations where there has been no preparation for it. It requires an infrastructure that consists of administrative support, attitudinal changes in terms of students and lecturer/supervisor practices, a willingness to engage in networking, access to and facility with the necessary technology, and a cultural and institutional commitment to make it work. There is still an assumption on the part of many policy-makers in education that e-learning is a cheaper, more efficient option to conventional learning. However, experience has shown that insufficient strategic planning, development time and resources, and underestimates of the time it takes for lecturers to give high quality responses to students, can result in unsuccessful projects on a large and small scale. An ecological approach means understanding that technological change is deeply implicated in social change, and vice versa.

We cannot underestimate, too, the importance of cross- and inter-cultural awareness when it comes to designing e-learning. Although, on the one hand, one of the great affordances of e-learning is that, with equal access to it and competence in its use, it can provide 'universal' or global coverage, bringing students together from a wide variety of contexts to enjoy intellectual exchange together, on the other hand there is the concomitant aspect of diversity and cultural difference. Such difference can be geographical, national, ethnic, gender, ability/disability, socio-economic and/or class-based. Key considerations that need to be taken into account include equality (or not) of access to hardware, software and wired or wireless connectivity, the degree of preparedness for offline and online educational activity, linguistic capability (we still have not seen enough bi- or tri-lingual e-learning programs), and education assumptions that are held by different cultures, for example with regard to types of argumentation and different forms of rationality.

Lastly, we wish to reiterate at the end of the chapter, and the end of this book, the importance of research in e-learning. We have characterized the two main types of research as research *about* e-learning and research *for* e-learning, suggesting that what is needed at present is a shift toward the latter. If research is to have more relevance in the field, it must get upstream of policy and practice.

We hope that this book provides a basis for further discussion, and that it will provoke and encourage new thinking and new practices in the field. In particular, we hope to have clarified some of the issues that need attention in e-learning, and to have provided at least the firm foundations for future theory and practice.

Further Reading

Anderson, T. and Kanuka, H. (2010). *E-research: Methods, Strategies and Issues*. Available online at: www.e-research.ca/index.htm

Andrews, R., Borg, E., Boyd Davis, S., Domingo, M. and England, J. (Eds.) (2011). *The Sage Handbook of Digital Dissertations and Theses*. London: Sage.

Conole, G. and Oliver, M. (Eds.), (2006). *Contemporary Perspectives in E-learning Research: Themes, Methods and Impact on Practice*. Abingdon: Routledge.

References

Adami, E. and Kress, G. (2010). 'The social semiotics of convergent mobile devices: New forms of composition and the transformation of *habitus*', in G. Kress, *Multimodality: A Social Semiotic Approach to Contemporary Communication*. Abingdon: Routledge. pp. 184–97.

Agarwal-Hollands, U. and Andrews, R. (2001). 'From scroll … to codex … and back again', *Education, Communication, Information*, 1(1): 59–73.

ALA Presidential Committee on Information Literacy (1989). *An Information Age School*. Retrieved 20 April 2010 from: http://www.ala.org/ala/mgrps/divs/acrl/publications/whitepapers/presidential.cfm

Allen, I. E. and Seaman, J. (2010). *Learning on Demand: Online Education in the United States 2009*. Babson Survey Research Group and The Sloan Consortium.

Allen, T. J. (1977). *Managing the Flow of Technology: Technology Transfer and the Dissemination of Technological Information within the R&D Organization*. Cambridge, MA: MIT Press.

Ally, M. (2004). 'Foundations of educational theory for online learning', in T. Anderson and F. Elloumi (Eds.), *Theory and Practice of Online Learning*. Athabasca: Athabasca University. pp. 3–31.

Alvermann, D. E. (2008). 'Why bother theorizing adolescents' online literacies for classroom practice and research?', *Journal of Adult and Adolescent Literacy*, 52(1): 8–19.

American Bar Association (2010). *Standard 306. DISTANCE EDUCATION*. Available online from: http://www.abanet.org/legaled/distanceeducation/Standard306.doc. Retrieved 20 April 2010 from: http://www.abanet.org/legaled/accreditation/acinfo.html

American Council of Learned Societies (2006). *Our Cultural Commonwealth: The Report of the American Council of Learned Societies Commission on Cyberinfrastructure for the Humanities and Social Sciences*. New York: American Council of Learned Societies.

Anderson, B. (1991). *Imagined Communities: Reflections on the Origin and Spread of Nationalism*, 2nd edn. London: Verso Editions/NLB.

Anderson, T. (2004). 'Toward a theory of online learning', in T. Anderson and F. Elloumi (Eds.), *Theory and Practice of Online Learning*. Athabasca: Athabasca University. pp. 33–60.

Anderson, T. and Elloumi, F. (Eds.) (2004). *Theory and Practice of Online Learning*. Athabasca: Athabasca University.

Anderson, T. and Kanuka, H. (2010). *E-Research: Methods, Strategies and Issues*. Retrieved 28 April 2010 from: www.e-research.ca/index.htm.

Andrews, R. (Ed.) (2004). *The Impact of ICT on Literacy Education*. London: RoutledgeFalmer.

Andrews, R. (2009a). 'Does e-learning require a new theory of learning?', paper given at European Conference for Education Research, University of Vienna, 29 September.

Andrews, R. (2009b). *Argumentation in Higher Education: Improving Practice through Theory and Research*. New York: Routledge.

Andrews, R. (2010). *Re-framing Literacy: Teaching and Learning in English and the Language Arts*. New York: Routledge.

Andrews, R. (forthcoming). *A Theory of Contemporary Rhetoric*. New York: Routledge.

Andrews, R. and Haythornthwaite, C. (Eds.) (2007). *The Sage Handbook of E-learning Research*. London: Sage.

Andrews, R., Borg, E., Boyd Davis, S., Domingo, M. and England, J. (Eds.) (2011). *The Sage Handbook of Digital Dissertations and Theses*. London: Sage.

Appadurai, A. (1996). *Modernity at Large. Cultural Dimensions of Globalization*. Minneapolis: University of Minnesota Press.

Arenas, M. B., Hitos, A., Perchiazzi, M. and Ugolini, S. (2010). 'People's empowerment through blended mentoring: The EMPIRE project experimentation in Spain and Italy', *European Journal of Online, Distance and E-learning*. 9 March. Retrieved 23 June 2010 from: http://www.eurodl.org/

Argote, L., McEvily, B. and Reagans, R. (2003). 'Managing knowledge in organizations: Creating, retaining, and transferring knowledge', *Management Science, 49*(4), special issue.

Argyle, M. (1991). *Cooperation: The Basis of Sociability*. London: Routledge.

Association of College and Research Libraries (2000). *Information Literacy Competency Standards for Higher Education*. Retrieved 12 February 2010 from: http://www.ala.org/ala/mgrps/divs/acrl/standards/informationliteracycompetency.cfm#ilhed

Atkins, D. E., Droegemeier, K. K., Feldman, S. I., Garcia–Molina, H., Klein, M. L., Messerschmitt, D. G., Messina, P., Ostriker, J. P. and Wright, M. H. (2003). *Revolutionizing Science and Engineering Through Cyberinfrastructure: Report of the National Science Foundation Blue-Ribbon Advisory Panel on Cyberinfrastructure*. Arlington, VA. Available online at: http://www.nsf.gov/publications/pub_summ.jsp?ods_key=cise051203

Aviv, R., Erlich, Z., Ravid, G. and Geva, A. (2003). 'Network analysis of knowledge construction in asynchronous learning networks', *Journal of Asynchronous Learning Networks, 7*(3): 1–23.

Baecker, R. (Ed.) (1993). *Readings in Groupware and Computer-Supported Cooperative Work*. San Mateo, CA: Morgan Kaufmann.

Bandura, A. (1977). *Social Learning Theory*. Englewood Cliffs, NJ: Prentice Hall.

Banks, J. A. (2008). 'Diversity, group identity, and citizenship education in a global age', *Educational Researcher, 37*(3): 129–39.

Bannon, L. (1989). 'Issues in computer supported collaborative learning', in C. O'Malley (Ed.), *Computer Supported Collaborative Learning*. Berlin: Springer-Verlag. pp. 267–82.

Bannon, L. and Schmidt, K. (1991). 'CSCW: Four characters in search of a context', in J. M. Bowers and S. D. Benford (Eds.), *Studies in Computer Supported Cooperative Work: Theory, Practice, and Design*. Amsterdam: Elsevier. pp. 3–16.

Barab, S. A., Kling, R. and Gray, J. H. (Eds.) (2004). *Designing for Virtual Communities in the Service of Learning*. New York: Cambridge University Press.

Baron, N. S. (Ed.) (2008). *Always On: Language in an Online and Mobile World*. Oxford, UK: Oxford University Press.

Barton, D., and Tusting, K. (Eds.) *Beyond Communities of Practice: Language, Power and Social Context*. Cambridge, UK: Cambridge University Press.

Baym, N. K. (1995). 'From practice to culture on Usenet', in S. L. Star (Ed.), *The Cultures of Computing*. Oxford: Blackwell. pp. 29–52.

Baym, N. K. (2000). *Tune In, Log On: Soaps, Fandom and Online Community*. Thousand Oaks, CA: Sage.

Bayne, S. (2008). 'Uncanny spaces for higher education: Teaching and learning in virtual worlds', *Alt-J Research in Learning Technology, 16*(3): 197–205.

Bayne, S. (2010). 'Academetron, automaton, phantom: Uncanny digital pedagogies', *London Review of Education, 8*(1): 5–13.

Bayne, S., Williamson, Z. and Ross, J. (2010). 'Reading screens: A critical visual analysis', in L. Dirkinck-Holmfeld, V. Hodgson, C. Jones, M. de Laat, D. McConnell and T. Ryberg (Eds.), *Proceedings of the 7th International Conference on Networked Learning*. Lancaster University. pp. 35–43.

Becker, H. S. (1953). 'Becoming a marijuana smoker', *American Journal of Sociology*, 59(3): 235–42.

Becker, H. S., Geer, B., Hughes, E. C. and Strauss, A. L. (1961). *Boys in White: Student Culture in Medical School*. Chicago, IL: University of Chicago Press.

Bell, G. and Gemmell, J. (2007). 'A digital life', *Scientific American*, 296(3): 58–65.

Benkler, Y. (2006). *The Wealth of Networks: How Social Production Transforms Markets and Freedom*. New Haven, CT: Yale University Press.

Berge, Z. L. (1997). 'Computer conferencing and the on-line classroom', *International Journal of Educational Telecommunications*, 3(1): 3–21.

Berger, P. L. and Luckmann, T. (1966). *The Social Construction of Reality*. New York: Anchor Books.

Berners–Lee, T., with Fischetti, M. (1999). *Weaving the Web: The Original Design and Ultimate Destiny of the World Wide Web by its Inventor*. New York: Harper-Collins.

Bhabha, H. (2004). *The Location of Culture*. New York: Routledge.

Bijker, W. E. (1995). *Of Bicycles, Bakelites, and Bulbs: Toward a Theory of Sociotechnical Change*. Cambridge, MA: MIT Press.

Bijker, W., Hughes, T.P. and Pinch, T. (Eds.) (1987). *The Social Construction of Technological Systems: New Directions in the Sociology and History of Technology*. Cambridge, MA: MIT Press.

Bishop, A. P. (2000). 'Communities for the new century', *Journal of Adolescent and Adult Literacy*, 43(5): 472–78.

Bishop, A. P., and Bruce, B. (2005). 'Community informatics: Integrating action, research, and learning', *Bulletin of the American Society for Information Science and Technology*, 31(6). Available online at: http://www.asis.org/Bulletin/Aug–05/bishopbruce.htm

Bishop, A. P., Bruce, B. C., Lunsford, K. J., Jones, M. C., Nazarova, M., Linderman, D., Won, M., Heidorn, P. B., Ramprakash, R. and Brock, A. (2004). 'Supporting community inquiry with digital resources', *Journal of Digital Information*, 5(3). Retrieved 25 June 2010 from: http://journals.tdl.org/jodi/article/viewArticle/140/138

Bishop, A., Van House, N. and Buttenfield, B. (Eds.) (2003). *Digital Library Use: Social Practice in Design and Evaluation*. Cambridge, MA: MIT Press.

Bolter, J. D. and Grusin, R. (1999). *Remediation: Understanding New Media*. Cambridge MA: MIT Press.

Bone, J. (2010). 'American lecturers banning laptops from the classroom', *The Times*, 11 March. Retrieved 21 March 2010 from: http://www.timesonline.co.uk/tol/news/world/us_and_americas/article7057511.ece

Bourdieu, P. (1986). 'The forms of capital', in J. G. Richardson (Ed.), *Handbook of Theory and Research for the Sociology of Education*. Santa Barbara, CA: Greenwood. pp. 241–58.

boyd, d. and Ellison, N. (2007). 'Social network sites: Definition, history, and scholarship', *Journal of Computer-Mediated Communication,13*: 210–30.

Bradner, E., Kellogg, W. and Erickson, T. (1999). 'The adoption and use of "Babble": A field study of chat in the workplace'. *Proceedings of the 6th European Conference on Computer Supported Cooperative Work*. Copenhagen, Denmark. pp. 139–58. Retrieved 7 April 2010 from http://www.research.ibm.com/SocialComputing/Papers/AdoptionOfBabble.htm

Bransford, J. D., Brown, A. L. and Cocking, R. R. (Eds.) (1999). *How People Learn: Brain, Mind, Experience, and School*. Washington, DC: National Academy Press.

Bregman, A. and Haythornthwaite, C. (2003). 'Radicals of presentation: Visibility, relation, and co–presence in persistent conversation', *New Media and Society*, 5(1): 117–40.

Brock, A. (2005). '"A belief in humanity is a belief in colored men": Using culture to span the digital divide', *Journal of Computer-Mediated Communication, 11*(1): article 17. Available online at: http://jcmc.indiana.edu/vol11/issue1/brock.html

Brock, A. (2007). 'Defining a community and a culture: Racial identity production by African American and mainstream websites'. Available online at: (2007) unpublished doctoral dissertation, University of Illinois at Urbana-Champaign, Champaign, IL.

Brown, J. S. (2000). 'Growing up digital: How the web changes work, education, and the ways people learn', *Change, 32*(2): 10–20.

Brown, J. S. and Adler, R. P. (2008). 'Minds on fire: Open education, the long tail, and learning 2.0', *EDUCAUSE Review, 43*(1): 16–32.

Brown, J. S., Collins, A. and Duguid, P. (1989). Situated cognition and the culture of learning. *Educational Researcher, 18*(1): 32–42.

Brown, J. S. and Duguid, P. (1991). 'Organizational learning and communities-of-practice: Toward a unified view of working, learning, and innovation', *Organization Science, 2*(1): 40–57.

Brown, J. S. and Duguid, P. (2000). *The Social Life of Information.* Boston, MA: Harvard University Press.

Brown, J. S. and Duguid, P. (2001). 'Knowledge and organization: A social-practice perspective', *Organization Science, 12*(2): 198–213.

Bruce, B. C. (2003). 'Distributed knowledge research collaborative', paper given at the Professional Development Workshop, Academy of Management Annual Meeting. Seattle, Washington.

Bruce, B. C. (2008). 'Learning at the border: How young people use new media for community action and personal growth', in C. Angeli and N. Valanides (Eds.), *Proceedings of the 6th Panhellenic Conference with International Participation: Information and Communication Technologies in Education (HICTE).* Nicosia, Cyprus: Department of Education, University of Cyprus. pp. 3–10. Available online at: http://hdl.handle.net/2142/13340

Bruce, B. C. and Bishop, A. P. (2008). 'New literacies and community inquiry', in J. Coiro, M. Knobel, C. Lankshear and D. Leu, (Eds.), *The Handbook of Research in New Literacies.* New York: Routledge. pp. 699–742.

Bruce, B. C. (2010). '"Building an airplane in the air": The life of the inquiry group', in B. Drayton and J. Falk (Eds.), *Creating and Facilitating Effective On–Line Professional Development for Educators.* New York: Teachers College Press.

Bruce, B. C. and Hogan, M. P. (1998). 'The disappearance of technology: Toward an ecological model of literacy', in D. Reinking, M. McKenna, L. Labbo and R. Kieffer (Eds.), *Handbook of Literacy and Technology: Transformations in a Post-Typographical World.* Hillsdale, NJ: Erlbaum. pp. 269–81.

Bruckman, A. (1997). '*MOOSE* crossing: construction, community, and learning in a networked virtual world for kids', unpublished doctoral dissertation, Massachusetts Institute of Technology, Cambridge, MA. Retrieved 8 April 2010 from: http://www.cc.gatech.edu/~asb/thesis/

Bruckman, A. and Jensen, C. (2002). 'The mystery of the death of Mediamoo: Seven years of evolution of an online community', in K. A. Renninger and W. Shumar (Eds.), *Building Virtual Communities: Learning and Change in Cyberspace.* Cambridge: Cambridge University Press. pp. 21–33.

Bruffee, K. A. (1993). *Collaborative Learning: Higher Education, Interdependence, and the Authority of Knowledge.* Baltimore: Johns Hopkins University Press.

Bryant, S. L., Forte, A. and Bruckman, A. (2005). 'Becoming Wikipedian: Transformation of participation in a collaborative online encyclopedia', paper presented at the International ACM SIGGROUP Conference. Sanibel Island, FL.

Budhathoki, N. R. (2010). 'Participants' motivations to contribute geographic information in an online community', unpublished doctoral dissertation, University of Illinois at Urbana–Champaign, Champaign, IL. http://hdl.handle.net2142/16956

Budhathoki, N. R., Bruce, B. C. and Nedovic–Budic, Z. (2008). 'Reconceptualizing the role of the user of spatial data infrastructure', *GeoJournal, 72*(3–4): 149–60.

Bundy, A. (Ed.) (2004). *Australian and New Zealand Information Literacy Framework: Principles, Standards and Practice, 2nd edn.* Adelaide: Australian and New Zealand Institute for Information Literacy. Retrieved 12 February 2010 from: http://www.caul.edu.au/info-literacy/InfoLiteracyFramework.pdf

Burt, R. S. (2000). 'The network structure of social capital', *Research in Organizational Behavior, 22*: 345–423.

Caldwell, B., Cooper, M., Reid, L. G., and Vanderheiden, G. (Eds.) (December 11, 2008). *Web Content Accessibility Guidelines (WCAG) 2.0.* W3C. Available online at: http://www.w3.org/TR/WCAG20/

Carroll, J. M. (Ed.) (2002). *Human–Computer Interaction in the New Millennium.* Upper Saddle River, NJ: Addison-Wesley.

Castells, M. (2001). *The Internet Galaxy: Reflections on the Internet, Business and Society.* New York: Oxford University Press.

CEC (Commission of the European Communities) (2005). *eInclusion Revisited: The Local Dimension of the Information Society.* Commission Staff Working Document.

Cheong, P. H. and Martin, J. N. (2009). 'Cultural implications of e-learning access (& divides): Teaching intercultural communication courses online', in B. A. Olaniran (Ed.), *Cases on Successful E-learning Practices in the Developed and Developing World: Methods for Global Information Economy.* Hershey, PA: IGI Global. pp. 78–91.

Cherny, L. (1999). *Conversation and Community: Chat in a Virtual World.* Stanford, CA: CSLI Publications.

Cho, H., Stefanone, M. and Gay, G. (2002). 'Social network analysis of information sharing networks in a CSCL community'. *Proceedings of the Computer-Supported Collaborative Learning Conference.* Boulder, CO.

Clark, H. H. (1996). *Using Language.* Cambridge, UK: Cambridge University Press.

Clark, H. H. and Brennan, S. E. (1991). 'Grounding in communication', in L. B. Resnick, J. M. Levine, and S. D. Teasley (Eds.), *Perspectives on Socially Shared Cognition.* Washington, DC: American Psychological Association. pp. 127–49.

Clarke, A. (1991). 'Social worlds/arenas theory as organizational theory', in D. Maines (Ed.), *Social Organization and Social Process: Essays in Honor of Anselm Strauss.* New York: Aldine de Gruyter. pp. 119–58.

Coakes, E., Willis, D. and Lloyd-Jones, R. (Eds) (2000). *The New SocioTech: Graffiti on the Long Wall.* Godalming, England: Springer-Verlag.

Cohen, W. M. and Levinthal, D. A. (1990). 'Absorptive capacity: A new perspective on learning and innovation', *Administrative Science Quarterly, 35*: 128–52.

Cohill, A. M. and Kavanaugh, A. L. (2000). *Community Networks: Lessons from Blacksburg, Virginia, 2nd edn.* Boston, MA: Artech House.

Collins, A. (2006). 'Cognitive apprenticeship', in K. R. Sawyer (Ed.), *The Cambridge Handbook of the Learning Sciences.* Cambridge, UK: Cambridge University Press.

Collins, R. (1998). *The Sociology of Philosophies: A Global Theory of Intellectual Change.* Cambridge, MA: Belknap Press/Harvard University Press.

Condry, I. (2006). *Hip-Hop Japan: Rap and the Paths of Cultural Globalization.* Durham, NC: Duke University Press.

Conole, G. and Oliver, M. (Eds.) (2007). *Contemporary Perspectives in E-learning Research: Themes, Methods and Impact on Practice.* London: Routledge.

Constant, D., Kiesler, S. B., and Sproull, L. S. (1996). 'The kindness of strangers: The usefulness of electronic weak ties for technical advice', *Organization Science, 7*(2): 119–35.

Contractor, N. S. and Eisenberg, E. M. (1990). 'Communication networks and new media in organizations', in J. Fulk and C. W. Steinfield. (Eds.), *Organizations and Communication Technology.* Newbury Park, CA: Sage. pp. 143–72.

Cook, S. D. N. and Brown, J. S. (1999). 'Bridging epistemologies: The generative dance between organizational knowledge and organizational knowing', *Organization Science, 10*(4): 381–400.

Cope, B. and Kalantzis, M. (Eds.) (2000). *Multiliteracies*. New York and London: Routledge.

Cope, B. and Kalantzis, M. (Eds.) (2009). *Ubiquitous Learning*. Champaign, IL: University of Illinois Press.

Cornford, J. and Pollock, N. (2002). 'The university campus as "resourceful constraint": Process and practice in the construction of the virtual university', in M. R. Lea and K. Nicoll (Eds.), *Distributed Learning: Social and Cultural Approaches to Practice*. London: RoutledgeFalmer. pp. 170–81.

Crabtree, A., Rodden, T. and Benford, S. (2005). 'Moving with the times: IT research and the boundaries of CSCW', *Computer Supported Cooperative Work, 14*(3): 217–51.

Crampton, J. (2004). *The Political Mapping of Cyberspace*. Chicago, IL: University of Chicago Press.

Crane, D. (1972). *Invisible Colleges: Diffusion of Knowledge in Scientific Communities*. Chicago, IL: University of Chicago Press.

Crook, C. (1989). 'Educational practice within two local computer networks', in C. O'Malley (Ed.), *Computer Supported Collaborative Learning*. Berlin: Springer-Verlag. pp. 165–82.

Crook, C. (2002). 'Learning as cultural practice', in M. R. Lea and K. Nicoll (Eds.), *Distributed Learning: Social and Cultural Approaches to Practice*. New York: RoutledgeFalmer. pp. 152–69.

Crutcher, M. and Zook, M. (2009). 'Placemarks and waterlines: Racialized cyberscapes in post Katrina Google Earth', *GeoForum, 40*(4): 523–34.

Crystal, D. (2001). *Language and the Internet*. Cambridge, UK: Cambridge University Press.

Cuthell, J. P. (2008). 'The role of a web–based community in teacher professional development', *International Journal of Web Based Communities, 4*(2): 115–39.

Daft, R. L. and Lengel, R. H. (1986). 'Organizational information requirements, media richness and structural design', *Management Science, 32*(5): 554–71.

Danaher, P., Moriarty, B. and Danaher, G. (2009). *Mobile Learning Communities: Creating New Educational Futures*. Abingdon: Routledge.

Danet, B. and Herring, S. C. (2007). *The Multilingual Internet: Language, Culture, and Communication Online*. Oxford, UK: Oxford University Press.

Danet, B., Rudenberg, L., Rosenbaum-Tamari, Y. (1998). 'Hmmm ... Where's all that smoke coming from? Writing, play and performance on Internet Relay Chat', in F. Sudweeks, M. L. Mclaughlin and S. Rafaeli (Eds.), *Network and Netplay*. Cambridge, MA: MIT Press. pp. 41–76.

Danziger, J. N., Dutton, W. H., Kling, R. and Kraemer, K. L. (1982). *Computers and Politics*. New York: Columbia University Press.

Davenport, J. (2007). 'Tens of thousands of CCTV cameras, yet 80% of crime unsolved', *London Evening Standard*. Last updated at 15:56pm on 19.09.07. Retrieved March 27, 2010 from http://www.thisislondon.co.uk/news/article-23412867-tens-of-thousands-of-cctv-cameras-yet-80-of-crime-unsolved.do

Davenport, T. H. (1997). *Information Ecology: Mastering the Information and Knowledge Environment*. New York: Oxford University Press.

Davenport, T. H. and Beck, J. C. (2001). *The Attention Economy: Understanding the New Currency of Business*. Cambridge, MA: Harvard Business School Press.

Dede, C. J. (1990). 'The evolution of distance learning: Technology-mediated interactive learning'. *Journal of Research on Computers in Education, 22*, 247–64.

DeSanctis, G. and Poole, M. S. (1994). 'Capturing the complexity in advanced technology use: Adaptive structuration theory', *Organization Science, 5*(2): 121–47.

DeSanctis, G., Poole, M. S. and Dickson, G. W. (2000). 'Teams and technology: Interactions over time', in T. L. Griffith (Ed.), *Research on Managing Groups and Teams, Volume 3: Technology*. Greenwich, CT: JAI Press. pp. 1–27.

de Vise, D. (2010). 'Wide Web of diversions gets laptops evicted from lecture halls', *Washington Post*. Retrieved 9 March 2010 from: http://www.washingtonpost.com/wp-dyn/content/article/2010/03/08/AR2010030804915.html?nav=hcmodule

Diesner, J. and Carley, K. M. (2005). 'Exploration of communication networks from the Enron email corpus', *Proceedings of the 2005 SIAM Workshop on Link Analysis, Counterterrorism and Security*, Newport Beach, CA. pp. 3–14. Retrieved October 30, 2008 from: http://research.cs.queensu.ca/home/skill/proceedings/diesner.pdf

Dirckinck-Holmfeld, L., Jones, C. and Lindström, B. (2009). *Analysing Networked Learning Practices in Higher Education and Continuing Professional Development*. Rotterdam: Sense Publishers.

Dladla, N. and Moon, B. (2002). 'Challenging the assumptions about teacher education and training in Sub-Saharan Africa: A new role for open learning and ICT', paper presented at the Pan-Commonwealth Forum on Open Learning International Convention Centre, Durban, South Africa. Retrieved 23 June 2010 from: http://www.open.ac.uk/deep/Public/web/publications/core.html

Dodge, M. and Kitchin, R. (2001). *Mapping Cyberspace*. New York: Routledge.

Dodge, M. and Kitchin, R. (2005). 'Code and the transduction of space', *Annals of the Association of American Geographers*, 95(1): 162–80.

Dodge, M. and Perkins, C. (2009). 'The "view from nowhere"? Spatial politics and cultural significance of high-resolution satellite imagery', *GeoForum*, 40(4): 495–700.

Domingo, M. (2010). 'Research into interactive multimodal texts', paper given at the ESRC Seminar series on New Forms of Doctorate, British Library, London.

Dornfeld, B. (1998). *Producing Public Television, Producing Public Culture*. Princeton, NJ: Princeton University Press.

Dutton, W. H. (1992). 'The ecology of games shaping telecommunications policy', *Communications Theory*, 2(4): 303–28.

Dutton, W. H. (2008). 'Social movements shaping the Internet: The outcome of an ecology of games', in M. S. Elliott and K. L. Kraemer (Eds.), *Computerization Movements and Technology Diffusion: From Mainframes to Ubiquitous Computing*. pp. 499–517.

Dutton, W. H., Cheong, P. H. and Park, A. (2004). 'An ecology of constraints on e–Learning in higher education: The case of a virtual learning environment', *Prometheus*, 22(2): 131–49.

Dutton, W. H., Helsper, E. J. and Gerber, M. M. (2009). *The Internet in Britain 2009*. Oxford: Oxford Internet Institute. Retrieved 25 June 2010 from: http://www.oii.ox.ac.uk/microsites/oxis/

Eastin, M. S. and LaRose, R. (2000). 'Internet self-efficacy and the psychology of the digital divide', *Journal of Computer-Mediated Communication*, 6(1). Available online at: http://jcmc.indiana.edu/vol6/issue1/eastin.html.

Eberle, J. and Childress, M. (2009). 'Using heutagogy to address the needs of online learners', in P. L. Rogers, G. A. Berg, J. V. Boettecher, C. Howard, L. Justice, and K. D. Schenk (Eds.), *Encyclopedia of Distance Learning*, 2nd Edn, Hershey, PA: IGI Global. pp. 2239–45.

Economist (2006). 'Wi-Pie in the sky'. *The Economist Technology Quarterly*, 11 March, pp. 22–4.

Ellis, K. and Kent, M. (forthcoming). *Disability and New Media*. Abingdon: Routledge.

Engeström, Y. (1987). *Learning by Expanding: An Activity Theoretical Approach to Developmental Research*. Helsinki: Orienta-Konsultit Oy.

Engeström, Y. (2009). 'Expansive learning: Toward an activity-theoretical reconceptualization', in K. Illeris (Ed.), *Contemporary Theories of Learning: Learning Theorists ... in their own Words*. London: Routledge. pp. 53–73.

Engeström, Y. and Middleton, D. (1996). *Cognition and Communication at Work*. Cambridge, UK: Cambridge University Press.

Engeström, Y., Miettinen, R. and Punamäki, R. (Eds.) (1999). *Perspectives on Activity Theory*. Cambridge, UK: Cambridge University Press.

Erickson, T. (1999). 'Persistent conversation: An introduction', *Journal of Computer-Mediated Communication, 4*(4). Available online at: http://www. ascusc.org/jcmc/vol4/issue4/ericksonintro.html

Ess, C. (2009). 'When the solution becomes the problem: Cultures and individuals as obstacles to online learning', in R. Goodfellow and M-N. Lamy (Eds.), *Learning Cultures in Online Education*. London: Continuum. pp. 14–29.

Eurostat (2010). Level of Internet Access – Households. Retrieved 25 June 2010 from: http://epp.eurostat.ec.europa.eu/portal/page/portal/product_details/dataset?p_product_code=TSIIR040

Fang, B. (2009). 'From distraction to engagement: Wireless devices in the classroom', *Educause Quarterly, 32*(4). Retrieved 4 June 2010 from: http://www.educause.edu/EDUCAUSE+Quarterly/EDUCAUSEQuarterlyMagazineVolum/FromDistractionto EngagementWir/192959

Finholt, T. (2002). 'Collaboratories', *Annual Review of Information Science and Technology, 36*: 73–107.

Fischer, C. (1992). *America Calling: A Social History of the Telephone to 1940*. Berkeley, CA: University of California Press.

Flowers, L. (2003). 'Talking across difference: Intercultural rhetoric and the search for situated knowledge', *College Composition and Communication, 55*(1): 38–68.

Ford, N. (2008). *Web-based Learning Through Educational Informatics: Information Science Meets Educational Computing*. Hershey, NY: Information Science Publishing.

Freire, P. (1970/2003). *Pedagogy of the Oppressed*. New York: Continuum.

Fried, C. B. (2008). 'In-class laptop use and its effects on student learning', *Computers & Education, 50*(3): 906–14.

Friesen, N. (2008). *Re-thinking E-learning Research*. New York: Peter Lang.

Fulk, J. and Steinfield, C. W. (Eds.) (1990). *Organizations and Communication Technology*. Newbury Park, CA: Sage.

Fulton, C. and Vondracek, R. (2009). 'Pleasurable pursuits: Leisure and LIS research', *Library Trends, 57*(4): 611–17.

Galegher, J., Kraut, R. E. and Egido, C. (Eds.) (1990). *Intellectual Teamwork: Social and Technological Foundations of Cooperative Work*. Hillsdale, NJ: Lawrence Erlbaum.

Gant, J. P., Turner-Lee, N. E., Li, Y. and Miller, J.S. (2010). *National Minority Broadband Adoption: Comparative Trends in Adoption, Acceptance and Use*. Washington, DC: Joint Center for Political and Economic Studies.

Garnett, F. and Ecclesfield, N. (2009). 'Proposed model of the relationships between informal, non-formal and formal learning', paper presented at the IADIS International Conference on Cognition and Exploratory Learning in Digital Age (CELDA), Rome, Italy.

Garrett, R. (2004). 'The real story behind the failure of UK eUniversity', *Educause Quarterly*, 4: 4–6.

Garrison, D. R. (2005). 'Learning collaboration principles', paper presented at the Sloan–C Summer Workshop, Victoria, BC, Canada.

Garrison, D. R. and Anderson, T. (2003). *E-learning in the 21st Century: A Framework for Research and Practice*. New York: RoutledgeFalmer.

Gaver, W. W. (1991). 'Technology affordances', in *Proceedings of the SIGCHI Conference on Human Factors in Computing Systems: Reaching Through Technology*. New Orleans, LA. pp. 79–84.

Gaver, W. W. (1996). 'Situating action II: Affordances for interaction: The social is material for design', *Ecological Psychology, 8*: 111–29.

Gee, J. P. (2003). *What Video Games Have to Teach Us About Learning and Literacy*. New York: Palgrave Macmillan.

Gee, J. P. (2005a). *An Introduction to Discourse Analysis*, 2nd edn. New York: Routledge.

Gee, J. P. (2005b). 'Semiotic social spaces and affinity spaces: From *The Age of Mythology* to today's schools', in D. Barton and K. Tusting (Eds.), *Beyond Communities of Practice:*

Language, Power and Social Context. Cambridge, UK: Cambridge University Press. pp. 214–32.

Gee, J. P., Hull, G. and Lankshear, C. (1996). *The New Work Order: Behind the Language of the New Capitalism*. Boulder, CO: Westview Press.

Gemmell, J., Bell, G. and Lueder, R. (2006). 'MyLifeBits: A personal database for everything', *Communications of the ACM*, *49*(1): 88–95.

Gibson, J. J. (1979). *The Ecological Approach to Visual Perception*. Boston: Houghton Mifflin.

Giddens, A. (1984). *The Constitution of Society: Outline of a Theory of Structuration*. Berkeley: University of California Press.

Gilbert, E., Karahalios, K. and Sandvig, C. (2008). 'The network in the garden: An empirical analysis of social media in rural life', *Proceedings of the CHI Conference*. Florence, Italy.

Girard, M. and Stark, D. (2007). 'Socio-technologies of assembly: Sense-making and demonstration in rebuilding lower Manhattan', in V. Mayer-Schönberger and D. Lazer (Eds.), *Governance and Information Technology: From Electronic Government to Information Government*. Cambridge, MA: MIT Press. pp. 145–76.

Goffman, E. (1986). *Frame Analysis*. Boston: Northeastern University Press.

Goldhaber, M. H. (1997). 'The attention economy and the net', *First Monday*, *2*(4). Available online at: http://firstmonday.org/htbin/cgiwrap/bin/ojs/index.php/fm/article/view/519/440/

Goldhaber, M. H. (2006). 'The value of openness in an attention economy', *First Monday*, *11*(6). Available online at: http://firstmonday.org/htbin/cgiwrap/bin/ojs/index.php/fm/article/view/1334/1254

Goodchild, M. F. (2007). 'Citizens as sensors: The world of volunteered geography', *GeoJournal*, *69*: 211–21.

Goodyear, P. (1998). 'New technology in higher education: Understanding the innovation process', keynote presentation at Integrating Information and Communication Technology into Higher Education (BITE) conference, Maastrict, NL. Retrieved 27 August 2010 from: http://domino.lancs.ac.uk/EdRes/csaltdocs.nsf/By%20Title/F9F42237151CCB0E8025696100579D60/$FILE/New+technology+in+higher+education.doc

Graham, S. (2004). *The Cybercities Reader*. London: Routledge.

Granovetter, M. S. (1973). 'The strength of weak ties', *American Journal of Sociology*, 78: 1360–80.

Greenhow, C. and Robelia, E. (2009a). 'Informal learning and identity formation in online social networks', *Learning, Media and Technology*, *34*(2): 119–40.

Greenhow, C. and Robelia, E. (2009b). 'Old communication, new literacies: Social network sites as social learning resources', *Journal of Computer-Mediated Communication*, *14*(4): 1130–61.

Greenhow, C., Robelia, E. and Hughes, J. (2009a). 'Web 2.0 and classroom research: What path should we take now?', *Educational Researcher, 38*(4): 246–59.

Greenhow, C., Walker, J.D. and Kim, S. (2009b). 'Millenial learners and net-savvy teens: Examining internet use among low-income students', *Journal of Computing in Teacher Education, 26*(2): 63–9.

Greeno, J. G. (2006). 'Learning in activity', in R. K. Sawyer (Ed.), *The Cambridge Handbook of the Learning Sciences*. New York: Cambridge University Press. pp. 79–96.

Gruzd, A. (2009). 'Automated discovery of social networks in online learning communities', unpublished doctoral dissertation, University of Illinois at Urbana-Champaign, Champaign, IL.

Gruzd, A. and Haythornthwaite, C. (forthcoming). 'Networking online: Cybercommunities', in J. Scott and P. Carrington (Eds.), *Handbook of Social Network Analysis*. London: Sage.

GSM World (2010). 'GSMA and the Cherie Blair Foundation for Women Publish "Women & Mobile: A Global Opportunity" Report', Retrieved 21 August 2010 from: http://www.gsmworld.com/newsroom/press–releases/2010/4644.htm

Gurstein, M. (2000). *Community Informatics: Enabling Communities with Information and Communications Technologies*. Hershey, PA: Idea Group Publishing.

Gutiérrez, K., Baquedano-Lopez, P. and Tejeda, C. (2000). 'Rethinking diversity: Hybridity and hybrid language practices in the third space', *Mind, Culture, & Activity: An International Journal, 6*(4): 286–303.

Hagar, C. (2005). 'The farming community in crisis: The information and social needs of Cumbrian farmers during the UK 2001 foot-and-mouth (FMD) outbreak and the role of information and communication technologies (ICTs)', unpublished dissertation, University of Illinois at Urbana Champaign, Champaign, IL.

Hagar, C. and Haythornthwaite, C. (2005). 'Crisis, farming & community', *Journal of Community Informatics, 1*(3). Available online at: http://ci-journal.net/index.php/ciej/article/view/246/210

Haines, V. A., Hurlbert, J. S. and Beggs, J. J. (1996). 'Exploring the determinants of support provision: Provider characteristics, personal networks, community contexts, and support following life events', *Journal of Health & Social Behavior, 37*(3): 252–64.

Haklay, M. and Weber, P. (2008). 'OpenStreetMap–User-generated street map', *IEEE Pervasive Computing, 7*(4): 12–18.

Hampton, K. (2001). 'Living the wired life in the wired suburb: Netville, glocalization and civil society', unpublished doctoral dissertation, University of Toronto, Toronto, Ontario, Canada.

Hampton, K. (2010). 'Internet use and the concentration of disadvantage: Glocalization and the urban underclass', *American Behavioral Scientist, 53*(8): 1111–32.

Hampton, K. and Wellman, B. (2003). 'Neighboring in netville: How the Internet supports community and social capital in a wired suburb', *City and Community, 2*(4), 277–311.

Harasim, L., Hiltz, S. R., Teles, L. and Turoff, M. (1995). *Learning Networks: A Field Guide to Teaching and Learning Online*. Cambridge, MA: The MIT Press.

Hargittai, E. (2007). 'Whose space? Differences among users and non-users of social network sites', *Journal of Computer-Mediated Communication, 13*(1): article 14. Available online at: http://jcmc.indiana.edu/vol13/issue1/hargittai.html

Hargittai, E. and Shafer, S. (2006). 'Differences in actual and perceived online skills: The role of gender', *Social Science Quarterly, 87*(2): 432–48.

Harrison, T. M. and Stephen T. (1996). (Eds.). *Computer Networking and Scholarly Communication in the Twenty-First-Century University*. Albany, NY: SUNY Press.

Hase, S. and Kenyon, C. (2000). 'From andragogy to heutagogy'. Retrieved 12 July 2010 from: http://ultibase.rmit.edu.au/Articles/dec00/hase2.htm

Hawisher, G. and Selfe, C. L. (Eds.) (1999). *Passions, Pedagogies, and 21st Century Technologies*. Logan and Urbana: Utah State University Press and NCTE.

Hawisher, G. and Selfe, C. L. (2007). 'On computers and writing', in R. Andrews and C. Haythornthwaite (Eds.), *The Sage Handbook of E-learning Research*. London: Sage.

Haythornthwaite, C. (2000). Online personal networks: Size, composition and media use among distance learners. *New Media and Society, 2*(2), 195–226.

Haythornthwaite, C. (2001). 'Exploring multiplexity: Social network structures in a computer-supported distance learning class', *The Information Society, 17*(3): 211–26.

Haythornthwaite, C. (2002a). 'Strong, weak and latent ties and the impact of new media', *The Information Society, 18*(5): 385–401.

Haythornthwaite, C. (2002b). 'Building social networks via computer networks: Creating and sustaining distributed learning communities', in K. A. Renninger and W. Shumar, *Building Virtual Communities: Learning and Change in Cyberspace*. Cambridge: Cambridge University Press. pp. 159–90.

Haythornthwaite, C. (2005a). 'Social networks and Internet connectivity effects', *Information, Communication and Society, 8*(2): 125–47.

Haythornthwaite, C. (Ed.) (2005b). 'Computer-mediated collaborative practices and systems', *Journal of Computer-Mediated Communication, 10*(4): article 11. Available online at: http://jcmc.indiana.edu/vol10/issue4/

Haythornthwaite, C. (2006a). 'Facilitating collaboration in online learning', *Journal of Asynchronous Learning Networks, 10*(1). Available online at: http://www.sloan-c.org/publications/jaln/index.asp

Haythornthwaite, C. (2006b). 'Articulating divides in distributed knowledge practice', *Information, Communication & Society, 9*(6): 761–80.

Haythornthwaite, C. (2006c). 'Learning and knowledge exchanges in interdisciplinary collaborations', *Journal of the American Society for Information Science and Technology, 57*(8): 1079–92.

Haythornthwaite, C. (2006d). 'The social informatics of elearning', paper presented at the Information, Communication and Society 10th Anniversary Conference, York, UK. Available online at: http://hdl.handle.net/2142/8959

Haythornthwaite, C. (2007a). 'Digital divide and e-learning', in R. Andrews and C. Haythornthwaite (Eds.), *The Sage Handbook of E-learning Research.* London: Sage. pp. 97–118.

Haythornthwaite, C. (2007b). 'Social networks and online community', in A. Joinson, K. McKenna, U. Reips and T. Postmes (Eds.), *Oxford Handbook of Internet Psychology.* Oxford, UK: Oxford University Press. pp. 121–36.

Haythornthwaite, C. (2008). 'Learning relations and networks in web–based communities', *International Journal of Web Based Communities, 4*(2): 140–58.

Haythornthwaite, C. (2009a). 'Crowds and communities: Light and heavyweight models of peer production', *Proceedings of the 42nd Hawaii International Conference on System Sciences.* Los Alamitos, CA: IEEE Computer Society.

Haythornthwaite, C. (2009b). 'Participatory transformations', in W. Cope and M. Kalantzis (Eds.), *Ubiquitous Learning.* Champaign, IL: University of Illinois Press. pp. 31–48.

Haythornthwaite, C. (2010). 'Ubiquitous Learning', Leverhulme Trust Public Lecture, London Knowledge Lab, London, 10 May. http://newdoctorates.blogspot.com/2009/10/leverhulme-trust-public-lectures.html

Haythornthwaite, C. (forthcoming). 'Online knowledge crowds and communities', in J. Echeverria, J. Zulaika, A. Alonso and P. Oiarzabal, P. (Eds.), *Knowledge Communities.* Reno, NV: Center for Basque Studies.

Haythornthwaite, C. and de Laat, M. (forthcoming). 'Social network informed design for learning with educational technology', in A. D. Olofsson and J. O. Lindberg (Eds.), *Informed Design of Educational Technologies in Higher Education: Enhanced Learning and Teaching.* Hershey, PA: IGI Global.

Haythornthwaite, C. and Kazmer, M. M. (2002). 'Bringing the internet home: Adult distance learners and their Internet, home and work worlds', in B. Wellman and C. Haythornthwaite (Eds.), *The Internet in Everyday Life.* Oxford: Blackwell. pp. 431–63.

Haythornthwaite, C. and Kazmer, M. M. (Eds.) (2004a). *Learning, Culture and Community in Online Education: Research and Practice.* New York: Peter Lang.

Haythornthwaite, C. and Kazmer, M. M. (2004b). 'Multiple perspectives and practices in online education', in C. Haythornthwaite and M. M. Kazmer, *Learning, Culture and Community in Online Education: Research and Practice.* New York: Peter Lang. pp. xiii–xxviii.

Haythornthwaite, C. and Kendall, L. (Eds.) (2010). 'Internet and community', *American Behavioral Scientist, 53*(8): Special issue.

Haythornthwaite, C. and Nielsen, A. (2006). 'CMC: Revisiting conflicting results', in J. Gackenbach (Ed.), *Psychology and the Internet*, 2nd edn. San Diego, CA: Academic Press. pp. 161–80.

Haythornthwaite, C. and Wellman, B. (1998). 'Work, friendship and media use for information exchange in a networked organization', *Journal of the American Society for Information Science, 49*(12): 1101–14.

Haythornthwaite, C. and Wellman, B. (2002). 'Introduction: Internet in everyday life', in B. Wellman and C. Haythornthwaite (Eds.), *The Internet in Everyday Life*. Oxford, UK: Blackwell. pp. 3–44.

Haythornthwaite, C., Andrews, R., Bruce, B. C., Kazmer, M. M., Montague, R-A. and Preston, C. (2007). 'New theories and models of and for online learning', *First Monday*, 12, (8). Available online at: http://firstmonday.org/htbin/cgiwrap/bin/ojs/index.php/fm/article/view/1976/1851

Haythornthwaite, C., Kazmer, M. M., Robins, J. and Shoemaker, S. (2000). 'Community development among distance learners: Temporal and technological dimensions', *Journal of Computer-Mediated Communication*, 6(1). Available online at: http://jcmc.indiana.edu/vol6/issue1/haythornthwaite.html

Haythornthwaite, C., Lunsford, K. J., Bowker, G. C. and Bruce, B. (2006). 'Challenges for research and practice in distributed, interdisciplinary collaboration', in C. Hine (Ed.), *New Infrastructures for Science Knowledge Production*. Hershey, PA: Idea Group. pp. 143–66.

Haythornthwaite, C., Lunsford, K. J., Kazmer, M. M., Robins, J. and Nazarova, M. (2003). 'The generative dance in pursuit of generative knowledge', *Proceedings of the 36th Hawaii International Conference on System Sciences*. Los Alamitos, CA: IEEE Computer Society.

Hearne, B. and Nielsen, A. (2004). 'Catch a cyber by the tale: Online orality and the lore of a distributed learning community', in C. Haythornthwaite, and M.M. Kazmer, (Eds.). *Learning, Culture and Community in Online Education: Research and Practice*. NY: Peter Lang. pp. 59–87.

Heath, S.B. (1983). *Ways with Words: Language, Life and Work in Communities and Classrooms*. New York: Cambridge University Press.

Heerwagen, J. H., Kampschroer, K., Powell, K. M. and Loftness, V. (2004). 'Collaborative knowledge work environments', *Building Research & Information*, 32(6): 510–28.

Heeter, C. (1992). 'Being there: The subjective experience of presence', *Presence: Teleoperators and Virtual Environments*, 1(2): 262–71.

Hembrooke, H. and Gay, G. (2003). 'The laptop and the lecture: The effects of multitasking in learning environments', *Journal of Computing in Higher Education*, 15(1): 46–64.

Herring, S. C. (2002). 'Computer-mediated communication on the Internet', *Annual Review of Information Science and Technology*, 36: 109–68.

Herring, S. C., Ogan, C., Ahuja, M. and Robinson, J. C. (2006a). 'Gender and the culture of computing in applied IT education', in E. Trauth (Ed.), *Encyclopedia of Gender and Information Technology*. Hershey, PA: Information Science Publishing.

Herring, S. C., Scheidt, L. A., Bonus, A. and Wright, E. (2004). 'Bridging the gap: A genre analysis of weblogs'. *Proceedings of the 37th Hawaii International Conference on System Sciences*. IEEE.

Herring, S. C., Scheidt, L. A., Bonus, S. and Wright, E. (2005). 'Weblogs as a bridging genre', *Information, Technology & People*, 18(2): 142–171.

Herring, S. C., Scheidt, L.A., Kouper, I. and Wright, E. (2006). 'A longitudinal content analysis of weblogs: 2003–2004', in M. Tremayne (Ed.), *Blogging, Citizenship and the Future of Media*. London: Routledge. pp. 3–20.

Hewling, A. (2009). 'Technology as "cultural player" in online learning environments', in R. Goodfellow and M-N. Lamy (Eds.), *Learning Cultures in Online Education*. London: Continuum. pp. 113–30

Hickman, L. A. (1992). *John Dewey's Pragmatic Technology*. Bloomington, IA: Indiana University Press.

Highsmith, J. (2002). *Agile Software Development Ecosystems*. Indianapolis, IN: Pearson Education.

Hiltz, S. R. (1994). *The Virtual Classroom: Learning Without Limits via Computer Networks*. Norwood, NJ: Ablex.

Hiltz, S. R. and Turoff, M. (1978). *The Network Nation*. Addison-Wesley (2nd edn, 1993). Cambridge, MA: MIT Press.

Hiltz, S. R., Turoff, M. and Harasim. L. (2007). 'Development and philosophy of the field of asynchronous learning networks', in R. Andrews and C. Haythornthwaite (Eds.), *The Sage Handbook of E-learning Research.* London: Sage. pp. 55–72.

Hinds, P. J. and Kiesler, S. (Eds.) (2002). *Distributed Work: New Research on Working Across Distance Using Technology.* Cambridge, MA: MIT Press.

Hine, C. (Ed.) (2006). *New Infrastructures for Science Knowledge Production: Understanding E-Science.* Hershey, PA: Idea Group.

Hjørland, B. (2004). 'Domain analysis in information science', in *Encyclopedia of Library and Information Science.* New York: Marcel Dekker.

Hofstede, G. (1983). 'The cultural relativity of organizational practices and theories', *Journal of International Business Studies 14*(2): 75–89.

Hofstede, G. (2001). *Culture's Consequences: Comparing Values, Behaviors, Institutions, and Organizations Across Nations.* Thousand Oaks, CA: Sage.

Hollingshead, A. B., Fulk, J., and Monge, P. (2002). 'Fostering intranet knowledge sharing: An integration of transactive memory and public goods approaches', in P. Hinds and S. Kiesler (Eds.), *Distributed Work: New Research on Working Across Distance Using Technology.* Cambridge, MA: MIT Press. pp. 335–55.

Holmes, B. and Gardner, J. (2006). *E-learning: Concepts and Practice.* London: Sage.

Horrigan, J. B. (2009). 'Home broadband adoption 2009'. 17 June. Retrieved 10 February 2010 from: http://pewresearch.org/pubs/1254/home–broadband-adoption-2009

Horrigan, J. B. (2010). *Broadband Adoption and Use in America*. OBI Working Paper Series No. 1. Federal Communications Commission. Available online at: http://online.wsj.com/public/resourses/documents/FCCSurvey.pdf

Howard, P. N. and Jones, S. (Eds.) (2003). *Society Online: The Internet in Context.* Thousand Oaks, CA: Sage.

Howard, R. M. (2009). *Writing Matters.* Chicago, IL: McGraw-Hill.

Hrastinski, S. (2006). 'Introducing an informal synchronous medium in a distance learning course: How is participation affected?', *Internet and Higher Education, 9*(2): 117–31.

Hrastinski, S. (2009). 'A theory of online learning as online participation', *Computers & Education, 52*: 78–82.

Hughes, G. (2010). 'Identity and belonging in social learning groups: The importance of distinguishing social, operational and knowledge-related identity congruence', *British Educational Research Journal, 36*(1): 47–63.

Hunsinger, J. and Krotoski, A. (2010). 'Learning and research in virtual worlds', *Learning, Media and Technology, 35*(2): special issue.

Hull, G., Zacher, J. and Hibbert, L. (2009). 'Youth, risk, and equity in a global world', *Review of Research in Education, 33*(1): 117–59.

Huysman, M. and Wulf, V. (2005). 'The role of information technology in building and sustaining the relational base of communities', *The Information Society, 21*(2): 81–9.

Illeris, K. (2007). *How We Learn: Learning and Non–learning in School and Beyond.* Abingdon: Routledge.

Illeris, K. (Ed.) (2009). *Contemporary Theories of Learning: Learning Theorists...in their own Words.* Abingdon: Routledge.

Indiana State University (2005). 'Indiana State to become notebook institution', News Release, 8 September. Retrieved 21 March 2010 from: http://www.indstate.edu/isu_today/archives/2005/sept/notebook.html

International Federation of Library Associations (2005). *The Alexandria Proclamation on Information Literacy and Lifelong Learning.* Retrieved 10 February 2010 from: http://archive.ifla.org/III/wsis/BeaconInfSoc.htm

International Telecommunications Union (2009). *Basic Indicators: Population, GDP, Ratio of Mobile Cellular Subscriptions to Fixed Telephone Lines.* Retrieved 10 June 2010 from: http://www.itu.int/ITU–D/ICTEYE/Indicators/Indicators.aspx

Internet World Statistics (2009). *World Internet Usage and Population Statistics*, 31 December 2009. Retrieved 25 June 2010 from: http://www.internetworldstats.com/stats.htm

Ito, M., Baumer, S., Bittanti, M., boyd, d., Cody, R., Herr-Stephenson, B., Horst, H. A., Lange, P. G., Mahendran, D., Martinez, K. Z., Pascoe, C. J., Perkel, E., Robinson, L., Sims, C. and Tripp, L. with A. Judd, M. Finn, A. Law, A. Manion, S. Mitnick, D. Scholssberg and S. Yardi (2009). *Hanging Out, Messing Around, and Geeking Out: Kids Living and Learning with New Media*. Cambridge, MA: MIT Press.

Jankowski, N. W. (Ed.) (2009). *E-Research: Transformation in Scholarly Practice*. New York: Routledge.

Jayakumar, U. M. (2008). 'Can higher education meet the needs of an increasingly diverse and global society? Campus diversity and cross-cultural workforce competencies', *Harvard Educational Review*, 4(78): 615–51.

Jenkins, C. (2004). The Virtual Classroom as Ludic Space, in C. Haythornthwaite and M. M. Kazner (Eds.) *Learning, Culture and Community in Online Education: Research and Practice*. New York: Peter Long. pp. 229–42.

Jenkins, H., with Clinton, K., Purushotma, R., Robinson, A. J. and Weigel, M. (2006). *Confronting the Challenges of Participatory Culture: Media Education for the 21st Century*. Chicago, IL: MacArthur Foundation. http://digitallearning.macfound.org/atf/cf/%7B7E45C7E0-A3E0-4B89-AC9C-E807E1B0AE4E%7D/JENKINS_WHITE_PAPER.PDF

Jewitt, C. (2008) *Technology, Literacy, Learning: A Multimodal Approach*. Abingdon: Routledge.

Jobbins, C. and Lenhart, A. (July 2, 2008). 'Pew Internet & American Life Project Reports 55% of adult Americans have home broadband connections', 2 July. The Pew Trusts: Washington, DC. Retrieved 24 June 2010 from: http://www.pewtrusts.org/news_room_detail.aspx?id=41002

Johnson, S. D., Benson, A. D., Duncan, J. R., Shinkareva, O., Taylor, G. D. and Treat, T. (2004) 'Internet-based learning in postsecondary career and technical education', *Journal of Vocational Education Research*, 29(2): 101–19. Available online at: http://scholar.lib.vt.edu/ejournals/JVER/v29n2/johnson.html

Jones, C. (2005). 'Nobody knows you're a dog: What amounts to context in networked learning?', in R. Land and S. Bayne (Eds.), *Education in Cyberspace* (pp. 105–16). London: Routledge.

Jones, C. and Healing, G. (2010). 'Learning nests and local habitations: Locations for networked learning', *Proceedings of the Networked Learning Conference*: Aalborg, DK.

Jones, I. and Symon, G. (2001). 'Lifelong learning as serious leisure: Policy, practice and potential', *Leisure Studies*, 20: 269–83.

Katz, J. E. and Rice, R. E. (2002). *Social Consequences of Internet Use: Access, Involvement and Expression*. Cambridge, MA: MIT Press.

Kaye, A. R. (Ed.) (1991). *Collaborative Learning Through Computer Conferencing: The Najaden Papers*. Berlin: Springer-Verlag.

Kaye, A. R. (1995). 'Computer supported collaborative learning', in N. Heap, R. Thomas, G. Einon, R. Mason and H. MacKay (Eds.), *Information Technology and Society*. London: Sage. pp. 192–210.

Kazmer, M. M. (2000). 'Coping in a distance environment: Sitcoms, chocolate cake, and dinner with a friend', *First Monday*, 5(9). Available online at: http://www.firstmonday.org/issues/issue5_9/kazmer/index.html

Kazmer, M. M. (2002). 'Disengagement from intrinsically transient social worlds: The case of a distance learning community, unpublished doctoral dissertation, University of Illinois at Urbana Champaign, Champaign, IL.

Kazmer, M. M. (2006). 'Creation and loss of sociotechnical capital among information professionals educated online', *Library & Information Science Research*, 28: 172–91.

Kazmer, M. M. (2007a). 'Community-embedded learning', in R. Andrews and C. Haythornthwaite (Eds.), *The Sage Handbook of E-learning Research*. London: Sage. pp. 311–27.

Kazmer, M. M. (2007b). 'Beyond C U L8R: Disengaging from online social worlds', *New Media and Society*, *9*: 111–38.

Kazmer, M. M. and Haythornthwaite, C. (2001). 'Juggling multiple social worlds: Distance students on and offline', *American Behavioral Scientist*, *45*(3): 510–29.

Kazmer, M. M. and Xie, B. (2008). 'Qualitative interviewing in internet studies: Playing with the media, playing with the method', *Information, Communication & Society*, *11*(2): 257–78.

Keeble, L. and Loader, B. D. (Eds.) (2001). *Community Informatics: Shaping Computer-Mediated Social Relations*. London: Routledge.

Keegan, D. (Ed.) (1993). *Theoretical Principles of Distance Learning*. London: Sage.

Kegan, R. (2009) 'What "form" transforms? A constructive-developmental approach to transformative learning', in K. Illeris (Ed.), *Contemporary Theories of Learning: Learning Theorists ... in their own Words*. London: Routledge. pp. 35–52.

Kendall, L. (2002). *Hanging Out in the Virtual Pub: Masculinities and Relationships Online*. Berkeley, CA: University of California Press.

Kiesler, S. B. (Ed.) (1997). *Culture of the Internet*. Mahwah, NJ: Lawrence Erlbaum.

Kiesler, S. B. and Sproull, L. S. (Eds.) (1987). *Computing and Change on Campus*. New York: Cambridge University Press.

Kim, A. J. (2000). *Community Building on the Web: Secret Strategies for Successful Online Communities*. Berkeley, CA: Peachpit Press.

King, A. (1993). From sage on the stage to guide on the side. *College Teaching*, *41*(1): 30–5.

King, E. (2005). 'Digitisation of newspapers at the British Library', *The Serials Librarian*, *49*(1–2): 165–81.

King, J. L, Grinter, R. E. and Pickering, J. M. (1997). 'The rise and fall of Netville: The saga of a cyberspace construction boomtown in the great divide', in S. Kiesler (Ed.), *Culture of the Internet*. Mahwah, NJ: Lawrence Erlbaum. pp. 3–33.

Kingsley, J. and Wankel, C. (2009). 'Introduction', in J. Kingsley and C. Wankel (Eds.), *Higher Education in Virtual Worlds: Teaching and Learning in Second Life*. Bingley, UK: Emerald. pp. 1–10.

Kirkland, D. (2009). 'Standpoints: Researching and teaching in the digital dimension', *Research in the Teaching of English*, *44*(1): 8–22.

Kling, R. (1999). 'What is social informatics and why does it matter?', *D-Lib Magazine*, *5*(1). Available online at: http://www.dlib.org/dlib/january99/kling/01kling.html.

Kling, R., Rosenbaum, H. and Sawyer, S. (2005). *Understanding and Communicating Social Informatics*. Medford, NJ: Information Today.

Knorr-Cetina, K. (1999). *Epistemic Cultures: How the Sciences Make Knowledge*. Cambridge, MA: Harvard University Press.

Knowles, M. S. (1968). Androgogy, not pedagogy! *Adult Leadership*, *16*: 350–52, 386.

Kolko, B. E., Nakamura, L. and Rodman, G. B. (Eds.) (2000). *Race in Cyberspace*. New York: Routledge.

Kominski, R. and Newburger, E. (1999). 'Access denied: Changes in computer ownership and use: 1984–1997', paper presented at the Annual Meeting of the American Sociological Association, Chicago, IL. Available online at: http://www.census.gov/population/socdemo/computer/confpap99.pdf

Korean Educational Development Institute (KEDI) (2007). *Understanding Korean Education. Vol. 2, ICT in Korean Education*. South Korea: The Korean Educational Development Institute.

Koschmann, T. (Ed.) (1996). *CSCL: Theory and Practice of an Emerging Paradigm*. Mahwah, NJ: Lawrence Erlbaum.

Koschmann, T., Hall, R. and Miyake, N. (Eds.) (2002). *CSCL 2: Carrying Forward the Conversation*. Mahwah, NJ: Lawrence Erlbaum.

Krackhardt, D. (1992). 'The strength of strong ties: The importance of *philos* in organizations', in N. Nohria and R. G. Eccles (Eds.), *Networks and Organizations: Structure, Form and Action*. Boston, MA: Harvard Business School Press. pp. 216–39.

Kramarae, C. (2001). *The Third Shift: Women Learning Online*. Washington, DC: American Association of University Women.

Kraut, R., Kiesler, S., Boneva, B., Cummings, J., Helgeson, V. and Crawford, A. (2002). 'Internet Paradox Revisited', *Journal of Social Issues*, 58(1): 49–74.

Kraut, R., Patterson, V.L., Kiesler, S., Mukhopadhyay, T. and Scherlis, W. (1998). 'Internet paradox: A social technology that reduces social involvement and psychological well-being?', *American Psychologist*, 53(9): 1017–31.

Kress, G. (2003). *Literacy in the New Media Age*. London: Routledge.

Kress, G. (2009). *Multimodality: A Social Semiotic Approach to Contemporary Communication*. London and New York: Routledge.

Kress, G. and Pachler, N. (2007). 'Thinking about the 'm' in m-learning', in Pachler, N. (Ed.) (2007) *Mobile learning: towards a research agenda*. London: Institute of Education, WLE Centre, Occasional Papers in Work-based Learning, 1: 7–32.

Kress, G. and van Leeuwen, T. (1996). *Reading Images*. London: Routledge.

Kress, G. and van Leeuwen, T. (2001). *Multimodal Discourse: The Modes and Media of Contemporary Communication*. London: Hodder Arnold.

Lakoff, G. and Johnson, M. (1980). *Metaphors We Live By*. Chicago, IL: University of Chicago Press.

Lam, W. S. E. (2006). 'Culture and learning in the context of globalization: Research directions', *Review of Research in Education*, 30: 213–37.

Land, R. and Bayne, S. (2005). *Education in Cyberspace*. New York: RoutledgeFalmer.

Lanham, R. (2006a). *The Economics of Attention: Style and Substance in the Age of Information*. Chicago: Chicago University Press.

Lanham, R. (2006b). 'An interview with Richard Lanham', University of Chicago. Available online at: http://www.press.uchicago.edu/Misc/Chicago/468828in.html

Lankshear, C., Peters, M. and Knobel, M. (2002). 'Information, knowledge and learning: Some issues facing epistemology and education in a digital age', in M. K. Lea and K. Nicoll (Eds.), *Distributed Learning: Social and Cultural Approaches to Practice*. London: RoutledgeFalmer. pp. 16–37.

LaRose, R., Eastin, M. S. and Gregg, J. (2001). 'Reformulating the Internet paradox: Social cognitive explanations of Internet use and depression', *Journal of Online Behavior*, 1(2). Available online at: http://www.behavior.net/JOB/v1n2/paradox.html

Latchem, C. and Jung, I. (2009). *Distance and Blended Learning in Asia*. Abingdon: Routledge.

Latour, B. (1987). *Science in Action: How to Follow Scientists and Engineers through Society*. Cambridge, MA: Harvard University Press.

Lave, J. and Wenger, E. (1991). *Situated Learning: Legitimate Peripheral Participation*. Cambridge, UK: Cambridge University Press.

Lawrence, P. R. and Lorsch, J. W. (1967). 'Differentiation and integration in complex organizations', *Administrative Science Quarterly*, 12: 1–47.

Lea, M. (2005). '"Communities of practice" in higher education: Useful heuristic or educational model?', in D. Barton and K. Tusting (Eds.), *Beyond Communities of Practice: Language, Power and Social Context*. Cambridge, UK: Cambridge University Press. pp. 180–97.

Lea, M. R. and Nicoll, K. (Eds.) (2002). *Distributed Learning: Social and Cultural Approaches to Practice*. New York: RoutledgeFalmer.

Leach, J. and Moon, B. (2002). 'Globalization, digital societies and school reform: Realizing the potential of new technologies to enhance the knowledge, understanding and dignity of teachers', keynote address at the 2nd European Conference on Information Technologies in Education and Citizenship: A Critical Insight, Barcelona, Spain. Retrieved 23 June 2010 from: http://www.open.ac.uk/deep/Public/web/publications/core.html

Leach, J., Ahmed, A., Makalima, S. and Power, T. (2005). *DEEP IMPACT: An Investigation of the Use of Information and Communication Technologies for Teacher Education in the*

Global South. London: Department for International Development (DFID). Available online at: http://www.open.ac.uk/deep/Public/web/publications/core.html

Leimeister, J. M., Schweizer, K., Leimeister, S. and Krcmar, H. (2008). 'Do virtual communities matter for the social support of patients?: Antecedents and effects of virtual relationships in online communities', *Information Technology & People, 21*(4): 350–74.

Lemke, J. and van Helden, C. (2009). 'New learning cultures: Identities, media and networks', in R. Goodfellow and M-N. Lamy (Eds.), *Learning Cultures in Online Education*. London: Continuum. pp. 151–69.

Lenhart, A. and Horrigan, J. B. (2003). 'Re–visualizing the digital divide as a digital spectrum', *IT&Society, 1*(5): 23–39. Available online at: http://www.stanford.edu/group/siqss/itandsociety/v01i05/v01i05a02.pdf

Lenhart, A. and Madden, M. (2007). 'Teens, privacy and online social networks: How teens manage their online identities and personal information in the age of MySpace'. Pew Internet and American Life Project. http://www.pewinternet.org/Reports/2007/Teens-Privacy-and-Online-Social-Networks.aspx

Lenhart, A., Horrigan, J., Rainie, L., Allen, K., Boyce, A., Madden, M. and O'Grady, E. (2003). 'The ever-shifting internet population: A new look at internet access and the digital divide'. Pew American Life and Internet Project. Retrieved 23 December 2005 from: http://www.pewinternet.org/pdfs/PIP_Shifting_Net_Pop_Report.pdf

Lessig, L. (2006). *Code: Version 2.0*. New York: Basic Books.

Levine, M. (1998, December 7–14). The juggler. *The New Yorker*, 72–80.

Levy, P., Ford, N., Foster, J., Madden, A., Miller, D., Nunes, M. B., McPherson, M. and Webber, S. (2003). 'Educational informatics: An emerging research agenda', *Journal of Information Science, 29*(4): 298–310.

Lin, N. (2001). *Social Capital: A Theory of Social Structure and Action*. Cambridge, UK: Cambridge University Press.

Lin, N. (2008). 'A network theory of social capital', in D. Castiglione, J. W. van Deth and G. Wolleb (Eds.), *Handbook of Social Capital*. Oxford: Oxford University Press. pp. 50–69.

Ling, R. (2004). *The Mobile Connection: The Cell Phone's Impact on Society*. San Francisco, CA: Morgan Kaufmann.

Ling, R. (2008). *New Tech, New Ties: How Mobile Communication is Reshaping Social Cohesion*. Cambridge, MA: MIT Press.

Liu, S. (2007). 'Assessing online asynchronous discussion in online courses: An empirical study'. *Proceedings of Technology, Colleges & Community Worldwide Online Conference*, 2007(1): 24–32. Retrieved 19 July 2010 from: http://etec.hawaii.edu/proceedings/2007/liu.pdf.

Livingstone, S. (2006). *UK Children Go Online: End of Award Report*. Retrieved 9 February 2009 from: http://www.lse.ac.uk/collections/children-go-online/

Livingstone, S. (2010). *Children and the Internet: Great Expectations, Challenging Realities*. Cambridge, UK: Polity Press.

Livingstone, S. and Bober, M. (2005). *UK Children Go Online: Final Report of Key Project Findings*. Economic and Social Research Council: UK. Retrieved 25 June 2010 from: http://news.bbc.co.uk/1/shared/bsp/hi/pdfs/28_04_05_childrenonline.pdf

Loader, B. and Keeble, L. (2004). *Challenging the Digital Divide: A Literature Review of Community Informatics Initiatives*. York, UK: Joseph Rowntree Foundation. Available online at: http://www.jrf.org.uk/publications/literature-review-community-informatics-initiatives

Luckin, R. (2008). 'The learner centric ecology of resources: A framework for using technology to scaffold learning', *Computers in Education, 50*: 449–62.

Luckin, R. (2010). *Re-designing Learning Contexts: Technology-rich, Learner-centred Ecologies*. Abingdon: Routledge.

Luckin, R., Akass, J., Cook, J., Day, P., Ecclesfield, N., Garnett, F., Gould, M., Hamilton, T. and Whitworth, A. (2007). 'Learner–generated contexts: Sustainable learning pathways through open content', in P. McAndrew and J. Watts (Eds.), *Proceedings of the Open Learn2007 Conference*. Milton Keynes, UK. pp. 90–4. Retrieved 13 June 2010 from: http://kn.open.ac.uk/public/getfile.cfm?documentfileid=12197.

Luckin, R., Clark, W., Garnett, F., Whitworth, A., Akass, J., Cook, J., Day, P., Ecclesfield, N., Hamilton, T. and Roberston, J. (2009). 'Learner–generated contexts: A framework to support the effective use of technology for learning', in M. J. W. Lee and C. McLoughlin (Eds.), *Web 2.0-Based E-Learning: Applying Social Informatics for Tertiary Teaching*. Hershey, PA: IGI Global. pp. 70–84.

Luff, P., Hindmarsh, J. and Heath, C. (2000). *Workplace Studies: Recovering Work Practice and Informing System Design*. Cambridge, UK: Cambridge University Press.

Lunsford, K. J. and Bruce, B. C. (2001). 'Collaboratories: Working together on the web', *Journal of Adolescent and Adult Literacy*, 45(1): 52–8.

Lyon, D. (2007). *Surveillance Studies: An Overview*. Cambridge, UK: Polity Press.

MacKenzie, D. and Wajcman, J. (1999). *The Social Shaping of Technology*. Buckingham, UK: Open University Press.

Madden, M. and Rainie, L. (2010). 'Adults and cell phone distractions', 18 June. Washington, DC: Pew Internet & American Life Project. Retrieved 25 June 2010 from: http://pewinternet.org/Reports/2010/Cell–Phone–Distractions.aspx

Mallen, M. J., Vogel, D. L., Rochlen, A. B. and Day, S. X. (2005). 'Online counseling: Reviewing the literature from a counseling psychology framework', *The Counseling Psychologist*, 33(6): 819–71.

Markus, M. L. (1983). 'Power, politics & MIS', *Communications of the ACM*, 26: 430–44.

Markus, M. L. (1990). 'Toward a "critical mass" theory of interactive media', in J. Fulk and C. W. Steinfield (Eds.), *Organizations and Communication Technology*. Newbury Park, CA: Sage. pp. 194–218.

Markus, M. L. and Bjorn-Andersen, N. (1987). 'Power over users: Its exercise by system professionals', *Communications of the ACM*, 30(6): 498–504.

Markus, M. L. and Robey, D. (1983). 'The organizational validity of management information systems', *Human Relations*, 36(3): 203–26.

Marriott, R. de C. V. and Torres, P. L. (Eds.) (2009). *Handbook of Research on E-Learning Methodologies for Language Acquisition*. Hershey, PA: IGI Global.

Marty, P. (2005). 'Factors influencing the co-evolution of computer-mediated collaborative practices and systems: A museum case study', *Journal of Computer-Mediated Communication*, 10(4): article 12. http://jcmc.indiana.edu/vol10/issue4/marty.html

Mathes, A. (2004). *Folksonomies – Cooperative Classification and Communication Through Shared Metadata*. Retrieved 19 July 2010 from: http://www.adammathes.com/academic/computer-mediated-communication/folksonomies.html

Mayadas, A. F., Bourne, J. and Bacsich, P. (2009). 'Online education today', *Science*, 323: 85–9.

Mayes, T. and de Freitas, S. (2006). 'Learning and e–learning: The role of theory', in H. Beetham and R. Sharpe (Eds.), *Rethinking Pedagogy for a Digital Age: Designing and Delivering E-Learning*. London: Routledge. pp. 13–25.

McCalla, G. (2004). 'The ecological approach to the design of e-learning environments: Purpose-based capture and use of information about learners', *Journal of Interactive Media in Education*, 7: 1–23. Available online at: www-jime-open.ac.uk/2004/7

McFarlane, A. (2007). 'Alone together, the experience of digital gamers', in R. Andrews and C. Haythornthwaite (Eds.), *The Sage Handbook of E-learning Research*. London: Sage.

McGrath, J. E. (1984). *Groups, Interaction and Performance*. Englewood Cliffs, NJ: Prentice-Hall.

McLeod, J.M. and Chaffee, S.H. (1973). 'Interpersonal approaches to communication research', *American Behavioral Scientist*, 16(4): 469–99.

Mehra, B., Merkel, C. and Bishop, A. P. (2004). 'The Internet for empowerment of minority and marginalized users', *New Media & Society*, 6: 781–802.

Merkel, C.B., Clitherow, M., Farooq, U., Xiao, L., Ganoe, C.H., Carroll, J. M. and Rosson, M. B. (2005). 'Sustaining computer use and learning in community computing contexts: Making technology part of "who they are and what they do"', *Journal of Community Informatics, 1*(2): 158–74.

Merriam, S.B. (2001). 'Andragogy and self-directed learning: Pillars of adult learning theory'. *New Directions for Adult And Continuing Education, 89*: 3–13.

Merton, R. K. (1957). *Social Theory and Social Structure.* NY: Free Press.

Mestre, L. (2006). 'Accommodating diverse learning styles in an online environment (guest editorial)', *Reference and User Services Quarterly, 46*(2): 27–32.

Meyer, J. H. F. and Land, R. (2005) 'Threshold concepts: an introduction', in J. H. F. Meyer and R. Land (Eds.), *Overcoming Barriers To Student Understanding: Threshold Concepts and Troublesome Knowledge.* London: RoutledgeFalmer. pp. 3–18.

Mezirow, J. (2009). 'An overview on transformative learning', in K. Illeris (Ed.), *Contemporary Theories of Learning: Learning Theorists...in their own Words.* London: Routledge, pp. 90–105.

Miller, C. (1994). 'Rhetorical community: The cultural basis of genre', in A. Freedman and P. Medway (Eds.), *Genre and the New Rhetoric.* Basingstoke, UK: Taylor and Francis. pp. 67–78.

Miller, M. H. (2010). 'How interactive technology can help minority students learn', *Chronicle of Higher Education,* 19 March. Retrieved 21 July 2010 from: http://chronicle.com/blogPost/How-Interactive-Technology-Can/21932/

Mishra, S. (2009). 'E-learning in India', *International Journal on E-learning,* 8(4): 549–60.

Mitchell, W. J. T. (1987). *Iconology: Image, Text, Ideology.* Chicago: Chicago University Press.

Miyake, N. (2007). 'Computer supported collaborative learning', in R. Andrews and C. Haythornthwaite (Eds.), *The Sage Handbook of E-learning Research.* London: Sage. pp. 263–80.

Miyata, K. (2002). 'Social support for Japanese mothers online and offline', in B. Wellman and C. Haythornthwaite (Eds.), *The Internet in Everyday Life.* Oxford, UK: Blackwell. pp. 520–48.

Monge, P. R. and Contractor, N. S. (2003). *Theories of Communication Networks.* Oxford, UK: Oxford University Press.

Montague, R-A. (2006). 'Riding the Waves: A Case Study of Learners and Leaders in Library and Information Science Education', unpublished doctoral dissertation, University of Illinois at Urbana-Champaign, Champaign, IL.

Moore, M. (1997). 'Theory of transactional distance', in D. Keegan (Ed.), *Theoretical Principles of Distance Education.* London: Routledge. pp. 22–38.

Moreland, R. (1999). 'Transactive memory: Learning who knows what in work groups and organizations', in L. Thompson, J. Levine and D. Messick (Eds.), *Shared Cognition in Organizations.* Mahwah, NJ: Lawrence Erlbaum. pp. 3–31.

Morgan, G. (2007). *Images of Organization,* updated edn. Thousand Oaks, CA: Sage.

Nakamura, L. (in press, a). 'Race and identity in digital media', in J. Curran, *Mass Media and Society,* 5th edn.

Nakamura, L. (in press, b). 'Feminist Issue', *Interacting with Computers,* special issue.

Nardi, B. (1996). *Context and Consciousness: Activity Theory and Human-computer Interaction.* Cambridge, MA: MIT Press.

Nardi, B. A. and O'Day, V. (1999). *Information Ecologies: Using Technology With Heart.* Cambridge, MA: MIT Press.

Nardi, B. A., Whittaker, S. and Schwarz, H. (2000). 'It's not what you know, it's who you know: Work in the information age', *First Monday,* 5(5). Available online at: http://www.firstmonday.dk/issues/issue5_5/nardi/

Nardi, B. A., Whittaker, S. and Schwarz, H. (2002). 'NetWORKers and their activity in intensional networks', *Computer Supported Cooperative Work,* 11(1–2): 205–42.

National Science Foundation Task Force on Cyberlearning (2008). *Fostering Learning in the Networked World: The Cyberlearning Opportunity and Challenge.* Arlington, VA: National Science Foundation. http://www.nsf.gov/pubs/2008/nsf08204/nsf08204.pdf

National Telecommunications and Information Administration (NTIA) (1999). *Falling through the net: Defining the digital divide*. U.S. Department of Commerce. http://www.ntia.doc.gov/ntiahome/fttn99/

National Telecommunications and Information Administration (NTIA) (2000). *Falling through the net: Toward digital inclusion*. U.S. Department of Commerce. http://www.ntia.doc.gov/ntiahome/fttn00/contents00.html

Neff, G. and Stark, D. (2004). 'Permanently beta: Responsive organization in the internet era', in P. E. N. Howard and S. Jones (Eds.), *Society Online: The Internet in Context*. Thousand Oaks, CA: Sage. pp. 173–88.

New London Group (1996). 'A pedagogy of multiliteracies', *Harvard Educational Review*, 66(1): 60–92.

New London Group (2000). 'A pedagogy of multiliteracies: Designing social futures', in B. Cope and M. Kalantzis (Eds.), *Multiliteracies: Literacy Learning and the Design of Social Futures*. London: Routledge. pp. 9–37.

Nie, N. H. (2001). 'Sociability, interpersonal relations, and the internet: Reconciling conflicting findings', *American Behavioral Scientist*, 45(3): 420–35.

Nie, N. H. and Erbring, L. (2000). 'Internet and society: A preliminary report', *IT&Society*, 1(1): 275–83. Available online at: http://www.stanford.edu/group/siqss/itandsociety/v01i01/v01i01a18.pdf

Nielsen, J. (1994). *Usability Engineering*. San Francisco, CA: Morgan Kaufmann.

Noble, F. and Newman, M. (1993). 'Integrated system, autonomous departments: Organizational invalidity and system change in a university', *Journal of Management Studies*, 30 (2): 195–219.

Noble, S. (in press). 'Technology design for social inclusion: A critical perspective', *Interacting with Computers*.

Nonaka, I. (1994). 'A dynamic theory of organizational knowledge creation', *Organization Science*, 5(1): 14–37.

Nonaka, I. and Takeuchi, H. (1995). *The Knowledge Creating Company*. New York: Oxford University Press.

Norman, D. (1988). *The Design of Everyday Things*. New York: Basic Books.

NTIA (2000) *Falling Through the Net: Toward Digital Inclusion*. US Department of Commerce. Available online at: http://www.ntia.doc.gov/ntiahome/digitaldivide/

Nunamaker, J. F., Sprague, R. H. and Briggs, R. O. (Eds.) (2009). 'Structure and complexity in sociotechnical systems', *Journal of Management Information Systems*, 26(1): special issue.

O'Malley, C. (Ed.) (1989). *Computer Supported Collaborative Learning*. Berlin: Springer-Verlag.

O'Reilly, T. (2005). 'What is web 2.0: Design patterns and business models for the next generation of software', 30 September. Retrieved 21 July 2010 from: http://oreilly.com/pub/a/web2/archive/what-is-web-20.html

O'Reilly, T. and Battelle, J. (2009). 'Web squared: Web 2.0 five years on', Web 2.0 Summit. Retrieved 21 July 2010 from: http://www.web2summit.com/web2009/public/schedule/detail/10194

Office for National Statistics (2009). 'Internet Access Households and Individuals 2009', *Statistical Bulletin*, 28 August. Retrieved 25 June 2010 from: http://www.statistics.gov.uk/pdfdir/iahi0809.pdf

Olaniran, B. A. (Ed.) (2009). *Cases on Successful E-Learning Practices in the Developed and Developing World: Methods for Global Information Economy*. Hershey, PA: IGI Global.

Oldenburg, R. (1989). *The Great Good Place: Cafés, Coffee Shops, Community Centers, Beauty Parlors, General Stores, Bars, Hangouts, and How They Get You Through The Day*. New York: Paragon House.

Oliver, M. (2005a). 'The problem with affordance', *E-Learning*, 2(4): 402–13.

Oliver, M. (2005b). Metadata vs educational culture: Roles, power and standardisation, in R. Land and S. Bayne (Eds.), *Education in Cyberspace*. Milton Park, UK: RoutledgeFalmer.

Oliver, M. and Carr, M. (2009). 'Learning in virtual worlds: Using communities of practice to explain how people learn from play', *British Journal of Educational Technology*, 40(3): 444–57.

Orlikowski, W. J. (1992). 'The duality of technology: Rethinking the concept of technology in organizations', *Organization Science*, 3(3): 398–427.

Orlikowski, W. J. (2002). 'Knowing in practice: Enacting a collective capability in distributed organizing', *Organization Science*, 13(3): 249–73.

Orlikowski, W. J. and Yates, J. (1994). 'Genre repertoire: The structuring of communicative practices in organizations', *Administrative Science Quarterly*, 39: 541–74.

Oliver, M. and Trigwall, K. (2005). 'Can blended e-learning be redeemed?', *E-learning*, 2(1):17–26.

Ospina, A., Cole, J. and Nolan, J. (2008). 'GimpGirl grows up: Women with disabilities rethinking, redefining, and reclaiming community', paper presented at the Internet Researchers 9.0 Conference. Copenhagen, Denmark.

Pachler, N. (Ed.) (2007). *Mobile Learning: Towards a Research Agenda*. London: WLE Centre, Institute of Education Publications.

Pachler, N., Bachmair, B. and Cook, J. (2009). *Mobile Learning: Structures, Agency, Practices*. New York: Springer.

Palloff, R. M. and Pratt, K. (1999). *Building Learning Communities in Cyberspace*. San Francisco, CA: Jossey-Bass.

Parnell, J. (forthcoming). 'Complexity Theory and E-learning', PhD thesis, University of London, Institute of Education.

Parsad, B. and Jones, J. (2005). *Internet Access in US Public Schools and Classrooms: 1994–2003* (NCES 2005–015). US Department of Education. Washington, DC: National Center for Education Statistics. Retrieved 17 July 2006 from: http://165.224.221.98/pubs2005/2005015.pdf

Pea, R. (1993). 'Practices of distributed intelligence and designs for education', in G. Saloman (Ed.), *Distributed Cognition*, Cambridge: Cambridge University Press. pp. 47–87.

Pelz, W. (2004). '(My) Three principles of effective online pedagogy', *Journal of Asynchronous Learning Networks*, 8(3): 33–46. Available online at: http://www.sloan-c.org/publications/jaln/v8n3/v8n3_pelz.asp

Perkins, D. (1999). 'The many faces of constructivism', *Educational Leadership*, 57(3): 6–11.

Perkins, D. (2006). 'Constructivism and troublesome knowledge', in J. H. F. Meyer and R. Land (Eds.), *Overcoming Barriers to Student Understanding: Threshold Concepts and Troublesome Knowledge*, London: RoutledgeFalmer. pp. 33–47.

Perrow, C. (1970). *Organizational Analysis: A Sociological View*. Monterey, CA: Wadsworth.

Pew Internet and American Life (2009a). 'Who's online: Demographics of Internet use', December. Retrieved 23 July 2010 from: http://www.pewinternet.org/Static-Pages/Trend-Data/Whos-Online.aspx

Pew Internet and American Life (2009b). 'Generational differences in online activities', 28 January. Retrieved 9 February 2009 from: http://pewinternet.org/Infographics/Generational-differences-in-online-activities.aspx

Pinch, T. J. and Bijker, W. E. (1984). 'The social construction of facts and artefacts: Or how the sociology of science and the sociology of technology might benefit each other', *Social Studies of Science*, 14: 399–441.

Polanyi, M. (1958). *Personal Knowledge: Towards a Post-Critical Philosophy*. Chicago, IL: Chicago University Press.

Polhemus, L., Shih, L. F. and Swan, K. (2001). Virtual interactivity: The representation of social presence in an online discussion paper presented at the Annual Conference of American Educational Research Association.

Poole, M. S. and De Sanctis, G. (1990). 'Understanding the use of group decision support systems: The theory of adaptive structuration', in J. Fulk and C. W. Steinfield (Eds.), *Organizations and Communication Technology*. Newbury Park, CA: Sage. pp. 173–93.

Poole, M. S. and Hollingshead, A. B. (Eds.) (2005). *Theories of Small Groups: Interdisciplinary Perspectives*. Thousand Oaks, CA: Sage.

Preece, J. (2000). *Online Communities: Designing Usability and Supporting Sociability*. New York: John Wiley and Sons.

Preece, J. and Maloney-Krichmar, D. (Eds.) (2005). 'Special Theme: Online Communities', *Journal of Computer-Mediated Communication, 10*(4): Articles 1–10.

Preston, C. J. (2008). 'Braided learning: An emerging process observed in e-communities of practice', *International Journal of Web Based Communities, 4*(2): 220–43.

Putnam, R. D. (2000). *Bowling Alone: The Collapse and Revival of American Community*. New York: Simon and Schuster.

Quan-Haase, A., Cothrel, J. and Wellman, B. (2005). 'Instant messaging for collaboration: A case study of a high-tech firm', *Journal of Computer-Mediated Communication, 10*(4): article 13. Available online at: http://jcmc.indiana.edu/vol10/issue4/quan-haase.html

Rafaeli, S. and Sudweeks, F. (1997). 'Networked interactivity', *Journal of Computer-Mediated Communication, 2*(4). Available online at: http://www.ascusc.org/jcmc/vol2/issue4/rafaeli.sudweeks.html

Rainie, L. (2006). '*Cell phone use*', April. Pew Internet & American Life Project. Retrieved 5 August 2006 from: http://www.pewinternet.org/pdfs/PIP_Cell_phone_study.pdf

Rainie, L. and Keeter, S. (2006). 'Pew internet project data memo: Cell phone use', April. Washington, DC: Pew Internet & American Life Project. Retrieved 25 June 2010 from http://www.pewinternet.org/~/media//Files/Reports/2006/PIP_Cell_phone_study.pdf

Rampton, B. (1995). *Crossing: Language and Ethnicity among Adolescents*. London: Longman.

Raymond, E. (1998). 'The cathedral and the bazaar', *First Monday, 3*(3). http://www.firstmonday.dk/issues/issue3_3/raymond/

Raymond, E. S. (1999). *The Cathedral & the Bazaar: Musings on Linux and Open Source by an Accidental Revolutionary*. Cambridge, MA: O'Reilly.

Rebaza, C. (2009). 'The technological continuum of coterie publication: Fan fiction writing communities on LiveJournal', unpublished doctoral dissertation, University of Illinois at Urbana-Champaign, Champaign, IL.

Reid, E. M. (1991). 'Electropolis: Communication and community on Internet Relay Chat', honours thesis, University of Melbourne.

Rennie, F. and Mason, R. (2004). *The Connecticon: Learning for the Connected Generation*. Greenwich, CT: Information Age Publishing.

Renninger, A. and Shumar, W. (Eds.) (2002). *Building Virtual Communities: Learning and Change in Cyberspace*. Cambridge, UK: Cambridge University Press.

Resnick, L. B., Levine, J. M. and Teasdale, S. D. (Eds.) (1991). *Perspectives on Socially Shared Cognition*. Washington, D. C: American Psychological Association.

Resnick, P. (2002). 'Beyond bowling together: Sociotechnical capital', in J. Carroll (Ed.), *Human – Computer Interaction in the New Millennium*. Upper Saddle River, NJ: Addison-Wesley. pp. 247–72.

Rheingold, H. (2000). *The Virtual Community: Homesteading on the Electronic Frontier*, revised edn. Cambridge, MA: MIT Press.

Rheingold, H. (2003). *Smart Mobs: The Next Social Revolution*. New York: Perseus Books.

Rice, R. E. (2002). 'Primary issues in internet use: Access, civic and community involvement, and social interaction and expression', in L. Lievrouw and S. Livingstone (Eds.), *The Handbook of New Media*. London: Sage. pp. 105–29.

Rice, R. and Katz, J. (Eds.) (2001). *The Internet and Health Communication: Experiences and Expectations*. Thousand Oaks, CA: Sage.

Rice, R. E. and Rogers, E. M. (1980). 'Reinvention in the innovation process', *Knowledge, 1*(4): 499–514.

Riel, M. and Polin, L. (2004). 'Online learning communities: Common ground and critical differences in designing technical environments', in S. A. Barab, R. Kling and J. H. Gray (Eds.), *Designing for Virtual Communities in the Service of Learning*. Cambridge, UK: Cambridge University Press. pp. 16–50.

Rizvi, F. (2009). 'Digital divide and higher education in sub-saharan Africa', in B. Cope and M. Kalantzis (Eds.), *Ubiquitous Learning*. Champaign, IL: University of Illinois Press. pp. 109–18.

Robins, J. (2002) 'Affording a place: The role of persistent structures in social navigation', *Information Research*, 7(3). Available online at: http://InformationR.net/ir/7-3/paper131.html

Robins, J. (2004). 'Affording a place: The persistent structures of LEEP', in C. Haythornthwaite and M. M. Kazmer (Eds.), *Learning, Culture and Community in Online Education: Research and Practice*. NY: Peter Lang. pp. 146–61.

Roethlisberger, F. and Dickson, W. (1939). *Management and the Worker: An Account of a Research Program Conducted by the Western Electric Company, Chicago*. Cambridge, MA: Harvard University Press.

Rogers, E. M. (1995). *Diffusion of Innovations*, 4th edn. New York: The Free Press.

Rogers, E. M., Eveland, J. D. and Klepper, C. (1977). *The Innovation Process in Organizations*, Department of Journalism, The University of Michigan, Ann Arbor. NSF Grant RDA 75-17952.

Rogoff, B. (1992). *Apprenticeship in Thinking*. New York: Oxford University Press.

Rudestam, K. E. and Schoenholtz–Read, J. (Eds.) (2002). *Handbook of Online Learning: Innovations in Higher Education and Corporate Training*. Thousand Oaks, CA: Sage.

Russell, D. R. (2002). 'Looking beyond the interface: Activity theory and distributed learning', in M. K. Lea and K. Nicoll (Eds.), *Distributed Learning: Social and Cultural Approaches to Practice*. London: RoutledgeFalmer. pp. 64–82

Russell, T. L. (2001). *The No Significant Difference Phenomenon*, 5th edn. IDECC. (see also http://www.nosignificantdifference.org/).

Ryberg, T. (2007). 'Patchworking as a metaphor for learning – understanding youth, learning and technology', PhD thesis published in e-Learning Lab Publication Series (Vol. 1: 1–477). Aalborg: Department of Communication and Psychology, Aalborg University.

Ryberg, T. and Dirckinck-Holmfeld, L. (2008). 'Power users and patchworking: An analytical approach to critical studies of young people's learning with digital media', *Educational Media International*, 45(3): 143–56.

Salaff, J. (2002). 'Where home is the office: The new form of flexible work', in B. Wellman and C. Haythornthwaite (Eds.), *The Internet In Everyday Life*. Oxford, UK: Blackwell. pp. 464–95.

Saltz, J. S., Hiltz, S. R. and Turoff, M. (2004). 'Student social graphs: Visualizing a student's online social network'. *Proceedings of the CSCW'04 Conference*. Chicago, IL.

Sandars, J. and Haythornthwaite, C. (2007). 'New horizons for e-learning in medical education: Ecological and web 2.0 perspectives', *Medical Teacher*, 29(4): 307–10.

Sawyer, K. R. (2006). 'Introduction: The new science of learning', in K. R. Sawyer (Ed.), *The Cambridge Handbook of the Learning Sciences*. Cambridge, UK: Cambridge University Press. pp. 1–19.

Sawyer, S. and Eschenfelder, K. R. (2005). 'Social informatics: Perspectives, examples, and trends', *Annual Review of Information Science and Technology*, 36(1): 427–65.

Sawyer, S. and Tapia, A. (2007). 'From findings to theories: institutionalizing social informatics', *The Information Society*, 23: 263–75.

Scardamalia, M. and Bereiter, C. (1996). 'Computer support for knowledge-building communities', in T. Koschmann (Ed.), *CSCL: Theory and Practice of an Emerging Paradigm*. Mahwah, NJ: Lawrence Erlbaum. pp. 249–68.

Schmidt, K. and Bannon, L. (1992). 'Taking CSCW seriously: Supporting articulation work', *Computer Supported Cooperative Work*, 1: 7–41.

Schneier, B. (2009). 'On London's surveillance cameras', Schneier on security blog, 31 August 2009. Available online at: http://www.schneier.com/blog/archives/2009/08/on_londons_surv.html

Schroeder, R. and Fry, J. (2007). 'Social science approaches to e-Science: Framing an agenda', *Journal of Computer-Mediated Communication*, 12(2): article 11. Available online at: http://jcmc.indiana.edu/vol12/issue2/schroeder.html

Schuler, D. (1996). *New Community Networks: Wired for Change*. Reading, MA: Addison-Wesley. Available online at: http://www.scn.org/ncn/

Scopes, L. J. M. (2009). 'Learning archetypes as tools of cybergogy for a 3D educational landscape: A structure for eTeaching in second life', unpublished masters thesis, University of Southampton, School of Education.

Scopes, L. (2010). 'Model of Cybergogy', VWBPE Video 12-03-10 – V1.0_0001. Available online at: http://blip.tv/file/3343043

Scott, W. R. (1992). *Organizations: Rational, Natural, and Open Systems*. Toronto: Prentice-Hall.

Seale, J. (2006). *E-learning and Disability in Higher Education: Accessibility Research and Practice*. Abingdon: Routledge.

Seale, J. (2010). *Digital Inclusion: A Research Briefing by the Technology Enhanced Learning Phase of the Teaching and Learning Research Programme*. University of London. Available online at: http://www.tlrp.org/tel/digital_inclusion_writing/

Searing, S. (2004). 'Reshaping traditional services for nontraditional learning: The LEEP student in the library', in C. Haythornthwaite and M. M. Kazmer (Eds.), *Learning, Culture and Community in Online Education: Research and Practice*. New York: Peter Lang.

Selfe, C.L. and Hawisher, G.E. (2004). *Literate Lives in the Information Age: Narratives of Literacy from the United States*. Mahwah, NJ: Lawrence Erlbaum Associates.

Selwyn, N. and Facer, K. (2007). *Beyond the Digital Divide: Rethinking Digital Inclusion for the 21st Century*. Futurelab. Available online at: http://www.futurelab.org.uk/resources/documents/opening_education/Digital_Divide.pdf

Senges, M., Brown, J. S. and Rheingold, H. (2008). 'Entrepreneurial learning in the networked age. How new learning environments foster entrepreneurship and innovation', *Paradigms*, 1(1): 125–40.

Sharples, M., Taylor, J. and Vavoula, G. (2007). 'A theory of learning for the mobile age', in R. Andrews and C. Haythornthwaite (Eds.), *The Sage Handbook of E-learning Research*. London: Sage. pp. 221–47.

Short, J., Williams, E. and Christie, B. (1976). *The Social Psychology of Telecommunications*. London: John Wiley and Sons.

Siemens, G. (2004). 'Connectivism: A learning theory for the digital age'. Retrieved 1 November 2009 from: http://www.elearnspace.org/Articles/connectivism.htm

Siemens, G. (2010). 'What are learning analytics?'. Retrieved 27 August 2010 from: http://www.elearnspace.org/blog/2010/08/25/what-are-learning-analytics/

Singel, R. (2005). 'A disaster map "wiki", is born', *Wired*, 2 September. Retrieved 23 July 2010 from: http://www.wired.com/software/coolapps/news/2005/09/68743

Smartmobs (2009). 'Emergent Social Revolution #iranelection' 13 June. Retrieved 24 January 2010 from: http://www.smartmobs.com/2009/06/13/breaking-news-emergent-social-revolution-iranelections/

Smedberg, Å. (2008). *Online communities and learning for health: The use of online health communities and online expertise for people with established bad habits*, doctoral dissertation, Computer and System Sciences, Stockholm University and KTH (Royal Institute of Technology), Stockholm, Sweden.

Smith, C. B., McLaughlin, M. L., Osborne, K. K. (1996). 'Conduct control on Usenet', *Journal of Compute-Medicated Communication*, 2(4). Available online at: http://jcmc.indiana.edu/vol2/issue4/smith.html

Smith, M. K., Doyle, M. E. and Jeffs, T. (Eds.) (2010). *The Encyclopedia of Informal Education*. Available online at http://www.infed.org/

Society of College, National and University Libraries (UK) (2008). 'Seven Pillars of Information Literacy'. Retrieved 12 February 2010 from: http://www.sconul.ac.uk/groups/information_literacy/headline_skills.html

Soylu, F. (2009). 'Designing online learning communities: Lessons from Eksisozluk', *European Journal of Online, Distance and E-learning*. Retrieved 15 July 2009 from: http://www.eurodl.org/index.php?article=366

Sproull, L. and Kiesler, S. (1986). 'Reducing social context cues: Electronic mail in organizational computing', *Management Science, 32*(11): 1492–512.

Sproull, L. S. and Kiesler, S. B. (1991). *Connections: New Ways of Working in the Networked Organization*. Cambridge, MA: MIT Press.

Star, S. L. (1995). *Ecologies of Knowledge: Work and Politics in Science and Technology*. Albany, NY: SUNY.

Star, S. L. (1999). 'The ethnography of infrastructure', *American Behavioral Scientist, 43*(3): 377–91.

Star, S. L. (2002). 'Infrastructure and ethnographic practice: Working on the fringes', *Scandinavian Journal of Information Systems, 14*(2): 107–22.

Star, S. L. and Bowker, G. C. (2002). 'How to infrastructure', in L. Lievrouw and S. Livingstone (Eds.), *Handbook of New Media*. Thousand Oaks, CA: Sage. pp. 151–62.

Star, S. L. and Griesemer, J. (1989). 'Institution ecology, translations, and coherence: Amateurs and professionals in Berkeley's museum of vertebrate zoology, 1907–1939', *Social Studies of Science,* 19: 387–420.

Star, S. L. and Strauss, A. (1999). 'Layers of silence, arenas of voice: The ecology of visible and invisible work', *Computer Supported Cooperative Work, 8*(1–2): 9–30.

Stebbins, R. A. (2006). *Serious Leisure: A Perspective for Our Time*. New Brunswick, NJ: Transaction.

Stebbins, R. A. (2009). 'Leisure and its relationship to library and information science: Bridging the gap', *Library Trends, 57*(4): 618–31.

Steeples, C. and Jones, C. (2002). *Networked Learning: Perspectives and Issues*. London: Springer.

Stern, M. J. and Wellman, B. (2010). 'Rural and urban differences in the internet society – real and relatively important', *American Behavioral Scientist, 53*(9): special issue.

Stoecker, R. (2005a). 'Is community informatics good for communities? Questions confronting an emerging field', *The Journal of Community Informatics, 1*(3): 13–26.

Stoecker, R. (2005b). *Research Methods for Community Change: A Project-Based Approach*. Thousand Oaks, CA: Sage.

Strauss, A. L. (1978). 'A social world perspective', *Studies in Symbolic Interactions,* 1: 119–28.

Suarez-Orozco, M. (Ed.) (2007). *Learning in the Global Era: International Perspectives on Globalization and Education*. Los Angeles: University of California Press.

Suchman, L. (1987). *Plans and Situated Actions: The Problem of Human–Machine Communication*. Cambridge, UK: Cambridge University Press.

Suchman, L. (Ed.) (1995). 'Representations of work. Guest edited section', *Communications of the ACM, 38*(9): 33–55.

Sudweeks, F., McLaughlin, M. and Rafaeli, S. (1998). *Network and Netplay: Virtual Groups on the Internet*. Cambridge, MA: MIT Press.

Swales, J. (1998). *Other Floors, Other Voices: A Textography of a Small University Building*. Mahwah, NJ: Lawrence Erlbaum.

Swan, K. (2001). Virtual interactively: design factors affecting student satisfaction and perceived learning in asynchronous online courses. *Distance Education 22,* 306–31.

Swan, K., Shen, J. and Starr, R. H. (2006). Assessment and Collaboration in Online Learning, *Journal of Asynchronous Learning Networks, 10*(1).

Swan, K. (2006). 'Online collaboration', *Journal of Asynchronous Learning Networks, 10*(1): special issue. Available online at: http://www.sloan-c.org/publications/jaln/v10n1/index.asp

Tang, T. and McCalla, G. (2003). 'Smart recommendation for an evolving e-learning system'. *Proceedings of the Workshop on Technologies for Electronic Documents for Supporting Learning*. International Conference on Artificial Intelligence in Education, Sydney, Australia.

Tapscott, D. (1998). *Growing Up Digital: The Rise of the Net Generation*. New York: McGraw-Hill.

Tapscott, D. and Williams, A. D. (2010). 'Innovating the 21st century university', *Educause Review*, Jan/Feb: 17–29.

Taylor, F.W. (1911). *The Principles of Scientific Management*. New York: Harper.

Thagard, P. (2005). 'Being interdisciplinary: Trading zones in cognitive science', in S. J. Derry, C. D. Schunn and M. A. Gernsbacher (Eds.), *Interdisciplinary Collaboration: An Emerging Cognitive Science*. Mahwah, NJ: Erlbaum. pp. 317–39.

Thompson, J. D. (1967). *Organizations in Action*. New York: McGraw-Hill.

Thompson, M. (2007). 'From distance education to e-learning', in R. Andrews and C. Haythornthwaite (Eds.), *The Sage Handbook of E-learning Research*. London: Sage.

Timmermans, S., Bowker, G. and Star, L. (1998). 'The architecture of difference: Visibility, discretion, and comparability in building a nursing intervention classification', in A. M. Mol and M. Berg (Eds.), *Difference in Medicine: Unraveling Practices, Techniques and Bodies*. Raleigh, NJ: Duke University Press. pp. 202–25.

Tönnies, F. (1887 [1955]). *Community and Organization*. London: Routledge and Kegan Paul.

Toulmin, S. (1958). *The Uses of Argument*. Cambridge: Cambridge University Press.

Trevino, L. K., Daft, R. L. and Lengel, R. H. (1990). 'Understanding managers' media choice: A symbolic interactionist perspective', in J. Fulk and C. W. Steinfield (Eds.), *Organizations and Communication Technology*. Newbury Park, CA: Sage. pp. 71–94.

Tripp, L. (2009). 'Teaching digital media production in online instruction: Strategies and recommendations'. *Proceedings of World Conference on Educational Multimedia, Hypermedia and Telecommunications 2009*. Chesapeake, VA: AACE. pp. 3106–11.

Trist, E. L. and Bamford, K. W. (1951). 'Some social and psychological consequences of the longwall method of coal-getting', *Human Relations*, 4(1): pp. 6–24, 37–8.

Turkle, S. (1995). *Life on the Screen: Identity in the Age of the Internet*. New York: Simon and Schuster.

Twidale, M. (n.d). 'Over-the-shoulder learning: Supporting brief informal learning embedded in the work context'. Available online at: http://www.lis.uiuc.edu/~twidale/pubs/otsl1.html

Twidale, M. B. and Ruhleder, K. (2004). 'Over-the-shoulder learning in a distance education environment', in C. Haythornthwaite and M. M. Kazmer (Eds.), *Learning, Culture and Community in Online Education: Research and Practice*. New York: Peter Lang. pp. 177–94.

van Dijk, J. (2005). *The Deepening Divide: Inequality in the Information Society*. Thousand Oaks, CA: Sage.

Varvel, V. (2010). 'Social engineering effects on instructors and students in an elearning environment', unpublished doctoral dissertation, University of Illinois at Urbana-Champaign, Champaign, IL.

Varvel, V. E., Montague, R.-A. and Estabrook, L. S. (2007). 'Policy and e-learning', in R. Andrews and C. Haythornthwaite (Eds.), *The Sage Handbook of E-learning Research*. London: Sage. pp. 269–85.

Vavoula, G., Pachler, N. and Kukulska-Hulme, A. (Eds.) (2009). *Researching Mobile Learning: Frameworks, Tools and Research Designs*. Oxford, UK: Peter Lang.

Volosinov, V. (1973). *Marxism and the Philosophy of Language*. Translated by L. Matejka and I. R. Titunik. Cambridge, MA: Harvard University Press.

Vygotsky, L. (1986). *Thought and Language*. Cambridge, MA: Harvard University Press.

Walker, J., Wasserman, S. and Wellman, B. (1994). 'Statistical models for social support networks', in S. Wasserman and J. Galaskiewicz (Eds.), *Advances in Social Network Analysis*. Thousand Oaks, CA: Sage. pp. 53–78.

Walther, J. B. (1996). 'Computer-mediated communication: Impersonal, interpersonal, and hyperpersonal interaction', *Communication Research*, 23(1): 3–43.

Warschauer, M. (2000). 'Language, identity, and the internet', in B. E. Kolko, L. Nakamura and G. B. Rodman (Eds.), *Race in Cyberspace*. New York: Routledge. pp. 151–70.

Warschauer, M. (2002). 'Reconceptionalizing the digital divide', *First Monday*, *7*(7): 1–15. Available online at: http://firstmonday.org/issues/issue7_7/warschauer/index.hmtl

Warschauer, M. (2003). *Technology and Social Inclusion*. Cambridge, MA: MIT Press.

Washington Post (2009). 'Iran's Twitter revolution: Witnessing a new chapter in the quest for freedom', 16 June. Retrieved 24 January 2010 from: http://www.washingtontimes.com/news/2009/jun/16/irans-twitter-revolution/

Watson, J., Gemin, B., Ryan, J. and Wicks, M. (2009). *Keeping Pace with K-12 Online Learning: An Annual Review of State-Level Policy and Practice*. Evergreen, CO: Evergreen Education Group.

Wegner, D. (1987). 'Transactive memory: A contemporary analysis of the group mind', in B. Mullen and G. Goethals (Eds.), *Theories of Group Behavior*. New York: Springer-Verlag. pp. 185–208.

Weick, K. (1976). Educational organizations as loosely-coupled systems. *ASQ*, *21*(1): 1–19.

Weick, K. E. (1990). 'Technology as equivoque: Sensemaking in new technologies', in P. S. Goodman, L. S. Sproull and Associates (Eds.), *Technology and Organizations*. San Francisco, CA: Jossey-Bass. pp. 1–44.

Weiser, M. (1991). 'The computer for the 21st century', *Scientific American*, *265*(3): 94–102.

Wellman, B. (1979). 'The community question', *American Journal of Sociology*, *84*: 1201–31.

Wellman, B. (1997). 'An electronic group is a social network', in S. Kiesler (Ed.), *Cultures of the Internet*. Mahwah, NJ: Lawrence Erlbaum. pp. 179–205.

Wellman, B. (Ed.) (1999). *Networks in the Global Village*. Boulder, CO: Westview Press.

Wellman, B. (2001). 'The rise of networked individualism', in. L. Keeble (Ed.), *Community Networks Online*. London: Taylor and Francis. pp. 17–42.

Wellman, B. (2002). 'Little boxes, glocalization, and networked individualism?', in M. Tanabe, P. van den Besselaar and T. Ishida (Eds.), *Digital Cities II: Computational and Sociological Approaches*. Berlin: Springer. pp. 10–25.

Wellman, B. and Berkowitz, S. D. (Eds.) (1997). *Social Structures: A Network Approach*, updated edn. Greenwich, CT: JAI Press.

Wellman, B. and Haythornthwaite, C. (Eds.) (2002). *The Internet in Everyday Life*. Oxford: Blackwell.

Wellman, B., Boase, J. and Chen, W. (2002). 'The networked nature of community: Online and offline', *IT&Society*, *1*(1): 151–65.

Wellman, B., Carrington, P. and Hall, A. (1988). 'Networks as personal communities', in B. Wellman and S. D. Berkowitz (Eds.), *Social Structures: A Network Approach*. Cambridge, UK: Cambridge University Press. pp. 130–84.

Wellman, B., Quan-Haase, A., Boase, J., Chen, W., Hampton, K., de Diaz, I. I. and Miyata, K. (2003). 'The social affordances of the internet for networked individualism', *Journal of Computer-Mediated Communication*, *8*(3). Available online at: http://jcmc.indiana.edu/vol8/issue3/wellman.html

Wellman, B., Salaff, J., Dimitrova, D., Garton, L., Gulia, M. and Haythornthwaite, C. (1996). 'Computer networks as social networks: Collaborative work, telework, and virtual community', *Annual Review of Sociology*, 22: 213–38.

Wenger, E. (1998). *Communities of Practice: Learning, Meaning, and Identity*. Cambridge, UK: Cambridge University Press.

Whitworth, A. (2007). 'Researching the cognitive cultures of e-learning', in R. Andrews and C. Haythornthwaite (Eds.), *The Sage Handbook of E-learning Research*. London: Sage.

Williams, R. and Edge, R. (1996). 'The social shaping of technology', *Research Policy*, 25: 856–99.

Willinsky, J. (2005). *The Access Principle: The Case for Open Access to Research and Scholarship*. Cambridge, MA: MIT Press.

Wulf, W. (1989). 'The national collaboratory', in *Towards a national collaboratory*. Unpublished report of a National Science Foundation invitational workshop, Rockefeller University, New York.

Yates, J. (1993). 'Co-evolution of information-processing technology and use: Interaction between the life insurance and tabulating industries', *Business History Review, 67*: 1–51.

Yates, J., Orlikowski, W. J. and Okamura, K. (1999). 'Explicit and implicit structuring of genres in electronic communication: Reinforcement and change in social interaction', *Organization Science, 10*(1): 83–103.

Zook, M. A. (2009). 'Digiplace and cyberscapes: Rethinking the digital divide in urban America', keynote presentation, eChicago conference, Chicago, IL. Available online at: http://www.ideals.illinios.edu/handle/2142/154

Zuboff, S. (1988). *In the Age of the Smart Machine: The Future of Work and Power*. New York: Basic Books.

Index

Added to a page number 'f' denotes a figure and 't' denotes a table.